Essay Index

ENVIRONMENTAL FACTORS
IN CHRISTIAN HISTORY

Shirley Jackson Case

ENVIRONMENTAL FACTORS IN CHRISTIAN HISTORY

Edited by

JOHN THOMAS McNEILL

MATTHEW SPINKA

HAROLD R. WILLOUGHBY

KENNIKAT PRESS

Port Washington, N. Y./London

ENVIRONMENTAL FACTORS IN CHRISTIAN HISTORY

Copyright 1939 by the University of Chicago
Reissued in 1970 by Kennikat Press by arrangement
Library of Congress Catalog Card No: 70-91047
SBN 8046-0657-9

Manufactured by Taylor Publishing Company   Dallas, Texas

ESSAY AND GENERAL LITERATURE INDEX REPRINT SERIES

PREFACE

THIS book of short studies is presented to Dr. Shirley Jackson Case, Dean Emeritus of the Divinity School of the University of Chicago, as a tribute to his scholarship and leadership. The writers are his former colleagues and students. The selection of topics is designed to illustrate an approach to the history of Christianity in which Dr. Case has done distinguished and pioneer service in his many books and articles. A list of his writings is appended, complete except for minor items, to the end of the year 1938; to this achievement in authorship we trust much will be added in years of freedom from administrative responsibility.

The papers are arranged substantially in the chronological sequence of their subject matter. Readers will quickly realize that necessary space limitation has compelled the authors to present their data and conclusions with the utmost condensation. The editors greatly appreciate the co-operative spirit in which contributors have adapted their material to meet this requirement. Though the studies range through widely varied fields, they are presented in the hope that together they may help to illumine the broad theme of the impact of non-Christian and nonreligious elements in culture and society upon the historical development of Christian thought, life, and institutions.

The publication of the book has been made possible by the work of a general committee led by Professor W. C. Bower and of a committee on subscriptions headed by Professor C. T. Holman, and by the generous and unfailing co-operation of the officers and editorial staff of the University of Chicago Press. Professor John Knox, editor of the *Journal of Religion*, has made many valuable suggestions and has corrected the page proof.

UNIVERSITY OF CHICAGO
June 17, 1939

v

TABLE OF CONTENTS

A BIOGRAPHICAL NOTE

THE contributions of Shirley Jackson Case to theological education in America began in 1905, when he was an instructor in New Testament Greek in Yale Divinity School. Three years later, after a period of teaching in Bates College, he joined the New Testament staff at the University of Chicago. In less than a decade he had become Professor of Early Church History as well as of New Testament Interpretation. Following his appointment to the chairmanship of the Department of Church History in 1923, he accomplished a well-balanced reorganization and enlargement of the department. His influence was nationally felt during the same period in guiding the policies of the American Society of Church History. As chairman of a deputation to the Orient in 1931–32, he surveyed the teaching of church history in mission schools of the Far East and made recommendations for its improvement and for the preservation of Christian records in those areas. His designation to the deanship of the Divinity School in 1933 immediately resulted in the effective co-ordination of divinity instruction with new trends in university education on the campus. He further contributed constructively and significantly to the progressive development of educational theory and practice, both in the Divinity School and in the University as a whole. At the very end of his half-decade of intensive administrative service (1938) he prepared a weighty report on the curriculum of theological education for the American Association of Theological Schools.

Undoubtedly the most significant results to date of his continuing career as a scholar and an educator have been the stimulation of sound researches carried through by competent students and the publication of a dozen major volumes recording the results of his own investigations. Dean Case himself indicates that, among them all, *Jesus: A New Biography* (1927) was the product of his most prolonged concentration on any nexus of historical problems. His students and friends would probably agree that his *Evolution of Early Christianity* (1914) is his most influential book; while his *Experience with the Supernatural in Early Christian Times* (1929) stands out as the finest example of his distinctive capacity for scholarly workmanship. The Rauschenbusch Lectures of Dean Case in 1933 dealing with *The Social Triumph of the Ancient Church*, and also his Lowell Institute Lectures of 1936, which traversed *The Highways of Christian Doctrine*, represent the more recent pioneering of his mind with social-historical methodology in the broad areas of early church history and the development of Christian thought.

THE SIGNIFICANCE OF JOHN THE BAPTIST FOR THE BEGINNINGS OF CHRISTIANITY

ERNEST WILLIAM PARSONS

Colgate-Rochester Divinity School
Rochester, New York

JOHN THE BAPTIST and his movement are slowly becoming the recipients of a more adequate interpretation than the long centuries have given them. Whether we shall ever be able to give them that which is rightfully theirs is a matter of doubt because of the scantiness of our sources and the character of most of them. The traditional and conventional view that John was the conscious forerunner of Jesus has so largely dominated the field that other interpretations have received comparatively slight consideration. The function of John the Baptist in relation to Jesus has, however, been the subject of a number of studies[1] in the past few decades, and he is gradually being freed from certain limitations of thought about him.

But his significance for the early Christian movement has not been so frequently explored. Two reasons for this are apparent. The first is the extreme difficulty of the sources. Fragmentary and casual as they are, they have been, wherever Christian in-

---

[1] Among works that may be consulted are the following: Wilhelm Brandt, *Die jüdischen Baptismen* (Giessen, 1910); Martin Dibelius, *Die urchristliche Überlieferung von Johannes dem Täufer* (Göttingen, 1911); Clayton R. Bowen, "John the Baptist in the New Testament," *American Journal of Theology*, January, 1912; Carl A. Bernoulli, *Johannes der Täufer und die Urgemeinde* (Leipzig, 1917); Maurice Goguel, *Jean Baptiste* (Paris, 1928); Clayton R. Bowen, "Prolegomena to a New Study of John the Baptist," in *Studies in Early Christianity*, ed. Shirley J. Case (New York, 1928); Ernest W. Parsons, "John the Baptist and Jesus," in *Studies in Early Christianity*; Ernst Lohmeyer, *Das Urchristentum, 1. Johannes der Täufer* (Göttingen, 1932). Two books which bear an imprimatur and which have some value in the consideration of sources and bibliography but which are barren of any historical interpretation are Theodor Innitzer, *Johannes der Täufer* (Wien, 1908), and Alexander Pottgiesser, *Johannes der Täufer und Jesus Christus* (Köln, 1911).

terpreters have touched them, so heavily overlaid with apologetic and tendential material as to render the task of getting the history behind the tradition one of difficulty. The other is the idea that, even if it be granted that the Baptist movement persisted for a longer time than was formerly thought, it was, nevertheless, a separate movement. There is, however, evidence that the movement came into contact with Christianity and that at least some of that contact was controversial.

There are four moments in the career of Jesus and in the movement of his followers in relation to which the Baptist and his cause affected Christianity in its early days. The first is the impact that John had upon Jesus himself. That he and his activities profoundly influenced Jesus is seen by the fact that Jesus went to him, apparently listened to his message, and presented himself for baptism at his hands. But this phase of the matter is rather obvious and has received consideration more than once in recent times.

With regard to the second point of influence, it can be said that little doubt remains that the message of John and of his followers had a definite influence upon the message of Jesus, upon that of his disciples during his life, and upon the proclamations of his followers in early post-resurrection days. There is no reason for questioning the essential historicity of the tradition which makes John herald the imminent end of the present age and the equally imminent coming of the new age and challenge his hearers to spiritual preparation for its coming in the call to repent. This message of John forms so important a part of the declaration of Jesus and of members of the Christian movement that it would not have been put on his lips and theirs had there not been necessity born of an actual occurrence. It is true that only in Matthew is the message given in these words, "And in those days cometh John the Baptist preaching in the wilderness of Judea, saying, Repent ye, for the kingdom of heaven is at hand" (Matt. 3:12).[2] But Mark gives the idea of imminence in that John is said to be the preparer of the messianic way and

[2] This and subsequent quotations from the American Revised Version of the Bible are used by the kind permission of the International Council of Religious Education.

his baptism is described as "the baptism of repentance unto remission of sins" (Mark 1:4). Both Matthew and Luke follow the earlier gospel in this respect. In the non-Markan material used by Matthew and Luke the elements of imminent judgment and a baptism connected with repentance are present. The "multitudes" come to his baptism and are challenged to repentance, and the chief sanction is the "wrath to come" and the "axe lying at the root of the tree." The imminence of a messianic kingdom the sharing of which was conditioned by repentance was the chief and the essential emphasis of the heralding of John.

The independent work of Jesus in its inception is characterized similarly by Mark and Matthew. "Jesus came into Galilee, declaring the good news about God and saying, The time is fulfilled, and the kingdom of God is at hand; repent ye, and believe in the good news" (Mark 1:14–15). "From that time began Jesus to preach, and to say, Repent ye, for the kingdom of heaven is at hand" (Matt. 4:17). Luke has another tradition regarding this beginning of independent work. But even in it Jesus is sent "to proclaim the year of the Lord's acceptance" and he declares, "To-day hath this scripture been fulfilled in your ears" (Luke 4:17 ff.). The early message of Jesus was essentially that of John with its two foci—the imminence of the kingdom of God and the ethical preparation for participation in it. And, as a result of his delivering this message, the popular success of John is paralleled by that of Jesus.

These two matters of the impending kingdom and the necessary spiritual preparation for its enjoyment appear again in a tradition very heavily burdened by later accretions. It is the story of the mission of the twelve. Mark's account is brief, but the essential elements of the message are to be seen in the injunction to take nothing for the journey and in the statement that "they went out and preached that men should repent" (Mark 6:12). Luke says that "he sent them forth to preach the kingdom of God" (Luke 9:2). Matthew's record is that Jesus sent them forth to preach to Israel alone, saying, "The kingdom of heaven is at hand" (Matt. 10:7). The fact that in each case the work of exorcism is added does not hide the fact that the message of the disciples of Jesus, whether they were twelve or not, was that of John and of Jesus himself. The tradition of the sending of the seventy in the Perean section of Luke records that they were to declare, "The kingdom of God is come nigh unto you" (Luke 10:9). The matter is emphasized in a later statement, "Nevertheless know this, that the kingdom of God is come nigh" (10:11). The element of repentance appears in this tradition in connection with the criticism of those cities which rejected the warning and the exhortation. This is true also of the tradition which Matthew has arranged around the mission of the twelve. These cities did not repent, but, if Tyre and Sidon had had this opportunity, "they would have repented." The various traditions concerning vigilance which may well have a germ that represents the thought of Jesus have as a constant factor the thought of imminence and readiness. The parables which are alleged to contain a developmental view of the kingdom are best interpreted in other ways. Even at the last, according to a Lukan tradition, Jesus expected the momentary inbreaking of the kingdom (cf. Luke 22:14–18).

Passing to those sources from which we must derive our knowledge of the message of the Christian movement immediately after the rise of the resurrection faith, we find the strain made familiar by John the Baptist persisting. The early chapters of the Acts of the Apostles strangely but fortunately preserve some primitive features. In the message ascribed to Peter on the day of Pentecost we have the elements of the imminence of the kingdom and of moral preparation for it. In that message the enthusiastic experience of the group is interpreted as the gift of the Spirit "in the last days." It proclaims the coming of "the day of the Lord . . . . that great and notable day." Salvation at that time is dependent upon calling "on the name of the Lord" (cf. Acts 2:16–21). Especially striking are the words of Peter in answer to a request for guidance in conduct, "Repent ye, and be baptized every one of you in the name of Jesus Christ unto the remission of your sins and ye shall receive the gift of the Holy Spirit" (Acts 2:38). Apart from some additions necessitated by the interpretation of Jesus as Messiah, this is essentially the Johannine message. In the address of Peter recorded in the third chapter of Acts we have the following exhortation ascribed to him, "Repent ye, therefore, and turn again, that your sins may be blotted out, so that there may come seasons of refreshing from the Lord and that he may send the Messiah who hath been appointed for you, even Jesus" (3:19–20). This is again the message of John with certain Christian additions. The connection between the gift of the Holy Spirit (an indication of the presence of the last days) and repentance appears again in Acts 5:31–32. Philip's message to the Samaritans is described as "preaching good tidings concerning the kingdom of God and the name of Jesus Christ" (Acts 8:12). The element of belief in the messiahship of Jesus is beginning to take the place of repentance. But repentance in connection with the gift of the Holy Spirit occurs in the story concerning Cornelius (Acts 11:15–18).

The letters of Paul were written to meet specific situations, and the thought of Paul is dominated to a large extent by his interpretation of the difficult fact of the death of his Messiah in terms of redemptive sacrifice. Nevertheless, the elements of the Johannine message with certain inevitable Christian alterations are to be seen as the message of Paul's missionary declarations. The results of his preaching to the Thessalonians are described as follows: "Ye turned unto God from idols to serve a living and true God, and to wait for his son from heaven . . . . who delivereth us from the wrath to come" (I Thess. 1:9–10). The thought of the imminent kingdom had been so impressed upon the Thessalonians by the Pauline preaching that a considerable portion of both letters is directed to the solution of problems and the correction of misunderstandings related to this part of the apostolic utterance. It is clear that they had "turned," that is, "repented," and that they were expectant of the messianic kingdom. Deliverance from "this present evil age" is the essence of Christian salvation as Paul describes it to the Galatians (Gal. 1:4). To the Corinthians he writes of his gladness that they "come behind in no gift, waiting for the

revealing of the Lord Jesus Christ . . . . that ye be unreprove-
able in the day of our Lord Jesus Christ" (I Cor. 1:7-8). The
thought of imminence is expressed in one of his latest writings
in the statement, "The Lord is at hand" (Phil. 4:5).

There can remain little doubt that the declaration of the
nearness of the kingdom of God and the call to moral and spiritual renewal in the light of that conviction which tradition
rightly placed upon the lips of John the Baptist had direct and
important influence upon the proclamation of Jesus and his
intimate associates and also upon that of his followers in the
early days of the Christian movement. It is within the bounds
of probability that a greater emphasis upon imminence and
consequent repentance appeared in the Pauline missionary work
than one might gather from his letters. The heavy burden of
proving that Jesus was the promised Messiah and of explaining
a messianic death might well tend to overshadow these matters
in writings addressed to practical and controversial situations.
The essential parts of the message of the Baptist appear in writings subsequent to Paul, such as the Epistle to the Hebrews
(10:36-39) and the Second Epistle of Peter (3:1-13). In fact,
the only document in the New Testament in which the vital
parts of the message of John do not appear is the Fourth
Gospel.

The third area in which John and his movement have been of
significant influence in early Christianity is that of the messianic interpretation of Jesus. It is probably true that this interpretation had its first roots in an enthusiastic but mistaken
estimate of Jesus on the part of some who were his intimate
associates during his earthly career. It was revived and revised
and given new strength and meaning by faith in his resurrection
and exaltation. It cannot be seriously doubted that the messianic explanation of Jesus antedated Pentecost. There is no intention to suggest that John or his followers had much if any
influence in originating the interpretation of Jesus as the Lord's
Anointed. But it is not without probability that certain claims
made for John and his movement had significance in making
more emphatic and precise the claims that Jesus was the ex-

pected Messiah and deliverer. There is not lacking evidence that John was considered by a persistent group to be a messianic leader and therefore a potential rival of Jesus.

Evidence as late as Justin Martyr and the Clementine *Recognitions* and Ephrem Syrus show that the disciples of John persisted and viewed their master as the Messiah. How they maintained this in the face of his tragic fate we do not know, but that they did it seems beyond dispute. Justin knows of a sect of "Baptists" whom he calls "Jews" (*Trypho* 80). The *Recognitions* offer specific evidence.

And behold, one of the disciples of John asserted that John was the Messiah, and not Jesus, inasmuch as Jesus declared that John was greater than all men and all prophets. "If then," said he, "he be greater than all, then he must be held to be greater than Moses and than Jesus himself. But if he be the greatest of all, then he must be the Messiah" [i. 60].

Ephrem Syrus is authority for the following: "The disciples of John also boast of John and declare him to be greater than the Messiah, who himself testified saying, He is not greater."[3]

Unless one treats this evidence as does Hans Lietzmann,[4] who considers it to have no historical value, it would seem clear that later than New Testament times there was a Baptist movement strong enough to be controversial and to make impressive claims for its founder. The evidence is tantalizingly inadequate to throw any light on the manner in which these claims for messianic dignity for John overcame the stern fact of his death. But the existence of the sect and its controversial claim are supported. If it were found necessary to abandon this evidence, there is other testimony which cannot be set aside. It is surprising that so many indications of a messianic interpretation of John should have survived in the New Testament. It is true that much of it is brought forward only to have it denied either by the writers or by John himself. The eagerness to deny messianic dignity and function to John manifest in the Fourth Gospel is well known. The author or editor can scarcely wait to

---

[3] For this reference see Goguel, *op. cit.*, p. 106 and n. 1. The evidence of the Zadokite fragments and of the Mandaean documents is too precarious to be adduced.

[4] *Geschichte der Alten Kirche*, I, 32, n. 4; English trans. B. L. Woolf, *The Beginnings of the Christian Church* (New York, 1937), p. 52, n. 4.

open his gospel before he tells his readers that "he was not the light" but that the true light was coming. John's function was not to reveal the light but to testify regarding the early coming of the revealing person. The testimony which he is said to have given to certain inquirers shows clearly that some had as late as this tradition been identifying him with the expected Messiah. To the question, "Who art thou?" he is made to reply most emphatically, "I am not the Messiah" (John 1:20). In this context no one had suggested that he was. The inevitable background is a messianic claim for John on the part of some. The same denial is made in an equally strange context in a later chapter (3:28). The persistent half-desperate attempt of this gospel to place John in a position inferior to Jesus is obvious.

The Synoptic Gospels also contribute evidence on the messianic interpretation of the Baptist. An examination of the infancy narrative of Luke raises important questions. The emphasis upon the extraordinary elements in connection with the birth of John makes that event as much of a divine intervention as that of Jesus with the exception of the Divine Spirit taking the place of a male parent. It is an incredible thing to Zacharias that a child should be born to his wife. But it is divinely ordained and is announced by the same archangelic messenger who later is to speak to Mary. The declaration that "he shall be filled with the Holy Spirit, even from birth. And many of the children of Israel shall he turn unto the Lord their God. And he shall go before his face in the spirit and power of Elijah, to turn the hearts of the fathers unto the children, and the disobedient to walk in the wisdom of the just; to make ready for the Lord a people prepared" (Luke 1:14–15), while not strictly messianic, is connected with Yahweh's deliverance. The utterance of Zacharias after the birth of the child connects him definitely with the divine redemption of Israel and in one phrase comes close to giving him a unique position with reference to it. The phrase is "the prophet of the Most High." It is almost instinctive to think of the prophet like unto Moses promised in the eighteenth chapter of Deuteronomy. But one recalls the denial of John himself in the Fourth Gospel: "Art thou the prophet?

And he answered, No." The similarities of function and circumstance with those which appear in the sections concerning Jesus are striking. The possibility, not to say probability, is very great that there is here a nativity story of John the Baptist in which he is portrayed as divinely born and divinely commissioned to a task which has remarkable points of contact with that ascribed to Jesus. It has been taken over by Christians and re-worked to the advantage of their Messiah.

If it should be objected that John's Levitical descent would bar him from messianic consideration, it needs only to be pointed out that there was in Judaism a strain of thought which expected the Messiah to come from the tribe of Levi. In the Wisdom of the Son of Sirach, Levi is exalted while the Davidic royal line gains but the slightest praise (45:6–26; 49:4–5). The priestly and prophetic representatives in Israel fare much better than the kingly ones. If there is any messianic messenger for this writer, it is probably Elijah (48:10–11). A certain precedence of Levi over Judah is exhibited also in the Book of Jubilees (31:9–20). In the *Grundschrift* of the Testaments of the Twelve Patriarchs there are a number of references to the Messiah as coming from the tribe of Levi. We quote but one, "And there shall arise unto you from the tribe of Levi the salvation of the Lord; and he shall make war against Beliar, and execute an everlasting vengeance on our enemies and turn disobedient hearts unto the Lord" (Test. Dan. 5:10).[5] In the Zadokite fragments there is to be found a comparison of the Levitic and Davidic strains in Judaism much to the advantage of the former.[6] It is thus evident that a messianic person of priestly descent would not be entirely strange to Jewish thought.

The prophetic work of John in calling men to a moral preparation for the divine deliverance is easily to be recognized in synoptic tradition under the Christian alterations in the interests of the messiahship of Jesus. Nowhere in the Synoptic Gospels, not even in the Christian re-working of the tradition, does

---

[5] Cf. R. H. Charles, *The Apocrypha and Pseudepigrapha of the Old Testament* (Oxford, 1913), II, 294.

[6] Cf. R. H. Charles, *Fragments of a Zadokite Work* (Oxford, 1912), pp. xii and 18.

John identify Jesus with the expected Messiah. That is true also of the tradition of Matt. 3:14-15, which is an attempt to ease the strain caused by the stubborn fact that John had baptized Jesus. It is probable that those passages which represent John as declaring himself unworthy to loose the thong of the Messiah's sandals are Christian interpretation. His work is to call men to repentance in view of the imminence of the divine kingdom. His later question to Jesus as to whether or not he was the "coming one," if it is actually a question of John, is the first indication of a connection in his mind between Jesus and the expected Messiah. The evasive answer of Jesus may have more than one explanation. The tribute of Jesus to John may well represent, apart from manifest additions, the esteem in which Jesus held his predecessor and contemporary in the heralding of the kingdom. "More than a prophet . . . . greatest among those born of women"—these are praise indeed. The clause which rules John out of the kingdom is an obvious interpolation. The popular appeal of John is seen in the statement that "all the people . . . . and the publicans, justified God, being baptized with the baptism of John" (Luke 7:29). It suggests an interesting parallelism to recall the declaration made in Mark 12:37 that the common people heard Jesus gladly. The importance of John and his movement can be inferred from the fact that "the days of John the Baptist" mark for Christian thought a most significant period for the kingdom of God (cf. Matt. 11:12; Luke 16:16). The question ascribed to Jesus, "The baptism of John, was it from heaven or from men?" (Mark 11:30) indicates in its context a high estimate of the mission and work of John.

The very definite attempt of the Fourth Gospel to have John relegate himself to a nonmessianic position and to give himself significance only in relation to Jesus is evidence of an estimate of John and claims for him that were disturbing to Christians of that day. It is no man of straw against whom the writer of the Gospel sets himself. It is a man whose messianic position and function are being asserted. This Gospel will not permit him to be a preparer of the way. His one task is to identify Jesus as the "Son of God." Having done that, he is to pass from the scene.

The evidence of the New Testament for the messianic interpretation of John and his movement is supported by an independent witness, namely, Josephus. In his *Antiquities* (xviii. 5. 2 [116–19]) he speaks of "John, that was called the Baptist." He states that he was a good man who commanded the Jews to exercise righteousness toward men and piety toward God and to "come to baptism." He asserts that the crowds that attended John's preaching and his great influence over them raised the apprehension in the mind of Herod Antipas that rebellion might result. Accordingly, he incarcerated him in Macherus and there put him to death. It is significant to note that Maurice Goguel thinks that Herod planned similar treatment for Jesus, compelling him to change some aspects of his ministry and finally to leave Galilee.[7]

The historical facts seem to be that John was hailed as Messiah and that this became an embarrassing matter for the followers of Jesus. It is probable that the emphasis on Davidic descent as a messianic credential for Jesus received at least an impetus from this claim of messiahship for one of Levitic origin. Through the royal line he comes to be the messianic king. This would enhance his dignity and importance in comparison with a priestly messiah, for the common messianic hopes envisioned a conquering king and a glorious kingdom. The Davidic descent had an advantage especially after the collapse of the Maccabean dynasty. Thus the Davidic descent of Jesus assumes importance in the opposition to a claim for one of priestly parentage. This descent is asserted in the Synoptic Gospels, the Pauline letters, the Epistle to the Hebrews, the Revelation of John, and the Acts of the Apostles; it is strongly implied in the Fourth Gospel. It appears in every major part of the New Testament. The reason for such an emphasis is not easy to discern when one remembers that the messiahship claimed for Jesus after the rise of the resurrection faith was of the transcendental type and did not require such emphasis. But, if it had been

---

[7] *The Life of Jesus*, trans. Olive Wyon (New York, 1933), pp. 346–60.

forced by a persistent claim for messianic position on behalf of a priestly person, this emergence of and emphasis upon the more popular idea of kingly descent for Jesus can well be understood. It is quite possible that a significant influence of the Baptist movement and of its founder was that it compelled a closer definition of the messiahship ascribed to Jesus. The relegation of John to the position of forerunner would stultify the claims made for him by devoted followers and would give Jesus the added support of the prophecy of Malachi regarding Elijah.

The mention of "the house of his servant David" in the utterance ascribed to Zacharias (Luke 1:69) does not bear strongly against the ascription of messiahship to a Levitic person. Though there is no textual evidence bearing on the matter, it is within the possibilities that the phrase may be an addition or an alteration in the interests of Davidic messiahship with an intent that it should be carried over to the one whom John was to foretell. Such alterations are well known in Jewish apocalyptic writings. Sometimes they were actuated by Jewish desires, sometimes by Christian wishes. If the composition known as the "Benedictus" were original in the Johannine nativity story, it is difficult to see how the priestly father of John could describe his son as of the "house of David." Either it is not original and thus existed independently where the reference to David was congenial or the phrase must be treated as an emendation.[8]

A fourth phase of primitive Christianity where John and his movement had significance is the rite of water baptism. With the very difficult questions concerning the baptism of John we are not here concerned. Such questions as to whether it was self-baptism or a baptism administered by another and the meaning of the phrase "unto remission of sins" are among the inviting problems which we must pass by. The probabilities are against the Johannine rite being self-baptism, and the interpretation of

---

[8] An interesting suggestion regarding this phrase and regarding the Lukan genealogy being originally a record of the descent of the Baptist is well presented by Clayton R. Bowen, *Studies in the New Testament: Collected Papers of Dr. Clayton R. Bowen*, ed. Robert J. Hutcheon (Chicago: University of Chicago Press, 1936), pp. 64-69.

the preposition "unto" as "in view of" or "for the purpose of" can be inconclusively debated.

The point of influence which we are suggesting is independent of these problems. A curious conjunction of water baptism and spirit baptism meets us in the traditions regarding the work of John. He is made to declare that one mightier and greater than he will follow him and that he would baptize John's hearers in Holy Spirit in contrast with the baptism in water which characterized John's movement. It is the clear intent of the evangelists to have John thus refer to Jesus as one whose work is not to be characterized by baptism in water. There is no record in the Synoptic Gospels that Jesus administered baptism of either kind. He himself is represented as endowed with the Spirit, but in the lone passage referring to others it is the Father who gives the Holy Spirit to them that ask him (Luke 11:13). In the early days of Christianity, however, the endowment of the Holy Spirit became important. The filling with the Holy Spirit of those who believed in the messiahship of Jesus (Acts 2:4) is interpreted by Peter as the fulfilment of the divine promise through Joel, "I will pour out my Spirit upon all flesh" (Acts 2:16–17). The gift of the Holy Spirit is closely connected with repentance and baptism in another statement by Peter made upon the same occasion (Acts 2:38). This Spirit baptism is a messianic act, for it is the risen, exalted Christ who has "poured forth this which ye see and hear" (Acts 2:33). Apparently the effects of this outpouring were temporary, for we are told that, after Peter and John had been released by the Sanhedrin, "they came to their own company" and reported the matter. Community praise and prayer followed, the result of which was the shaking of the room in which they were and the filling of them all with the Holy Spirit (Acts 4:31). It is in this fulness of the Holy Spirit that Stephen speaks. The Spirit had not fallen upon the Samaritan believers until Peter and John communicated it, then "they received the Holy Spirit" (Acts 8:16–17). Through Ananias Paul receives this filling of the Spirit (Acts 9:17). The Holy Spirit falls upon Cornelius and those around him when they hear Peter's declaration of the messiahship of Jesus. It is this possession of the Spirit that actually admits them to the Christian fellowship. In his defense of his action Peter makes no mention of their baptism in water but is made to say, "I remembered the word of the Lord how he said, John indeed baptized with water; but ye shall be baptized with the Holy Spirit" (Acts 11:16). Characteristic of at least some of Paul's missionary work is this filling with the Holy Spirit upon acceptance of the messiahship of Jesus (cf. Acts 13:52; 19:6). The first letter of Paul to the Corinthians offers evidence to show the important place which Spirit baptism and control had come to hold in some, if not all, of the primitive Christian communities. Dealing with a difficult and factional situation, he exhorts his hearers to unity of purpose and effort, part of his argument being, "For in one Spirit we were all baptized into one body . . . . and were all made to drink of one Spirit" (I Cor. 12:13). Further argument is not needed to show that possession of the Holy Spirit, designated by "pouring out upon," "being filled by," "baptized in," was a distinctive mark of the members of the communities which were bound together by a belief in the messianic position and salvation of Jesus. Wherever it is in any way connected with baptism in water, the superior quality and advantage of the gift of the Spirit is made clear.

Because the traditions suggest it, the general conception is that baptism in water is a rite which characterized Christianity from its inception. This is a questionable view. It is very improbable that Jesus carried this feature of John's work over into his own activity. No synoptic tradition even suggests that Jesus baptized his followers or that his followers practiced baptism in water. The one synoptic reference to baptism in relation to Jesus, other than John's baptism, refers to baptism neither in water nor in Spirit but to a task and an endurance (cf. Luke 12:50; Mark 10:38–39). It is true that in the Fourth Gospel we have a tradition to the contrary, but it is used in a theological interest and has contradictory elements. The statements are as follows. "After these things came Jesus and his disciples into the land of Judea and there he tarried with them and baptized.

And John also was baptizing in Aenon near to Salim because there were many waters there" (John 3:22–23). "When therefore the Lord knew that the Pharisees had heard that Jesus was making and baptizing more disciples than John, although Jesus himself baptized not, but his disciples" (John 4:1–2). In spite of this tradition, the historical probability is great that baptism in water did not constitute any part of the activity of Jesus. The story of the occurrences on Pentecost in the second chapter of Acts has Peter revert to the message of the Baptist. The synoptic message of Jesus and his disciples has but two elements, the imminence of the kingdom and the urgency of moral preparation for participation in it. But in the record of Peter's address at the inauguration of the Christian message he is made to exhort his hearers to baptism (Acts 2:38). The result of this proclamation and exhortation was, we are told, the reception of the apostolic word and the acceptance of baptism on the part of "three thousand souls." It is difficult to imagine such a procedure taking place in Jerusalem. A tradition concerning the Jerusalem group of hearers, preserved for us in a later chapter (Acts 4:4), omits the matter of baptism and puts belief in the apostolic word to the front. Baptism appears in the account of the Samaritan mission of Philip, here antedating and separate from the descent of the Holy Spirit upon them (Acts 8:14–17). It is part also of the story of the conversion of the man of Ethiopia (Acts 8:37–39) and is a constant factor in the Acts of the Apostles after this. That it was the practice of at least some of the communities founded by Paul as well as some otherwise founded is clear from many statements: "Or are ye ignorant that all we who were baptized into Christ Jesus were baptized into his death? We were buried therefore with him through baptism into death" (Rom. 6:3–4); "For as many of you as were baptized into Christ did put on Christ" (Gal. 3:27); "Else what shall they do who are baptized for the dead?" (I Cor. 15:29). These passages with others show the prevalence of water baptism in the early churches. As indicated earlier in this discussion there is in this same letter to the Corinthians an utterance that reflects the persistence of the view that Christians had something of surpassing value and importance in Spirit baptism. For in its context it seems more than probable that this is what Paul had in mind when he said, "For in one Spirit were we all baptized into one body, whether Jews or Greeks, whether bond or free, and were all made to drink of one Spirit" (I Cor. 12:13). A comparison with I Cor. 10:1–3 in this respect is not without interest.

But there is a declaration by this man which discloses what is apparently a decidedly secondary valuation of baptism in water. While dealing with the divisions in the Corinthian church, he asks, "Were ye baptized into the name of Paul? I thank God that I baptized none of you, save Crispus and Gaius, lest any man should say that ye were baptized into my name. . . . . For Christ sent me not to baptize but to preach the gospel" (I Cor. 1:13, 15, 17). It is true that there is an interpretation of this passage which considers it to be testimony to the high estimate which Paul placed upon baptism. The emphasis in this interpretation is on the phrases "into the name of Paul" and "into my name." But the statement that his apostolic mission is to herald the good news and not to baptize is a high hurdle for this interpretation to take.

Thus we have a Christian emphasis on baptism in the Spirit as superior to water baptism, a Jesus who does not practice water baptism, and a movement of his followers which does practice it. Behind all this there is the rival movement of John, with which Jesus had been associated and from which he had parted, and in which baptism in water was an essential element. Spirit baptism seems to have been of temporary effect; it was concrete only through manifestations some of which, at least, fell into poor repute and were coarsely interpreted by non-Christians. It was connected with an emotional enthusiasm which, no matter of how high a character, would inevitably become difficult to maintain. The Baptist and his followers might well be considered to have an advantage over the Christians in this respect. Did the concrete action of baptism in water make a deeper impression on the simple souls who devotedly espoused the faith in Jesus as the messianic savior? Did baptism in water come into the post-resurrection movement which centered in Jesus from the Baptist group? Did the followers of Jesus adopt this concrete symbolism as of more direct appeal to many than the superior but at times more difficult baptism in the Spirit? Water baptism with various symbolisms was present in Judaism and in many of the contemporary religions. In these latter, however, it was not of eschatological significance as it was in Judaism and in the Baptist movement and later in Christianity itself. It was beyond doubt a central element in a movement which in early days was a rival to Christianity and which must have caused not a little embarrassment to Christian leaders. It is in all likelihood beyond definite proof that baptism in water was adopted into Christianity from the practice of John and his adherents, but it is within the realm of probabilities. The hypothesis would help to explain a number of difficult situations among which are the recurring contrasts of Spirit and water baptism[9] in the traditions of a movement that has come to practice both.

Thus in the influence which the leader of the Baptist movement had upon his temporary adherent, Jesus of Nazareth, in a dominant element both of the message of Jesus and of his early followers, in the closer definition of the messianic descent and function of Jesus, and in the acceptance of baptism in water as a symbol of certain phases of religious experience—in these matters John the Baptist proved deeply significant for the Christian movement in its early days.

[9] Two valuable monographs in this field are Johannes Leipoldt, *Die urchristliche Taufe im Lichte der Religionsgeschichte* (Leipzig, 1928), and Hans Leisegang, *Pneuma Hagion* (Leipzig, 1922).

RELIGIOUS HEALING IN FIRST-CENTURY PALESTINE

S. VERNON McCASLAND

University of Virginia, Charlottesville, Virginia

FROM a remote antiquity Palestine had a vigorous life of its own, but it was a bridge over which most of the culture of the ancient world passed at one time or another, and much of it took root and flourished there. As a result of military conquest, commercial relations, or some less clearly defined means of cultural exchange, probably very few things in first-century Hellenistic culture would have been strange to its indigenous life. Its ideas about healing would be largely indebted to the Old Testament, but perhaps more to Jewish beliefs of a popular nature which never found expression in canonical sources. Influence of Persian dualism was strong. Many ideas were held in common with Semitic peoples generally. The cultures of Greece and Rome were struggling for a footing and had, indeed, been widely accepted. The conquest of Alexander brought Palestine within the orbit of Hellenism; subsequent events kept it there. Whether from the Ptolemies, Seleucids, Nabateans, or Romans, external influences were continuous. When the Maccabeans yielded to Pompey, Roman culture poured through open doors. But, although Palestine accepted many things from foreign sources, she usually succeeded in making them her own.[1]

PREVENTIVE MEDICINE

We may designate as preventive medicine all devices, procedures, herbs, medicines, or objects of any kind expected to ward off disease and preserve good health. First of all, we may infer, was the requirement of living a devout, righteous life.

---

[1] A penetrating study of healing in Hellenistic times, with particular attention to theories of disease, was presented by S. J. Case, "The Art of Healing in Early Christian Times," *Journal of Religion*, III (1923), 238–58.

God was believed to send illness as punishment for sin. This belief was held by the early Christian community as well as by the Jews, as shown, for example, by the question of the disciples concerning a blind man—who had sinned, the man or his parents? (John 9:2)—or the death of Ananias and Sapphira, a divine punishment visited on them for dishonesty (Acts 5:1). The belief was maintained and elaborated in rabbinic thought until it was held by some that all the calamities of man's life, such as the death of his children,[2] illness,[3] and all suffering,[4] result from sin, although this never became the only interpretation of suffering in Jewish life. A rabbinic proverb runs: The door which is not open to alms will be opened to the physician.[5]

The inspection and isolation of persons and houses with contagious diseases by Jewish priests was another phase of preventive medicine in Palestine, for the Levitical regulations on this subject were still observed in the first century.[6]

AMULETS

Another widely used preventive device was amulets of various types and materials, whose function was to protect the person or animal wearing them, or the object, building, or locality where they were placed or on which they were suspended, against marauding evil spirits or the baneful influence of the evil eye, constant sources of danger and threats against the health and welfare of human beings. These objects are parallel in function to the modern practices of sanitation, hygiene, vaccination, and other protective measures against disease. In general use for this purpose were either material objects endowed with protective powers or a potent formula or charm, either spoken or written, usually calling by name, and invoking the aid of, some deity or other powerful spiritual being, often several spirits and deities at the same time. As an illustration of this practice from

---

[2] H. L. Strack and P. Billerbeck, *Kommentar zum Neuen Testament aus Talmud und Midrasch* (Munich, 1922), I, 365 (*Schab.* 32b Bar.).

[3] *Ibid.*, p. 479 (*Ned.* 41a).

[4] *Ibid.*, p. 495 (*Schab.* 55a).

[5] *Ibid.*, IV, 558 (*Midr.* HL 6, 11 [125a]).   [6] *Ibid.*, pp. 751 f.

ancient times, we may note this passage from a Leyden magical papyrus:

> Thou art I and I am thou; whatever I say must come to pass, for I bear thy name as an amulet in my heart; all the storms of Styx will not overwhelm me; nothing, whether spirit or demon or any other horror of Hades, will oppose me because of thy name which I have in my soul, which I invoke; hear me then, O Merciful One, in all things; grant me health proof against all bewitchment; grant me happiness, prosperity, honour, victory, power, lovableness; hold in check the evil eye of all my adversaries; grant me grace in all my works.[7]

The belief in the evil eye was widespread in ancient times although not much evidence with reference to it in Palestine has survived. It was so general in Egypt that a reference to it is not unusual in ordinary personal letters, especially in regard to children, and the eye of Horus was one of the commonest amulets in Egypt.[8] Belief in the evil eye is widespread in Palestine today, and a glass factory at Hebron specializes in evil-eye beads. Amulets of this and various other types are worn by people and animals and hung on houses, automobiles, and other objects of value. Hand beads made by the same Hebron concern, said to be the hands of Fatima, Jacob, or the Virgin Mary, according to the purchaser's religion, are another popular type. That this modern use of amulets is a continuation of an ancient practice is shown by the beads and pendants found in excavations, many of them definitely from the Hellenistic level. To take just one example, the Harvard excavation at Samaria found, along with many other objects recognized as amulets, several eye beads.[9]

In first-century Palestine it was believed that certain herbs formed potent amulets and that Noah had been taught their use by angels.[10] Solomon was also said to have received knowledge of such things from God; and a particular rue which grew in a

[7] Otto Pfleiderer, *The Early Christian Conception of Christ* (London and New York, 1905), p. 115. Quoted by permission of G. P. Putnam's Sons, publishers.

[8] Cf. B. P. Grenfell and A. S. Hunt, *The Oxyrhynchus Papyri* (London, 1898–1914), No. 292; G. Milligan, *Selections from the Greek Papyri* (Cambridge, England, 1910), p. 38; E. Budge, *Egyptian Magic* (London, 1899), p. 55.

[9] G. A. Reisner, *Harvard Excavations at Samaria* (Cambridge, Mass., 1924), I, 376, 379, 380, 381, 382.

[10] Bk. Jub. 10:10–14.

wadi near the castle of Machaerus east of the Dead Sea was highly prized for this purpose.[11] The general use of potent names in charms is indicated not only by the secret powerful names revealed in Enoch, chapters 40 and 69, but also in the reference of Josephus to the angel names held in secret by the Essenes.[12] The story of the exorcism in the Book of Tobit (8:1-3) shows that the liver and heart of a fish burned on incense served the same purpose. Phylacteries and mezuzahs, while they had the more general purpose of reminding the Jew of the Law and his obligation under it, appear also to have served as amulets to protect against demons, the name *phulakteria* itself, derived from *phulassein*, "to guard" or "protect," indicating this, and in later rabbinic thought this specific function is definitely attributed to the phylacteries.[13]

CURATIVE MEDICINE

Coming to the treatment of actual disease, we pass logically from the preceding to demon possession and exorcism. "Possession," as we use the term here, refers to certain types of mental derangement, not to other disorders of the body attributed to demons. There are different types or degrees of possession. The affliction is characterized by a partial or complete change of personality. The patient may manifest a different voice, facial expression, moral character, and even knowledge which he does not normally seem to possess; or he may on occasion assume several different roles successively, each with its peculiar and definite characteristics. In some cases the afflicted person retains consciousness of his own identity but feels at times that a strange personality enters into him, dominates him, usurping his functions of speech, sight, etc., and then departs, probably to return from time to time. In other cases the stranger takes up a permanent abode in the patient, but without smothering out the normal consciousness entirely, so that the normal and abnormal selves function alternately. Or the demon completely overwhelms the normal self for a period, so that the person com-

---

[11] Josephus *Antiquitates Judaiorum* viii. 2. 5.   [12] Josephus *Bellum* ii. 142.
[13] Strack and Billerbeck, *op. cit.*, IV, 275 (*Berakh.* 23a).

pletely identifies himself with the strange personality. Finally, in the most severe cases, the domination is complete and permanent, so that the individual experiences no more lucid moments but consistently assumes and manifests the role of the demonic invader and master.

The exorcist is a person who attempts, by invoking powerful names over the demon or by amulets, herbs, or other potent devices, or his own authority, to strip the demon of his power, drive him out, and restore the patient to his normal consciousness and functions. Regardless of the scientific standing of the theory of personality involved, the symptoms themselves and many cures are well authenticated in both ancient and modern times.[14]

The exorcism of the first century in Palestine is related to the demonology of older Semites and Egyptians, as well as Greeks and Romans, but true possession, in the Mediterranean world, may not be much older than the first century. The ancient Semites had an elaborate demonology, one of the best-known figures being Lamashtu, a blood-sucking demoness, who emerges in Greece as Lamia, and then survives in the vampire conceptions of Europe.[15] Then there is the ancient Semitic group of seven demons, who probably appear in the story of Mary Magdalene.[16] But, while diseases are attributed to demons by the ancient Semites, we are not aware of any case which presents the change of personality required in true possession. The earliest definite cases of real possession with which we are familiar involve Jews and early Christians and are associated with Palestine. That there was much traffic with the occult among the ancient Hebrews is shown by the laws against such practices;[17] but the story of the evil spirit which tormented

[14] Cf. T. K. Oesterreich, *Die Besessenheit* (Halle, 1921); English trans. *Possession, Demoniacal and Other* (New York, 1930); John L. Nevius, *Demon Possession and Allied Themes* (Chicago, 1894).

[15] Stephen H. Langdon, *Semitic Mythology* (Boston, 1931), pp. 85, 366–68.

[16] G. A. Barton, in *Encyclopedia of Religion and Ethics*, IV, 570; R. C. Thompson, "Assyrian Prescriptions for the Head," *American Journal of Semitic Languages and Literature*, October, 1937.

[17] Cf. Deut. 18:10; Exod. 22:17; Lev. 20:27; II Chron. 33:6.

Saul is the only close approach to possession in the Old Testament, and it does not clearly present the change of personality demanded, although that may possibly have been present. The same must be said about the case of Sarah in the Book of Tobit. It is not unusual for a possessed woman to be in love with the demon and loath to give him up, which may well have been the case with Sarah; but no specific statement is made to show the phenomena manifested by true possession, and the narrative is so overlaid with legend, if it be not pure fiction, that we cannot now be certain of what happened in this instance. Nevertheless, Tobit does throw light on Jewish demonology, possibly in Egypt about the second century before Christ, indicating not only beliefs about the evil work of demons but also devices for their control revealed by angels.

In first-century Palestine, however, as related by Josephus, there was widespread exorcism of apparently real possession, and the Jews were proud of the skill which they possessed in this art.[18] Solomon is said to have been the great authority in this field, and he had received his knowledge from God. Josephus describes exorcisms performed in the presence of Vespasian and his staff; and the fact that he wrote in Rome under the patronage of Vespasian and his sons, even if there were no other evidences of his reliability, is a strong substantiation of his authenticity. The exorcist to whom Josephus refers is a certain Eleazar. What he says about exorcism applies to the years of the war against Rome, that is, A.D. 66–70. His account agrees with what rabbinic tradition relates about a rabbi of Palestine, Chanina ben Dosa, from the same period, a friend of Jochanan ben Zakkai and a contemporary also of the Apostle Paul and other Christians of the last half of the first century. He is said on one occasion to have exorcised Agrath bath Machlath, identified by some as Lilith, the reputed mother of Ahriman, known among the Hebrews as early as Isa. 34:14. The conception of this female leader of demons, with luxuriant hair and wings, terrifying specter of night, as reflected in rabbinic thought, is consistent with what we otherwise know of first-century demonol-

18 Josephus *Bellum* vii. 178–85; *Ant.* viii. 2. 5.

ogy in Palestine.[19] Another rabbi, Schimon ben Jochai, while he was on a mission to Rome about the middle of the second century, is said to have cast out a demon from the emperor's daughter.[20] That the Pharisees of the time of Jesus were accustomed to cast out demons is shown by his words, "If I cast out demons by Beelzebub, by whom do your sons cast them out?" (Matt. 12:27; Luke 11:19, from the Q document). One of these sons of the Pharisees is to be seen in Bar Jesus the Jewish sorcerer met by Paul at Paphos (Acts 13:6). At Ephesus Paul came in contact with certain of the itinerant exorcists of the Jews who even attempted to use the name of the Lord Jesus to cast out demons (Acts 19:13). The fact that seven of these exorcists were sons of a Jewish high priest connects them with Palestine. The casual reference to these traveling Jewish exorcists apparently assumes that they belonged to a recognized Jewish profession at the time. A somewhat similar situation existed in Egypt in the time of Hadrian. In a letter to the Consul Servianus he writes scornfully: "There those who worship Serapis are in fact Christians, and those who call themselves bishops of Christ are, in fact, devotees of Serapis. There is no chief of the Jewish synagogue, no Samaritan, no Christian presbyter, who is not an astrologer, a soothsayer, an anointer."[21] About the middle of the second century Justin Martyr freely admits that Jews are successful exorcists.[22] While his *Dialogue with Trypho the Jew* was probably written at Ephesus, Justin was a native of Palestine, born at Shechem, and Trypho the Jew is thought to be Rabbi Tarphon of Lydda, who had attended temple services in Jerusalem in his youth, a rabbi who was known for his hostility to Christianity.[23]

Simon Magus, the Samaritan encountered by Philip and

[19] Strack and Billerbeck, *op. cit.*, IV, 514–15.

[20] *Ibid.*, pp. 534–35.

[21] David Magie, *Scriptores historiae Augustae* (London and New York, 1922), Vol. III (viii. 1–4).

[22] Justin *Dialogus* 85.

[23] O. Stählin, *Die altchristliche griechische Litteratur* (Munich, 1923), pp. 1283 f.; H. L. Strack, *Einleitung in Talmud und Midrasch* (Munich, 1930), pp. 125 f.

Peter at Samaria, was a Palestinian sorcerer. Still another is referred to by Lucian of Samosata in northern Syria as the "Syrian from Palestine," adept in the art of exorcism.[24] Lucian, who wrote about the middle of the second century, shows a wide acquaintence with Semitic exorcism.

The best-known Palestinian exorcists of the first century, of course, are Jesus and his first disciples, all of whom were Jews. Even Paul, who was a native of Tarsus, was educated in Palestine. Jesus cast out demons and gave his disciples power to do the same thing, in this way destroying the power of Satan and preparing for the messianic kingdom. The essential authenticity of the Gospel records in this respect appears to us to be beyond reasonable question. Exorcism was thus deeply rooted in first-century Palestine, first among Jews, then among Jewish Christians, from whom the heritage was passed on to more recent times.

Palestine appears to have been the chief source of exorcists and exorcism of the time. Such writers as Strabo, the elder Pliny, Cicero, and Pausanias, although much interested in religious things, appear not to be acquainted with the phenomena. The ancient Greeks regarded epilepsy as the "sacred disease" and treated it by purification and incantation. In an essay under that title Hippocrates ridiculed both the diagnosis and the treatment. Here we have what closely resembles demon possession and exorcism, but it is not the same. The disease is caused not by demons but by one or another of the gods, and the idea of the replacement of human personality by divine is not presented. Another close approach to the conception among the Greeks is made by Plutarch in his discussion of the *Oracles of the Pythia* and the *Decadence of Oracles*. His idea of inspiration is close to possession but not identical with it, nor does exorcism appear. Incantations were widely used among the Greeks, but their use does not necessarily imply real possession. The *Life of Apollonius of Tyana* presents real possession and exorcism, but it was written in the third century and is so legendary that its testimony is of doubtful value faced by the

[24] *Philopseudes* 16.

silence of the above-named reputable authorities. The Greeks and Romans were certainly ready for the appearance of these phenomena in the first century; in fact, the absence of positive evidence of their existence is surprising; but the great outburst of possession and exorcism during early Christian times seems to have begun in Palestine. Of course, the phenomena were soon generally known all over that world. The cause of this strange development at that time is not certainly known, but Harnack has connected it with the breakdown of the old religions and the emergence of the individual with his fears.[25]

Exorcism is not the only type of healing attributed to Jesus and his disciples, the documents listing such diseases as leprosy, blindness, paralysis, fevers, withered members, raising the dead even being included, thus continuing the Jewish traditions associated with Elisha and the popular legends about Solomon, who had now become a great healer. The already mentioned Chanina ben Dosa, in addition to exorcisms, is said to have cured at least two fevers by prayer.[26] A similar cure is attributed also to Judah, the Prince of Galilee, early in the second century.[27] These Palestinian healings have many parallels among Greeks and Romans of the time, not to mention those at the great shrines of Asklepios and other healing deities. The legends associated with Apollonius of Tyana have been referred to. Vespasian is said to have cured blind and lame in Alexandria sent to him by Serapis in dreams.[28] Hadrian did similar things.[29] So did Pyrrhus.[30] Vespasian is said to have cured blindness by the application of spittle to the cheeks and eyes and lameness by the impress of his foot. Pyrrhus is also said to have cured by the touch of his foot. A blind woman is said to have been cured after she had kissed the knees of Hadrian and then bathed her eyes in water in a temple.

[25] A. Harnack, *Texte und Untersuchungen* (Leipzig, 1892), VIII, Heft 4, 37–147, "Medicinisches aus der ältesten Kirchengeschichte."

[26] Strack and Billerbeck, *op. cit.*, II, 441 (*Berakh.* 34b Bar.).

[27] *Ibid.*, I, 526 (*Chag. 3a*).   [28] Tacitus *Historia* iv. 81.

[29] Magie, *op. cit.*, Vol. I (Hadrian xxiv. 3–4; xxv. 1–2).

[30] Plutarch *Life of Pyrrhus* iii.

SACRED SPRINGS

The story of the healing of Naaman's leprosy in the water of the Jordan indicates the curative powers attributed to certain waters in ancient times. There are natives in Palestine today who still believe that the Jordan's water has a medicinal value. It is quite generally believed in Palestine that springs and wells are inhabited by spirits, in some cases by good spirits and in others by evil, some being ordinary jinn, others saints, Moslem or Christian. Dr. Canaan has made a study of no less than one hundred and twenty-five of these inhabited springs, indicating several which the natives believe have healing powers. He suggests with great probability that the spirits in many cases may represent survivals under modern names of supernatural beings associated with these springs in antiquity.[31] While most of the popular beliefs of this kind in ancient Palestine have perished, a few intimations of them, nevertheless, have come down to us. The Pool of Siloam may be a case in point. According to John 9:1–7, Jesus anointed a blind man's eyes with clay made with spittle and sent him to wash in this pool, and he was healed. The Siloam fountain is still thought to have healing properties today. The Pool of Bethesda is a good illustration of the belief in the first century not only that certain pools were inhabited by divine beings but that they possessed miraculous power to heal. John 5:2–9 relates that a multitude of the sick were accustomed to lie in its porches waiting for the troubling of the water, when the first one to step in was cured. The popular belief is preserved by an interpolator, who says an angel came down and troubled the water and cured the first one to step in. The Bordeaux Pilgrim (A.D. 333) mentions healings at this pool and says that Solomon had bound demons there.[32]

ASKLEPIOS AND HYGIEIA

Dr. Canaan states that all hot baths today are thought to be inhabited, for example, the one at Tiberias, famous in the first

[31] T. Canaan, "Haunted Springs and Water Demons in Palestine," *Journal of the Palestine Oriental Society*, I (1922), 153–70.

[32] P. Geyer, *Itinera Hierosolymitana saeculi IIII–VIII* (Vienna and Leipzig, 1898), p. 21.

century,[33] by jinn who heat the water.[34] The religious belief about these hot springs at Tiberias in the first century is shown by a bronze coin struck by the city in A.D. 99, on the obverse of which is the bust of Trajan, but on the reverse is Hygieia seated on a rock, from beneath which water breaks forth, holding in her right hand the serpent of Asklepios, which feeds from a phial in her left. The coin was again struck in A.D. 108.[35] Thus the cult of the famous Greek healing deity Asklepios had taken root here on the Sea of Galilee in the first century, probably absorbing an older local healing cult. There are several springs in Palestine today believed to be inhabited by serpent spirits.[36] Sacred springs in association with healing shrines were well known in Greece. Pausanias found a spring sacred to Asklepios at Gythium in Laconia, another sacred to Amphiaraus at his healing shrine in Oropus, whose altar was shared by Hygieia among others, and still others presided over by healing nymphs on the Lower Anigrus in Trephylia.[37] Another Hygieia coin was struck at Tiberias during the reign of Commodus in A.D. 189.[38] The biblical name of the springs at Tiberias was Hammath; the Greeks called the village Emmaus; and today it is Al Hummam. Hammath or Emmaus appears to have been the usual designation for hot springs in Palestine.[39]

A few miles around the south end of the Sea of Galilee from Tiberias, beyond the Jordan in the valley of the Yarmuk, with Gadara on a high hill above to the south, is another Hammath, today Al Hammeh, with even more famous hot springs. Eunapius affirms that, next to those at Bajae, they are the most important baths in the world.[40] Strabo says that when cattle

---

[33] Josephus *Bellum* ii. 21. 6; *Ant.* xviii. 2. 3; Pliny *H.N.* v. 15.

[34] Canaan, *op. cit.*, p. 23.

[35] G. F. Hill, *Greek Coins of Palestine* (Oxford, 1914), p. 6, Pl. I, No. 10.

[36] Canaan, *op. cit.*, p. 24.

[37] Pausanias iii. 21. 8; i. 34. 4; V. 5. 10.

[38] Hill, *op. cit.*, p. 10, No. 38, Pl. II, No. 6.

[39] G. A. Smith, *Historical Geography of the Holy Land* (4th ed.; New York, 1896), pp. 450 f.

[40] E. Schuerer, *Geschichte des juedischen Volkes* (4th ed.; Leipzig, 1901–11), II, 158.

drank the water they lost their horns and hooves.[41] The *Onomasticon* of Eusebius refers to them as cleansing springs. Epiphanius says that a festival was celebrated there each year when men and women bathed together, that polyandry was practiced there, and that the waters were good for various diseases.[42] Antonius Placentius (A.D. 570) refers to them as the "baths of Elijah, where lepers are healed." He says that there was a great bathing pool into which the lepers were sent with lights and incense, where they sat down all night long, that the one to be cured saw some vision, that while he recited it the springs were restrained seven days, and that on the seventh day he was cured.[43] Thus, in his time, not only are springs thought of as inhabited by a holy man but the healing has taken on the incubation feature so characteristic of the Asklepios cult. This late development here may well be an elaboration of a first-century practice parallel to that at Tiberias.

A first-century site equally famous for its fresh waters and fruits and its hot baths was Livias, across the Jordan twelve miles east of Jericho, the Beth-Haram of the Old Testament.[44] We do not know that religious healing was performed here in the first century, but in the fourth century St. Silvia was shown here beautiful springs which Moses gave the Israelites when he struck the rock, and also hot springs in which Moses bathed.[45] In the sixth century Theodosius said not only that Moses bathed in these hot springs but that lepers were cured there.[46] Gregory of Tours gives the same information.[47]

The hot baths at Callirhoe, east of the Dead Sea, were also a famous resort in the first century, to which Herod the Great went in desperation, only to die a few days later at Jericho, but we have no evidence of a religious interpretation of healings there.[48]

[41] Strabo xvi. 2. 45.

[42] Epiphanius *Adv. Haer.* i. 131.   [43] Geyer, *op. cit.*, p. 163.

[44] Josephus *Ant.* xviii. 2. 1; Pliny *H.N.* xiii. 4. 44.

[45] Geyer, *op. cit.*, p. 52.

[46] *Ibid.*, p. 145.

[47] *De gloria martyrum* i. 18.   [48] Josephus *Bellum* i. 33. 5; Pliny *H.N.* v. 16. 72.

The spring at Jericho, known as Elisha's Fountain, had a healing function at least from the time of that prophet, who is said to have transformed its deadly waters with salt (II Kings 2:19–20). Josephus refers to this and says its waters made both land and women fertile.[49] In the sixth century Theodosius reported that the grave of Elisha was there and that a church was built over it.[50] This spring is now believed to be inhabited by a young woman.[51]

Jacob's Well, near Sychar and Neapolis, modern Nablus, where Jesus asked the Samaritan woman for a drink (John 4:5–6), a gift of the Patriarch Jacob and from which he himself is said to have drunk, may well have had healing properties even in the first century. At any rate, in the sixth century, Antonius Placentius reports that the sick were cured there from a water bucket from which the Lord had drunk.[52] The cult of Asklepios also took root in Neapolis. Whether in the first century or not we do not know, but Asklepios and Hygieia coins were struck there under Antoninus Pius and again during the reigns of Philip Senior and Gallus a century later.[53]

The Asklepios cult is also indicated at Ascalon. Proclus, head of the Neo-Platonist school at Athens in the fifth century, celebrated the Asklepios Leontouchos of Ascalon in a hymn.[54] How early this Greek deity appeared there is unknown; but, if we may judge by other cases, Asklepios probably absorbed the cult of an older native healing deity here, possibly indicated by the epithet "Lion-keeper."

Asklepios was well known at Sidon in Phoenicia in the first century, where he had absorbed the native cult of Eshmun, one of the chief deities not only of Sidon but of all Phoenicia, with numerous temples, the one at Sidon dating at least from the fourth century before Christ.[55] Strabo mentions the Tamyrus

[49] Bellum iv. 8. 3.   [51] Canaan, op. cit., p. 15.

[50] Geyer, op. cit., p. 137.   [52] Geyer, op. cit., pp. 162 f.

[53] Hill, op. cit., pp. 47, 65, 66, 71.

[54] Schuerer, op. cit., p. 31; Marinus Vita Procli 19.

[55] F. C. Eiselen, Sidon (New York, 1907), p. 166; an inscription from 396–383 B.C.

River between Berytus and Sidon with its grove of Asklepios.[56] Antonius Placentius refers to the Asklepios River at Sidon.[57] Pausanias met a man of Sidon at Aegium in Achaia, who contended that the Sidonians understood Asklepios and Apollo better than the Greeks did, affirming that Apollo was the sun and Asklepios the air, both essential to health.[58] The Eshmun temple at Sidon was excavated in 1900, and numerous votive inscriptions to Eshmun were uncovered, with at least one to Asklepios.[59] A trilingual inscription of Sardinia identifies the two deities.[60] The Eshmun temple in the Phoenician colony of Carthage in the time of Strabo was devoted to the worship of Asklepios.[61] It seems probable that, wherever the Phoenician Eshmun was worshiped, at home or in the colonies, he was absorbed in the Hellenistic period by Asklepios. This not only testifies to the healing character of Eshmun but indicates the wide prevalence of religious healing in Phoenicia from early times. The way for the coalescence of the two deities was prepared also by the reverence for serpents which existed in Phoenicia, as reported by Philo Byblius,[62] so that Asklepios with his sacred serpents would not seem strange there. Even the youthful nature of Eshmun was paralleled in Greece by certain beardless statues of Asklepios.[63] This Eshmun-Asklepios cult must have been well known in Palestine. Jesus and his disciples, when they retired into the borders of Tyre and Sidon, to say the least, were close to the Asklepios shrine at Sidon. The proximity of Phoenicia and Palestine to each other and the similarity of their languages made extensive commercial and cultural intercourse between them inevitable, and it was fur-

---

[56] Strabo xvi. 2. 22.   [57] Geyer, op. cit., p. 159.   [58] Pausanias vii. 23, 7–8.

[59] Eiselen, op. cit., p. 135; Mitteilungen der vorderasiatischen Gesellschaft (Berlin, 1904), p. 316, No. 12.

[60] G. A. Cooke, North-Semitic Inscriptions (Oxford, 1903), p. 108.

[61] Strabo xvii. 3. 14.

[62] Philo Byblius 41a, 41b, in C. Mueller, Fragmenta historicorum Graecorum (Paris, 1849), pp. 572 f.

[63] Pausanias ii. 13. 5; ii. 10. 2.

thered no doubt by the generally peaceful relations between them, even from ancient Hebrew times.

PAN

One of the most interesting of the healing shrines of Palestine was Caesarea Philippi, Paneas, the modern Banias, its name indicating that it was sacred to the Greek Pan. In the nature of the case, Pan was not original here but had some Semitic predecessor, possibly Baal Gad, Lord of Good Fortune.[64] The popularity of Pan there is shown by numerous coins carrying his symbols. From this site we have an inscription to Nemesis set up by a priest of Pan; likewise, one by Agrippa, king of Judea, to Echo,[65] showing that other deities were associated with Pan here. The first-century importance of this place is shown by the fact that, when Augustus added that region to the kingdom of Herod the Great, Herod built a temple there dedicated to Augustus; that the site was further embellished by Herod Philip, who named it Caesarea, and again by King Agrippa, who named it Neronias; that Vespasian visited there; and that Titus celebrated his victory over the Jews there.[66] Josephus says that the place was called Pannium (Paneion) and that it contained a great cave in a mountain full of still water but that underneath the caverns arose the springs of the Jordan. The original deity there would have been the god of the source of that river. Eusebius relates that the mountain was called Panius and describes a sacrifice made on certain days to the spirit of the spring. He also describes what he thought was a statue of Jesus there, set up in gratitude by the woman healed of an issue of blood before her house, and says that a strange plant climbed up on the bronze statue which was a remedy for all kinds of diseases and that before the statue knelt a supplicating woman.[67] The statue was certainly not of Jesus, and likely not of Asklepios, as Harnack thought,[68] but probably of one of the emperors honored there. In any case, it testifies to the cult

---

[64] J. Hastings, *Dictionary of the Bible*, I, 337.   [65] *CIG*, 4537 and 4539.

[66] *Ant.* xv. 10. 3; xvii. 8. 1; xx. 9. 4; *Bellum* iii. 9. 7; vii. 2. 1.

[67] *H.E.* vii. 17-18.   [68] *Op. cit.*, p. 141.

of healing at Paneas. While the statue of a healer which stood there did not represent Pan, it is not improbable that he functioned as a healer at Paneas. Neither the grotto, nor the spring, nor the mountain sacred to Pan, nor his healing function is unusual in the cult of that Arcadian deity.[69] Peter the Deacon says there was not far from Mount Hermon a fountain blessed by the Savior which healed all diseases.[70] Thus what was probably first a Semitic and then a Greek healing shrine was absorbed into the healing cult of the Christian Lord.

SERAPIS

Another deity who may have had a cult of healing in Palestine was Serapis, whose role as a healer in Egypt, especially in association with Asklepios in the Serapeum at Memphis, is well known.[71] The healing shrines of Asklepios at Epidaurus, Rome, and numerous other places around the Mediterranean, with their dreams and votive inscriptions, were familiar to all in the first century; and Serapis in certain regions was equally famous. Cicero recognizes this when he groups together Aesculapius and Serapis as objects of his satire because of their dream healings.[72] We have no specific testimony to Serapis as a healer in Palestine, but an inscription to Serapis, now built into the pier of the Zion gateway in the south wall of Jerusalem, was set up by a standard-bearer of the Third Legion of Cyrene about A.D. 115.[73] Numerous Serapis coins from Jerusalem (Aelia Capitolina) appear from the time of Antoninus Pius, at Caesarea from the time of Hadrian, and at Neapolis from the time of Marcus Aurelius.[74] It is not unreasonable to suppose that his cult of healing so popular in Egypt was maintained in Palestine, brought there probably by soldiers from Egypt who served in the Roman armies.

[69] Pausanias ii. 10. 2; ii. 32, 6; i. 34. 1–5. [70] Geyer, op. cit., p. 112.

[71] Cf. F. C. Kenyon, Catalogue of Greek Papyri in the British Museum (Oxford, 1893), p. 27.

[72] De divinatione ii. 59.

[73] F. J. Bliss, Excavations at Jerusalem (London, 1898), p. 251.

[74] Hill, op. cit., pp. 57 ff., 84–85.

It is thus clear that we have a considerable amount of evidence of religious healing in first-century Palestine. There were both preventive and curative procedures. On the one hand, there were the indigenous practices involving amulets, charms, incantations, exorcism, sacred springs, prayer, piety, and the names of angels and of the Deity. On the other hand, there was a penetration of Palestine by foreign cults, such as those of Asklepios and Hygieia, Pan, and Serapis. There was religious healing in Judaism, Greco-Roman and Phoenician cults, and also in emerging Christianity. Healing was one of the most important functions of religion in first-century Palestine. No religion could have supplied all the needs of that world without it, even if it had been desirable. Although Palestine had no healing shrines comparable to those of Asklepios at Epidaurus, Memphis, and Rome, it appears to have surpassed other Mediterranean lands in the activity of individual religious healers, particularly in the exorcism of demons from possessed persons, a practice which, in both Judaism and Christianity, was to continue in regions beyond.

THE HELLENIZATION OF JEWISH MESSIANISM
IN EARLY CHRISTIANITY

CLYO JACKSON

St. Stephen's College, Edmonton, Alberta

CHRISTIANITY is a historical religion. It had its rise in Palestine and among Jews whose sacred scriptures were mainly in Hebrew and whose daily speech was Aramaic. Jesus was a Jew, as were his earliest followers. The estimate which these primitive Christians formed of their fellow-Jew who had become central in their religious life was expressed by the Jewish term "Messiah," i.e., "anointed." For centuries this word had been gathering up into itself the hopes and ideals of this proud people, who were now experiencing the bitterness of their subjugation to Rome as earlier their fathers had chafed under the domination of other world-empires. There were other characterizations at hand which might have become controlling in their evaluation of Jesus and which did contribute in part to their expression of his religious significance for them; but "Messiah" surpassed all other attempts to classify Jesus.

Christianity remained for only a generation in Palestine. Early within that generation the new movement was attracting Greek-speaking Jews and Gentiles beyond Palestine. In that new, strange world Jesus of Nazareth remained supreme in the religion of the Christian groups over the Greco-Roman world. The Hebrew and Aramaic term "Messiah" was retained in its Greek equivalent "Christ"; the Greek form went into the very name of the new religion. This essay asks what changes in the conception of savior and salvation took place when the religion whose Savior had been acclaimed "Messiah" on Jewish soil for Jewish people with Jewish hopes and ideals came to have the value of "Christ" for people of gentile heritage.

35

Jewish messianism has become the technical term for the varied hopes of this dejected people—hopes that the golden age for which they yearned would surely come; that Yahweh was in control and would not disappoint his own.

Messianism has a long history even antecedent to the Old Testament. The genesis of the idea of a happy deliverance from the ills of life has been traced to the elemental characteristics of early man, namely, superstitious fear due to animistic conceptions in the presence of the stern forces of nature, the sense of dependence consequent thereon, and the desire to be happy ingrained in the heart of man. This combination of traits in primitive man has resulted in the widespread pictorial representation of the eventually happy issue of that struggle which seems to characterize life. Man, least at home on the water yet forced to live by the water, looked upon the forces which produced the catastrophes he knew, floods and storms at sea, as antagonistic; man's salvation must perforce come from one who would overcome these sea monsters; the consummation was in the daydreams of a golden age, yearnings and aspirations handed on from generation to generation, until the tradition came to be regarded as the echo of something that had once upon a time actually happened. In the Old Testament are preserved reflections of these primitive philosophical ventures in the myths which the Hebrews shared with other peoples, not through some common source or original, it is thought, but because of common experience; these the Hebrews utilized and adapted in conformity with their developing spiritual conceptions. In historical times they had effected a unification of these stories: to Yahweh they ascribed the role of both destroyer and deliverer. In monotheistic Israel Yahweh had become the cause of all supernatural activities, beneficent and malevolent. The problem of suffering was a pressing one for the devout Jew.

Jewish messianism is thus the dream of a glorious future rid of those factors which now make life hard. From the thought of deliverance and the vision of a blessed age on ahead their religious teachers turned to speculate as to how this redemption would be brought about. Of course it would be Yahweh who would effect the transformation: "We hope in God, our deliverer" (Ps. Sol. 17:3). But He would have a helper, one "anointed" to his task as they knew their kings and priests anointed with oil to theirs. This "Anointed One" or Messiah of later Jewish thinking has lent his name to the earlier formulations. It is doubtful if the word "Messiah" is used in this technical sense in the Old Testament at all. Many passages there and in the inter-Testament literature speak of a glorious future but have no Messiah agent; Yahweh alone is the deliverer. Yet such passages are spoken of as messianic. Some scholars have thought it desirable to delimit the term so that it would express only such hopes as imply a personal Messiah. And for the other, the earlier and more vague concept, no word is conveniently at hand; "messianic age without a Messiah" has been suggested, an "unhappy phrase" in George Foot Moore's judgment.[1]

When one turns to the inter-Testament passages which picture a personal Messiah, no definitive portrait can be reconstructed. Jewish religious teachers—prophet, apocalyptist, sage—all sought to make real the nebulous faith that Yahweh would come in rescue. For clarity these imaginative representations of the coming "Messiah" have been grouped as (i) national, or Davidic; and (ii) eschatological, or supernatural and apocalyptic; a third merits mention if only to be dismissed, namely, the priestly Messiah of the line of Levi, as in the Testaments of the Twelve Patriarchs.

The inter-Testament Jewish writings which have survived are as varied in form as the books of the Old Testament: translation, history, poetry, didactic romance, wisdom, apocalypse; one cannot escape the inference that these uncanonical works mirror a vigorous religious life in that period. Of these in that milieu the apocalyptic writing seems to have flourished most; this type was more popular than the mere listing of the known apocalypses beside the titles of the other Jewish literature of their producing would indicate. Judaism rejected this genre eventually, as did Christianity; it is difficult now to appreciate

[1] *Judaism in the First Centuries of the Christian Era* (Cambridge, Mass.: Harvard University Press, 1927), II, 327.

the popularity of what seems to us bizarre pictorial writing, which was such a radical departure from the more direct and canonized "Thus saith the Lord" of the prophets. Extant apocalypses are all composite, as if made up of fragments of earlier works of the same type. And there survive in the New Testament traces of apocalyptic details not found in the known apocalypses (e.g., Rom. 8:22).

When the title "Messiah" came to be used of the historical Jesus, many of the characterizations which the reverent imagination of Jewish religious teachers had created were not immediately applicable. The reason is obvious: Jesus had lived a human life, and many of these Messiah portraits presented a supernatural and pre-existent being. But of these pictures of the coming Messiah one was at once applicable, namely, the Davidic Messiah. If this title were applied to anyone who was living his life in Palestine, such ascription would be understood by the Roman authorities as sedition. The inflammable nature of messianism led early Christian writers to indicate pointedly their loyalty to the empire.

Messianic hopes seem not to have flourished in the later Tannaite age; the rise of Christianity and events in Palestine about A.D. 70 and A.D. 135 would not furnish a favorable environment. The absence of messianic ideas in the Mishnah is not to be wondered at; Palestinian Jews would not remember the word "Messiah" kindly. "The new sect [Christianity] . . . . pointed to an array of passages [in the Old Testament] in which they found prediction of their 'Messiah.' The messianic application of all such passages was thenceforward repudiated, as a matter of course, by the Jewish authorities, as far as this could be done."[2]

When the Messiah title was applied to one who had lived a human life, there would be much freedom of selection as to details, for there was no agreement in the inherited Messiah portrait.

Without the neglected Jewish writings of the inter-Testament

[2] C. C. Torrey, "Outcroppings of Jewish Messianism," in *Studies in Early Christianity*, ed. S. J. Case (New York: Century Co., 1928), p. 303.

period the Gospel background would be unintelligible. The apocalypses especially which had cheered the Jews in days of distress were cherished by the Christians of the first century and neglected, even disowned, by later Judaism.[3] The political events about A.D. 70 left this people without Zion and Temple and Altar. Judaism determined to set itself steadfastly against denationalization, and only in the refinements of the Torah was this happily done. Resultant rabbinism, work of the Pharisees, kept the Jewish people together after the Sadducean activities about the Temple had ceased and the sect had disappeared, and their religious activity found expression in the formal canonization of the Hebrew scriptures and the codification of the Talmud. In the formative years of the Christian movement within Judiasm apocalyptic messianism was the popular expression of religious life.

When early Christians called Jesus "Messiah," the title would call up no unified or standard portrait. Later when Paul speaks of Jesus as "of the seed of David" (Rom. 1:4), it is not probable that he intended the Romans to visualize an overlord who would do for Israel what their great David had done; the epithet is taken quite from its original setting in an effort the better to do justice to Jesus, risen and exalted. Similarly, in the Gospels the assertion that Jesus is of David's line is made with no thought that he was a revolutionist. The title had drawn to itself all the desirable qualities of the many idealizations of the inter-Testament Jewish writers.

The possibility that environment would modify religious conceptions has come to be recognized slowly. The little verse in the vigorous epistle of Jude about "the faith once for all delivered" unto the Christians has seemed to preclude the idea that "the environment of early Christianity" contributed to the expression of that vigorous faith. But even in Judaism the cult practices of Galilee differed from those of Judea; there were slight differences in respect of marriage laws (*Ketuboth* iv. 12a; v. 9; xiii. 10); there was a difference in the observation of the

---

[3] Excepting, of course, Daniel, which had so honorable a place in the life of the Maccabees that the list of the canonical books could not fail to include this.

fourteenth of Nisan: in Judea one worked until noon; in Galilee not at all (*Pesachim* iv. 5). Judea had Jerusalem and the Temple and priests and sacrifices; Galilee must be content with synagogue instruction and the long pilgrimage to the Holy City: "O Galilee, Galilee, thou hatest the Torah" was Ben Zakkai's lament.[4] Thus within rabbinic Judaism which glorified the Torah, now that the Temple and sacrifices were abolished, modifications had grown up.

Early Christianity was at the outset Palestinian. The transition from Palestinian to extra-Palestinian Christianity was not so abrupt as might at first glance appear. Jesus' life had been spent largely in Galilee: his intimate friends were Galileans; in Galilee they had lived together; from Galilee he had gone up with them to that fateful Passover, apparently for his first visit to the city and the Temple (Mark 11:11). When the officials took Jesus into custody, his companions "all forsook him and fled" (Mark 14:50) back to Galilee, it would seem. In Galilee again they learned that they could not thus put him out of their lives, that he who had become central in their lives was vital still. Galilee was the cradle of the Christian faith.

This most northerly province of Palestine, separated as it was from Judea and the capital city by schismatic Samaria, was "a half-way house between the Judaism of Jerusalem and that of the Dispersion."[5] "Judea was on the road to nowhere, Galilee was covered with roads to everywhere" is George Adam Smith's terse way of putting it.[6] Or, with Schürer, "He who wandered among the hills and valleys of Galilee was never far from some great and populous city."[7]

The largest cities of Galilee were Tiberias, Sepphoris, and Gabara, all "Hellenistic" cities. Sepphoris, politically for a time the capital, "ornament of all Galilee" (Josephus *Antiq.* xviii.

[4] Quoted in the *Jewish Encyclopaedia*, art. "Johanan ben Zakkai."

[5] W. K. L. Clarke, *The Parting of the Roads*, ed. F. J. Foakes Jackson (London, 1912), p. 178.

[6] *Historical Geography of the Holy Land* (London, 1909), p. 425.

[7] E. Schürer, *History of the Jewish People* (Edinburgh, 1898), Vol. II, chap. i. pp. 103, 139, 146.

2. 1) thanks to Herod Antipas, who had rebuilt it, was but an hour's walk north and west of Nazareth. The presence of these Greek towns spoke persistently to the Galilean Jew of the greater Greek world beyond to which many of his own countrymen had gone.[8]

The study of early Christianity must start with Paul; his letters are our earliest literature and have the value of scientific documents as other New Testament writings do not have. The possibility of editorial manipulation when the letter collection was being prepared for the canon is present; some letters, it would seem, were put together under the one heading, and in the process modification might creep in. But the canon-making church, which was unwilling to accept a harmonized gospel story and which insisted on the fourfold gospel with its self-evident differences, would not yield to the desire to change Paul materially in the interests of any dogma, however advantageous such change might then seem.[9] The great epistles bear authentic marks of the very situation in Corinth and Ephesus of A.D. 50–70. From Paul comes our most reliable picture of the early church.

Paul was of the great world beyond Palestine. The impact of that Greek environment had long been making itself felt on the Jewish people who had found their place there. They had adopted the Greek language; they had done their sacred scriptures into Greek; within the oldest portion of the Septuagint are marks of non-Jewish religious ideas in the rendering of the Hebrew.[10]

As soon as the earliest Christians left Galilee and Judea, they stepped out from the shelter which an indigenous ethnic faith, passionately particularistic, had provided into a busy, jostling world. The influences which had made extra-Palestinian Ju-

---

[8] See R. Otto, *Kingdom of God and the Son of Man*, trans. Filson and Woolf (London: Lutterworth Press, 1938), for Persian and Indian Aryan influences upon Galilee of Jesus' day.

[9] See below, p. 51.

[10] H. B. Swete, *Introduction to the Old Testament in Greek* (Cambridge, England, 1914), pp. 326 ff.

daism distinguishable from Palestinian Judaism would now similarly surround the new religious movement.

Paul, of that world, accepted the primitive Christian's characterization of Jesus as Messiah, but accepted only after struggle. His difficulty would arise because of the difference between the Jesus whom Christians termed Messiah and the Messiah of his inherited Jewish hopes. For, though of extra-Palestinian Judaism, Paul was Hebrew of the Hebrews. To him at first it must have seemed sacrilegious that anyone should say that one born of woman, born under the Law, crucified by the Romans upon the cursed tree, was Messiah. His first major problem was to find place for this Jesus of history alongside his messianic conceptions. Would Paul subordinate the Jesus of history to his inherited theological ideas of the coming Messiah or would he mold his thought of Messiah to the lowly Jesus of whom he had learned from the Christians, from Peter and from Jesus' brother James?

There are many passages in the letters which show that Paul had accepted, apparently from the primitive church, the apocalyptic interpretation of Jesus as Messiah.[11] The recovery of the inter-Testament Jewish literature, made accessible by Kautzsch in 1900 and Charles in 1913, gave to this strangely new aspect of Jewish background something of the nature of a discovery. Forthwith zealous scholars seized upon apocalyptic eschatology as the key to the understanding of Jesus and Paul: Jewish environment was the explanation of early Christianity. The work of these apocalyptic interpreters, e.g., Schweitzer, was influential over a long period in part because of the outbreak of the World War; in that catastrophe the apocalyptic hopes seemed to bring comfort to many. Apocalypticism spoke from distress to distress, and the Revelation of John was searched for guidance.[12] While the contribution of this aspect of the Jewish environment to the expression of the significance of Jesus is

[11] [See the author's unpublished thesis in the University of Chicago Libraries: "Hellenization of Christian Messianism" (1923), where the apocalyptic references in Paul are listed along with the parallels in the inter-Testament literature.—EDITORS.]

[12] Cf. C. Jackson, "The Seminary Professor and New Testament Research," *Journal of Religion*, XVII (April, 1937), 183–94.

now generally recognized, other aspects of Paul's Jewish heritage from contemporary Jewish thinking contributed. But no longer is Jewish apocalyptic messianism regarded as the controlling factor in Paul's Christianity.

Contemporaneous with the discovery of the apocalyptic in early Christianity was the recovery of the Hellenistic background. For Christianity could not be confined to Palestine any more than Judaism could be; but extra-Palestinian Judaism did not harbor the new religion long. At Corinth, where the first bit of Christian writing that has survived was done, and at that very time, Paul had begun his ministry in the synagogue, after his custom; but before long he was out of the Jewish synagogue, at Ephesus now, and was using the schoolhouse of Tyrannus, "when that lecture-hall was free," to adopt the Codex Bezae gloss (Acts 19:9). So, twenty years after the death of Jesus, Judaism and Christianity were parting company.

Thus two streams united to form the cultural heritage of Christianity: Judaism and Hellenism.[13] For, before Paul, Christianity had become Greek. To do into Greek the Aramaic sayings of Jesus which the primitive church had preserved was the difficult task which the widening horizons had put upon the early Christian preachers. In that they would no doubt unconsciously color their story of Jesus by their own background, just as the Septuagint translators had done.

More potent in influence upon the new religion than language would be the impact of the pagan world with its picturesque and varied religious rites. Harnack's often-quoted words about Christianity being a Greek movement for the first two centuries has reference to more than language. The interaction of the practices of one worshiping community upon the practices of another has been observed in modern missionary activities; the Commission of Appraisal has set down their judgment that, "whenever two vigorous religions are in contact, each will tend to borrow from the other—terms, usages, ideas, even gods and

[13] See G. H. C. Macgregor and A. C. Purdy, *Jew and Greek, Tutors unto Christ* (New York: Charles Scribner's Sons, 1936), pp. 193–348. Professor Macgregor lists as qualities characteristic of Hellenism, individualism, humanism, intellectualism, beauty, moderation, and naturalism.

articles of faith."[14] Hinduism and Buddhism, they report, show a readiness to appropriate Christian ideas and methods such as modes of worship, preaching, Sunday schools, hymns, etc., learned from the missionary. A situation pregnant with like results was present in the early decades of the Christian Era. The discovery of this aspect of the extra-Palestinian environment of early Christianity was intoxicating. Of the many religious forces, the mystery religions seemed peculiarly close to Christian cult practices; originally nature religions in which were celebrated the miracle of returning spring and the consequent revival of all nature with the promise of fertility to the soil after the dreary winter, the mysteries disclosed to the novitiate through the initiatory rites the meaning of life and death. The dramatic portrayal of the sufferings of the god, the baptismal cleansing, the sacred meal—all seemed to anticipate the crux of the Christian gospel. Startled by the parallels, some New Testament scholars saw the Christianity even of Paul as a mystery religion—a religion which gave to its devotees through magical sacraments the assurance of salvation and the promise of a blessed immortality. Paul may have had no thought of appropriating such pagan concepts; the people to whom he spoke must have understood him in the way they had been accustomed to understand similar religious rites with which they were familiar: Paul's "mystery" (I Cor. 15:51) and baptism for the dead (I Cor. 15:29), and the sacred meal, which had had tragic consequences for some (I Cor. 11:29), are details which might suggest that Paul's Christianity was a mystery religion. Apparently, Christian baptism was being performed for the dead, and some had died because they had partaken of the "Lord's meal" unworthily; the sacred elements had become as poison to them, like opium, medicine for some but poison for others.

Early in the second century Ignatius had spoken of the bread of the Lord's Supper as the "medicine of immortality, the antidote that we should not die but live forever in Jesus Christ"

[14] Commission of Appraisal, W. E. Hocking, chairman, *Re-thinking Missions* (New York, 1932), pp. 43 f.

(Eph., chap. 20). Justin (*ca.* A.D. 150) noted that in the practice of the church after the Eucharist "a portion is sent to those who are absent." Justin was aware of the parallel, for he accuses the devotees of Mithra of imitating Christian usage: "The wicked devils have imitated [this rite] in the mysteries of Mithras, commanding the same thing to be done. For you either know or can learn that bread and a cup of water are placed in the mystic rites of one who is being initiated" (*First Apology*, chap. 67).

The significance of the Jewish background for early Christianity was obvious to all; the discovery of the Hellenistic environment was not so generally welcomed. Yet some scholars seized upon this as the clue to the understanding of Paul: Paul's Christianity was a mystery religion which mediated salvation in magically efficacious sacraments; eventually it supplanted the pagan mysteries.[15]

The years of this century have given to the students of the Jewish environment in which Christianity had its rise and of the Hellenistic environment in which it flourished a sense of perspective. Now it is seen that neither background alone will account for the new religion, nor will both together.[16] Clothes, Carlyle wrote, give us individuality, but they do not make the man; the "Jewish old-clothes of Christianity," to appropriate his figure, and the Greek felt hats, which Antiochus would require all to wear (II Macc. 4:12), were "threatening to make clothes-screens" of the reality. One has only to read the Jewish Enoch beside the letters of Paul to realize that Christian apocalyptic differed from its Jewish prototype: I Corinthians, despite its many references to apocalyptic, throbs with life; Enoch seems so removed from things mundane that there is ever present an element of unreality, the greater because of its pseudepigraphic authorship; Paul put himself in his letters as few do. In the

[15] E.g., A. Loisy, "The Christian Mystery," *Hibbert Journal*, October, 1911, pp. 45–64; K. Lake, *Earlier Epistles of St. Paul* (2d ed.; London, 1914).

[16] Cf. E. F. Scott, *The Kingdom and the Messiah* (Edinburgh, 1911), p. vi, and *The Kingdom of God in the New Testament* (New York, 1931), pp. 58 and 60; cf. Lake, *op. cit.*, pp. 215, 233, 385, and 435, and *Paul, His Heritage and Legacy* (New York, 1934), pp. 106 f.

same way the moral requirements in Paul seem strangely new when put alongside the ethical aspects of the mysteries, oriental in origin, but influential in the Greco-Roman world.[17] The reasons for the more restrained view of the early environmental factors in Christianity now seem so obvious.

Certain considerations keep one from viewing the apocalyptic as central and controlling in Paul's interpretation of Jesus as the Christ. Paul has introduced conceptions which are alien to apocalyptic Judaism—conceptions which are so unlike the messianism of contemporary Judaism that it would seem nearer the truth to regard these as primary and fundamental, and the apocalyptic as secondary. New traits appear in the picture which Paul drew of the Messiah; these new aspects take precedence over Paul's inherited conception of Messiah, and this change brought about for Paul, Pharisee of the Pharisees though he was, the revolutionary struggle that made him Christian.

What are the features in Paul's new Messiah portrait which are not in his inheritance but which seem to be basic? Those which come from the life of Jesus. Jesus had lived humbly the life of a Galilean itinerant preacher; after his crucifixion his disciples came to think of him as risen, at God's right hand; when Paul applied the epithet "Messiah" to this Jesus, something had happened to his conception of Messiah. Jesus had come to be for Paul a charismatic personality, in Otto's phrase, i.e., a religious and moral genius; in him Paul saw the realization of his people's dreams of messianic succor: the realization was quite unlike the dream, and the title inadequate; but no other near-adequate category seemed at hand.

Paul had opportunity to know the story of that life; and the inference is well-nigh inescapable that Paul had actually taught his hearers the story of that life in its essential aspects.[18] The

---

[17] See F. Cumont, *Oriental Religions in Roman Paganism* (Chicago: Open Court Publishing Co., 1911), pp. xii–xiii; H. R. Willoughby, *Pagan Regeneration* (Chicago: University of Chicago Press, 1929); M. Enslin, *Ethics of Paul* (New York: Harper & Bros., 1930), esp. pp. 45 ff.

[18] He speaks of two events of that earthly life—the Last Supper and the death, burial, and resurrection—quite by accident, for difficulty had arisen at two points where, in seeking solution, Paul finds it helpful to refer to what he had previously taught: "Which also I delivered unto you" is his courteous reminder to them that they should have re-

character of Jesus, "born of woman," meek and sweetly reasonable (II Cor. 10:1), was an ideal not hinted at in the masterful, militaristic, apocalyptic Messiah: he has "loved us" (Rom. 8:37), and we ought in return to love him (I Cor. 16:22). The impression which the story of that life made upon Paul was that here was a way of living worthy and capable of imitation (II Cor. 11:1)—a way at heart the reversal of current ideals, but in effect a conception of God which had brought Paul an emancipation he had not attained in Pharisaic Judaism.

In telling the story of that life for others in our gospels the early church had itself a large, even a creative, part. Their background was that of eschatology and apocalypticism, as it was for Jesus and for Paul; more significant was the background in morals and religion which through the centuries Judaism had been achieving. With this rich inheritance—apocalyptic, eschatological, ethical, religious—Jesus had pushed forward the frontiers in the moral and religious aspects of human life; the church understood that the high demands—demands which Jesus had himself met—were really incumbent upon all. In it all Jesus is of the nature of the genius; to his challenge Paul

---

membered his narrative of the institution (I Cor. 11:23), and of the Easter story (I Cor. 15:3; 15:1).

Similarly, though the occasion to rehearse the details did not present itself, he must have told of the crucifixion (Gal. 3:1-2; I Cor. 2:8; I Thess. 2:15, meaningless if Paul had not known that the readers were already familiar with the death of Jesus). The date of the event (I Cor. 5:7), the suffering and humiliation (Gal. 6:17; Mark 15:15; Rom. 8:17; Phil. 3:10; Gal. 5:11; 6:14); the spirit in which this was endured (II Cor. 13:4; Phil. 2:8), a spirit to be copied (Phil. 3:17)—all is told so casually that it can mean only that he knew they would recall what he knew they knew.

Traits of Jesus' character reflected in the letters show that Paul must have acquainted his hearers with that life: sinlessness, postulated, it is true, of the apocalyptic Messiah, had been realized in One "in the likeness of flesh of sin" (Rom. 8:3), humble (Phil. 2:6), obedient (Rom. 5:19), forgetful of self (II Cor. 8:9; Rom. 5:19), lovable as loving (Rom. 8:37; I Cor. 16:22; II Cor. 5:14; Eph. 3:19), meek and reasonable (II Cor. 10:1), a trait hitherto proper only in slaves.

Many words of Paul recall sayings ascribed to Jesus in the Synoptics: I Cor. 13:2, cf. Matt. 17:20; 21:21; Rom 2:1, cf. Matt. 7:1 f.; Rom. 12:10, cf. Mark 9:34 ff.; Rom. 12:14, cf. Matt. 5:39.

A few sayings about "inheriting the Kingdom of God," an expression which Paul uses rarely, are introduced in such way as to bring to mind Matthew's expression (25:34), and in such way as to imply that Paul had communicated the matter previously (e.g., "I told you before," Gal. 5:21; I Cor. 15:50; Rom. 14:17; Eph. 5:5).

Cf. F. C. Porter, *The Mind of Christ in Paul* (New York: Charles Scribner's Sons, 1930); C. H. Dodd, *History and the Gospel* (New York, 1938), esp. pp. 57–68.

had yielded assent. While it is in part true that it was Jesus' "eschatology which was decisive in carrying Jesus beyond the span of his natural life to the post-resurrection company of his disciples, resulting in their giving him a unique status as a veritable messenger of God, the fulfilment of Israel's hope, the true Messiah,"[19] apocalyptic eschatology of itself would not have stood the test of time and shortly must have petered out.[20] Basically, it was the life of Jesus, lived among his fellow-Jews within the limitations of first-century ideas and ideals, that made the Christian church. To his intimate followers that life came as the revelation of God. In it they saw the possibilities of their own lives; to that goal they gave themselves without stint in the spirit they had caught from him; and through the years a growing cloud has gathered, witnessing to the fact that his is the way to live.

When Paul accorded this Jesus of Galilee, crucified and risen at God's right hand, the title "Messiah," his inherited thinking regarding messianism had to undergo change; apocalyptic Judaism could not inclose the Jesus of Paul's redemption.

Monotheism has difficulties. Paul, monotheist that he was, had yielded himself "slave" to this Jesus; he prays to him (II Cor. 12:8), loves him (I Cor. 2:9; 16:22; etc.), places him beside God (I Thess. 1:1) as of Yahweh's class ("in the form of God" [Phil. 2:5]). He often uses the same expression for what God has done and what Christ has done (I Cor. 15:10 and II Cor. 12:9; Rom. 15:15 f. and Rom. 5:11). Sometimes it is impossible to say whether Paul's Kyrios is Yahweh or Jesus (Rom. 14:6–9 and Rom. 14:8 and 14); sometimes that most intimate relationship is oddly expressed: "if God's spirit dwells in you" (Rom. 8:9), "if any one has not the spirit of Christ" (Rom. 8:39). A prayer to God is also addressed to Jesus Christ

---

[19] C. C. Morrison, "Jesus Christ as God and Savior," *Christendom*, Autumn, 1938, p. 593.

[20] For an examination of C. H. Dodd's "realized eschatology," i.e., that "the kingdom of God *has come*" (Mark 1:15) within the lifetime of Jesus, a position which implies that Jesus did not hold to a future consummation within, or at the end of, our aeon, see James Campbell in the *Expository Times*, XLVIII, 91–94, 138–41, 184 f.; and Clarence T. Craig in *Journal of Biblical Literature*, LVI (1937), 17–26.

(I Thess. 3:11). He called Jesus by the title for Yahweh in his Greek Bible—Kyrios, as others gave Serapis or the Emperor Nero the same title.

Such was Paul's practice; but in his theology Paul does subordinate Jesus to God: face to face with the inescapable problem of Jesus' relation to Yahweh, he declared himself a strict monotheist. He nowhere calls Jesus God;[21] there is only one God (I Cor. 8:4; I Cor. 8:6: "One God the Father, and one Lord Jesus Christ" [Col. 1:3]); several expressions enforce this subordination of Jesus under the form of sonship: "the God and Father of our Lord Jesus Christ" (Rom. 15:5). In the picture of what is to come the Son is subjected to Him "that God may be all in all" (I Cor. 15:28; II Cor. 5:18). Manifestly, Paul subordinates Jesus Christ to God; yet he has divine functions. Paul was moving in the direction of the Logos solution of the dilemma: "To us one God the Father from whom all things .... and one Lord Jesus Christ through whom all things are" (I Cor. 8:6; cf. Col. 1:15–18). Some Christians, as at Colossae, wished further to subordinate Jesus by putting Jesus below the divine beings which filled the upper world; but Paul will not be party to further humiliation: "In Christ all this hierarchy of emanations dwells bodily" (Col. 2:9).

Paul seems conscious of the dilemma, but his experience permits him to set the two things—devotion to Yahweh and devotion to the Lord Jesus Christ—side by side as not incompatible. He does not sublimate Jesus Christ into a hypostasis in the divine substance; that remained for the Greek theologians of the fourth century.

It was the impact of the human life of Jesus, exemplifying even unto death the life of love and humility to which Paul's being gave assent that this is the true life, not Pharisaism, not apocalypticism, not the mysteries, which most accounts for the new Messiah portrait which Paul has left. It was Jesus, who had walked with his feet so firmly upon this earth, who knew children as they are, that they do sometimes sulk, who viewed

---

[21] Rom. 9:5 can be punctuated to mean that Christ as to the flesh is God, but the passage when punctuated as in Westcott and Hort is not different from Paul elsewhere.

human relations as they are and not with blind idealism, certain that brothers do quarrel over the inheritance and do strive for the best places, who knew so well "what was in man," and who notwithstanding put forth the ideal of love and humility; it is this Jesus who is central in Paul's Christianity. In Paul Christianity has historical relations with the surrounding life, but there is also something not elsewhere. One may turn in the wrong direction and discover what was not new in Paul; the thing that was new Paul had learned from Jesus: he may not consciously have known that his portrait of the Master was drawn from that earthly life.

One aspect of Jewish messianism Paul has used to resolve the theological dilemma in which his acknowledgment of Jesus as Messiah had placed him, namely, pre-existence. Pre-existence had been posited of the apocalyptic Messiah (I Enoch 48:2 and often; IV Ezra 13:26); with Paul's acumen the problem of this relation must present itself; Paul finds a way out in maintaining that Jesus' earthly life was one of humiliation, a kenosis; that before his earthly life Jesus' status had been on an equality with Yahweh.

The question has been investigated in recent years. F. C. Porter[22]—convinced that basic in Paul's Christianity are the life and teachings of Jesus—has urged that the two passages, Col. 1:15–17 and Phil. 2:6–11, so fundamentally different from the rest of Paul's letters in attitude of mind to Jesus, are, one, a Logos interpolation (pp. 196 f.) and, the other, a quotation from a hymn (p. 207).

In 1932 E. Barnikol published two volumes on the question of the pre-existence of Paul's Christ: *Mensch und Messias* and *Philipper 2*.[23] Barnikol lists nine passages in Paul which have been understood to imply the pre-existence of his Christ;[24]

---

[22] *Op. cit.* E. Lohmeyer (*Kyrios Jesus* [Heidelberg, 1928]) also judges the pre-existence section in Philippians not Paul's but earlier, a Jewish hymn, which Paul quotes.

[23] *Mensch und Messias* (Kiel: Walter G. Mühlau, 1932); *Philipper 2: Der Marcionitische Ursprung des Mythos-Satzes Phil. 2:6–7* (Kiel: Walter G. Mühlau, 1932).

[24] Phil. 2:1–11; Gal. 4:4; I Cor. 2:8, 8:6, 10:4; II Cor. 8:9; Rom. 8:3, 8:32; 9:5.

against these he puts twenty-five passages which point the opposite way.[25] When in *Mensch und Messias* Barnikol examines the eight passages (excepting Phil. 2:1–11), the pre-existence of Paul's Christ yields to a post-resurrection interpretation rather than to pre-existence, or the passages are to be understood proleptically. Barnikol judges the Colossian epistle deutero-Pauline.

In his *Philipper 2* Barnikol concludes that the passage in question, Phil. 2:6–7, is not from Paul but has been interpolated from Marcion. The ground for deleting it is the fact that no Christian writer before Clement of Alexandria makes use of the section; Irenaeus quotes Phil. 2:8 but neglects the two verses which precede, as though 2:6–7 were not in his text. The vocabulary of the two verses contains words not found elsewhere in Paul, or not so used.[26] Barnikol calls attention to the editorial work necessary in preparing the letter collection for the canon, as in Romans and II Corinthians, and hints at the ease with which interpolation might occur. Marcion made use of the passage (Tertullian *Adv. Mar.* v. 20), for it fitted his heretical views.

The two volumes raise the christological problem, but the Marcionite origin of Phil. 2:6–7 is not demonstrated. There are reasons why Irenaeus need not quote the earlier portion of the passage: the kenosis part (2:6–7) was not so apt for his purpose as 2:8 was; and, as M. Dibelius has indicated,[27] the passage in Paul did provide Marcion orthodox support for his heresy. Paul was critical of many items in Christianity which had come from Judaism—the Judaism he knew so well—but he was less critical in appropriating Hellenistic modes of religious expres-

---

[25] I. Thess. 2:15, 4:14; Gal. 1:8, 4:14; I Cor. 1:22–9, 3:11, 15:3 ff., 15:13, 15:28, 15:45; II Cor. 5:15 f., 5:21, 11:4, 13:3 f.; Rom. 1:3, 5:6, 5:12, 6:3–5, 6:9–10, 8:19, 8:29 ff., 8:38 f., 9:23, 10:6 ff., 11:34.

[26] μορφή in both verses and not elsewhere in Paul. εἰκών is found in Rom. 1:23; 8:29; I Cor. 11:7; 15:49 (bis); II Cor. 3:18; 4:4. δοῦλος often in Paul, as a "slave" of Jesus Christ; never elsewhere of Jesus himself. κενοῦν in Rom. 4:14; I Cor. 1:17, 9:15; II Cor. 9:3, meaning "to destroy"; never elsewhere in Paul does it mean "to empty," as here. ἁρπαγμός is a New Testament *hapax legomenon*.

[27] *Handbuch zum Neuen Testament: An die Philipper* (Tübingen, 1925), *ad loc.* esp. p. 73.

sion like μορφή and ἐν ὁμοιώματι and σχήματι. . . . ὡς. The church soon did regard Jesus Christ as pre-existent and accepted the Logos Christology. Believing, as I do, that the historical Jesus was basic in Paul's Christianity, one might wish to be able to delete these Logos and pre-existent foregleams as not by Paul; but that only postpones the solution which the church did adopt. The problem of the relation of Jesus of Nazareth, Messiah, to Yahweh remains. It seems more likely that Paul himself attempted the solution than that the canon-making church has interpolated into Philippians from Marcion.

On gentile soil, where dying and rising saviors were already in favor, such worshiping communities would influence nascent Christianity where they seemed to have common ground, namely, the sacramental rites. Of this, considerations of space forbid discussion.

POPULAR REACTIONS AGAINST CHRISTIANITY
IN THE ROMAN EMPIRE

ERNEST CADMAN COLWELL

Divinity School, University of Chicago

THE story of popular opposition to Christianity in the Roman Empire cannot be written entirely aside from the history of official persecution.[1] The interrelation of popular and official reactions to Christianity is seen first of all in the fact that popular opposition preceded and underlay all official opposition to Christianity in the first two centuries and a half. That there was before Decius no empire-wide rigorous attempt to crush the Christian religion is generally admitted today.[2]

Before Decius strong popular opposition preceded governmental opposition and was in most cases the reason for it. Tacitus says, "Those who were called Christians by the mob and were hated for their crimes."[3] Pliny notes that an anonymous accusation containing many names was presented to him, and

---

[1] I have tried to expound elsewhere the reaction of the upper classes to Christianity in this period (E. C. Colwell, *John Defends the Gospel* [Chicago, 1936]).

[2] For discussions of the persecutions see S. J. Case, *The Social Triumph of the Ancient Church* (New York, 1933); A. Harnack, *The Mission and Expansion of Christianity in the First Three Centuries*, trans. J. Moffatt (2d ed.; London and New York, 1908); E. T. Merrill, *Essays in Early Christian History* (London and New York, 1924); L. H. Canfield, *Early Persecution of the Christians* (New York, 1913); H. B. Workman, *Persecution in the Early Church* (London, 1906); K. S. Latourette, *A History of the Expansion of Christianity: The First Five Centuries* (New York and London, 1937); A. D. Nock, *Conversion . . . . from Alexander the Great to Augustine of Hippo* (Oxford, 1933); P. C. Labriolle, *La Réaction païenne* ... (Paris, 1934).

The debate among scholars as to the legal basis of these early popular persecutions still goes merrily on. The continuance of this dispute is evidence of lack of conclusive evidence on this point. In such circumstances the expression of one more opinion is not important, but it seems to the author that the case for a Neronian edict is unconvincing, that in definite times and places all the various other bases alleged played a part, and that the accusation of treason-atheism played an important role only from the last part of the second century on.

[3] *Annals* xv. 44.

the rescript of Hadrian to Minicius Fundanus was evidently called forth by a petition which claimed to represent the inhabitants of a province. In each of these cases it is clear that popular dislike of the Christians preceded the action of the officials. Nero would not have found the Christians a scapegoat had they not incurred the dislike of the populace. Pliny's correspondence with Trajan shows him to be a temperate official restraining the violence of the enemies of Christianity.

The early Christian sources present the same picture. From the Gospels through the incidents of the Book of Acts it is the mob that strikes first; official action becomes necessary to preserve the peace and restrain disorder. The Fourth Gospel, at the beginning of the second century, assumes as a well-known fact that Christians are "hated by the world." The same statement is made in the Epistle of James (4:4), "The friendship of the world is enmity with God." In the apocryphal Acts official opposition is regularly a result of individual protest to the authorities. In the earliest martyrdoms the crowd is violently against the Christians; note, for example, the cries of "Away with the atheists" in the *Martyrdom of Polycarp* (iii. 2, xii. 2). Thus also in Eusebius *Church History* iii. 32 (under Trajan): "A persecution was stirred up against us in certain cities in consequence of a popular uprising." Athenagoras *Plea for the Christians*, chapter i: "You allow us to be driven, harassed, and persecuted, the multitude making war upon us for the name alone." The mobs at Lyon are credited by the Christian narrator with hostility surpassing that of the Roman officials in that they are responsible for the return of Attalus to the arena.[4] Both Tertullian and Eusebius cry out against Roman officials who slay the Christians merely for the sake of gratifying the outcries of the populace.[5]

There is a strong, long-continued Christian tradition that the Jews were responsible for the outbreaks of mob violence against

[4] *Letter of the Churches of Vienne and Lyon* i. 50; cf. i. 17.

[5] Eusebius *Church History* iv. 8; Tertullian *Apology* ii. 37; cf. also *II Clement* vi. 3; Justin *I Apology* i. 1; iv. 5, xiv. 3, xx. 3, xxiv. 1, lvii. 2; *II Apology* i. 2, viii. 1-5; Tatian 25; *Epistle to Diognetus* v. 11, 17.

the Christians. The Passion story in the Gospels, the persecutions in the Book of Acts, and the early Christian martyrdoms all support one of the best-known lines in Tertullian, "The synagogues are the source of persecution." When the early Christian authors do not blame the Jews with direct responsibility for the persecutions, they still hold them responsible by ascribing to them the creation of slanders which were spread abroad against the Christians. Justin, Origen, and Tertullian are in agreement on this.[6]

This early picture cannot be accepted uncritically. Adequate recognition must be given to the apologetic interest of early Christian authors. It is now generally admitted that the author of Acts had as one purpose the conciliation of Roman officialdom. His consistent presentation of Roman as friend and Jew as enemy puts pressure upon the Roman leader not to align himself with the despised Jew. For it should not be forgotten that the Jew was the victim of prejudice then as now; and when early Christian authors try to place the major responsibility for persecution upon him, they are impelled by that desire to associate their persecutors with objects of popular dislike which led also to their portrayal of Nero and Domitian as persecutors and of the good emperors as nonpersecutors. It is therefore reasonable to assume that the Jewish part in this persecution has been overstated.[7]

The letters of Paul themselves indicate that he suffered from Gentiles as well as from Jews.[8] In I Thess. 2:14–15 he speaks forcefully of the persecutions which he had suffered from the Jews, but it is often overlooked that this is said to emphasize the persecutions which the Thessalonians had suffered from their own countrymen.[9] The implication of this important verse is

[6] Justin *Dialogue* 16, 17, etc.; Origen *Celsus* vi. 27; Tertullian *Scorp.* 10; *Nations* i. 14; *Marcion* iii. 23.

[7] That the chief opposition to Christians came from Gentiles after the first century is the position of Latourette, *op. cit.*, p. 121.

[8] Cf. II Cor. 11:24–25.

[9] "For you, brethren, became imitators of the churches of God which are in Judaea in Christ Jesus; for you also suffered the same things *of your countrymen* even as they did of the Jews."

that the early Christians in Paul's day were persecuted by the people among whom they lived: Palestinian churches by Jews, missionary churches by the Gentiles. Nor need it be assumed that the early identification of the Christians with the Jews—a confusion that lasted no more than one generation—was the sole cause of their being slandered. They earned these slanders in the same way that the Jews did. The characteristics of the Jewish religion that brought these slanders upon it in pre-Christian days were present also in Christianity to make it the object of slander independent of any connection with Judaism. A clear statement of the grounds on which the popular hatred of the Jews stood occurs in the *Life of Apollonius of Tyana*. Philostratus (v. 33) indicts them for an unsocial existence, for living as a foreign nation within the empire.

But Philostratus was an intellectual and speaks of real causes for prejudice where a member of the mob would have reported in detail the gross slanders which circulated against the Jews. These slanders were briefly that the Jews were cannibals, that they were atheists, that they preached and practiced sexual license, were guilty of ritual murder, etc. These same slanders, with no more modification than is necessary to transfer the murder meal from the Passover to the Lord's Supper, were frequently directed against the Christians in the first few centuries of the Christian Era. There is hardly a calumny directed against the Jew which was not later directed against the Christian.

These slanders were in no important way the causes of popular opposition to Christianity. They sprang out of it and were caused by it more than they contributed to it. When the conditions which made the slanders possible or credible died, the slanders died with the opposition.

The soil out of which these slanders grew was widespread popular hatred of the Christians. The Christians in some of their writings protest against it, although in many of the early documents it is assumed as part of the nature of things. Most interesting is their analysis of the reason for the opposition. Within the books of the New Testament itself we find the statement that Christians are persecuted for the name, that is, merely for being Christian.[10] "By the invocation of the name of Jesus Christ who was crucified under Pontius Pilate there is a separation and division among mankind."[11] However questionable may be the accusation of Christian apologetics that the Roman courts condemned the Christians merely for the name, there can be no doubt that the mob condemned the Christians as Christians. It was not only the existence in Christianity of disturbing elements, peculiar practices, and peculiar beliefs but the more general matter of Christianity's conception of itself as distinctive that led to opposition.

Christianity was born with this conviction. It inherited it from Judaism. The identification of Jesus, the Lord of the Christian cult, with the Jewish Messiah led inevitably to the early Christian doctrine of the third race. The strong Jewish influence upon the Christian church in the first generation of its existence made the first of the Ten Commandments a primary commandment for Christianity. The rejection of Jesus as the Messiah by the Jewish people before the year 60 made the Christians the third race.

They are a third or a new race religiously, as almost all the early Christian writers insist, because they profess a new religion that is distinguished from Judaism by their faith in Jesus as Messiah and distinguished from polytheism by their monotheistic inheritance from Judaism. This is plainly said in the *Preaching of Peter:* "He [God] hath made a new one [covenant] with us; for the ways of the Greeks and Jews are old, but we are they that worship him in a new way in a third race, even Christians."[12] This was the basic distinction—they worshiped God in a new way. It is with this in mind that Justin says in *Dialogue* 116, "We are the true high-priestly race of God."

But even before this period the basis of the third-race doctrine is plainly expressed in the canonical books. It rests on the division of humanity into two groups—Christians, who are

[10] I Pet. 4:14–16; cf. Hermas *Vision* iii. 1. 9; 2. 1; 5. 2.

[11] Irenaeus *Demonstration of the Apostolic Preaching* 97.

[12] See Clement *Strom.* vi. 5. 39 in M. R. James, *The Apocryphal New Testament* (Oxford, 1924), p. 17.

good, and non-Christians, who are wicked.[13] In I Peter a description of the rejection of Jesus is followed by a doctrine of the new race:

> But you are an elect race, a royal priesthood, a holy nation, a people for God's own possession, that you may show forth the excellencies of him who called you out of darkness into his marvellous light; which in time past were no people but now are the people of God: who had not obtained mercy, but now have obtained mercy [2:9–10].[14]

This conception of the Christians as a distinct people which arose inside the church at least as early as Paul (II Cor. 6:14—7:1) is found throughout the same period in pagan criticisms of Christianity. Suetonius in his brief statement on the Christians (*Nero* xvi. 2) refers to them as a race.[15] Out of this Christian conception arose the practices and attitudes which alienated the people of the empire. Foremost in the list of these alienating products comes the Christian attitude of aloofness and separation. "Be not unequally yoked with unbelievers, for what have righteousness and lawlessness in common, or what fellowship has light with darkness? and what harmony has Christ with Beliar, or what part has a believer with an unbeliever?"[16] This exhortation to separation is based on the conception of Christians as God's peculiar people. The Christians are to hold themselves aloof because they are the temple of God, says Paul, who quotes Lev. 26:11–12 and Ezek. 37:27 to support his position.

We have seen that the author of the Fourth Gospel sees the Christians as being in the world but not of the world (15:19). Hermas urges the Christians to flee from this world and its affairs (*Similitude* i; *Vision* iv. 3. 4). The sayings of Jesus found at Oxyrhynchus contained the warning that "unless you fast to the world you shall in no wise find the Kingdom of God." Tertullian with characteristic fanaticism expressed this Christian aloofness in its most extreme form. It was his pious wish that Christians might not even inhabit the same world with non-

---

[13] Cf. Gal. 1:4; Acts 2:40, etc.

[14] Cf. Apoc. 1:6; 5:9–10; Aristides 16; *Diognetus* i; Irenaeus *Demonstration of the Apostolic Preaching* 92 f.; Justin *I Apology* xiv. 67; Tertullian *Apology* 39.

[15] Cf. Nock's summary, *op. cit.*, p. 207.   [16] II Cor. 6:14.

Christians, but the exhortation to aloofness is not limited to extremes or to extreme phrasing.[17]

Christian preachers often proclaimed the doctrine of the third race in an arrogant manner. Granted that they did not speak with conscious conceit, what they said must have sounded arrogant in the ears of the nonbelievers.[18] By definition the heathen, that is, the non-Christians of the first two races, were wicked. Some of the New Testament passages already quoted make this claim explicit. The doctrine reaches classic expression in the Fourth Gospel, where wickedness consists of the rejection of Jesus.[19] Other Christian writers say specifically that a virtuous life outside the church will not save one from torture. In the apocalyptical writings these denunciations are rather strong. The Apocalypse of John, e.g., characterized the non-Christians as idolaters, murderers, sorcerers, fornicators, thieves, dogs, and liars (9:20–21; 21:8; 22:15).

The expression of such accusations did not make the Christians exceedingly popular with the people thus described. The Christians not only indicted the heathen with all the crimes in the calendar but they also promised them swift and terrible punishments for these crimes. "For the sinners shall be burnt because they sinned and did not repent, and the heathen shall be burnt because they did not know their creator."[20]

Many of the manuals suggest that the tone in which these early Christians replied to their persecutors was that of Stephen, the first martyr, who prayed for those who did the wrong.[21] But this is not always true, for the reaction of the persecuted against their persecutors is often expressed in statements of bitterness and severe condemnation which served as at least a minor cause of further opposition.

It is generally admitted that the apocalyptic writings come out of the rank and file of the early church. In them bitterness is piled upon bitterness in denunciation of the persecutors, and Christian author after Christian author exults gleefully over the

[17] Tertullian *Shows* 15. [18] Hermas *Vision* i. 4. 2; ii. 4. 1.

[19] Cf. Acts 2:40; Gal. 1:4; Eph. 5:16; Heb. 11:7.

[20] Hermas *Similitude* iv. 4. [21] Latourette, *op. cit.*, p. 135.

prospective damnation and torture of his enemies. In this re-spect the Apocalypse of John is typical. The least that it prom-ises the enemy is destruction (11:17–18; 13:10). The saints are patient and endure because they foresee the sad fate of the enemy, tortured endlessly with fire and brimstone (14:9–12). Those who pour out the blood of the saints are to be given blood to drink (16:6); and, although some writings make the punish-ment correspond to the crime, the author of this apocalypse will be satisfied with nothing less than double (18:6). In the *Epistle of the Apostles* the Christians are urged to rebuke the people who lead them astray, and the Christians are assured that those who do not accept the admonition will be despised and rejected by God.[22]

As the Christian apocalypses conformed in their content to the pattern of Greco-Roman descriptions of the afterlife, they became more specific in the identification of crime, sin, and punishment. But in their catalogue of sinners they do not neg-lect the false witnesses, the slanderers, and the persecutors of the church.

And some there were there hanging by their tongues; and these were they who blasphemed the way of righteousness, and under them was a flaming fire, tormenting them. . . . . And other men and women were being burned up to their middle and cast down in a dark place and scourged by evil spirits, and having their entrails devoured by worms that do not die. And these were they that had persecuted the righteous and delivered them up.

As a final bonus the righteous were assured that they would be allowed to enjoy the sufferings of the persecutors.[23]

That not all the martyrs shared in the spirit of Stephen can be demonstrated from the Acts of the martyrs themselves. When Polycarp, for example, offered to explain Christianity to the proconsul,

[he said:] "Persuade the people." Polycarp answered: "I would have counted you worthy to be reasoned with; for we have been taught to give answer as is fit, where we can without harm, to governments and powers established by God, but the people I do not deem worthy to hear any defence from me." . . . . Then [the proconsul said] say . . . . "Away with the atheists." But Polycarp,

---

[22] *Epistle of the Apostles* 38 in James, *op. cit.*, p. 409.

[23] *Apoc. of Peter* 22, 27, 28, 29.

gazing with a steadfast countenance on all the crowd of lawless heathen in the stadium, waved his hand at them, groaned, and looking up to heaven said: "Away with the atheists."[24]

This bitterness against the persecutors and contempt for the crowd so unexpected in the mild Polycarp breaks through again in the martyrdom of Carpus. After Carpus was nailed to the stake, he smiled at the crowd. When the bystanders in astonishment asked him why he smiled, he said, "I saw the glory of the Lord, and I was glad, and at the same time I was freed from you and am not a party to your misdeeds."[25]

Out of the conception of the Christians as a distinct people came also the frequent accusation that the followers of Jesus were haters of mankind. The Christian group was defined in two ways: first, by the establishment of internal relationships and, second, by the repudiation of attitudes and practices of the enveloping social groups. The charge that the Christians were antisocial rises out of this latter element for the most part and is commonly advanced with reference to the repudiation of pleasure, the breaking of home and family ties, the ruining of business, the abandonment of religion, and the avoidance of civic duties.

A fair statement of the pagan indictment against the Christians as joy-killers is given in the *Octavius* of Minucius Felix (viii), where they are said to lead a gloomy existence, losing all joy in this life for fear of the life to come. The Christians admitted their opposition to pleasure. "The flesh hates the soul and wages war against it, although it has suffered no evil, because it is prevented from enjoying its pleasures; and the world hates the Christians although it has suffered no evil, because they are opposed to its pleasures."[26]

The pleasures to which the Christians were opposed are usually described as the theater, the races, the gladiatorial combats, etc. Yet there is an occasional sentence in early Christian literature that suggests a more rigorous puritanism. In the *Similitudes* (vi. 5. 5) Hermas asks for an identification of the luxuries

---

[24] Cf. i. 2; *Martyrdom of Polycarp* x. 2; ix. 2.

[25] *Acts of Carpus, Papylus, and Agathonica.*   [26] *Epistle to Diognetus* vi. 5.

which have been forbidden. "Sir," said I, "what sort of luxuries are harmful?" "Every act," said he, "which a man does with pleasure is a luxury." It is, however, worth noting that in the context the only luxuries attacked by name are evil temper, adultery, drinking, slander, lying, covetousness, and theft.

The Christian objection to heathen pleasures rested at least in part on the distinctive ethical standards of the new religion. This ethical basis underlies another famous passage—I Pet. 4:1–4. Separation from the pleasures of the heathen is here recognized as a cause for the hatred and slander with which Christianity was greeted by the masses. Its ethical basis is clear, and loyalty to the standards of the new race is urged in a later passage of the same book (4:14–15).

The Christians, who because of their loyalty to their own group's standards would not attend any of the public festivals of the day, came naturally into the title "haters of mankind."[27] The bitterness that led to this charge would be produced, we may be sure, not only by their conspicuous absence as a group from these affairs but also in individual cases by a Christian's refusal to accompany a neighbor to the stadium or the theater. This bitterness accumulated. One of its tributaries was the friction caused in family life by the ethical teaching of the church on the relation of husband and wife.[28]

Even more reprehensible than the repudiation of pleasures was the repudiation of family. In the first two centuries of its history Christianity broke up many homes. Many a pagan first heard of Christianity as the disintegrating force that had wrecked a neighbor's home.

The church's right to disrupt families was canonized with the gospels. In them the founder of the religion set loyalty to himself above and against family ties. One who would follow him after he had buried his father was told to leave his father unburied and follow Jesus (Matt. 8:21–22; Luke 9:57–60). Jesus said he came with the purpose of breaking up homes—to set a man at variance against his father and his own household (Matt.

[27] Tertullian *Apology* 35, 38, 42; *Shows*, *passim*.

[28] Justin *II Apology* 2; Tertullian *Apology* 3; *Nations* i. 4.

10:35–37; Luke 12:51–53). He told his followers to call no man "father" (Matt. 23:9); he repudiated his own family and accepted his followers as a substitute (Mark 3:31–35; Luke 8:19–21; Matt. 12:46–47). In a society in which the family was important and the father claimed a high degree of authority, the proclamation of these teachings was naturally regarded as an attack on the home.

The story of the collapse of homes under the stress introduced by the conversion of the wife or children to Christianity is told in the chapter by Professor Oborn (pp. 131–48), who discusses the economic strain caused by Christian objection to abortion and infanticide, by Christian almsgiving, etc. Tertullian's description of the activities expected of a Christian woman goes far toward explaining the action of the non-Christian husband. A wife who went out regularly at night to secret meetings, who sometimes spent the whole night in prayer with the brethren, who visited criminals in jail, etc., would (as the modern reader can easily imagine) have difficulty convincing a jealous husband of the exalted nature of the motives that lay behind these actions. Even after the Christian member of the family had died, the Christian religion would cause division; for the Christians insisted upon being buried together. They were a new race, a special people.

In this early period there was no established and recognized authoritative spokesman for Christianity. This meant that the extravagances of extremists were blamed upon the more moderate majority. It often happened, therefore, that Christianity appeared as opposed to marriage since there were individual Christians who preached the most rigorous sexual continence. In the apocryphal Acts official opposition to Christianity is the result of an individual's protest to the authorities—a protest based on the breakup of marriages due to the conversion of the wife and her subsequent continence or to the conversion of the fiancée and her refusal to marry. The Acts of Paul (about A.D. 160) furnishes examples of both. Thecla's rejection of her betrothed is the classic example of the latter type,[29] and the newly

[29] Cf. the English translation in James, op. cit.

recovered story of Paul at Ephesus records the conversion of the wife of a minor official and his protest as the beginning of Paul's trouble with the governor. The conversion of the governor's own wife and her separation from her husband carry on the monotonous theme, enlivened in this narrative by Paul's informal chat with the baptized lion.[30] These apocryphal Acts, it is now believed, came from the Christian masses; their strong sexual asceticism was another basis for the popular hatred of the Christians as antisocial in that they were against the home.

Christians manifested their hatred to society, so the heathen said, not only by opposing pleasure and breaking up families but also by ruining business. That economic interests led to popular opposition is certain, but it is equally certain that this was a minor element in the total complex of heathen hostility. The general causes of economic opposition (ban on trades, ruin of temple trades, individual competition between Christian and heathen) must have been operating more strongly after A.D. 250, when popular opposition was dying out, than they were before this date, when popular opposition was strongest. That is to say, the economic stresses introduced by Christianity increased in force as Christians increased in numbers, but popular opposition to Christianity decreased as Christians increased in numbers.

This is not to deny that the spark that fired the hostility of individuals or mobs into action against the Christians was economic in many instances. This is explicit in the statements of both Christians and heathen; e.g., in Paul's healing of a soothsaying girl in Philippi (Acts 16:19–20), and in the silversmiths' riot in Ephesus (Acts 19:23–24). The extent of the image-making industry is indicated in an incident related by Philostratus in which a shipload of images is described.[31]

The epistle of Pliny to Trajan has been frequently quoted as an indication of the economic opposition to Christianity. Pliny is speaking of the efficacy of the repressive measures directed against the Christians.

[30] C. Schmidt and W. Schubart, *Acta Pauli* (Hamburg, 1936), pp. 22 f.

[31] *Life of Apollonius of Tyana* v. 20.

It is quite evident that the temples which were nearly deserted have begun to be crowded, and the customary rites long neglected are being resumed, and the meat of sacrificial animals, for which until now only an occasional buyer could be found, is once more being sold. . . . .[32]

Labriolle sanely accepts the comment of Bubet that Pliny's statement was based on the complaints of the temple priests, of the butchers, and of all the little world which was busied with the cultic ceremonies and made money from them; they did not hesitate to paint in the blackest colors the disaffection from which their interests suffered.[33] But, though Pliny's strong statements need discounting, the unfavorable effect of Christian expansion upon the temple trades cannot be questioned. It is supported by the incident at Ephesus cited above and by Tertullian's statement that the temple revenues were decreasing.[34] Even so, it is no more than a minor, an incidental, and an inciting cause in the persecution of the Christians by the mob before the middle of the third century.

The same thing must be said of individual acts of hostility to Christians which led directly to financial profit. Eusebius tells the story of a soldier who denounced his comrade Marinus as a Christian when Marinus was due for promotion.[35] Informers were at times motivated by the desire of sharing in the property of accused Christians.[36] But this does not deserve classification as a general, widespread, and basic cause of popular opposition to Christianity.

Nor does the Christian ban on various trades and professions merit such classification. The number of occupations prohibited by one or another Christian writer is so great as to convey the impression that there was little that a Christian could do.[37] Yet these bans created little popular opposition. It must be borne in mind not only that the most lengthy bans are the expression of leaders' wishes rather than the description of the practice of the

[32] Pliny *Epistles* x. 96. 10.

[33] Labriolle, *op. cit.*, p. 34, n. 2.

[34] Tertullian *Apology* 42.

[35] *Church History* vii. 15. 2.

[36] Clement *What Rich Man* . . . . 25; Melito in Eusebius *Church History* iv. 26. 5.

[37] Tertullian *Idolatry* 4–6, 8–12, 17, 19; *Crown* 11; B. S. Easton, *The Apostolic Tradition of Hippolytus* (Cambridge, 1934), 11–13, 15, pp. 42 f.; Origen *Celsus* viii. 68, 73; Cyprian *Epistles* lx (2).

rank and file[38] but also that these leaders are extremists in the rigor of their opposition to heathenism. In addition, it must be remembered that in the first two centuries the numbers of the Christians in any particular trade or occupation were (with some local exceptions) too small to create a shortage of workers if the ban were strictly obeyed. As we shall see later, aloofness and separation were ideals that were never more than approximated in practice.

Christian attitudes on poverty and wealth and the acceptance of slaves as brothers and officers within the new race are sometimes listed as economic bases for opposition to Christianity. This seems to be due either to confusion or to overstatement. Until Christianity had attained social prestige, the appearance of slaves as officers within its ranks would not disquiet officialdom; nor would the championing of poverty for Christians disquiet the rich who were outside the new group. It was only as these factors affected social behavior that they roused opposition, and their influence here was not large.[39]

Much more important among the causes of popular opposition to Christianity was the "atheism" of the new religion.[40] It was, as we have seen, in the area of religion, in the matter of worship, that the Christians were a new race distinct from Jews and polytheists. The Christians "do not regard as gods those who are considered to be so by the Greeks, nor do they observe the superstition of the Jews."[41] In this area the aloofness and negative nature of the religion was most obvious to the general public.

It is hard for the modern man to realize that the early Christians were invisible as Christians; that is to say, their activities as members of a religion did not come to the attention of the mass of their fellow-citizens. Religions were ancient; Chris-

[38] This practice can be glimpsed in the list of Christian occupations derived from Christian inscriptions in Case, *op. cit.*, pp. 69 f.

[39] There is no evidence that either Christian or pagan enemy in the first three centuries saw Christianity as a threat to the institution of slavery.

[40] Cf. Harnack, *TU*, XXVIII, 4; Drachmann, *Atheism in Pagan Antiquity* (London, 1922); Workman, *op. cit.*

[41] *Epistle to Diognetus* i.

tians were a novelty. Gods were worshiped in temples—the most impressive public buildings of the towns; no one had seen a Christian temple. Most of the cults had impressive public processions; there were no Christian processions. The gods were visible in their images, but no one had seen an image of Jesus. The Christian cult services were secret and, to a heathen spy, would not have been recognizable as religious services. These people who claimed that the world had been made for them were the heralds of an intangible, invisible religion.

Not only were the Christians nonreligious in a negative sense; they were antireligious in a positive manner. The quiet Christian might be content with abstaining from kissing his hand before a shrine; the fanatic tore down the image of the god. From the Christian viewpoint all the heathen worshiped idols or demons, and the Jews were bound in superstition. Since religion permeated most areas of ancient life and all other cults save Judaism were tolerant if not syncretistic, the translation of the doctrine of the third race into abstention from all the manifold religious activities of the time on the part of the increasing number of Christians not only won them the title "atheists" but also generated intense dislike.

There is no need here to labor the point that the prosperity and welfare of citizen and community and empire were regarded as dependent on religious forces.[42] The obvious atheism and hostility to the reverenced cults manifested by the Christians made popular opposition inevitable. There was sincere feeling behind the cry of the mob that filled the ears of Polycarp: "Away with the atheists!" The Christians were a liability; they were the most probable cause of any mysterious natural disaster. "If the Tiber floods the City, if the Nile does not overflow the fields, if it does not rain, if there is an earthquake, a famine, a plague, immediately the cry is raised: 'The Christians to the lions!'"[43] To be an atheist was to be sure of

[42] See, e.g., S. J. Case, *Experience with the Supernatural in Early Christian Times* (New York, 1929), and *The Social Triumph of the Ancient Church.*

[43] Tertullian *Apology* 40; *Nations* i. 9; Minucius *Octavius* vii; Cyprian *Epistles* lxxiv. 10 (75), *Demetrius* 2, 3; Arnobius *Heathen* i. 1, 2, 13–16; Eusebius *Church History* iv. 13. 1–7; Origen *Celsus* iii. 22, vii. 62.

incurring the violent dislike of the mob. Atheism was universally unpopular—as unpopular with the government as with the mob. The road that the Christians traveled from the period when major opposition was popular to the period when major opposition was governmental led from atheism to sedition.[44]

We have already had occasion to note that through the first part of the third century the opposition to Christianity originated with the mob and that the role of the government was largely that of the policeman. But even within this period the records indicate that the Christians so acted as to alienate patriots and officials. I have sketched elsewhere the extent to which the doctrine of the kingdom of God and Christian eschatology were liabilities to the growth of the movement.[45] In addition to the references given there, the acts of the martyrs show a belligerence on the part of an occasional Christian that must have alienated any patriot or official. The extreme statements of the Scillitan martyrs, for example, can only be described as provocative. They are paralleled by the affirmation of two later Palestinian martyrs who said, "Jesus Christ is Emperor."[46]

In addition to the proclamation of Lord Jesus as a rival to Lord Caesar, the early Christians as members of a new race were not good citizens. "For here we have no continuing city, but we seek one that is to come."[47]

"You [said Hermas to the Christians] as the servants of God are living in a foreign land, for your country is far from this country." And again ".... make no further preparations for yourself beyond a sufficient competence, as though you were living in a foreign country, and be ready in order that, whenever the ruler of this country wishes to expel you for resisting his law, you may depart from his country, and without insult to others, exultantly follow your own law."[48]

[44] This process is well summarized by Professor Case, *The Social Triumph of the Ancient Church*, pp. 145–68.

[45] Colwell, *op. cit.*, chap. vii.

[46] Eusebius *Martyrs of Palestine* i. 5; cf. Justin *Apology* 11.

[47] Heb. 13:14; cf. 11:13; Phil. 3:20; I Pet. 2:11; Tertullian *Apology* 1, 41; *Epistle to Diognetus* v. 5, 9.

[48] *Similitude* i. 1, 6.

In this regard the antisocial aloofness of Christianity noted above became an especial liability. A h́eathen critic of the church says of the Christians, "They scorn public office and purple attire."[49] There are passages that imply that the Christians avoided military service.[50] But in both of these matters there is convincing evidence that the Christians were far from completely loyal to the extravagant statements of Tertullian.

None of these aggravations would have led to imperial persecution had the popular opposition to the Christians overcome this third race. When, on the contrary, the members of the new race overcame the popular opposition, the government was forced to act. In the words of Merrill, "There finally came a time when it [the government] must either fight or tamely acknowledge a super-power within its own borders."[51]

Although popular opposition was still occasionally strong as late as the days of Decius,[52] there are evidences that it is already defeated by a Christianity that is rapidly increasing the number of its adherents. The attitude of the heathen at the martyrdom of S. Fructuosus in A.D. 259 is significant: "And when Bishop Fructuosus and his deacons were being led to the amphitheater, the crowd began to sympathize with Bishop Fructuosus, since he was indeed greatly loved not only by the brethren but also by the heathen."[53] In several of the later martyrdoms we find the military or the officials associated with the stirring up of the mobs, an item unparalleled in the earliest stories.[54] In the life of Cyprian there is a record of a plague in Carthage without any popular outbreak against the Christians; in the *Acts of Cyprian* the mob is friendly; in the *Passion of S. Procopius* (A.D. 303)

---

[49] Minucius *Octavius* viii. 4; cf. Tertullian *Apology* 42, and Workman, *op. cit.*, pp. 179 f., esp. n. 6.

[50] See the references in Workman, *op. cit.*, p. 181, n. 1, and Harnack, *Militia Christi*, pp. 46 f.

[51] *Op. cit.*, p. 68.

[52] Oborn refers to Eusebius *Church History* vi. 41. 1–8; Cyprian *Epistles* lii. 1, 2 (56), xxxv. (7), iv. 2 (5), liv. 6 (59); Pontius *Life* . . . . 7.

[53] *Acts of Fructuosus* iii.

[54] E.g., *The Passion of SS. James and Marian* ii. 2.

there is no note of popular opposition. The slanderous charges of cannibalism and incest disappear after Celsus.[55]

How were the slanders silenced and the popular opposition overcome? Not by the rhetorical periods of apologists, or by the conversion of men of the mental caliber of Pantaenus and Clement of Alexandria. It was the life of the common man, the ordinary Christian, that overcame the opposition of the heathen masses.[56] This triumph of the laymen was made possible by their failure to live as separately and aloof as their leaders desired. It is possible to take up each of the specific areas in which the Christians were accused of being antisocial and note some participation by Christians in the allegedly "heathen" activities.

There was from the beginning some intercourse between Christian and heathen. The Christian was supposed to let his light shine on the pagan darkness; pagans came to some Christian meetings; Christians ate dinner with pagans, and, although they could not associate with Christian sinners, they could with pagan sinners. Even the rigorous Tertullian can be called to the witness box to testify to the extent to which Christians shared the life of their heathen neighbors.[57] Some Christians attended the shows; some served in the army; some held public office; even some Christian ministers made idols; many Christians made money.[58] In the third century, a time of severe economic depression in the empire, the church at Rome supported about one hundred clergy and fifteen hundred poor people: widows, orphans, sick, poor, and disabled.

[55] Cf. Oborn's statement in his chapter below (pp. 131-48). Nock admits that the petition from the people of Lycia and Pamphilia to Maximinus in 311-12 was "probably inspired." His statement that it crystallizes a popular attitude might be qualified by the note that that attitude was now vanishing (*op. cit.*, p. 208).

[56] On the part played by the ordinary men and women see Harnack, *Mission and Expansion of Christianity in the First Three Centuries*, I, 366-68; C. J. Cadoux, *The Early Church and the World* (Edinburgh, 1925), pp. 95 f.

[57] Phil. 2:15; I Cor. 9:22, 10:27-28, 5:9-11, 14:23-24, 10:14-21; Tertullian *Apology* 42.

[58] Pseudo-Cyprian *Shows* 1, 2; Tertullian *Idolatry* 14; Cadoux, *op. cit.*, pp. 276-80; Tertullian *Crown* 12; *Idolatry* 7. Case has traced the increase in the economic strength of the Christians in *The Social Triumph of the Ancient Church*, chap. ii.

The concept of the third race, of the Christians as a new and distinct grouping of mankind, was the basic cause of popular opposition in the first few centuries; it was also the victory that overcame the world. The Christians were a self-conscious brotherhood, an ecumenical brotherhood from the days of Paul on. Christians belonged to the brotherhood wherever they traveled in the empire; a letter from the group they left admitted them to full privileges in the neighborhood church in their new town.[59] Within this brotherhood the poor man found recognition, affection, insurance for his wife and children, decent burial, victory over sin, and the assurance of immortality.[60] Before there was canon or creed or priesthood, the brothers found their relationship strongly based on their common devotion to the Lord Jesus through whose activities all these benefits were mediated to them. By claiming to be a new race they aroused the hatred of the masses; by living as members of this third race they won over the masses. This is the paradox of the first and greatest triumph of the church.

[59] Cf. the early church letters in E. J. Goodspeed and E. C. Colwell, *A Greek Papyrus Reader* (Chicago, 1935), Nos. 5 and 10.

[60] Cf. the social-ethical brotherhood of Hermas *Mandates* viii. 10.

ROMAN RELIGIOUS SURVIVALS
IN CHRISTIANITY

GORDON J. LAING

University of Chicago

THE Romans of the first century of the Empire, when Christianity appeared among them, were a distinctly religious people. To be sure there were then, as there had been in preceding generations, many skeptics, and it is obvious that the beliefs of the faithful lacked many of the ethical ideals associated by later ages with religion. Nevertheless, the masses of the people were profoundly religious, intensely anxious to establish right relations with the supernatural powers. The empire of Augustus was to a considerable extent built on the religious consciousness of the people.

There were many elements in the religious situation of the period. It was indeed a curious complex; beliefs of varying age and origin existed side by side. There were many survivals of that animism which constituted the chief feature of the oldest Roman religion known to us; there were flourishing cults of Greco-Roman provenience; there were cults from the Orient; there was already the beginning of emperor worship; there was belief in divination, in astrology, in miracles.

In general, the Romans were tolerant of foreign cults, and, although they refused official recognition to some of them and excluded others from the sacred boundary of the city (*pomerium*), they did not interfere with their adherents. There were some exceptions, the cult of Isis for example, and Christianity, but in both these cases the objections were not exclusively religious.

It was this interest in religion, this almost universal quest for religious satisfactions, this willingness to hear the advocates of a new cult, and the familiarity with various ideas that most

72

Romans had acquired from the manifold nature of their religious environment which gave Christianity its opportunity and contributed so largely to its ultimate success. The ground was well prepared.

But not every religion could have seized the opportunity as Christianity did, and doubtless one of the chief reasons for its victory lay in its adaptability. The instructions which Gregory the Great is said to have given to a missionary to the Saxon heathens is of notable significance not only as indicative of the policy of the church in the sixth century but also of that of the preceding centuries. For he told him, "Remember not to interfere with any traditional belief or religious observance that can be harmonized with Christianity."[1] Surely Gregory was not thinking merely of his own time; the whole history of the church must have been in his mind. For his predecessors, far from attempting to uproot such deep-set beliefs, allowed them to remain, perhaps even encouraged their growth but gave them a different direction. Adaptability was a natural characteristic of Christianity; from its very beginning it had been a religion for all peoples. If it had been afflicted with that unyielding rigidity generally characteristic of tribal cults, there would have been no possibility of its ever becoming a world-religion.

Such in outline was the nature of the new faith, and such was the character of the religious environment in which it had to compete for place and recognition with many long-established cults. To what extent did its environment influence it? When it emerged triumphant after the long centuries of struggle, what traces were there of the contacts to which it had been exposed? To what extent did its adaptability react upon itself? How did it differ from the religion that had come out of Palestine? These are the questions which this chapter endeavors to answer.

The changes were numerous. Some of them were in matters of fundamental Christian belief; others consisted of accretions to the body of doctrine; the remainder belonged to the external forms of worship, or to organization and administration.

Of these three types of change or development, the first, i.e.,

[1] F. Legge, *Forerunners and Rivals of Christianity* (Cambridge, England, 1915), I, 85.

change brought about in the fundamental doctrines of the Christian faith, is least noticeable. In a good many cases indeed, such influence as can be found is of an indirect and secondary nature. For example, it would be folly to say that the idea of Christ as a redeemer God can be traced to any pagan redeemer god, such as Attis, associate of the Mother of the Gods, or Mithras, or any other. And yet these redeemer gods, overlaid though they sometimes were with a crude and revolting mythology, did serve to accustom men's minds to the idea. In the same way it would be wholly beside the mark to seek a specific pagan prototype for the doctrine of the Trinity, such as the Egyptian group, Isis, Serapis, and the child Horus; or the Indian Brahma, Siva, and Visnu; or that triad, the Good, the Intelligence, and the World-Soul which, in the theory of the Neo-Platonist Plotinus, made up the Supreme Reality. But it would be equally erroneous to decline to recognize the strong probability of these ideas having had some influence in the formulation and acceptance of the Christian doctrine as set forth in the Nicaean and Athanasian creeds.[2]

In the idea of communion more influence is apparent. We know that communion with the god and participation in the divine nature were the final objective of the elaborate ceremonies of initiation in such oriental cults as those of Isis and Mithras. Moreover, the Romans were familiar with the idea of communing with deity long before any oriental cult had been introduced among them, and the medium they used was that of sacred meals.[3] The best known of these was the one held on the Alban Mount on the occasion of the Latin festival. Delegates of all the peoples belonging to the Latin League took part in a meal in honor of Jupiter of the Latins and, by eating parts of the sacrificial victim, entered into communion with him. There were many other sacred meals of the same kind in the old Roman religion, some of them of great antiquity. But the idea of communion did not develop to the point of giving the indi-

[2] *Ibid.*, pp. 88–89.

[3] Ruth Thomas, "The Sacred Meal" (University of Chicago doctoral dissertation [Chicago, 1937]).

vidual the sense of communing with his god. The emphasis was on the relation of the state to the god, and the rigid sacerdotalism that burdened the Roman system prevented its ever serving as a satisfactory medium for the growth of a personal religion.

In this deficiency of the native Roman religion lay one of the chief opportunities of the oriental cults, which with their elaborate initiations and other spectacular ceremonies offered close personal communion with their deities.

From this communion came regeneration for the individual with its concomitants of spiritual purity, happiness in this world, and eternal felicity in the world beyond the grave. The doctrine of regeneration became a commonplace of the foreign cults in Rome.[4] One of the striking examples is furnished by the ceremony of the Taurobolium, which was connected with the worship of the Mother of the Gods at least as early as the second century of our era. From this baptism in the blood of the sacrificed bull, the participant emerged "born again" (*renatus*) and as a result was said to be purified from sin, made eligible for close communion with the divine, and assured of everlasting life. Communion and regeneration were elements in the teaching of the Isis cult also; and both were stressed by the Mithraists. There is an interesting relief of what seems to be a Mithraic communion on a monument found at Konjica in Bosnia in which Mithras, the sun-god, and initiates are shown at a table, eating and drinking.[5] Moreover, regeneration appears in the philosophy of the Neo-Pythagoreans, who had taken it from the Orphics. It has an important place in the Hermetic literature, some of which goes back to the first century, although the corpus was not compiled until the end of the third. It is found in the system of the Neo-Platonists, who had so profound an influence on the thought of the third century. It turns up also in the philosophic system of the Stoics.

It is then clear that the doctrine of regeneration was of the

[4] For a detailed discussion see H. R. Willoughby, *Pagan Regeneration* (Chicago, 1929).

[5] F. Cumont, *Textes et monuments* (Brussels, 1899), I, 175, Fig. 10.

very essence of the religious thinking of the time, and its appearance in the Christian system was but one among many. Christianity did not take it from any of the others. It, and all that went with it—purification, absolution, spiritual progress and the happiness it brings, everlasting life—formed part of a common stock of religious ideas. Not only was the general idea of regeneration widespread but some of the methods of attaining communion with God were the same in different cults: baptism, initiation, the sacred meal. Of these, the Christians laid most stress on baptism and the sacred meal. The latter showed an amazing development. What had been in the beginning nothing but a commemorative meal of Hebrew origin became from one cause or another—influence of environment, religious emotionalism, mystic obscurantism—the elaborate doctrine of transubstantiation.

To pass to another phase of the subject, it can hardly be doubted that Christian conceptions of life after death were definitely influenced by the ideas current in the Roman Empire. It is of course true that the Jews placed the souls of the dead under the earth, and it is only reasonable to suppose that on this point the Christians were following Jewish precedent. But the details of the life after death which the Christians visualized were largely pagan. It was not the paganism of the indigenous Roman religion, whose conceptions of the next world were of the vaguest, but the beliefs and legends of the Greco-Roman and oriental cults that determined Christian eschatology. In the Eleusinian mysteries as well as the Orphic doctrines, the idea of hell involves not only punishment but also purgatorial atonement. These were doctrines that had wide currency, and known also were the pagan stories of descents into hell; for example, those of Orpheus, Dionysus, Theseus and Pirithous, Castor and Pollux, and Virgil's hero Aeneas. The Isiac cult contained similar ideas of punishment and felicity after death.

In the preceding paragraphs the discussion has centered in doctrines which, already existent or implicit in the earliest forms of Christianity, were changed or developed by contacts with its pagan rivals. But the influence of the Roman environ-

ment was not confined to modifications or developments of doctrines of the Christianity of Jesus and Paul. Accretions of magnitude appeared and flourished in the new milieu. Among these
was the veneration of saints, which owed its origin and the development it showed in subsequent centuries to a number of
converging influences inherent in Roman religion. One of these
was that pandemonism which was the most notable feature of
the earliest Roman religion about which we have any definite
information; another was the affection which the Romans always had for minor deities. There were other influences also:
belief in intermediate divinities, readiness to accept miracles
without hesitation, and familiarity with the idea of the man-
god. The first two influences mentioned were, it will be observed, indigenous Roman attitudes; in the others there are
some Greek or oriental elements.

These influences have been mentioned in the order of their
ultimate importance. Undoubtedly, although at first thought
it may seem a far cry, the old Roman pandemonism made the
largest contribution to the establishment of the idea of the
veneration of saints. For it is a mistake to think that pandemonism died out of Roman religion in its early days. It was
doubtless overshadowed by some of the more spectacular cults,
but it never disappeared. It persisted in many forms, especially
among the uneducated classes, during the whole period of
Roman history. The Italian masses believed that the world
swarmed with spirits (*numina*), each one of which was potent
in a particular place or field of activity. The degree of specialization was carried to the extreme. For example, relays of spirits
watched over a person from the period of his gestation and
birth to his death. The same kind of specialization is seen in the
prayer addressed at the beginning of the sowing season to the
twelve spirits who presided over the successive stages of the
preparation of the soil, the sowing of the seed, and the growth
of the crop. These were all minor spirits, but the simple folk
felt on more familiar terms with them than with remote and
powerful gods who could only be approached through elaborate
ritual.

A good example of the affection and reverence which the Romans always felt toward the minor divinities is furnished by their attitude toward their household gods (*Lares domestici*), protecting spirits of the home, with whom the whole life of the family was intimately connected. Their statuettes were placed in little shrines in the private houses or in niches in the wall of less pretentious homes. Offerings were regularly made to them in the course of the dinner, and special honors were paid to them on the occasion of any event of importance in the family, as for example, a wedding. "Little gods" they were sometimes affectionately called.

Plutarch mentions spirits who were intermediaries between men and the higher gods; Maximus of Tyre describes lesser deities who healed disease, gave assistance in crises, guarded cities; Aristides (who lived in the time of Marcus Aurelius) relates in his *Sermones sacri* stories of miraculous cures in temples; and the Neo-Platonists of the third century encouraged belief in innumerable subordinate and intermediate deities.

Nor to the minds of the common people of Rome did there seem anything incongruous in regarding some human beings as more than mortals. There were generations of tradition behind such an attitude. Had not Aeneas, the founder of the Latin race, been deified? Had not Romulus, the first of the Roman kings, been caught up into heaven?

Lucian's ridicule in his *De dea Syria* shows how widespread some of the beliefs were in the Greco-Roman world of the second century. And no one can be surprised that simple people, with their inherited ideas and under the influence of their environment, should honor the saints.

Obviously there was something here that could not be disregarded by the founders of the church. It was part of the religious feeling of the time and must be dealt with as such. And it was in this spirit that the Christians met the situation. They encouraged the veneration of men whose virtues and achievements had placed them near God. The abounding polytheism of the pagans found vent in the veneration of the saints, who from this time on took the place of the old minor and subordinate spirits. They became the intermediaries between man and God, not themselves divine but with intercessional powers of unusual efficacy through the humanity that had been theirs and the divinity to which through their holiness they drew near. What resulted has sometimes been called a new polytheism, but such a term is not justified, for, while the church approved the veneration of saints, it never taught the worship of saints.

There were, of course, always some of the Church Fathers who protested against the growth of the doctrine. They said that they did not find it in the teaching of Jesus. But there were others who approved and supported it. It would, indeed, be interesting to know whether it ever needed much encouragement or guidance on the part of the authorities of the church. The need of the intermediate powers was there in the minds of the people as the result of centuries of religious experience, and the opportunity was there in the glorious careers of the saints. The development was a wholly natural one.

In another respect, also, the institution of the veneration of saints showed a striking resemblance to the old Roman polytheism, and that was in the high degree of specialization accorded to many of the saints, if not in the formal teaching of the church, at least in the minds of the illiterate peasantry of southern Italy and Spain. From the lists cited for these countries it would almost seem as if some saint or other had special efficacy in the case of every one of the diseases to which mankind is subject. Nor is this specialization confined to pathology or found only in southern Europe.

But it was not always these minor divinities—"departmental spirits," *Sondergötter*, as they are variously called—to whose functions the saints succeeded. Sometimes they took the place of more powerful gods. St. Elmo, to whose presence sailors in the Mediterranean attribute the electric phenomena that appear about the spars of a ship after a storm, has taken the place of the Greco-Roman divinities, Castor and Pollux, patrons of sailors. St. Nicholas has succeeded the Greco-Roman god Poseidon-Neptune as the patron of boatmen and fishermen. At

Sorrento there is a statue of St. Nicholas, with the attribute of a dolphin, once the symbol of Poseidon-Neptune; and at Bari in the festival of St. Nicholas boatmen and fishermen have an important part. One of the features of the cult of the Greco-Roman god Aesculapius was the practice of incubation. The belief was that, if one suffering from some disease slept within the precincts of a temple of the god, he would be told in a dream what he should do to be cured. Many saints succeeded to this power, and incubation was practiced in their churches, e.g., in the Middle Ages, St. Martin at Tours, St. Julian at Avernus, St. Maximinus at Trèves, SS. Peter and Paul at Cambridge; and, in modern times, St. Andrew at Amalfi, St. John in Calabria and Sardinia, Santo Ciro at Portici near Naples, San Roque in Campania.

Even the cult of Egyptian deities may have contributed to the list of the saints. Isis, among many other things, was a goddess of the sea and in this capacity was called Isis Pelagia, and the suggestion has been made that we have traces of this cult in the legends of St. Pelagia.[6] More probable is the theory that the representation of Isis' son Horus on horseback killing a crocodile with a spear has had a direct influence on the well-known group of St. George and the dragon.[7]

Another accretion in Christianity to which its contacts with Roman paganism at least contributed was the cult of the Virgin Mary. The case is not so clear as in the veneration of the saints and calls for careful analysis. For instance, while a number of pagan prototypes for the Virgin have been suggested (Diana of Ephesus, the Mother of the Gods, and the Egyptian Isis), it could not be said that Mary reproduces or even represents any of these. Yet, on the other hand, these pagan divinities did play their part in making the masses familiar with the idea of both virgin goddess and mother goddess.

Moreover, there were contacts between the Christian Mary and her pagan predecessors. It can hardly have been merely a

[6] H. K. Usener, *Die Legende der h. Pelagia* (Bonn, 1879).

[7] Meyer, in W. H. Roscher, *Ausführliches Lexikon der griechischen und römischen Mythologie* (Leipzig, 1884), I, 2748.

coincidence that one of the oldest churches of the Madonna was built on the site of the famous temple of Diana at Ephesus. It was there that Mary was declared Mother of God in 431, and it may even be assumed that the procession on the occasion of that ceremony, with its smoking censers and flaring torches, differed but little in externals from the processions once held in honor of the Roman Diana or her predecessor on the same site, the Greek Artemis, or the still more remote oriental goddess who had preceded her. The site has had a long religious history, and the familiar manifestation of cult treading on the heels of cult is well illustrated there. Such a procession may still be seen in many parts of the world on the occasion of the crowning of a Madonna.

That Diana's appellation of queen of heaven is the source of Mary's designation of queen or sovereign of the universe cannot be demonstrated. This was a descriptive term common to a fairly large group, and so was applied to Mary among many others. The Roman Juno, the Greek Hera, the Carthaginian Dea Caelestis, the Egyptian Isis, the Phoenician Astarte, and the Babylonian Mylitta had all been queens of heaven.

The contacts with the Mother of the Gods, the Phrygian deity whom the Romans had introduced into Italy toward the end of the third century before Christ, were still more limited. To be sure, there is a shrine of the Virgin on Monte Vergine near Avellino in the Apennines not far from Naples, where there once was a temple of the Mother of the Gods and where the processions now held doubtless show some points of resemblance to pagan ceremonial, but such similarity as there may be is in externals only. Neither is there much significance in the resemblance between the Virgin's title, Mother of God (*Gran Madre di Dio*), and that of the pagan divinity, Mother of the Gods, nor in the similarity between statues of the two. All the world over the sculptured representations of mother-goddesses have features in common. The contacts between the Virgin Mary and Isis are both more numerous and more striking than those mentioned in the case of Diana or the Mother of the Gods. For, while some of the parallel epithets listed by Beauregard[8] have but little appropriateness, others cited by him do seem to indicate direct influence; e.g., Mater Domini = Isis Mater, Madonna Addolorata = Isis Furva, Regina Maris = Isis Pelagia, Maria della Potenza = Dea Potens, and Madonna del Ajuto = Isis Soteira. Moreover, some images of the Madonna bear a notable resemblance to images of Isis, e.g., the statue of the goddess described in the inscription found in Spain and published in *CIL*, II, 3386. MacKenzie Wallace[9] mentions an icon of the Madonna that was taken to private houses in Moscow, just as the image of the holy Bambino of the Church of Ara Coeli in Rome was sometimes transferred to private houses there. And we know that the same thing was done with images of Isis in antiquity. Some statuettes and figurines of Isis nursing the child Horus resemble statuettes of the Madonna and Child so closely that they have been mistaken for them and worshiped in Christian churches.[10]

But Isis contributed more than cult epithets or sculptured models to the worship of Mary. The attitude of the devotees of Isis, the adoration with which they regarded her, so different in emotional content from anything that the indigenous Roman religion had ever offered, doubtless helped to build up a belief in divine compassion and so served to prepare the way for the worship of Mary. This spirit of adoration is well exemplified in Lucius' prayer to Isis after his initiation into her mysteries.[11] Here are some of the phrases which he applies to Isis: "sancta et humani generis sospitatrix perpetua, semper fovendis mortalibus munifica, dulcem matris affectionem miserorum casibus tribuis . . . . et depulsis vitae procellis salutarem porrigas dexteram." Not a thousand tongues, he cries, could express the adoration of his heart.

But it was in the external forms of worship that the Roman environment showed its influence most clearly, and of this Christian festivals furnish many illustrations. For example, the Feast of the Purification of the Virgin, held on February 2, and

---

[8] *Les Divinités égyptiennes* (Paris, 1866), pp. 174, 175, 341.

[9] In his book *Russia* (London, Paris, and New York, 1877), p. 408.

[10] Drexler in Roscher's *Lexikon*, II, 431.   [11] Apuleius *Metamorphoses* xi. 25.

called Candlemas, has some connection with the Lupercalia which the Romans used to celebrate in the same month. An analysis of some parts of the pagan festival indicates a special relation to the fertility of women, and in some celebrations of the modern festival this aspect of it has been emphasized: in the north of England the festival used to be called "The Wives' Feast Day."

The Litania Maior as it was once celebrated by the church showed many similarities to the old Roman festival of the Robigalia. Both were held on the same day (April 25); both included a procession and a prayer. The Christian procession, starting from San Lorenzo in Lucina, had a station at San Valentino outside the walls and another at the Milvian Bridge. Then it turned left and, after stopping at a station of the Holy Cross, proceeded to St. Peter's Basilica.[12] The pagan procession left the city by the Porta Flaminia, crossed the Milvian Bridge, and went on to the grove of Robigus at the fifth milestone on the Via Claudia, where the sacrifice was made. The purpose of both processions was the same, namely, to win the blessing of heaven on the crops.

The Roman Ambarvalia has left a deep impression on subsequent religious history. It was held at the end of May and consisted of procession, prayer, and sacrifice. A pig, a sheep, and a bull, representing the farmer's most valuable stock, were driven three times around the fields and then sacrificed. The hope was that through this ceremony hostile spirits would be excluded and fertility assured for the farm. It is one example of a common type of lustral ceremony. It furnishes, moreover, a clearer case of direct survival than can be found in any other phase of church history. In southern Italy today on the Rogation days before Ascension, priests and parishioners pass around the fields and with the Litania Minor ask a blessing on the farms and households. There is even similarity between the Christian and the pagan prayer.

Fowler,[13] writing in 1899, speaks of similar processions in

---

[12] *Liber pontificalis*, ed. L. Duchesne (Paris, 1886), II, 4, "Life of Leo III" (795–816).

[13] W. W. Fowler, *Roman Festivals* (New York, 1899), p. 127.

some parishes in England on one of the three days before Ascension. The minister, officials of the church, and parishioners passed around the bounds of the parish and prayed for divine blessing on the farms and people. This was called "beating the bounds." From Fowler's account, however, the practice is in decline at present. But processions of this kind, in which the cross is carried, are held in Holland and other parts of Continental Europe. A procession of this type has been reported for both Lutheran and Catholic groups in the neighborhood of Fox Lake, Wisconsin, as late as the beginning of this century.

The church festival of All Souls' Day has obviously been influenced by the Roman festival of the dead called the Parentalia. There is, it is true, a difference of date, the former taking place on the second of November, while the latter was celebrated from the thirteenth to the twenty-first of February. On those days the ancient Romans, partly from motives of affection and desire to pay to the spirits of their ancestors what was their due and partly from a fear that neglect of such duties would make the spirits hostile, visited the family tombs and made offerings there. On All Souls' Day in our own time great numbers of people go to the cemeteries and adorn the graves of their relatives with flowers and candles, the service having to do with the repose of their souls.

Our Christmas has inherited many of its features from pagan festivals. The date is the day of the festival of the Invincible Sun-god, whose worship had been introduced into Rome from Palmyra in Syria by the Emperor Aurelian. The identity of date was not a mere coincidence. A sort of parallelism between Christ and the sun had grown up in the minds of the Christians and, as Usener has suggested, it may have developed into the idea that the festival of the Invincible Sun on the twenty-fifth of December was the appropriate date for the celebration of the nativity of Christ, who was the Sun of Righteousness.

It is, however, to the Roman festival of the Saturnalia that most of our Christmas customs go back: e.g., the merriment, the eating and drinking, the exchange of gifts, and the use of candles. The length of the holiday season of the Saturnalia, moreover, lasting from the seventeenth to the twenty-first of December, corresponds fairly well to our Christmas week. In North Staffordshire in England the farm servants' holiday lasts a full week, and it is of some interest to find in the same region that interchange of roles between masters and servants that was one of the distinctive features of the Saturnalia.

In various details of worship we find pagan influence also. One of these is prayer. For instance, there may be some Roman influence in our grace at meals. This was a custom of the Romans, but it was by no means confined to them. Both the Greeks and the Hebrews gave thanks at meals.

Fowler[14] aptly points out a more specific survival in the prayer of a peasant of the Roman campagna today, who, turning to the east and using holy water, prays for the safety and increase of his flocks; while the pagan shepherd, at the festival of the Parilia on the twenty-first of April, according to the account of Ovid,[15] prayed for the same things, wetting his hands with dew and turning to the east. Only the divinity addressed is different; the pagan prayed to Pales, the Christian to the Madonna.

A common form of adoration in ancient times was the kissing of sacred objects. This was a practice of some oriental peoples, as for instance the Arabs, and of the Greeks and Romans. Cicero in one of his Verrine orations mentions a statue of Hercules at Agrigentum whose mouth was worn away by the kisses of his devotees, and Lucretius[16] speaks with scorn of similar manifestations of misguided piety. It is, therefore, a continuation of a widespread ancient practice rather than an exclusively Roman custom that we find in such survivals as kissing the foot of the statue of St. Peter in his basilica at Rome, or the ring of a cardinal, or the Bible in taking an oath.

Prayer and adoration had an important place in the daily services in the temples of Isis in Rome, Pompeii, and other centers of her worship. At the early service, after the priests had thrown open the gates of the temple precinct, they drew aside the curtains before the image of the goddess, and the devotees

---

[14] *Ibid.*, p. 81.   [15] *Fasti* iv. 703 ff.   [16] *De rerum natura* i. 317.

prayed to her or sat in silent adoration. The bench before the statue of Horus in the temple at Pompeii was obviously for this purpose. In a well-known fresco found at Herculaneum in which a priest stands at the top of the steps leading to a temple of Isis, holding up a jar, we may have an example of the adoration of the holy water of the Nile.

There are a few survivals of Roman or at least Greco-Roman forms of sacrifice. The practice of *ex voto* offerings, so common among the pagans, did not pass away after the official recognition of Christianity by the Roman state. Persons whose hearts were set on possessing something or attaining some aim, or who were hopeful for the occurrence of a certain event, or were faced with danger to themselves or their household, still promised that, if their prayer were granted, they would make an offering to the divine powers. And, if the prayer was answered, they acted in accordance with their vow (*ex voto*), their offerings ranging from candles to churches. Shrines of SS. Cosma and Damiano, where incubation is practiced, show many examples of wax representations of parts of the body healed through the curative efficacy of the saints. These *ex voto* offerings differ in no essential respect from those that used to be placed in the temples of Aesculapius and other gods. Sometimes the pagan worshiper in limited gratitude or on account of lack of means confined himself to a votive tablet, and that custom also passed over into the Christian church. The objects deposited in many churches in southern Europe furnish clear enough evidence of the survival. The history of the church shows votive churches just as Greco-Roman religion had its innumerable votive temples. The Church of San Gennaro in Naples was built on the occasion of a plague, and the Church of San Paolo in the same city was also built *ex voto*.

Of the great mass of expiatory sacrifices that characterized the Greco-Roman background of Christianity, there are but few survivals. Under the new religion, the whole attitude toward atonement was radically changed. There are, however, some traces of survival of certain practices connected with the oriental cults in Rome. The Greek Orphists trafficked in indulgences as far back as Plato's time, and it is highly probable that they continued to do so in southern Italy, where they were influential in relatively early times, and in Rome itself. Moreover, according to Juvenal, there was sale of indulgences in the cult of Isis in Rome. Whether this phase of her worship was recognized by its authorities or whether it was carried on by delinquent priests, we do not know. Nor did this abuse disappear with the passing of paganism, as the abuse of indulgences during long periods of church history abundantly shows. For, while the decrees of various councils from medieval to modern times have demonstrated the repugnance of the church to what its enemies have always called "the traffic in indulgences," especially the acceptance of alms in reparation for pardoned sins, it has only been through constant vigilance on the part of the high ecclesiastical authorities that alms-gatherers have been controlled and the evil suppressed.

In the institution of monachism, also, there is pagan influence, and one of the important sources is found in the cult of Isis and Serapis. While some scholars deny this, and Cabrol[17] asserts that monasticism was of exclusive Christian origin, their position is not supported by the facts.

Among the latter may be mentioned especially the fragments of papyrus found as far back as 1820 and containing information about the hermits of the Serapeum in Egypt. The papyrus, in the opinion of Kenyon,[18] belongs to the second century before Christ. Moreover, we are informed that, when the religion of Isis and Serapis passed away toward the end of the fourth century, some of the recluses who had lived in the Serapeum became Christians. It should be remembered also that St. Anthony, regarded by many as the father of Christian monasticism, had been an Egyptian hermit, and St. Pachomius, who established his monastery near Dendera in southern Egypt about A.D. 320, was not without his influence in Roman monasticism. Perhaps other sources of influence may be found in

[17] *ERE*, VIII, 783.

[18] Sir F. G. Kenyon, *The Palaeography of Greek Papyri* (Oxford, 1899), pp. 4 and 38; cf. Legge, *op. cit.*, I, 84.

Neo-Platonism, Druidism, Orphism, Buddhist asceticism, or Jewish monasticism with special reference to the Essenes. But whether any or all of these contributed, the influence exerted was far less than that of the recluses of Isis and Serapis.

In other institutions of the church, also, survivals of paganism may be found. In the rite of marriage, for example, the veiling of the bride may be Roman, and the wearing of a garland by both bride and groom that still obtains in some parts of Germany and Switzerland and in countries under the jurisdiction of the Eastern church may also be of Roman origin. That Roman custom contributed to the wedding-feast is doubtless true, but here, as in the case of the garlands, there may have been some Jewish influence. In any case, a modern wedding procession in the rural regions of Italy today reproduces many of the features of the old Roman celebration.[19]

In funeral rites, likewise, many of the pagan customs were preserved by the early Christians, and some of them have survived to our own time. In the lighted candles placed beside the corpse or carried in the procession we see the funeral torch of the Romans, the original use of which was due to the fact that in the early period of Rome funerals were held at night. The professional mourners (*praeficae*) that appeared at Roman funerals are employed today at funerals in Campania and Calabria. The funeral oration that is still so common in many contemporary church groups goes back through dignitaries like Gregory, Jerome, and Ambrose to imperial, republican, and then, presumably, regal Rome. Few institutions have shown more durability than this dismal concomitant of a dismal occasion.

In a number of other miscellaneous usages connected with the external forms of Christian worship there are traces of pagan survivals. For example, it seems certain that the extensive use of music in many of the oriental cults in Rome had its influence in the development of the Christian service. It is even possible that the music of the Ambrosian chants continued the tradition of Greco-Roman melodies, although sufficient data for the establishment of such a theory are not available. We do not really know whether what we call the music of Ambrose and

[19] W. B. McDaniel, *Roman Private Life* (New York, 1929), p. 50.

Gregory reproduces with any degree of accuracy their original systems.

Bells, gongs, and other noise-making instruments were commonly used in ancient Rome, as also in India, China, Greece, Etruria, and other countries, on the occasion of eclipses. The purpose was to frighten away the evil spirits that were supposed to be the cause of the celestial disturbance. The pagan custom of ringing bells at funerals was based on the same belief that evil spirits could thus be kept away, and this is obviously the origin of our passing and funeral bells.

The use of the *sistrum* in many of the ceremonies of Isis probably had a similar purpose. This does not preclude the possibility of its serving also to draw the attention of the devotees to some important point in a ceremony, and the suggestion that has been made that it is the prototype of the little bell (the *sanctus*) rung at the celebration of the Mass is reasonably plausible. Possibly the bell found at Tarragona in Spain and apparently connected with the ceremonies of emperor worship was used in the same way.

The use of candles in church services was avoided by the early Christians. To them lights seemed to suggest pagan ritual, but from the end of the third century there was a marked change of attitude, and lights came to be widely used in many Christian rites. It is an interesting example of the growth of externalism in church services.

The same sort of development is seen in the case of incense. It was used in many of the Greco-Roman and oriental cults in Italy, but the early Christians excluded it from their services. For a long time, indeed, the burning of incense served to mark off a pagan from a Christian. In periods of persecution it was one of the tests employed to determine whether a person accused of being a Christian was really one. But, by the end of the fourth century, it had come to be used ritually. It is attested at that time for Jerusalem, and in the sixth century for Antioch. By the fourteenth century it was established in the West in the Mass and other services. Nor is the practice static even now. For, although it was abolished in the Church of England at the Reformation, it was resumed about the middle of the nineteenth century, and it is increasing at the present time.[20]

Another instance of the growth of externalism along lines that suggest a recession to paganism is furnished by the attitude of the church toward the use of garlands. As we know from Tertullian's *De corona* and other sources, the early Christians were bitterly opposed to them. They thought of them as symbols of paganism. But little by little their feeling changed, and statues of the Madonna adorned with a garland became frequent.

A similar change of attitude is found in the matter of the tonsure. This was one of the characteristics of the priests of Isis, and from Jerome's denunciation of it we may infer that the authorities of the church in the fourth century were opposed to it. And yet the very fact that he spoke against it shows that it was known at that time, and its use gradually spread. To Christian as to pagan, its symbolism was the same: separation from the world, penitential devotion, dedication to divine service. It was firmly established among orders of monks by the fifth century, although it does not seem to have been recognized by the church until the seventh century.

The Isiac cult unquestionably made many contributions to the external forms of Christian worship. The white linen robes of the Egyptian priests have persisted in Christian vestments, and it is possible that the rule that all women must be veiled during Isiac ceremonies is the source of the modern custom of women's heads being covered in church. Other points of resemblance between Christian and Isiac practices have been indicated by various scholars. Indeed, if we may judge from the letter which the Emperor Hadrian wrote to the Consul Servianus, it was not always easy to distinguish between the adherents of Isis and her consort Serapis and those of Christ: "Illic [i.e., in Alexandria] qui Serapem colunt Christiani sunt, et devoti sunt Serapi qui se Christi episcopos dicunt."[21]

---

[20] E. G. C. F. Atchley, *History of Use of Incense in Divine Worship* (London, 1909).

[21] *Historia Augusta*, Saturninus (Teubner ed., Hohl) ii. 227.

CURRENT CONTRIBUTIONS FROM ARCHEOLOGY TO EARLY CHRISTIAN HISTORY

HAROLD R. WILLOUGHBY
Divinity School, University of Chicago

THE year 1938 saw the freeing of Shirley Jackson Case from the exacting responsibilities of a divinity deanship. Most happily he has returned to research in the history of early Christianity. By a peculiar coincidence the same year was exactly the one-hundredth anniversary of the active entry of American scholarship into archeological field work in Palestine. There is, accordingly, a timely appropriateness to summarizing in Dean Case's honor the outstanding and current contributions of archeology to our understanding of early Christianity.

In the month of April, 1838, Professor Edward Robinson, of Union Theological Seminary, entered the land of Palestine at its southern extremity at Beersheba.[1] He came with his mind systematically crammed with all available information concerning Palestinian topography. For two short months, only, he traveled through the country, following all available leads, recording important observations, and accomplishing an incredible number of place identifications. These, published in the first of his *Biblical Researches* in 1841,[2] immediately won the recognition of the gold medal of the London Geographical Society and ultimately the distinction of Professor Robinson as the "Father of Biblical Archeology."

[1] The Society of Biblical Literature and Exegesis appropriately celebrated the Robinson centennial by devoting the programs of an entire afternoon and evening at the very end of the year, December 30, 1938, to archeological papers and discussions. This was in conjunction with the Archeological Institute of America and the American Schools of Oriental Research.

[2] Edward Robinson, *Biblical Researches in Palestine, Mount Sinai and Arabia Petraea* (3 vols.; Boston, 1841).

I

In spite of chaotic conditions in Palestine today, the centennial of Professor Robinson's initial survey finds an American School of Oriental Research actively at work in this area, operating from a strategic base just north of the Damascus gate of Jerusalem, and achieving results that bear striking and most favorable comparison with the pioneering work done in his day by Professor Robinson.

The American School stands literally on the north wall of mid-first-century Jersualem, the "third wall" of Herod Agrippa I and Josephus.[3] A part of the wall itself is actually included within the school grounds. Standing on the balcony over the entrance to the main building of the school, one can trace the line of Agrippa's important fortification, as Professor Robinson traced and described it sketchily a century ago,[4] across open spaces up to the slender Sienese tower of the Italian Hospital, and then along the height of land through the Russian Compound, to the northwest corner of the present medieval walls of Jerusalem. The very site of the American School is a constant and stimulating incentive to significant work in archeology.

Two 1938 field operations of the school deserve prominent placement at the very forefront of this résumé: (1) the comprehensive archeological survey of eastern Palestine and (2) the completed excavation of Khirbet et-Tannûr. The systematic exploration of Transjordania is being carried forward personally by Director Nelson Glueck himself.[5] Its main objectives are to locate and date as many archeological sites as possible, to define the limits of ancient culture areas, to determine the character of the cultures that occupied them, and to trace the course of their historical development. This is a survey project that is many times more than a modern equivalent for the topo-

---

[3] Sukenik and Mayer, *The Third Wall of Jerusalem* (Jerusalem, 1930).

[4] *Op. cit.*, I, 314 and 315.

[5] Nelson Glueck, "Explorations in Eastern Palestine, I–III," *Annual of the American Schools of Oriental Research*, Vols. XIV, XV, and XVIII (1934, 1935, 1938).

graphical meanderings of Professor Robinson a hundred years ago—revolutionary in influence though the latter proved to be.[6]

The excavation of Khirbet et-Tannûr, completed in 1938 by Director Glueck and Mr. Lankester Harding, discloses one of the most strategically important religious sites in the southern Transjordan area.[7] It is a Nabatean temple-complex of the Roman period, superbly situated at the peak of a steep and isolated hill in the Wadi Hesa, the River Zered of biblical narratives,[8] which empties into the southern end of the Dead Sea. Built of white limestone, and standing in lofty isolation at the confluence of two great valleys, the temple was visible for vast distances. It suffered much from earthquakes, was several times rebuilt, and was finally left covered with debris and undisturbed save for a small squatters' settlement. In addition to the structural remains and inscriptions, the most important of the discoveries on the site were plastics in the round and in relief. These are so very numerous as to constitute a sizable gallery of first-century Nabatean religious art.

The chief cult statue was a Hadad with the clear attributes of Zeus. But a more dominating piece of sculpture was a massive relief of his consort Atargatis as the goddess of fruits and vegetation that was ensconced over the entrance to the inner court. Numerous other carved representations of this divine pair were found, characterized by a surprising variety of attributes, and indicating the multifarious functioning of the cult itself. When these monuments are comprehensively recorded and interpreted, a new chapter in the history of religions will have been written for that region in which Paul of Tarsus spent

[6] One prime historical and geographical determination of Professor Glueck's explorations deserves summarization in the discoverer's own words from a personal letter: "The results already achieved have amazed me. . . . . I can now trace the major political boundary line of the Nabatean kingdom as sharply as if one cut a loaf of bread in two. North of a line nearly parallel with the north end of the Dead Sea, Nabatean sherds cease as if by magic!"

[7] Glueck, "A Newly Discovered Nabataean Temple of Atargatis and Hadad at Khirbet et-Tannûr, Transjordania," *American Journal of Archaeology*, XLI (1937), 361–76, Figs. 1–15; "The Early History of a Nabataean Temple (Khirbet et-Tannûr)," *Bulletin of the American Schools of Oriental Research*, No. 69 (February, 1938), pp. 7–18.

[8] Num. 21:12; Deut. 2:13.

the crucial three years of his life immediately after his conversion experience at Damascus.[9]

During the closing weeks of 1937 the Dominican Fathers of the Ecole biblique at St. Stephen's Convent were responsible for a singular disclosure of early Christian mosaics at Maʿin near Medaba in Transjordania.[10] The floors of the nave and septentrional annex of a sixth-seventh century church were uncovered, revealing extensively preserved mosaics. Decorative patterns occupied the large central panel of the nave; but around the border were depicted twenty-four contemporary churches in the Holy Land, with their names recorded. Almost half of these are extant in whole or in part. They include the following churches: Nicopolis, [Eleuthero]polis (?), Ascalon, Maiumas, [Ga]za, Od[roa], [Cherachm]uba, Areopolis, Gadoron, Es[bus], and Belemunim. In the early eighth century the nave mosaic was badly damaged and crudely restored in an operation dated by inscription in 719-20. It would be exaggeration to assert equal archeological importance for these church mosaics in comparison with the neighboring Medaba map. It is accurate, however, to say that they constitute an invaluable document for the recovery of Christian institutions and architecture and mosaic painting in the Holy Land during the early pilgrimage period.

In Palestine proper of late some very excellent work has been accomplished by means of soundings, surveys, and partial excavations within and beneath famous structures that are still extant. The most productive example of this procedure is the reconstruction of the Constantinian basilica in Bethlehem from explorations made within and beneath the present church, which dates from Justinian's period. Plans for the Constantinian building have recently been published by such masters of archeological reconstruction as Père Vincent, of the Ecole biblique, and Mr. E. T. Richmond, of the Department of Antiqui-

[9] Gal. 1:17.

[10] R. P. de Vaux, "Une Mosaïque byzantine à Maʿin (Transjordanie)," *Revue biblique*, XLVII, No. 2 (April, 1938), 227-58, Pls. XI-XVI.

ties.[11] Substantial agreement between them gives confidence in their results.

The Nativity Church of Constantine is shown to have consisted of an atrium, arcaded on all four sides; a nave only a little less ample than the present nave; and a domed octagon that crowned the sacred grotto itself. This last-named construction was the remarkable feature of the complex. It was virtually separate from the nave, though communicating with it through three entrances. Its shape and position made it comparable to the Constantinian *Anastasis* in relation to the *Marturion* at the Holy Sepulcher in Jerusalem. Also it had affinity with the centralized Constantinian *Analepsis* out on the Mount of Olives.

The Bethlehem Octagon is believed to have been destroyed during the Samaritan insurrections of the fifth–sixth century. After order was restored in A.D. 529, Justinian rebuilt the Bethlehem basilica, enlarged the nave somewhat to its present proportions, and replaced the original octagon with the majestic trefoil apse that is the great glory of the Church of the Nativity of today.[12]

By far the most promising excavation being carried forward under Jewish auspices in Palestine at present is the exploration of the famed rabbinic necropolis at Beth Shearim,[13] the Sheikh

[11] E. T. Richmond, "The Church of the Nativity," *Quarterly of the Department of Antiquities in Palestine*, VI (1938), 63–72, Figs. 1–3; L. Hughes Vincent, "Aux origines de l'architecture chrétienne," *Quantulacumque* (London, 1937), pp. 55–70; "Bethléem: Le Sanctuaire de la Nativité," *Revue biblique*, XLV (1936), 544–74, Pls. I–XI; *ibid.*, XLVI (1937), 93–121, Pls. I–XXI. For the affirmation that the Octagon was a pre-Constantinian construction see M. Vionnet, "Les Eglises de la Nativité à Bethléem," *Byzantion*, XIII (1938), 91–128, Pls. I–VII.

[12] Decidedly deserving notation among substructural explorations in Jerusalem are Père Vincent's recent additions to our knowledge of the Pretorium of Pilate (see Vincent, *Le Lithostrotos* [Jerusalem, 1933]; also *Revue biblique*, XLVI [1937], 563–70).

The discoveries in progress within the medieval citadel of Jerusalem, for which C. N. Johns is responsible, have unusual importance for pre-Herodian history and military architecture (see *Quarterly of the Department of Antiquities in Palestine*, V [1936], pp. 127–31, Pls. LXVIII–LXXIII).

[13] *Quarterly of the Department of Antiquities in Palestine*, VI (1938), 222 and 223; *Bulletin of the Jewish Palestine Exploration Society*, IV (1936–37), 79–82, Figs. 1–4; pp. 117, 118, Figs. 1, 2; *ibid.*, V (1937–38), pp. 49–97, Pls. I–XVI; pp. 109–16; *Bulletin of the American Schools of Oriental Research*, No. 67, pp. 35 and 36; *American Journal of Archaeology*, XLII, No. 1 (1938), 168 and 169.

Ibreik of today and the Gaba of Josephus.[14] It is located on the Plain of Esdraelon not far from Nazareth, where the Plain of Megiddo begins to drop down to the coastal plain. The catacombs are not dissimilar structurally from those of the same period in Alexandria. They date from the second and third centuries, the period of the early Amoraim and the Mishna and the Gemara. From all over the Diaspora the remains of leading Jewish personages were brought here for burial—from as far west as Italy even. Nabatean pottery indicates a personage from Petra; and the burials from Palmyra are particularly numerous. The inscriptions vary accordingly. These are mainly in Koinē Greek, with a frequent admixture of Palmyrene and Hebrew epigraphs.

More important is the wealth of decorative and representative designs incised or painted on the walls. Twenty-seven different varieties of the Menorah design have been isolated, together with representations of the torah shrine, synagogue portals, the oil jar, the shofar, the boat of Charon, fruits, rosettes, plants, animals, and even human figures. In period these parallel or antedate the great cycle of frescoes unearthed in the synagogue at Dura Europos, and they precede by a great deal the bulk of synagogue decorations—mosaics, reliefs, and paintings —previously known. These relationships lend to the Beth Shearim materials of enhanced importance for the history of Jewish art through a difficult period, and also for the history of early Christian art at its very beginnings. The Sheikh Ibreik excavation has only just started. It will take years to dig out the whole network of catacombs.

Typical of a large amount of good work accomplished of late in this area in uncovering early Christian and Byzantine churches is the recently published report concerning the churches at Bosra and Samaria-Sebaste.[15] The late Howard Crosby Butler wrote regarding the cathedral church of SS. Sergius and Bacchus at Bosra: "At the time of its erection it was one of the largest domed churches in the world." The time

---

[14] Josephus *Jewish War* ii. 459; iii. 36.

[15] J. W. Crowfoot, *Churches at Bosra and Samaria-Sebaste* (London, 1937).

of its construction was A.D. 512–13. The work of Mr. J. W. Crowfoot has demonstrated that the church probably did not have a dome but a no-less-interesting timbered cupola, conical or octagonal in shape. The cathedral retains very considerable distinction as an unusually large congregational church, built on a peculiar, centralized plan, about which an exceptional amount of information is available. The peculiarity of its plan is an inner colonnade, quatrefoil in shape, within a virtually square exterior. It is a ground plan that should be studied in relation to such problematic structures as the middle church of St. John the Prodromos at Jerash, the stoa church within the library of Hadrian in Athens, the San Lorenzo Church in Milan, not to mention the incomparable SS. Sergius and Bacchus in Constantinople itself.

The large group of early Christian churches at Jerash, with their wealth of mosaic pavements and ecclesiastical sculpture, are still awaiting final publication.[16] Meanwhile the study of these diverse structures in relation to the monumental city architecture about them continues to go forward. Some most amazing adaptations and transformations are already clear. The use of the great central viaduct of the city, immediately in front of the propylaea to the Artemis temple itself, to serve as the foundation and structural skeleton for a Christian basilica, is a metamorphosis without parallel anywhere else in the world. The viaduct gate, with its arched middle opening, supplied the triumphal arch to the church. The viaduct colonnade served to separate the nave of the basilica from the side aisles; and the exedrae of the viaduct made an enveloping framework for the atrium.

A more significant metamorphosis from the religious standpoint was accomplished at the Dionysus temple of pagan Jerash, with its monumental stairway mounting up from the colonnaded main street of the city. The temple was reconstructed as the very cathedral church of Christian Jerash. Its

---

[16] Crowfoot, *Churches at Jerash: A Preliminary Report* (London, 1931); Fisher and McCown, "Jerash-Gerasa 1930: A Preliminary Report," *Annual of the American Schools of Oriental Research*, XI (1931), 1–59, Pls. 1–16; Carl H. Kraeling (ed.), *Gerasa, City of the Decapolis* (New Haven, 1938).

charming fountain court became the atrium for the church. Around the fountain, where formerly the Dionysus wine festival was celebrated, there was later enacted the ecclesiastical pageant of the turning of water into wine at Cana!

In briefest summary it may be affirmed that no other city in the Mediterranean world except Rome has yielded more varied and specific monumentalizations of the successful manner in which the triumphant Christian church possessed itself of the institutions and buildings of a declining pagan city, and adapted them to its own purposes, than has Jerash-Gerasa of the Decapolis.

As Jerash provides an unusual opportunity for studying the functioning of religious institutions in the total environment of a great city, so also does ruined Palmyra, the "caravan city" in the Syrian desert off to the northeast.[17] There has been in progress here a most difficult project in modern social and civil engineering that has archeological value and deserves very hearty appreciation. The French mandatory power has moved the entire modern native town outside the limits of the ancient city and has left the majestic Palmyrene ruins free for excavation and consolidation. Since the Palmyra of Roman times occupied the whole of the local oasis, the creation of a livable new town in the desert outside has been no insignificant engineering accomplishment. Today the only modern buildings within the ancient ruins are the police post, the archeological headquarters, and the romantic Hotel Zenobia. Since the removal of the native population special attention has been concentrated on the vast pile of the central sun temple and its surrounding precinct.[18] The temple itself is being reconstructed and rendered secure, and the sacred area is being completely explored. This was a major sanctuary of the oriental sun cult that was favored by the Syrian emperors of the third century, and even by Constantine himself, the "first Christian emperor." Explorations

---

[17] M. I. Rostovtzeff, *Caravan Cities* (Oxford, 1932), pp. 91–152.

[18] See particularly the series of reports on "Antiquités syriennes" by M. Henri Seyrig, appearing in *Syria: revue d'art oriental et d'archéologie* from 1931 to date. Cf. Theodor Wiegand, *Palmyra* (Berlin, 1932).

on this site should tell us much more about one of the last great henotheisms of paganism and of its final competition and coalescence with triumphant Christianity.

An early Christian center of maximum importance, where current archeological operations are being carried out properly on a city-wide scale, is Antioch-on-the-Orontes, where "the disciples were first called Christians," and where Emperor Julian "the Apostate" had a very bad time with his pagan revival. The work here is being carried forward by a group of co-operating American institutions under the vigorous leadership of the Princeton Department of Art and Archeology.[19] One main objective of the work is to recover the ancient city plan of Antioch, now largely lost in the expanse of the fertile plain of the Orontes. A most effective co-ordination of library research and field work *in situ* has been accomplished. In the archeological laboratory at Princeton the documentary data regarding Antiochene topography are being compiled, systematized, and interpreted. On the site itself soundings, exploratory digs, and excavations have already established the following major features of the ancient city plan: the circumference of the Justinian and the Tiberian walls; the location of the citadel—on Mount Staurin rather than on Mount Silpius as was formerly supposed; the limits of the city island—lost by the silting-up of one branch of the Orontes; the plan of the great circus; various Roman baths and aqueducts; the line of the colonnaded main street; and most recently the forum of Valens.

The renewed concession for excavation at Antioch includes the port of Seleucia. There Professor W. A. Campbell has uncovered the concrete wharves of the habor—now a marshland—and the market gate of the port. Historically, this site is most closely associated with the missionary expansion of Hellenistic

---

[19] Charles R. Morey, *The Mosaics of Antioch* (Princeton, 1938); George W. Elderkin, *Antioch-on-the-Orontes*, Vol. I (Princeton, 1934); Richard Stillwell, *Antioch-on-the-Orontes*, Vol. II (Princeton, 1938). Cf. E. S. Bouchier, *A Short History of Antioch* (Oxford, 1921); V. Schultze, *Altchristliche Städte und Landschaften*, Vol. III: *Antiocheia* (Gütersloh, 1930). See also Walther Eltester, "Die Kirchen Antiochias im IV Jahrhundert," *Zeitschrift für die neutestamentliche Wissenschaft*, XXXVI (1937), 251–86, Pls. 1 and 2.

Christianity[20] as well as with the development of Levantine trade.

The most important of the specifically ecclesiastical remains uncovered at Antioch is a complex of four basilicas, radiating cruciform fashion from a central square court which contained a martyr's shrine. It is dated by a mosaic inscription to A.D. 387, and M. Jean Lassus has identified the *marturion* as of St. Babylas, the martyr-bishop of the Decian persecution.[21] The architectural student recognizes the ground plan at once as the prototype for the near-by pilgrimage church of St. Simeon Stylites, built about A.D. 450. This underscores the consequential quality of the Antioch *marturion*. If now the famed octagon of Constantine can be recovered, another major addition to our repertoire of early Christian churches will have been made.

II

In approaching the work currently progressing on Christian archeological sites in Greek lands, it is convenient to do as Paul himself did: land at Kavalla, the ancient Neapolis, proceed up the Via Egnatia, and cross the immense plain of Philippi, where Antony and Octavius destroyed the Roman republic and avenged the assassination of Julius Caesar. The modern auto road enters the Byzantine walls of Philippi, at the eastern gate, and duplicates the exact line of the Roman roadway through the city, some ten feet above its excellent pavement. From the steep sides of the acropolis, just below the triple fortresses that gave the city its plural name, one can get a bird's-eye view of the excavations being conducted by the French School under the direction of M. Lemerle.[22]

They have uncovered the entire periphery of the Roman forum, a small market beyond that, and the monumental basilica of the Derekler farther on. The huge piers of that gigan-

---

[20] Acts 13:4; 14:26.

[21] *Antioch-on-the Orontes*, II, 5-14. This was the martyr whose relics desecrated the Apollo temple at Daphni at the time of Emperor Julian's unhappy visit.

[22] For the most recent accomplishments at Philippi see various reports by M. Paul Lemerle in *Bulletin de correspondence hellénique*, particularly LXI (1937), 86-108, Pls. IX–XIV.

tic fifth-century church still dominate the site as they have done continuously for the last fifteen centuries. In surface area the Derekler is far larger than the small market beside it and almost as inclusive as the great Roman forum itself. At an early date in its history, however, the Christian community was sharply decimated in numbers. Then an apse was built across the main entrance. What formerly had been only the narthex was now commodious enough for the entire congregation.

On a wide terrace above the forum and beyond the Via Egnatia, the French have uncovered other Christian churches[23] even earlier than the Derekler. At higher levels rock-cut pagan sanctuaries have been cleared; and hundreds of strange votive reliefs, carved on the faces of cliffs, have been cleaned and recorded and catalogued. Already there is visible here an exceptionally extensive record of the religious life of the city, Christian and pagan, where Paul established his first community in Europe.

In Thessalonica, Paul's next important propagandist center for Macedonia, the Via Egnatia is still the main street of the modern city, running straight through the heart of Salonica from east wall to west wall, and dividing in two the ample civic center. It is still spanned by a triple Roman arch of the early fourth century—that of Galerius, who instigated the last great persecution of the Christians and at the very end promulgated the first imperial edict of toleration in their favor. Originally, this was a companion to the Vardar arch on the other side of the city, which incorporated one of the decisive "Politarch" inscriptions of Thessalonica;[24] but the latter arch was torn down in 1876 in the name of civic improvement. Below the modern Via Egnatia, on the gently sloping shore of Salonica's harbor, lies the ultramodern international town, as was the case in the Roman period. Above the main street, climbing the steep slopes of the enveloping hills up to the Monastery of the Blateon and the citadel, crowd the native quarters of the town, with houses

[23] These include a baptistry and a memorial chapel, the latter associated with the tradition of Paul's Philippian imprisonment (Acts 16:22-40).

[24] Acts 17:6.

higgledy-piggledy and narrow streets leading nowhere—again as was the case in Paul's time.

What one most admires in modern Salonica is the grand scale of city planning carried out since the disastrous fire of the war period. It is archeologically valuable that the main lines of this plan, represented specifically by the chief new streets, follow exactly the original Roman quadrangular plan for the city. However, the Roman right angles are being broken by the diagonal streets characteristic of French city planning and most familiar to Americans from the L'Enfant plan for the city of Washington.

In Salonica today the restoration of the Roman quadrangular scheme has served to focus travel at exactly the most prominent ancient monuments and buildings still standing in the city. Thus one important street passes immediately in front of the fifth-century domed church of Hagia Sophia and another leads directly into it! A restored street is projected to run straight from the Arch of Galerius to the dominating domed tower of St. George's, and so to make clear once again the effective relationship that once obtained between these two signal structures. Finally, the chief perpendicular street of Salonica, shooting up from the port, ends exactly in the open atrium in front of the basilica of St. Demetrius, the patron saint of the city.

By far the most important project in specific archeological restoration in progress at Salonica—perhaps the most worthwhile project of the kind in all the Christian world—is the rebuilding of the fifth-century basilica of St. Demetrius.[25] When in August, 1917, the world learned that the very last structure to catch fire in that terrific conflagration was the church of the patron saint, and that the most important of Salonica's important churches was entirely gutted, just after it had been freshly restored, there were those who were broken-hearted. But the ruin was not complete or irreparable loss. As one result, a long-forgotten crypt was rediscovered, out of which came treasures and valuable vestments. The final result is yet in process—the restoration of the basilica to all its ancient splendor.

[25] G. Sotiriou, *The Church of St. Demetrius* (Athens, 1920).

The architects are doing an archeologically correct piece of work and a far better job of building with much better materials than was accomplished in the first instance.

In Salonica's massive Hagia Sophia, a domed basilica of the late fifth century, searching investigations have been carried through even while the church itself has been in continuous use as the chief cathedral of the city.[26] Particularly the successive pavements beneath the main floor have been explored, and also the roof construction above has been examined. Accordingly, it is now possible to reconstruct the initial aspect of this singular experiment in ecclesiastical architecture that antedated that other great compromise structure, the Hagia Sophia of Byzantium itself.

St. George's cupola in Salonica is perhaps the most problematic of the fascinating group of the centralized churches of Christendom. Recently it has been secularized. Its mosaics have been cleaned and made secure. In the various niches in its circumference the different floor levels of the rotunda have been exposed; and in the apse a charming Byzantine Ascension has been uncovered. Marked stages in the historical development of the structure have thus been accentuated; but its ultimate origin and function remain as obscure as ever. Probably it was once a Roman tomb.

Current operations in Paul's Thessalonica have served to emphasize its convenience and importance as a center for the study of early church architecture and decoration.[27] Only the Eternal City itself affords more numerous and advantageous opportunities for such investigations.

The two major Pauline centers in Greece proper, Athens and Corinth, are at present the foci of supremely successful archeological operations, conducted by the American School of Classical Studies in Greece. A prime division of labor between American and Greek archeologists in Athens is that the latter are responsible for uncovering the efficiently systematized and

[26] M. Kalliga, *Die Hagia Sophia von Thessalonike* (Würzburg, 1935).

[27] Diehl, Le Tourneau, and Saladin, *Les Monuments chrétiens de Salonique* (Paris, 1918); Tsimas and Papahatzidakis, *Mosaïques des églises de Salonique* (Athens, 1933).

highly commercial Roman Agora, while the former are excavating the more casual and more conspicuously religious Hellenistic Agora. The Roman project lags somewhat from lack of funds; but the Hellenistic excavation proceeds at a great rate.[28] The area uncovered extends from the Stoa Basilikē on the north, where the Council of the Areopagus met in Paul's time, up to the Hill of the Areopagus on the south, at the base of which are the foundations of the early Christian basilica of St. Dionysius the Areopagite.

To date the most considerable results have been topographical discoveries. It is most fascinating to follow through Pausanias' itinerary, confirming his descriptions in detail by the monuments actually uncovered in the Agora. Here one can view today the foundations of that majestic series of ancient sanctuaries that monumentalized the remarkable religiosity of the Athenians: the altar of the Twelve Gods, the temple of the Paternal Apollo, the Metroön, the Tholos, the Eleusinion, etc. In general, the Agora excavations enable us to reconstruct the setting that gave stimulus to Paul's very unsuccessful attempt to philosophize early Hellenistic Christianity and make it intellectually appealing.[29] This, in turn, contributed in a negative way to the success of his more emotional and picturesque and religious presentation of Christianity at Corinth.[30]

The excavation of the Hellenistic Agora, involving as it has the expropriation of the most densely populated section of modern Athens, is perhaps the most ambitious effort of the kind ever undertaken by a privately supported archeological society. The work has been in progress for nine seasons, now; and it is expected that it will be complete in two seasons more—a truly colossal performance in an amazingly brief period of time!

Contrasting with the rapidity of the Athenian accomplishments are the long-drawn-out American operations centering

[28] Up-to-date reports regarding the Agora operations appear regularly and currently in the *American Journal of Archaeology* and in *Hesperia*, the journal of the American School in Athens.

[29] Suzanne Halstead, "Paul in the Agora," *Quantulacumque* (London, 1937), pp. 139–43.

[30] Cf. Acts 17:16–34 with I Cor. 2:1–5.

on the Roman Agora in Corinth.[31] For over forty years, now, the American School has been digging intermittently on this site. Not until 1937 was the last modern building (of the Turkish period), standing within the Agora itself, finally demolished. With the expanse cleared at last, it is possible to know life at the center of Roman Corinth rather better than in most Pauline cities.[32] One can now examine a large number of important sites and structures at the civic center that Paul undoubtedly knew very well indeed: the Propylaea, the world-famed Fountain of Pirene, the basilicas Roman and Julian of Gallio's period, the public Bema, the Senate House, the shops bordering the Agora, the Apollo Temple, and various other sanctuaries less positively identified. The southern end of the Lecheum Road, where the [CUNAIΓWΓHEBPIAIWN] inscription was found, has been cleared as far as the limits of the modern village allow; but as yet the synagogue itself has not been located. Outside the Agora area a pavement laid by Erastus the aedile, together with his appreciative inscription, has been uncovered.[33]

American work at Corinth has been exceedingly wide-ranging, as well as concentrated at the center. The complete circumference of the city walls to a distance of six miles, including Acrocorinthus as well as the city proper, has been continuously traced and explored at all crucial points. Of the outlying sites that have been accorded complete excavation, the most productive have been the theater, the odeum, the Asclepeum, and the Christian basilica in the Craneum quarter.

The Asclepius precinct, located on the north edge of the plateau, where it had the constant benefit of fresh breezes from the Gulf of Corinth, was found to be swept bare to bedrock of all monumental remains, presumably by Christian fanaticism.

[31] American School of Classical Studies, *Corinth: Results of Excavations*, Vols. I–X (Athens, 1929–38); Carpenter and Morgan, *Ancient Corinth: A Guide to the Excavations* (Athens, 1936³).

[32] In the memorial number of *Ephemeris Archaiologike*, celebrating the centennial of the University of Athens (1937–38), Professor Oscar Broneer has just published a study of the Corinthian Agora of Paul's time. "The Topography of Corinth at the Time of St. Paul," *Ephemeris Archaiologike*, C (1937), 125–33, Figs. 1–6.

[33] Rom. 16:23. See Henry J. Cadbury, "Erastus of Corinth," *Journal of Biblical Literature*, L (1931), 42–58; "The Macellum of Corinth," *ibid.*, LIII (1934), 134–41.

Only numbers of eloquent ex-votos in terra cotta, representing all parts of the human body, were exhumed from hollows and crevices in the rock. Some of these were even life-size, and were thus unique for Greece.

The early Christian church uncovered at the east gate of Corinth stood beside the road leading off to Phoebe's town of Cenchreae on the Saronic Gulf. It was a huge affair with a peculiar trefoil chapel, surrounding a large *marturion*. The size of this and many other early basilicas in Greece gives one a much enlarged conception of the vigor of the Christian church in the Balkan peninsula at this early period. Moreover, such sizable early basilicas are likely to be found at almost all the great classical religious centers of Greece, such as Daphni or Delphi or Epidaurus or Olympia. Here, then, Greece offers an unusual opportunity to investigate the metamorphosis and Christianization of pagan cults localized on sites of great sacredness and prime historical importance.

III

The student who is interested in large-scale archeological operations that have significance for early Christian history should by all means acquaint himself with what is going on in Rome and Italy at the present time. More archeological work is being done there in a more adequate manner than anywhere else on earth just now. In part this is due to the circumstance that the contemporary fascist regime in Italy regards itself as the political and cultural heir to the Roman Empire at its best and greatest. Italian interest in Roman archeology from Augustus to Trajan—the general period of early Christianity's emergence—is correspondingly intense. Moreover, there is keen appreciation in government circles of the propagandist value of archeological discoveries and restorations, both for stimulating patriotic fervor and for inviting tourist travel.[34] Accordingly, government support in Italy for archeological research is today generous to the point of being lavish.

[34] Ente Nazionale Industrie Turistiche (ENIT), *Die toten Städte Italiens* (Rome, 1938); Francesco Pellati, *The Latest Archaeological Discoveries in Italy* (Bergarno, 1935²); V. Macchioro, *A Lightning Spark for Pompeian Visitors* (Naples, n.d.).

What has most stimulated Italian effort during the past year has been the Bimillennium Augustanum. The founder of the Roman principate, in whose reign Jesus of Nazareth was born, was himself born in the year 63 B.C. Accordingly, the year from the twenty-third of September, 1937, to the twenty-third of September, 1938, was grandly celebrated in Rome as the two-thousandth anniversary of Augustus. The program was a most far-reaching one; but in Rome it focused rather sharply on the Mausoleum of Augustus near the Tiber, on the Palazzo delle Esposizioni on the Via Nazionale, and finally on the Ara Pacis Augustae itself.

At the imperial burial vault between the Flaminian Way and the Tiber, the world-famous concert hall of the Augusteo has been dismantled and the mausoleum itself completely excavated to its innermost core. Its exterior has been widely cleared of encumbering buildings and systematized in a manner to recall for the classicist the *silvas et ambulationes* that originally enhanced the tomb.[35]

The Augustan Exposition on the Via Nazionale concerned itself mainly with monuments from the Roman provinces.[36] Because of its comprehensiveness it was extensively revealing to the student investigating the Mediterranean milieu that conditioned the genesis and early development of the Christian movement. Also it gave generous space—an entire gallery—to the display of specifically Christian monuments.[37] Probably it was the best-arranged archeological exhibition ever staged; and it gave rise to a variety of distinctive events.

The culmination of the entire celebration came on September 23, 1938, when Il Duce rededicated the Ara Pacis Augustae, recovered fragment by fragment from the mud of the Campus Martius through the last four centuries. With its restoration, the prime monument of Augustus' wedding of religious revival

---

[35] Suetonius *Augustus* c. 4.

[36] Bimillenario della Nascita di Augusto, *Mostra Augustea della Romanità* (Rome, 1938[2]).

[37] Catullo Mercurelli, "I Monumenti cristiani alla Mostra Augustea della Romanità," *Rivista di archeologia cristiana*, XV (1938), 123-39, Figs. 1-16.

and Roman imperialism stands before the world in its original dignity.

Undoubtedly, the Rome of Mussolini presents the most grandiose co-ordination of comprehensive city planning with provision for preserving the monuments of antiquity that one can see anywhere today. The supreme example of this procedure is the construction of the Via dell'Impero from the Colosseum to the Piazza Venezia, straight through the entire line of the gigantic Imperial Fora up to Hadrian's Temple to the divine Trajan. Included are such stupendous monuments as Julius Caesar's Temple to Venus Genetrix, Trajan's mercantile hemicycle, and Augustus' Temple of Mars Ultor. Enough remains of these structures, with their monolithic columns and veneered walls, to give one a brilliant impression of the "grandeur that was Rome" when Christianity came into being.[38]

While one is bewildered by the magnitude and cleverness of this vast accomplishment, one cannot close his eyes to certain obvious defects in the plan. In the first place, Vespasian's important Forum and Temple of Peace—a tragic landmark in the history of the Jews—were left buried out toward the Colosseum. In the second place, the axis of the Via dell'Impero does not parallel either the axis of the Imperial Fora or that of the old Republican Forum alongside. It is a disquieting third axis between the two. In the third place, as between the rights of ancient monuments and the opportunities for modern propaganda, archeology is too frequently sacrificed to propaganda.

The treatment accorded two independent monuments at the Colosseum end of the Via dell'Impero has created no little comment among archeologists. The Basilica of Maxentius and Constantine has been consolidated and rendered structurally secure. It is now regularly used as an outdoor concert hall; its apse and semi-dome being acoustically very effective. One can scarcely take exception to the concerts. But it is patently inappropriate when the back wall of the basilica is used as a billboard to dis-

[38] A. W. Van Buren, *Ancient Rome as Revealed by Recent Discoveries* (Rome, 1936), pp. 45–55, Pl. V; Grant Showerman, *Monuments and Men of Ancient Rome* (New York, 1935), pp. 1–73.

play propagandist marble maps of the extent of the Roman Empire, ancient and modern.

Next to the basilica stands the double temple of Venus and Roma, built by Hadrian and finally rebuilt by the much-depreciated Maxentius. This has recently been restored in a most original manner with the aid of landscape-gardening. Carefully trimmed hedges have been grown to replace the structural units that have disappeared. Straight hedges are walls, stratified hedges are long flights of steps, round hedges with marble bases are columns, and cubical hedges are altars. Here are the monuments of the dead past made literally alive once more! It is all done with such cleverness and accuracy that criticism of it is disarmed.

A structural peculiarity of the great temples along the Via dell'Impero deserves special study for the contribution it may have to make to architectural origins in early Christian churches. It is the appearance of the enlarged niche or apse at the end of the cella as an architectural enframement for the cult statue.[39] This peculiarity is present on the inside of Julius Caesar's temple to Venus Genetrix and in Domitian's temple to Minerva. It is evident on both the interior and the exterior of Augustus' vast dedication to Mars Ultor. It is duplicated in Maxentius' double temple to Venus and Roma.

Now it is well known that an apse is a foreign formation in a classical temple. The Greeks regularly located their cult statues in a free-standing position in the cella, so they could be seen from the back as well as from the front. Italians of the republican period located their cult images flat against the back wall of the cella—to be viewed from the front only. Neither Greeks nor Italians typically made use of the apse in public temples.

There are in the city of Pompeii, however, frequent instances of large curvilinear niches for cult statues in sanctuaries of the Lares, or the genius of the imperial family, i.e., in shrines that had household character in combination with public function. This connection with the imperial family seems at present to be

---

[39] Van Buren, *op. cit.*, pp. 56–57. Professor Van Buren first made the suggestion here developed in a terse communication to the Congress of Roman Studies in 1935.

the explanation of the temple apses in the imperial Fora; for Venus Genetrix was the divine ancestress of the Julian house, as Mars Ultor was both its divine ancestor and its potent protector. Similarly, Domitian adopted Minerva as the patroness of his household. In each instance the power of the princeps in state affairs made these imperial household cults to be of great public significance as well.

It is quite possible that conspicuous imperial temples such as these may have made contribution to the later prominence of the apse in Christian basilicas. Of course, it is not proposed that this was the sole group of archetypes for Christian apses. Architectural origins are almost never so simple as that. Earlier and other apsidal structures are known to have had their influence in the matter. Religious function, however, is certainly in favor of supplementary influence from the imperial household temples such as those along the Via dell'Impero.

Outside the imperial city, in such productive excavations as those at Pompeii and Ostia, a start is being made in tracing the beginnings of Italian Christianity in the Campanian city and the Latin port. At Pompeii only the merest problematic traces of the Christian movement have as yet been found.[40] Since the city was finally destroyed in A.D. 79, this scantiness of Christian remains was surely to be expected.

The caricaturistic fresco of the judgment of Solomon and the Sodom-Gomorrah inscription of Pompeii are well-known data. Did they possibly have Christian and eschatological connections, as well as Jewish background? Two years ago, in the freshly excavated palaestra west of the amphitheater, Cavaliere della Corte recognized a complete copy of the famous ROTAS-SATOR square, one of the most familiar magical inscriptions of late antiquity. Is this, as Professor Rostovtzeff avers, a specifically Christian cryptogram, concealing the dual Greco-Latin confession: ΑΩ *pater noster?*[41] When immediately after its dis-

---

[40] R. C. Carrington, *Pompeii* (Oxford, 1936), pp. 116–29.

[41] M. Rostovtzeff, *The Excavations of Dura-Europos* (New Haven, 1934), V, 159–61. See also Franz Dornseiff, "Das Rotas-Opera-Quadrat," *Zeitschrift für die neutestamentliche Wissenschaft*, XXXVI (1937), 222–38.

covery the matter was discussed before the Naples Academy and the Pontifical Academy in Rome, there were scholars who were willing to assert the probable Christian character of the rebus, and there were others who dissented. A priori it is not the least improbable that there was a Christian community in Pompeii when Vesuvius exploded its summit in A.D. 79. The author of Acts relates that, when Paul landed in Italy two decades earlier, a Christian group welcomed him in the neighboring port of Puteoli.

In Ostia, the port of Rome, Christian monuments are beginning to become noticeable.[42] Indeed, a group of early Christian chapels has already been uncovered that may yet rival in numbers and interest the well-known Mithraic sanctuaries of the port. The visitor simply cannot avoid the remains of the early Christian oratory beside the Decumanus Maximus, immediately back of the theater. Here was found a sarcophagus inscribed *Hic Quiriacus dormit in pace.* Probably this Quiriacus was a companion of the martyrs who suffered the extreme penalty *ad arcum ante theatrum Ostiae.*[43]

Farther down the main street of Ostia, directly in front of the great markets of the city, are the apses of a former bathing establishment that was later transformed into a Christian church. There are indications that the metamorphosis took place after the triumph of the church in the fourth century.

Still farther on, almost at the Forum itself and adjoining the Piazza dei Lari, is a well-built though small basilica, with a sizable apse and a large entrance. In a niche in a stairhall back of the apse was found a relief of Christ as the Good Shepherd. The bricks of which the basilica was constructed show date stamps between A.D. 113 and 123. Its plan fully justifies the designation of the building as a basilica; but its small size suggests it was a private construction. Probably it was used as a pagan chapel before it was put to Christian use. Thus, by the gradual recovering of modest monuments that are recognizably

---

[42] Guido Calza, *Ostia: Historical Guide to the Monuments* (Milan, 1937).

[43] *Acta Bollandiana,* XXXVIII, 757 ff.

Christian, the beginnings of the church in the imperial port are taking on definite features.

Inclusive of work on particular locations, there is in progress throughout Italy today a comprehensive program of archeological restoration that is of very great promise indeed. Its objective is nothing short of restoring all important early Christian churches to their original state, as nearly as possible. Almost anywhere in Italy at present, in large cities or on deserted sites even, one is likely to find such work in progress. Sometimes the Catholic church is financing it, and sometimes the fascist government is responsible. The total process involves the removal of all incongruous medieval and modern additions, the fundamental security of the original structure, the careful preservation of all early frescoes or mosaics or decorations, the accurate reproduction of lost parts—in short, the comprehensive restoration of the building to its early state. Such work, so very widespread, involves huge sums of money, varied technical skills, detailed historical and archeological knowledge, an honesty that is willing to sacrifice everything to accuracy, and patience beyond belief. The results being actually achieved at the present time are frequently above praise.

The early Christian restorations are particularly conspicuous in Rome itself, where the dignity and simplicity of early basilicas are a needed antidote to the ill-restrained license of the domineering baroque churches that crowd the Eternal City. Yet it is in the Ravenna of Honorius the Weak and Theodoric the Great that one can get his most consistent and harmonious impressions of early church architecture and furnishings and decoration.[44] This is because the main monuments that still dominate the city were first built in the major early periods of the city's history, during the fifth century and the sixth.

Restorations of the very highest order of excellence, completed or in process, monumentalize the three golden eras in Ravennate life. The Roman imperial period of Honorius and Galla Placidia is summarized by Santi Nazario e Celso, the

---

[44] Guiseppe Gerola, *I Monumenti di Ravenna bizantina* (Milan, 1937). Cf. Corrado Ricci, *Ravenna* (Bergamo, n.d.); Charles Diehl, *Ravenne* (Paris, 1927).

mortuary chapel of the crumbling imperial court, and the tomb of Galla Placidia herself. One notes with concern, however, that in an adjacent weed-grown lot the very court church itself, the Basilica of Santa Croce, stands now ignored and neglected. The Gothic period of Theodoric is epitomized not only by the tomb of that great *Führer*, but also by Sant' Apollinare Nuovo, built by Theodoric to be his court church and the Arian cathedral. Finally, the period of the Byzantine exarchate is represented by that most subtle and daring of central churches, San Vitale, with its splendid presbyterium mosaics portraying Justinian and Theodora visiting the church in imperial state.

For the student of the history of Christianity during these centuries, the grouping of restored Ravennate churches according to their historical origins has comprehensive import. He recalls that the Christian movement itself had main phases during the fifth and sixth centuries corresponding exactly to the main groupings of early monuments in Ravenna. As Catholic, Christianity was the religion of the declining Roman Empire of the West. As Arian, it was the religion of the vigorous barbarians from the north. As Orthodox, it was the religion of the cultured East Christian empire of Byzantium. Thus, the past and the present and the future of Ravennate Christianity about A.D. 500 may be thought of as typifying the greater past and the more chaotic present and the more uncertain future of North Mediterranean Christianity for that same period.

THE IMPACT OF GNOSTICISM ON EARLY
CHRISTIANITY

JAMES THOMAS CARLYON

Southern Methodist University
Dallas, Texas

FOLLOWING its rise in Palestine in the first century, Christianity moved out from its Jewish origin and environment to become the accepted religion of the Roman Empire, and that within three short centuries. Whatever Jewish elements remained, the movement is likely to have taken to itself generous gentile enrichments before it secured the patronage of Constantine and the Romans. Among the cultural influences of these centuries Gnosticism takes its place.

While a very precise and accurate determination of the characteristics of Gnosticism may yet elude us, it is possible to understand its general nature. In addition to the controversial writings of the Church Fathers, we now have a third-century manuscript of a genuine Gnostic writing, the *Pistis Sophia* (Codex Askewianus in the British Museum). It is probable that we have here Gnostic materials that belong to the second century of the Christian Era. It is generally agreed that Valentinus and his Egyptian followers represent the mature expression of the Gnostic schools in their challenge to orthodox or traditional Christianity. They flourished also in the second century. From a careful scrutiny of the systems of Valentinus and Marcion and the *Pistis Sophia* this contemporaneous rival of early Christianity becomes fairly well known to us. Its interpreters in our day include such names as Legge, Mead, Reitzenstein, Burkitt, Lake, Scott, and Case. A field once known by only a few expert scholars has through their labors become attractive and interesting to every student of early church history.

Gnosticism seems to have been a highly complex religio-philosophical movement of antiquity, bearing in its current the vital forces of East and West—a movement never definitely organized into a single school or church and never clearly systematized as a philosophy or a theology. It rather represents gentile peoples in their quest for redemption: a dualistic worldview unwilling to rest in permanent division, inquiring minds that refused to believe the riddle of the universe was insoluble, lost souls crying out for salvation, human hearts hungry for divine fellowship, good life that felt clear intimations of its immortality, serious minds seeking some rational interpretation of man in his relation to the cosmos. The Gnostic teachers and preachers announced the good news of a divine revelation, but secret within the esoteric circle of the initiated, a revelation of heavenly realities and of the passwords by which the soul of the illumined might surely escape its superhuman foes in its ascent from the material and the temporal to the spiritual and the eternal. Over against the simple Hebrew trust in Providence, the Gnostics offered a highly speculative cosmology in which the supreme deity was far removed from an evil world. Creation itself had been a mistake, and the distance between God and man was covered only by a series of emanations, moving ever farther from the heavenly throne down to the female deity whose defection gave rise to the creation of man in whom a bit of heaven was imprisoned in the mass of earth. Salvation was really the escape of this divine spark and its return to its proper heavenly home.[1]

Much of Gnosticism paralleled Christianity as a separate religious and cultural expression of gentile life and at times sought to contradict or destroy the church which it would supersede. Other Gnostics were Christians who sought to sublimate the moral and historical elements of their faith to the rational and mystical emphases of Gnosticism. The most prominent and capable of these Christian Gnostics were Basilides, Valentinus, Heracleon, and Ptolemy. After presenting the significant traits in these schools, H. Lietzmann suggests the focal point of the attack upon orthodox Christianity:

[1] Irenaeus *Adv. Haer.* i. 1; Tertullian *The Five Books* iv. 7; *Pistis Sophia.*

Gnosis has been described as the "acute Hellenization of Christianity": we must recognize in addition an equally acute "re-orientalization," but it was not the many coloured figures of the Greek and oriental divine world which threatened Christianity. These were easily overcome. In gnosticism the god of oriental mysticism rose up in power and might against the Father in Heaven to whom Jesus had taught His disciples to pray.[2]

I

From an analysis of the fully developed Gnostic schools of the second century one turns back to the New Testament to discover clear evidence there of just such Gnostic ideas and practices in the environment of the first Christians.

It is significant that the earliest New Testament writer appears in radical contrast with Jesus of Nazareth. Instead of a Heavenly Father's attitude of understanding and friendly relation with the Son, Paul conceives of God as far away and of man as lost and in his evil nature banished from the presence of a justly angry deity. Under the pen of the apostle the humble and lowly teacher of Nazareth was transformed into the figure of a divine redeemer. The good news of God's gracious favor gave way to a theology of atoning sacrifice. The Gospel of Jesus became a gospel about Jesus.

It was as a myth, as a story of a God who had descended from heaven, that the Greeks immediately accepted it. It is not God, but the Son of God alone, who thus descends into this world; the Jesus of history is completely smothered up by the myth of the heavenly son of God.[3]

Keeping the language and ideas of the later Gnostics in mind, one follows the missionary apostle in his pastoral correspondence with his churches to find a terminology far different from that of the Synoptic Gospels and much like that with which he is already familiar. The distinctive Gnostic words recur again and again, not in a single letter alone but in almost every piece of his writing. The central Gnostic term *gnōsis* ("knowledge") occurs twenty-one times, *mustērion* ("mystery") nineteen times,

---

[2] *The Beginnings of the Christian Church*, trans. B. L. Woolf (New York: Charles Scribner's Sons, 1937), p. 397. Quoted by permission of the publisher.

[3] P. Wernle, *The Beginnings of Christianity*, trans. G. A. Bienemann (New York: George Putnam's Sons, 1903), p. 252. Quoted by permission of the publisher.

and *sophia* ("wisdom") twenty-eight times. R. Reitzenstein[4] lists with these, as Gnostic, many words which have come to be accepted almost as distinctively Christian in our time: body, flesh, holy one, *plērōma* ("fulness"), power, salvation, spirit, truth. The secrets of man's salvation have been revealed to the Christian preacher as a bequest of his divine Lord. This mystery of redemption was committed forever to the care of the church, and its gracious benefits are limited to those who are "in the Spirit" and so make up the true "Body of Christ." The fullest expression of this notion occurs in the Ephesian letter which is post-Pauline and records a further development of certain phases of the apostle's thought (1:23; 2:20 ff.; 4:12 ff.; 5:23 ff.).

The deliverance by Christ was conceived by Paul in cosmic terms. The Christian shared in the victory of his Lord, who proved himself supreme among the superhuman forces of the world (Gal. 1:20 ff.; 5:23 ff.). The whole cosmos had been under the dominance of demonic hosts until Christ engaged them in combat and deprived them of their authority and power. No longer did the believer need to fear, since he belonged by union with his Lord to the new creation (Rom. 8:18 ff.). All the angelic hosts recognized their subjection to him (I Thess. 3:13; 4:16). The two dread foes of man's hopes and dreams, Sin and Death, chief ministers of Satan, lost their dire control over destiny with the overthrow of their chief.[5]

Paul met the Gnostic demand for the immortality of the soul by showing that the Christian had already become a spirit-person and had assumed a heavenly nature even while remaining upon the earth. He need have no fear of his place in the future life, since he had achieved a present union with Christ which was essentially the life of the redeemed in heaven (Col. 2:13; Rom. 6:13 ff.).

The ascent of the soul to the divine realm had been realized

---

[4] *Die hellenistischen Mysterienreligionen* (Leipzig: B. G. Teubner, 1910), pp. 138 and 144.

[5] H. B. Carré, *Paul's Doctrine of Redemption* (New York: Macmillan Co., 1914) p. 13.

for the apostle in his experience of mystical fellowship with Christ. The continuing life which he claimed was not really his own. He lived and yet it was his Lord who really lived in him. His was life "in Christ" (Rom. 8:1; II Cor. 5:17). This mystical union with a divine Savior was accomplished either by the act of faith or through the sacraments of Baptism and the Supper. In one Sacrament there occurred an initiation into the mystery, while in the other there was found a full assurance of the consummated union as well as a means of sustenance in the new order of life.[6]

The wide prevalence of Gnostic terms and ideas in the Pauline literature is a strange phenomenon only to those who forget that the first of the apostles was born in Tarsus of Cilicia and that he grew to manhood in a country teeming with Gnostic religionists. He is known to us today as Paul the Hellenist. Jew by birth and Pharisee by choice when in Jerusalem, yet this man wrote with sympathy and with understanding of things that belonged in the religious culture of Gentiles. It is possible that he was more Greek than he knew. It is probable that the Stoic university in his native city, famous because of the connection of Athenodorus with it, and the popular mystery of Mithras which was well established there made Tarsus uniquely equipped to prepare Saul of Tarsus for acceptance of a commission to preach Christ among the Gentiles. In fact, he came to feel that God had set him apart from his very birth to this task.

The evidence of Gnostic elements in the environment of other New Testament writers varies considerably with the several books. Of the Gospels, Mark reflects a possible Gnostic point of view in the baptism of Jesus and in his conflict with supernatural foes as presented in the first three chapters. There is little question, however, of a rather fully developed Gnostic situation confronting the writer of the Fourth Gospel. The anti-Semitism of the book, its contrast of light and darkness, the doctrine of the incarnation and return to the Father, the stress on guidance into truth, the straining at emphasis upon the full

[6] S. J. Case, *The Social Origins of Christianity* (Chicago: University of Chicago Press, 1923), pp. 140 and 146.

humanity of its Hero—all suggest to the critical student that the writer, while appreciating certain aspects of Gnosticism, was really intent upon correcting its mistaken conceptions of Christ. Students of the canon are inclined to think that this affinity with the heretical movement along with the book's popularity among Gnostic Christians made its acceptance by the church quite problematical for some years after the other three gospels had found wholehearted reception.

In the Fourth Gospel we overhear the writer, in the name of the Church, replying to such questions as these: Is Jesus only one of the aeons? Is he a vice-God or a higher Logos? . . . . But the aversion to Gnosticism, which begins with the prologue, continues through the whole book, and is only thrown into relief by the author's use of Gnostic phrases and formulas. The Gnostic tendencies which were operating at the time when this writing was composed, tended to resolve revelation into a process of aeons, semi-mythological and semi-metaphysical, by means of which God and the world came into relations; they further developed an ethical barrenness by their intellectualism.[7]

The First Epistle of John even more clearly sets itself against a false gnosis. The writer is particularly severe with those who claim knowledge but who fail to keep the ethical requirements of the church (2:3-6).

The Epistle to the Hebrews glorifies orthodoxy. It opens with an enthusiastic declaration of the superiority of the Christian revelation. The following chapters tell the story of the Son of God come to earth as a pioneer of salvation, taking his place among men to share with them their lowliness that they in turn might share with him his exaltation. Enlightened souls could scarcely reject the fulness of salvation in Christ for the lesser compensations in other faiths. The emphasis upon the genuine humanity of Jesus would be a definite answer to the Docetae who reduced the fleshly form of the Lord to a mere phantom (10:19-24).

The Pastoral and the Catholic Epistles feel likewise the presence and threat of Gnosticism. The unique mediatorship of Christ between God and man (I Tim. 2:5 ff.), the security of

---

7 J. Moffatt, *Introduction to the Literature of the New Testament* (New York: Charles Scribner's Sons, 1911), pp. 530 f. Quoted by permission of the publisher.

heaven (II Tim. 4:18), and the stress upon true knowledge (Titus 1:1-4) are indicative of the sub-Pauline author's answer to the Gnostic constituency. The heretics of Jude are pictured in verse 8 as they who "set at nought dominion and rail at dignities." They seem to be the same opponents who are more fully described in II Peter (chaps. 2 and 3).

This cursory survey of the New Testament does not pretend completeness but illustrates a literature rather generally charged with Gnostic elements. Heffern[8] concludes from a comprehensive examination of the whole New Testament that the canon reveals at least eleven of the distinctive marks of the Gnostic movement, which the Christian leaders of the age were compelled to challenge in the name of the historic Jesus and the Christian church. On the negative side there are indications of the denial of the primitive eschatology, of a future resurrection, of the anticipated enjoyment of messianic happiness as well as of the rightful authority of the state. On the positive side the Christians made the same but superior claims of inner illumination, accepted more or less fully the prevailing gentile dualistic world-view, engaged in controversies with leaders on the basis of individual guidance as against constituted church authorities, were inclined toward moral laxity because of a false sense of freedom from law and from other external control, rejected the social and divine duty of marriage, tended toward undue exaltation of the Spirit-Christ to the disparagement of the historic and human features in the Master, and finally struck at the heart of Christianity by undue stress upon the mediation of angels who usurped the solitary grandeur of Jesus Christ, the world's Redeemer. Paul seems to me to have typed the Christian response to the challenge and competition of Gnosticism under four general pronouncements: the Christian religion offered first-century inquirers a supernatural salvation supernaturally revealed, a superior faith-knowledge that emancipated them from fear of the evil spell of demonic forces, a confident assurance of immortality already begun in the Spirit,

---

[8] A. D. Heffern, *Apology and Polemic in the New Testament* (New York: Macmillan Co., 1922), pp. 363 f.

and an ascent to deity through union with the Son of God in whom dwells all the Pleroma (Col. 1:19; 2:3 ff.).

II

It is generally agreed by students of early Christianity that Gnosticism made its impact upon Christian life and practice primarily by indirection, or at least without conscious intent. It was a species of mental culture, perhaps the most vigorous cultural factor in the life of antiquity. Gnostics were the thinkers of the time, serious-minded men who combined genuine religion and piety with healthy intellectuality.

Gnosticism was one of the greatest efforts ever made to satisfy the religious needs by seeking a religion which would conserve the maximum of the past and yet adjust itself to the contemporary outlook. It was the religious reaction of the syncretistic centuries to the intellectual forces of the time. It was a long-sustained attempt to reconcile religion and culture and to make religion at once rational and uplifting and enthusiastic. It was the natural evolution of the persistent Hellenic demand "Know thyself" and thereby "thou shalt know God and the universe" and obtain salvation.[9]

These men were theologians and philosophers and, as such, represented the sort of interest with which Christian leaders were compelled to cope. They afforded an atmosphere, a climate in which the awakening Christian society had to live. Many of them made no effort to win Christian people to their organizations. Theirs was a genuine and vigorous cultural movement whose *raison d'être* was within itself. Their leaders were men who felt themselves under compulsion to answer the deep questions which their own minds and hearts entertained. They were seeking salvation for themselves; answering inquiries which their cosmos thrust upon them; their concern was their own destiny. From their point of view their relation to Christianity was quite a secondary thing, just as was their traffic with Jews and with the various mystery cults.

It is necessary to remind ourselves that behind the streams of Christian Gnosticism there lies a vast dim hinterland of purely pagan Gnosticism, which may be in part explored by a study of Christian Gnosticism and a comparison of the latter with the Hermetic writings and what we know of the mystical

---

[9] S. Angus, *The Religious Quests of the Graeco-Roman World* (New York: Charles Scribner's Sons, 1929), pp. 378 f. Quoted by permission of the publisher.

philosophies of Babylonia, Persia, and Egypt. The way of Gnosticism had been mapped out in all its essential features before the Christian era had begun.[10]

Thus we are to think of Gnosticism as the larger and more pervasive cultural movement having varied and multiplied contacts with the total religious life of antiquity. Christianity was but one of the many faiths or organized religions with which Gnostics had intimate dealings.

Nevertheless, the impact upon Christianity was significant and specific, and church historians have little difficulty in enumerating at least the more permanent effects of this fellowship (or competition) of faiths. The letters of Paul and the Epistle to the Hebrews had made in the first century a beginning of Christian theology. But as yet there had been achieved no adjustment of those two rival world-attitudes represented in the Hebrew religion and Greek philosophy. Both were present in the Christian church. Paul, to be sure, had sought to make certain compromises such as his doctrine of the resurrected spirit body and the dual deities. He had insisted that the church make room for both Jews and Greeks. He had at best only postponed the day when Gentile should meet Jew face to face and have it out. The Gnostics forced the issue. They demanded that the practical way of life offered by the Christian preacher be supplemented by a theoretical solution of the deep intellectual problems of alert minds of the day. Man's salvation must be coupled with a respectable system of thought. Within Christianity itself there arose men who set themselves to a reinterpretation of the Gospel. Such is Lietzmann's explanation of the Fourth Gospel; John combines Paul with Gnosticism:

It [Gnosticism] was not thrust back now in an unreasoning fashion, but greeted as a new form of the affirmation of God and valued for purposes of filling out and shaping the inherited tradition of Christianity. This is the source of many changes in the traditional presentation of the gospel story: the heightened glory of the figure of Jesus, the increase of the miraculous element, the evolution of Christ-mysticism into God-mysticism, the tendency to advance conceptions like truth, love, light, life to the point of personification, and especially the introduction of the formula "to see God" and "to

[10] G. H. C. Macgregor, *Jew and Greek: Tutors unto Christ* (New York: Charles Scribner's Sons, 1936), p. 309. Quoted by permission of the publisher.

know God"; also the ceremonial "hieratic" style of the gospel with the striking monotony of its speeches, the "meandering" turns of its course of thought, and the "I am" pronouncements of the Son of God.[11]

In even more detail and completeness the Christian Gnostics of the second century undertook this task. Professor Burkitt pays them proper tribute in his exposition of their work as "an attempt to set forth what a generation ago would have been called 'the New Theology'; that is to say, a reformulation of Christianity in terms of 'modern' science and philosophy."[12] He speaks this terse word: "Their merit was in recognizing that some new theory of religion was called for."[13] Christianity must either accept a theology already at hand or make its own. The Church Fathers fought Gnosticism within and without the church for the preservation of the institution itself. Theological research and philosophical reflection became the mental habit of second- and third-century Christendom. For this advance we must give praise to the Gnostics who stirred Christian minds to action.

One of the first tasks thrust upon the Christian church in this intellectual endeavor was the selection of a Christian canon of Scripture. From its inception the church had used the Hebrew Scriptures as if they were its own. Yet even the most superficial acquaintance with these books revealed their tension with much that was integral to Christianity. Paul had emphasized the contrast of law and gospel in no uncertain terms; one invited to slavery, the other to freedom. The Gnostic Christians threw their weight against Judaism, the Hebrew Scriptures, and their implications for religion. They showed the contrast between Jewish exclusiveness and the expansiveness of Christianity, between the primitive ethics of Yahweh and the Grace of the Lord Jesus Christ, between the legal strictures of the Lord of Hosts and the generous understanding of the Father of Jesus, between the destructiveness and the vengefulness of the one as

[11] *Op. cit.*, pp. 312 f. Quoted by permission of the publisher.

[12] F. C. Burkitt, *Church and Gnosis* (Cambridge: At the University Press, 1932), p. 91.

[13] *Ibid.*, p. 90.

against the forgiving redemptiveness of the other, between the act of creation which degraded divinity by breathing heavenly life into earthly matter and the incarnation which had as its goal the release of the soul from the flesh. In line with this reaction against the older canon the Gnostics set to work to choose a truly Christian list of books for use in the churches. The most famous of these lists was selected by Marcion of Sinope, son of a bishop of orthodox Christianity, and a man of deep piety. It included the Gospel of Luke and the Epistles of Paul, modified so as to omit their Jewish features. The Fathers recognized the insidious challenge to the very life of the church. For, however imperfect Judaism and her Scriptures were, they had given birth to Christianity: they had produced Peter and Paul and Jesus; they had contributed an ethical monotheism far superior to the antinomian and licentious religious practices of paganism. Not only did the Docetae party question the true historical character of Jesus but the Gnostic attack threatened to cut the whole church from its historic roots and to classify it among new and unworthy things. The one adequate answer to the Gnostic offer of a canon was given by the church in choosing a list of books acceptable to the church as a whole and adding these to the sacred books already in use. The Muratorian Fragment testifies to the immediate results of the countermovement. A Christian canon was on its way before the close of the second century. In paradoxical truth the Gnostic Marcion has earned the title, "the Father of the Canon."

One of the influences leading to the formation of the canon was the literary activity of the Gnostics. During the major part of the second century these earnest religionists were composing hymns and writing gospels and other books to incorporate their ideas. M. Dibelius counts among their significant literary products the following books: the Ebionite Gospel, the Nativity Gospels, the Apocryphal Acts of the Apostles, and the Psalms of the Naassenes. Among the books of "Acts" he singles out particularly those of John, Peter, and Andrew. Besides these there must have been considerable literature that has disappeared from view.

Gnosticism represents a marked secularization of Christianity, for the occurrence of lyric poetry, even if still "popular" though possessing artistic value, is a kind of symbol of an approximation to literature as such. On the other hand, the fact that the new poesy flourished among the very heretics was altogether ominous to non-canonical poetry. For it turned out after the middle of the second century that the non-biblical hymns were entirely suppressed in the Church. It is on this account that our knowledge of primitive Christian hymns is so sparing.[14]

While much of the literary work of the period was thus destroyed, the positive influence of these writings is preserved in the liturgy of Christendom. The Gnostics doubtless played a part in the creation of a church calendar, in the inception of the observance of the Feast of Epiphany, in the "Virgin" devotional works. W. D. Niven traces their influence, by way of the Ophite serpent ceremony, upon the sacramental doctrine of transubstantiation.[15]

In the rejection of Gnostic books and a frank acceptance of the Hebrew Scriptures (though these were often interpreted allegorically to escape their contradiction of Christian teachings) the Church Fathers adopted the high ethical ideals of Judaism, carried forward somewhat to allow for the emphasis upon innerness of motive, as required by Jesus. Between the rival claims of a workable ethics and a rational philosophy the church preferred the former, leaving to time and councils the development of the latter. The Hebrew way of life had immediate reference to the daily conduct of men who were endeavoring to be "the Body of Christ" and whose conduct must measure up in some degree to the example set by their Lord in his earthly ministry. Occasional persecution served to throw the balance in favor of the Hebrew tradition, since the interests that were in large part theoretical suffered the more under this pressure. Plato, the Stoics, and the Epicureans joined battle against the childish fear of superhuman foes in the heavens and summoned

[14] M. Dibelius, *A Fresh Approach to the New Testament and Early Christian Literature* (New York: Charles Scribner's Sons, 1936), p. 254. Quoted by permission of the publisher.

[15] *The Conflicts of the Early Church* (London: Hodder & Stoughton, 1930), pp. 164–65.

men to freedom and self-reliance akin to the simple Hebrew faith.

Over against the self-centeredness of Judaism the Christian church set itself with increasing confidence to the task of cultivating the inhabited world. Whence this missionary enthusiasm? Jesus himself had never traveled outside the boundaries of Palestine; the Twelve had remained in Jerusalem after the dispersion of the first disciples on the occasion of Jewish persecution in their capital city; Paul had begun as a messianic evangelist rather than a missionary in the true sense of the word. From the time of Alexander the Great Hellenism had been on the march. Each of the mystery cults had a mission and particularly did the oriental mysteries outbid the native Greek cults for popular favor. Even more continuously and ingratiatingly did Gnosticism seek both individual believers and a group or institution to which it might become attached in healthy parasitism. Into Judaism, into Hermeticism, and into many other religions did it insinuate itself. Its devotees would be satisfied with nothing short of world-conquest, and its eclectic theosophy was well calculated to appeal to many peoples. Religion as well as politics was imperial. Its union with Christianity seemed natural and providental. The church, like the Gnostic sects, was in the first century otherworldly, concerned with saving men from a bad world. A casual reading of the letters to the seven churches as given in the first chapters of the Revelation of John makes clear the Christian judgment upon any who participated in the mundane affairs of the time. It is probable that this conflict with dualistic Gnosticism drove Christian leaders to two major decisions: the church must adopt the Gnostic and Greek world-encompassing enthusiasm, but at the same time it must honor this present social and economic order in which it lived. This latter followed logically from the adoption of the Old Testament canon.

Hence it became incumbent upon Christian leaders to think more highly than had formerly been their custom of the material world that God himself had created. . . . .

Spiritual values remained supreme, and the quest for worldly goods was always to be made subservient to moral and religious ideals, but a moderate prosperity was no longer inconsistent with the aims of the church. The manner by which material possessions were acquired and the ways in which they were used now became the focal points of chief concern to the Christian moralists.[16]

The church of the second century arrived at the full concept of universality, foregleams of which had already appeared in the vision of the Apostle to the Nations. Instead of striving to keep themselves unspotted from the world, the second-century bishops thought of themselves as world-figures, and the Roman church found many believers in its proclamation of a Petrine foundation that implied authority and divine control over the Western world. The sense of world-destiny lent confidence to the Christian imagination which leaped from local bishoprics and district synods to world-councils and a church spreading through the race.

We have in this chapter been referring to "the church" when in exactness we should rather have written "churches." Each bishop was supreme in his own metropolitan area. But the danger from without had the natural result of uniting separate and rival churches and of giving them a sense of common history, common interests, and common goals. The serious threat of heresy intensified the strong sense of loyalty to Christ and prepared the way for aggressive leadership in church affairs. In the West a succession of strong bishops gradually lifted the bishop at Rome to pre-eminence among the bishops of Africa, Italy, and Gaul. Here was the power needed to overthrow heretical influences such as Gnosticism and Montanism. Not only was Rome strong; it was also apostolic.

Irenaeus' view of the episcopacy completed his structure of arguments against the Gnostics. His basic idea was apostolicity. Exercised in three ways, through the Scriptures, the traditions, and the episcopacy the apostolic succession was regarded as the bulwark of orthodox Christian doctrine.[17]

In the East likewise the movement toward authoritative leadership was quickened by attacks from without and by heretical

[16] S. J. Case, *The Social Triumph of the Ancient Church* (New York: Harper & Bros., 1933), p. 54. Quoted by permission of the publisher.

[17] William Scott, *A History of the Early Christian Church* (Nashville: Cokesbury Press, 1936), p. 311. Quoted by permission of the publisher.

dangers within. In fact, there seems to have been a keener interest in correct thinking in the East than in the West. Bishops here also claimed the apostolic succession. Ignatius makes the appeal for honor to the bishopric not for himself but for the church, in whose service he was ready to lay down his life.

These episcopal leaders early recognized the necessity of establishing some official system of doctrine. Under the threat of Gnostic speculation they summoned the scholars of Christendom to theological research and statement. If both the Father and the Son, a Christianized Yahweh and the Lord Jesus Christ, were to be worshiped, then both their mutual relations and their contact with the cosmos must be clarified. If the Christian's lord had lived a real and full manhood, then his kinship to deity must be made clear. A Christology and a theology became imperative. The simple beginnings of Paul and John were no longer adequate. They might have developed into the Gnostic position almost as well as into that coming to be held by traditional Christianity. Once this task was understood, it was undertaken. Over against the post-resurrection emphasis of the Gnostic Christians the Church Fathers set the historical life and teachings of Jesus of Nazareth. The sacrifice upon Calvary was genuine and accomplished something both in the conquest of demons and also in the salvation of men. His resurrection body was the first fruits of the resurrection of Christian believers of all ages. Jesus took his place with Plato and the philosophers as the world's master-mind. And yet the Gnostics won, in part. The simple monotheism of Judaism gave way to a learned doctrine of a three-person deity, of which the second and third persons in their relationship to the first were markedly similar to what the Gnostics had called emanations (Irenaeus *Adv. Haer.* i. 2. 5–6). The Son and the Spirit were for many Christians subordinates and in some way derivatives from the Father God. The mediatorship of Christ and the comforting presence of the Holy Spirit were likewise concessions to the heretical polytheism of opponents of orthodox theology. The developed doctrine of the Logos, the high teaching of the incarnation, these are precious possessions of Christianity for which theologians have been most grateful to their inspirers, whoever they may have been. The Gnostics take their place with others in this significant development.

Thus a rational theology developed to satisfy the demands of reason in a thoughtful time. But reason was not enough; authority also was necessary. The new doctrine of apostolicity was called into action, and the Twelve plus Paul became the arbiters of Christian thought. A canonical rule of faith took its place by the side of the apostolic canon of Scripture. The Apostles' Creed came into being as a forerunner of the later conciliar symbols such as those of Nicaea and Constantinople. While the creeds claimed a basis in revelation via apostolic experience and expression, they became less and less testimonies of faith and more and more statements of truth. *Gnōsis* was usurping *pistis* in the realm of orthodoxy. What had begun as a way of life, simple and clearly marked, became a way of knowledge or correct doctrine which the ordinary layman was not expected to understand and which was but dimly seen by the technical scholar. Under the aegis of Paul the Pastoral Epistles stoutly supported orthodoxy, while the bitterest attacks upon false teaching were launched against the heretics in the names of Peter and Jude. The church won its controversy with Gnosticism, but the church itself was changed.

Not only was it [the church] thus deprived of influences that would have proved helpful, but it suffered a partial arrest of development. The extravagance of Gnosticism was only the other side of that freedom which was the birthright of Christianity, and which breathes through the New Testament like a living air. To check the inroads of Gnosticism the church had to prohibit freedom. Dogma was made rigid: the idea of new revelation was forbidden, ecclesiastical government became official and oppressive.[18]

As canon and creed emerged, they added to the prestige of their manufacturer. Back of them both appeared the clear lines of the Catholic church. Out of rich varieties of Christian worship and spontaneous praise of Christ there was crystallized the cultus of Catholicism: the simple order of the synagogue serv-

[18] E. F. Scott, "Gnosticism," *Hastings Encyclopedia of Religion and Ethics* (New York: Charles Scribner's Sons, 1914), VI, 241. Quoted by permission of the publisher.

ice gave way to punctilious arrangements for initiation into a mystery which possessed divine secrets surpassing the passwords and formulas of pagan mysteries. Clearly defined and carefully ordered as a hierarchy the ministers of the church took their place in a highly organized ecclesiastical system. Mystery, sacramental miracles, and an effective liturgy lifted the church service into a supernatural affair of dread possibilities for the unfaithful as well as of gracious and divine blessing for the devout. So grew the power and sanctity of the priesthood and the gradual separation of clergy from laity.

The new faith could not escape the religious influences so powerful around it: in the new cosmopolitanism it could not remain a sect partitioned off. The points of view shared with its contemporaries were so numerous that they exposed it to the inroads of other ideas. Despite the obvious advantage of Christianity in making a new beginning as a religion, it was soon drawn into the currents of asceticism, dualism, demonology, and the mythologizing of its historic content. Indeed Christianity offered a more promising field than elsewhere to those who sought Gnosis. There are many reasons why the Christian Church should become the home of the Gnostic movement.[19]

The Catholic and true church thus became the important achievement of these early centuries; a church holding in its keeping the keys that unlock heaven and hell, a church that should one day hold undisputed power on the earth also.

Gnosticism was by no means the only influence that must be held responsible for the Hellenizing of Christianity. It was, however, one of the major factors in the change which made the church more than a messianic sect of the Jews and which equipped it to become a church of the nations. The foregoing statement is not intended to imply that its influence was wholly evil. Much that it accomplished was good. Because of this historic fact Gnosticism perhaps deserves better of the church which it has helped to produce. The contributions of Judaism may not have been altogether perfect, and surely the impact of Gnosticism is not entirely to be regretted. Each of these major influences in early Christianity merits discriminating appraisal.

[19] Angus, *op. cit.*, pp. 384-85. Quoted by permission of the publisher.

ECONOMIC FACTORS IN THE PERSECUTIONS OF THE CHRISTIANS TO A.D. 260

GEORGE THOMAS OBORN

Taylor University
Upland, Indiana

THROUGHOUT the course of history economic factors have played a fundamental role in every social upheaval, and, since the early persecutions of the Christians undoubtedly may be included in the category of violent social disturbances, it may be taken for granted that material considerations were of basic importance. But how important? It is the purpose of this essay to summarize the data in answer to that question. Clearly, it must be kept in mind that we are dealing here with only one, but a very significant, aspect of the causes of the persecutions. Social and religious forces also played important roles, but they have been more frequently expounded, and the necessity for brevity forces us to ignore them altogether in this present treatment.

In dealing with the economic motivation of the persecutions, it will be convenient to divide them into two periods: the first, extending from the beginning of the Christian movement to the reign of Decius (A.D. 249–51), during which period the persecutions were local and sporadic and, with four possible exceptions, were instigated by popular hostility; and the second, beginning with the reign of Decius and ending, by the limitation of this article, with the edict of Gallienus in A.D. 260. During this latter period popular hostility almost completely disappeared as a cause of the persecutions, and imperial action became the instigating force. Hence the persecutions during this second period were general and affected the whole church.

The four possible exceptions to instigation by popular hostility during the first period demand a brief explanation. The first of these is the persecution under Nero which, it may be asserted, was due to imperial action, and, in a sense, that is true; but it was odium already attaching to the Christian name in the mind of the masses that made the action of Nero feasible. It is to be classified under the head neither of imperial action nor of mob violence. Its instigation is to be found primarily in the personal character of Nero. In the second instance the death of Domitian cut short the persecution that had been begun under his rule and threatened widespread suppression of Christianity. If it had continued, it might have constituted imperial action against the Christians, but, as under Nero, the personal element was an important factor in the situation, and no final conclusion can be drawn. The situation under Septimius Severus is much more difficult to interpret. Here we have the issue of an edict definitely in opposition to Christianity which aroused considerable persecution and resulted in some famous martyrdoms. But it is significant to note that the edict was not directed at Christianity as a whole and did not aim to exterminate Christianity but merely to check its growth. Septimius Severus had been favorable to Christianity, which had enjoyed nearly a century of relative peace, with the result that the new faith was rapidly becoming a powerful element in society and of increasing importance to the state authorities. Hence Septimius Severus had more opportunity than any of his predecessors to observe the inherent danger to the state of the Christian organization. But Septimius Severus must have valued much too highly the large and influential body of Christians to have had any desire to exterminate them. Nor had the time yet arrived in the financial affairs of the Empire when drastic action to save the state from total collapse seemed imperative. Therefore, Septimius adopted the much milder method of inhibiting the increase of what must have seemed to him a cancerous growth in the body politic. The fourth difficulty is the outbreak under the emperor Maximinus. But this persecution was clearly a policy not of suppressing Christianity as such but of wiping out influential leaders under the former emperor and was only local and intermittent in its effect.

In taking up the economic factors that entered into the motivation of the popular hostility to the Christians, we will be able to do little more than indicate the more important sources of friction and some of the materials that substantiate this line of interpretation. Space will not permit the indication of how these causes of friction were eventually overcome.

The first area of economic conflict between Christianity and paganism is to be seen in the *familia*. When the encroachments of Christian propaganda split the *familia* into pagan and non-pagan elements, this disruption caused more than merely social disharmony; it interfered positively with the economic structure of the group. The very fact that a woman had adopted a faith that was alien to that of her husband destroyed the pagan ideal of the home. Such action on the part of one of the heads of the *familia* disrupted the family cult and endangered the prosperity of the group, for we must remember that it was "an age of supernaturalism" when men sought and believed in supernatural aid in every undertaking and interest of life. Small wonder, then, that pagan husbands not uncommonly disowned their Christian wives.[1]

But the difficulty was not always occasioned by the conversion of the female side of the household. There is an intimation, at least, that when Cyprian became a Christian he proceeded to dispose of a considerable portion of his property in the interest of his new cause and that this action was taken in spite of the objections of his wife.[2] Cyprian himself urgently and repeatedly counsels the heads of Christian households not to abstain from almsgiving because they have families to provide for.[3] Cyprian's advice must have had considerable influence, and, in case the entire family were not Christian, this jeopardizing of the family exchequer would cause a deal of trouble.

There is another matter that would cause no little economic difficulty in the case of a pagan husband and a Christian wife. The practice of abortion and infanticide was widespread in the pagan world. The life of the newly born child lay at the mercy

[1] Tertullian *Apol.* 3; *Ad nationes* i. 4; Arnobius *Adversus nationes* ii. 5.
[2] Pontius *Vita Cae. Cyp.* 3.　　　　[3] *De op. et Elee.* 16–20.

of the father. If birth had not been prevented by abortion and the child was undesirable in the eyes of the father, it would be disposed of by exposure or other methods. The girl infants were the most usual victims of this procedure, and the only conceivable basis for this action is economic. The Christian conscience abhorred this practice then as today. What would be the outcome when the Christian wife objected to the exposure of her infant daughter? Most certainly the pagan husband would know whence had come this marked change in the attitude of his wife; formerly she had acquiesced, but now it was quite different. This economic difficulty must have engendered much hostility on the part of pagan husbands and their associates.

In the cases of families split between parents and children we find similar difficulties. The story of Paul and Thecla[4] furnishes a pertinent example. It does not matter here whether the "Acts" are genuine or not, since they were accepted as depicting a true situation and the writer believed them to be truly representative. In these Acts Thecla is persuaded by the preaching of Paul to renounce her approaching nuptials and remain a virgin. She was the daughter of wealthy but pagan parents, and her betrothed was probably also well to do. She had been betrothed by her mother, and her refusal to go ahead with the arrangements caused her mother and also the disdained suitor great consternation. It cannot be asserted that the mother's anguish was purely economic, but neither can it be gainsaid that a "good" match for her daughter, as this seems to have been, would certainly be economically advantageous. On the other hand, marrying a daughter of a well-do-do family was not to be blithely rejected by any young man, regardless of the possible actual affection involved. Thus the refusal of Christian daughters to marry the choices of their pagan parents would antagonize two groups: the parents and the suitors. And this antagonism had a considerable economic foundation. But apart from this matter of advantageous marriages the disaffection of the children in the home would cause trouble. Eusebius gives us an account coming from the fourth century of a son who

[4] See C. Schmidt, *Acta Pauli* (Leipzig, 1904).

returned home from school only to find that he could not adjust himself to the existing conditions and left his home eventually to suffer martyrdom.[5] Tertullian and Arnobius tell us that sons were often disinherited or cast out.[6] The Clementine *Homilies* and *Recognitions* advise the separation of families where the parents are pagan, as the children would profit them nothing if they remained.[7] Many parents, then as now, depended upon their children to contribute to the family income. In many cases they must have constituted the only old age insurance available. When the son refused to learn, or to continue in, the pagan trade or occupation of his father, which was so often intimately linked up with idolatrous beliefs and practices, the father must have felt not only that he was losing a son but that his future welfare hung in the balance. What was more natural then than that the disobedient son should be angrily cast out or disinherited.

There is still another feature in the disruption of the *familia* which demands our attention. The *familia* of every well-to-do citizen contained a number, if not a large number, of slaves. Christianity early encroached upon this fruitful field for propaganda.[8] The situation was repeatedly at the breaking-point, and only a match was needed to set off the conflagration. As a rule masters governed their slaves with an iron hand, and it is to be expected that, when they ascertained that any of them had taken up with a new "superstition" that taught absolute equality (and practiced it!), they would take drastic measures to let their slaves know their true position. Here was a closely knit organization instilling a psychology of equality very detrimental to slave economy and conducive to revolts and consequent economic disasters. The slaveowners as a whole could hardly be expected to appreciate the fact that actually Christianity was a force making for stability in this section of the social structure. As a matter of fact, we have positive evidence

[5] Eusebius *Martyrs of Palestine* iv. 5.

[6] Tertullian *Ad nat.* i. 4; *Apol.* 3; Arnobius *Adv. nat.* ii. 5.

[7] Clement *Homiliae* xi. 19, 20; *Recognitions* vi. 4.

[8] P. Allard, *Les Esclaves chrétiens* (Paris, 1914).

that pagan masters did take drastic action against their Christian slaves. Tertullian tells us that pagan masters sent their Christian slaves to the slave prisons,[9] and Arnobius informs us that Christian slaves were tortured by their masters.[10] In theory Christianity certainly threatened the breakdown of slave economy, and this would be readily perceived by slaveowners in the pagan world, with its consequent opposition.

Of the nature of propaganda may be mentioned the millenarianism of the Christian society. In the early generations the Christian writers and preachers spoke with confidence and exultation of the coming day when all would be transformed, their enemies and all unbelievers would be overthrown, and the Christians would reign supreme in a glorified world. This view was prevalent even in the days of Cyprian, who believed that the Lord would avenge the sufferings of the faithful and in the apocalyptic kingdom the believers would reign with Christ.[11] The economic significance of this teaching is almost too obvious to need expression. In a world in which pagans were to be visited with eternal damnation or subject to the yoke of Christian rulers, the former had nothing to gain and everything to lose. How important this matter was in stirring up hatred against the Christians it is impossible to say, but its influence must have been considerable, especially among the uncultured masses. The fiery maledictions of irresponsible radicals, who would not be differentiated by the crowd from "orthodox" Christians, must have contributed appreciably to the suspicion of the masses.[12]

No consideration is more important in understanding the popular opposition to Christianity than the full comprehension of the intense and widespread superstition. Heathens and Christians alike sought a supernatural explanation for all untoward events such as floods, storms, famines, earthquakes, and plagues. To both, such disasters were caused by the displeasure of the supernatural. The Christians as "atheists" in

---

[9] *Ad nat.* i. 4; *Apol.* 3.   [10] *Adv. nat.* ii. 5.

[11] Cyprian *Ep.* lv. 2, 7, 10 (58); *De Dominica oratione*, 13; *Ad Demet.* 17, 21, 22.

[12] Origen *Con. Cel.* vii. 9.

the opinion of the pagan world were repeatedly accused of angering the gods and thus causing the disastrous public calamities.[13] The Christians, on the other hand, tended to defend themselves in a measure by asserting that the disasters were due to the wickedness of the heathen which had angered the one true God.[14] These great physical disasters are always primarily economic. Even pestilences have their economic residue, and in the other disasters the loss of life is directly dependent upon the economy of the calamity. Arnobius gives us an economic interpretation of these misfortunes[15] and tells us that the failure of the corn crop was often the cause of popular hostility.[16] The importance of this superstition in causing repeated opposition to the Christians can hardly be overemphasized.

Our next problem is to show to what extent the conduct of Christians rent directly certain economic realms of social activity. There is considerable evidence, though not abundant, for the direct interference of the Christians with the heathen temples. Along with other references, we find in the writings of Origen a suggestion that some Christians were taking destructive action against idols.[17] The Synod of Elvira felt called upon to pass a law that anyone who died as the result of the destruction of idols should not be considered a martyr.[18] Apparently such conduct was much too prevalent. To whatever extent this activity occurred it constituted definite economic destruction and would necessarily arouse strong opposition.

The Christians also interfered with the temples in other ways. The situation in Bithynia-Pontus is enlightening.[19] We are told that the temples there had been deserted and that the markets were at a standstill. Such interference with temple revenues would be certain to arouse violent hostility on the part of those concerned, and this must have been the case to a greater or less

[13] Tertullian *Apol.* 40; *Ad nat.* i. 9; Cyprian *Ep.* lxxiv. 10 (75); *Ad Demet.* 2, 3; Eusebius *H.E.* iv. 13. 1–7.

[14] Tertullian *Ad Scapulam* 3; Hermas *Simil.* vi. 3; Cyprian *Ad Demet.* 6–11, 17, 21.

[15] *Adv. nat.* i. 1, 3.   [17] Origen *Con. Cel.* viii. 38.

[16] *Ibid.* 16.   [18] Synod of Elvira *Canon* 60.   [19] Plinius *Epist.* 96.

degree wherever Christianity gained a firm foothold. Tertullian had to meet the accusation in his day that the temple revenues were daily falling off.[20] The Christians might seek to defend their conduct with regard to the heathen temples, but that would not fill the empty coffers or satisfy those dependent upon them.

Closely allied with this phase of economic disruption was the Christian opposition to all trades and professions connected in any way with idolatry. This feature is such an outstanding characteristic of early Christianity that it needs no detailed delineation. The list of prohibited trades and professions leaves one wondering indeed what means the pious Christian could employ in order to earn a living.[21] A striking example of how the conduct of Christians tended not only to cripple certain trades by their withdrawal but also to hinder the remunerative practice of certain professions is seen in the account given by Lucian of Alexander of Abonouteichus, the oracle-monger. By daring and deceit he had built up a very lucrative trade in oracles, but he found that the presence of Christians or Epicureans interfered with his rites (and his profits!), and so he and his followers called upon all such persons to be off![22]

In the opposition of Christianity to antisocial occupations we find an attitude that would alienate what is always a powerful element in the social organization: the vice and gangster combine. The Christian, says Tertullian, takes pride in his opposition to such as pimps, panders, bath-suppliers, assassins, poisoners, sorcerers, soothsayers, diviners, astrologers.[23] This was the characteristic Christian attitude which we find expressed in various canons of the church. The prevalence of these corrupting trades in Roman society made these conflicts numerous and important. An interesting illustration of the opposition of white-slavers to the Christians is found in the story of the maiden of Corinth and Magistrianus.[24] It is impossible to esti-

---

[20] Tertullian *Apol.* 42.

[21] Tertullian *De idol.* 4-6, 8-11, 19; *De corona* 11.

[22] Lucian of Samosata *Alexander the Oracle-monger* 38.

[23] Tertullian *Apol.* 43.   [24] Hippolytus *Fragments.*

mate the extent and the violence of this hostility, but, whatever its potency, it was certainly based on economic considerations.

Another prominent feature of early Christian social life was its aloofness from the world. The Christian idealists desired to keep the believers from all contact and association with pagans whether in business or pleasure. Tertullian wishes that they might not even inhabit the same world.[25] It is not to be imagined that this ideal of aloofness was ever completely attained, but it seems to have been more effective sometimes than even the idealists desired. The Christians were accused of being useless in the affairs of life, and there must have been real basis for the charge. Even Tertullian resents this accusation and seeks to refute it.[26] His is a classic treatment and worthy of the most careful consideration. The point that we wish to emphasize is that this chapter in Tertullian's Apology brings out in sharp outline the economic bearing of the withdrawal of the Christians from pagan society. They are accused of not engaging in commerce or trade with pagans or of purchasing a great many of the common articles offered for sale by the pagan merchants. The fact that Tertullian denies this accusation does not neutralize the effect that had been produced upon the popular mind, which was undoubtedly an important cause of the hostility of the populace.

A further consideration of significance is the economic competition of the Christians in the pagan world. In contrast to the Roman attitude was the Christian insistence upon work as a duty; one should be ashamed of idleness.[27] The keener competition of the Christian in comparison with his pagan rival was based not only upon the Christian ideal of industry, honesty, and frugality but equally vitally upon his better habits of daily living. The Christians were not yet as fortunate as the Jews, who had a recognized holy day on which they were excused from labor in order to visit their houses of worship. The Christians had to meet for worship before or after their daily

[25] Tertullian De spec. 15.

[26] Tertullian Apol. 42; cf. Ep. to Diog. 5; Origen Con. Cel. viii. 5.

[27] Didache 12; Ignatius Ep. to Philad. 4; Apost. Const. ii. 63.

labor. They soon came to have special services once a week, but those who were employed by pagans, at least, had to work just the same. Consequently, the Christian community assembled at sunrise for a brief service of worship and again after the day's work was done. There is abundant evidence to show that this was not only a weekly but a daily program of widespread practice all through the period which we are considering. If the Christian was so situated that he could not attend some sunrise service or for some reason or other none was to be held, he was urged to rise before daybreak nevertheless to read the scriptures and pray before going to work.[28] This practice, coupled with a high moral standard which included honesty, industriousness, and frugality, was bound to make the Christian a powerful and dangerous competitor in the labor market. The labor market in the Roman world was in a precarious condition. The upper classes had only disdain for labor, trade, and commerce and relegated all such matters to their slaves. The proletariat had no industrial ideal. This made Christian competition all the more effective. The only redeeming elements in the pagan situation were the freedmen. The freedmen had learned industriousness, trades, and commerce while they were slaves and necessity had wiped out any innate aversion. They seem to have lived normal, healthful lives by the heathen standard and rapidly came into virtual control of the economic affairs of the Empire. Their numbers were constantly on the increase, and, while it is impossible to form any certain judgment, it appears that they constituted the majority of the working population during the Christian Era. It seems to us that this is the class with which the Christians came into most active competition, they numbering many freedmen in their own group. But even the freedman could hardly compete successfully with the Christian, for he too often dissipated his energies in riotous living. The Christian who was prompt (because he had arisen early to go to church), sober, frugal, honest, reliable, and efficient would naturally have the edge in any competitive market. The chances are that the Christian could find steady employ-

[28] *Egyptian Church Order* (Connolly, pp. 96, 100, 191, 192).

ment while the pagan would be drifting from one job to another. This would not make for a friendly attitude on the part of the pagan worker. The story of the stone masons who aroused the ire of their fellow-workers is an illustration in point though it comes from the fourth century. Celsus does not seem to have appeciated the Christian workers who were employed in pagan homes.[29] It would appear also that certain Christians entered into business enterprises which were in direct competition with their pagan neighbors and were dependent upon a pagan constituency to a considerable extent, otherwise their confession of the faith would not have ruined their business irrevocably.[30] It does not require a great stretch of the imagination to perceive how such competition would arouse considerable hostility. But Christians were not merely day laborers, artisans, traders, and retailers; they were also big businessmen. They carried on world-wide enterprises, and there is even an indication that they may, at times, have cornered the grain market![31] The possibilities for friction in such a situation are quite obvious. Its actuality may be taken for granted.

The task of delineating the economic factors in the imperial persecutions of the third century is more difficult than in the case of the popular hostility but nonetheless rewarding. Here also it will be possible to consider only the more important aspects.

In the fall of the year A.D. 249 Caius Messius Decius, a Roman of the old school, became head of the Roman Empire. His was not an enviable task. A strong army was needed on many fronts, but how were the soldiers to be paid? Decius does not seem to have been one who acted hastily. He probably realized that, if the imperial treasuries were low, it would bring no permanent relief to increase taxation. Much more fundamental measures were called for. The basic reason for the precarious situation was obvious: the traditional gods of Rome were angered. Philip, the predecessor of Decius, had been a syncretistic orientalist in matters of religion; no wonder, then,

[29] Origen Con. Cel. iii. 55.   [30] Cyprian Ep. xxxvii. 1 (41).

[31] Cyprian De Lapsis, 6; Arnobius Adv. nat. i. 16.

that the Empire was crumbling. The surest way to restore permanent prosperity, according to such a Roman as Decius,[32] would be to revive the worship of the Roman religion throughout the Empire, and the favor of the gods would assure the future. The consequence was that Decius, probably early in January of the year 250, issued an edict to the effect that all Roman temples should be reopened and all citizens of the Empire should show their allegiance to the gods of Rome by worshiping at these shrines. There is indication, also, that there was a general religious revival at this time.[33] Thus the measure adopted by Decius was a religious action in its conception and execution. However, this step was not motivated by any personal, pious, religious devotion on the part of Decius but by the threatening economic ruin of the Empire. The primary and fundamental cause of the imperial action taken by Decius was economic. It does not matter in the least whether he was fully conscious of that fact or not. Decius saw that, unless forces could be assembled that would enable him to combat effectively the threatening dissolution, within and without, the Empire would collapse. It is very significant that the first imperial persecution of the Christians on a general scale was instigated at the time when the Roman Empire was tottering on the brink of complete economic disaster. It would be apparent to any wide-awake citizen that immediate and drastic action was imperative.

It is very difficult to say how much the prospect of immediate financial returns to be derived from the confiscation of the property of those who would refuse to conform operated in the motivation of Decius in undertaking his reform action. We do not believe that it can be established that the opportunity for pecuniary acquisitions constituted any appreciable motive in his instigation of persecution, but of course it may be confidently assumed that he would be nothing loath to make use of all such opportunities to refill the empty coffers of the state.

[32] See Dio Cassius *Roman History* lii. 36 for a brief exposition of this point of view.

[33] A. D. Nock, "A diis electa," *Harvard Theological Review,* XXIII (1930), 251-54.

He must have been fully aware of the general prosperity of the Christians.

There is another phase in the action of Decius that deserves to be considered in this connection. Martyrdoms were not numerous during this persecution, and this fact has significance in two ways. In the first place, it indicates that Decius was not obsessed with the opportunity that would have been offered for financial gain by the wholesale massacre of those who refused to obey his edict. In the second place, it shows an appreciation on the part of the emperor of the economic loss that would have been incurred by unrestrained executions. It is not unreasonable to impute such understanding to Decius, since it is known that others realized the situation.[34] Decius had no desire to suppress Christianity by means of bloodshed and thus further to jeopardize the economic welfare of the Empire through the depletion of its population.

What would have been the outcome for Christianity if the policy of Decius had continued to be effectively administered can never be determined. Its enforcement was cut short by the death of Decius, who lost his life in the late summer of the year 251 while he was attempting to stem the tide of northern invasion. He left the Empire not one whit improved, and the disastrous plague which soon after swept throughout the Mediterranean world was but another sign and cause of internal decay.[35] This plague was the occasion for an edict by the new emperor, Gallus, calling upon all the citizens of the Empire to offer sacrifice to the gods in order that the latter might be appeased and the plague checked. This once more brought the Christians under the condemning arm of the imperial government as religious and political objectors. It has already been pointed out that plagues have vital economic significance and, in so far as they have such, they are to be reckoned as economic forces in the causes of persecution. However, the persecution

---

[34] Tertullian *Apol.* 44.

[35] Eusebius *H.E.* vii. 1; Pontius *Vita Cae. Cyp.* 9; Cyprian *Ep.* liii (57), liv. 6 (59), lv. 7 (60), lvi (60); *Ad Demet.* 5, 7.

under Gallus was but momentary and not to be classed as an important action on the part of the Roman government.

The accession of Publius Licinius Valerianus to the headship of the Roman world introduces another significant period in the relation of the Roman government to Christianity. Valerian was a man of the same stamp and attitudes as Decius, and the arguments offered concerning the motivation of Decius apply also in the case of Valerian. We refer the reader to that discussion, as we feel that the point of view there emphasized is vital to a true understanding of the motivation of these two major persecutions. However, the action of Valerian is a little more difficult to understand because he took no action against the religious recusants of the Empire for some years. We have only conjecture to guide us in this difficulty, but again the economic interpretation comes to our assistance. While Valerian was too busy with external matters concerning the Empire to pay much attention to the internal affairs during the early years of his reign, yet he could have continued the persecuting policy of Decius if he had seen fit. It will be permissible to suggest that Valerian observed that, instead of the condition of the Empire improving after the policy of Decius and Gallus had been put into execution, the situation had continued to grow worse. Possibly he may have decided that the policy was in error and so determined to abandon it. With what result? The economic status of the Empire continued on the downward grade! What was to be done? We must not forget that Valerian, like Decius, would be firmly convinced that the welfare of the Empire was dependent upon the favor of the gods. Perhaps, Valerian may have reasoned, the lack of improvement in the Empire was due not to the policy of Decius but to its ineffectiveness! Possibly a more stringent enforcement would produce results. The outcome was that he issued an edict which differed from that of Decius chiefly in this respect: that it was aimed directly at the Christian organization itself.

The confiscations that occurred constitute a further problem in the persecutions of Valerian. In this connection it is important to bear in mind that two edicts were issued by Valerian about a year apart which contain important variations. The first, which was issued in the year 257, aimed at crippling the Christian organization by sending the bishops into exile and forbidding all Christian assemblies. No general confiscations or executions were called for. Certainly Valerian, as well as Decius, had no desire to destroy, unnecessarily, large numbers of the population and thus further to endanger the already tottering resources of the Empire; it can hardly be imagined that any Roman emperor would hesitate to shed blood through any feeling of human compassion. But the first edict of Valerian failed signally to bring the desired result. The bishops could direct their flocks almost as well from exile as from their home headquarters, and the Christians continued to assemble for their meetings of worship in spite of the danger resulting from the interdict. The logical consequence was a second edict more drastic than the first. It specified the recall and execution of the bishops along with other members of the clergy; senators and other laymen of high rank were to be degraded, their property seized, and themselves executed later if they persisted as recusants; matrons were to be deprived and banished; the Christian servants in the household and employ of the emperor were to be deprived of their property and sent in chains to work on the imperial estates. The former edict against the assembling of Christians was still in effect, and its enforcement was continued. The corporate property and funds of the church were appropriated.

That there is a strong economic element here can easily be perceived, but how far it was an active factor in motivating the persecution is quite another matter. M. Allard makes much of the desire of Valerian to seize the wealth of the individual Christians and the corporate property and funds of the church.[36] But, if this was an important factor, it did not become effective until the second edict. The first edict was not only bloodless but without important confiscations. We feel that this inconsistency in the action of Valerian cannot be allowed. His pri-

[36] P. Allard, *Les dernières persécutions du troisième siècle* (Paris, 1907), pp. 36–57; *Le Christianisme et l'empire romain* (Paris, 1907), pp. 107–10.

mary motive, fired, it is important to remember, by the economic crisis of the Empire, was to crush the power of the Christians by destroying their organization. Having failed in his first attempt, he had either to abandon his efforts altogether or to take more stringent measures. He adopted the latter course and sought to disable the recalcitrant body by destroying its material resources and by depriving it of both its clerical and its lay leadership. This move showed real acumen, but he did not appreciate the inherent power of Christianity. An important part of his policy was to cripple the organization economically, and it can be readily granted that he would not bemoan the increase that might come thereby to the imperial treasury. Many of the Christians were wealthy, as Valerian must have known, and he aimed at the wealthiest. But the contention, on this basis, that Valerian was motivated by any special avarice is unwarranted. We find ourselves, therefore, in practically the same position with regard to Valerian as we are with regard to Decius: no direct economic motive can be imputed to either of these emperors.

Nevertheless, we wish to reiterate emphatically the interpretation which we have already expounded: that economic factors were fundamental in the instigation of all these imperial persecutions. While we do not agree with those writers who point to the confiscations by these emperors as indicating their avariciousness, we insist that their action can be explained only on the basis of economic considerations. The economic cataclysm which threatened the Roman Empire during the middle of the third century is well known to all students of Roman history. This, and this alone, constitutes the major explanation for the edicts of Decius and Valerian. They both sought, with much anxiety, to avert the impending economic ruin. Apart from this element the first universal persecutions of Christianity remain genuine enigmas. The fact that these emperors adopted religious methods for accomplishing their purpose is satisfactorily explained, as already pointed out, by the superstitious warp and woof of ancient society. The provocation of the first general imperial persecutions of Christianity was economic.

The capture of Valerian by the Persians was followed by the reign of his son Gallienus. The edict of Gallienus relative to the Christians was one of toleration and forms a fitting climax to the evidence we are presenting in favor of an economic interpretation of the imperial actions against Christianity. The content of the edict is preserved for us by Eusebius:[37] the Christians were to be once more allowed to assemble, their corporate property was to be restored, and they were to be protected from molestation. One question only is pertinent for our purpose: Why did Gallienus reverse the edict of his father? No satisfactory answer can be given, especially on the basis of the customary practice of mercilessly maligning the character and intelligence of Gallienus. But, if we accept, even to a limited extent, the defense of the statesmanship of Gallienus urged by M. Homo,[38] it will help us to understand the action which he took. Valerian, his father, had tried a soft answer, but the wrath had not been turned away from the Empire. Then he had tried two measures of repression, the second more drastic than the first, and both had failed. The Christians were still powerful and the Empire was worse off than ever; Valerian himself was enduring an ignominious captivity. Might not Gallienus have observed that, if toleration was useless, repression was worse than useless, for it simply piled up disasters and internal ruptures when the Empire was already at the breaking-point? If Gallienus had given the matter no thought, why did he take any action at all? The evidence that he was influenced by his wife is quite unsatisfactory.[39] If his attitude had been one of complete indifference, he would simply have done nothing and so allowed the former edicts to be carried out or to fall into abeyance wherever they would. Instead, he took definite action in favor of Christianity. Most of this is mere conjecture, of

[37] Eusebius *H.E.* vii. 13. How far this rescript of Gallienus was a genuine edict of toleration and what the consequent status of Christianity was is a moot question, but that problem is of minor importance in this connection. The vital point is merely that Gallienus took some favorable action with regard to Christianity. More than that is nonessential to the validity of our interpretation.

[38] L. Homo, "L'Empereur Gallien," *Revue historique*, CXIII (1913), 1–22, 225–67.

[39] P. J. Healy, *The Valerian Persecution* (Boston, 1905), p. 271.

course, but, if guesses are worth anything historically, our guess is that material considerations played their customary part.

We have endeavored to point out that there were numerous and deep-rooted economic factors that occasioned continual friction between the early Christians and their contemporaries. These are of first importance in affording a fundamental explanation for the popular hostility to the Christians and the resultant persecutions. We have also sought to show the basic importance of underlying economic forces in the first imperial persecutions. Deductions, being of doubtful value, may be left to the inclinations of the reader, but we feel that no delineation of the causes of the Christian persecutions can be satisfactory without according to the economic factors a primary role.

THE SOURCES OF CHRISTIAN ASCETICISM[1]

MERVIN MONROE DEEMS

Bangor Theological Seminary
Bangor, Maine

WHEN the disillusioned disciples returned to Jerusalem with renewed confidence and zeal because of the appearances of their risen Lord, they constituted a Jewish group which had every reason to turn from the world in the expectation of the new age to be introduced by the return of the heaven-ascended Messiah.

The earthly mission of this Messiah had been to get people to prepare themselves for the coming kingdom; and the things of this world must not be permitted to interfere with the attain-

[1] For those who wish to pursue this study further the following articles and books are recommended:

For background consult: P. Arbesmann, *Das Fasten bei den Griechen und Römern* (Giessen, 1929); W. Capelle, "Altgriechische Askese," *Neue Jahrbücher für das klassische Altertum, Geschichte und deutsche Literatur und für Pädagogik*, Vol. XXV (1910); E. Fehrle, *Die kultische Keuschheit im Altertum* (Giessen, 1910); O. Hardman, *The Ideals of Asceticism* (New York, 1924); J. Haussleiter, *Der Vegetarismus in der Antike* (Berlin, 1936); J. W. Swain, *The Hellenic Origins of Christian Asceticism* (New York, 1916); T. Wächter, *Reinheitsvorschriften im griechischen Kult* (Giessen, 1910).

For Christian asceticism see H. Achelis, *Virgines subintroductae* (Leipzig, 1902), *Das Christentum in den ersten drei Jahrhunderten* (Leipzig, 1912); E. Buonaiuti, *Le Origini dell'ascetismo cristiano* (Pinerolo, 1928); M. M. Deems, "Social Aspects of Early Christian Asceticism" (University of Chicago dissertation [1928]); G. Dellung, *Paulus Stellung zu Frau und Ehe* (Stuttgart, 1931); Ph. Gobillot, "Les Origines du monachisme chrétien et l'ancienne religion de l'Egypte," *Recherches de science religieuse*, Vol. X (1920); *ibid.*, Vol. XI (1921); *ibid.*, Vol. XII (1922); K. Heussi, *Der Ursprung des Mönchtums* (Tübingen, 1936); H. Koch, "Virgines Christi," *Texte und Untersuchungen zur Geschichte der altchristlichen Literatur*, Vol. I (3d ser.; Leipzig, 1907), *Quellen zur Geschichte der Askese und des Mönchtums in der alten Kirche* (Tübingen, 1933), *Virgo Eva-Virgo Maria* (Berlin, 1937); F. Martinez, *L'Ascétisme chrétien pendant les trois premiers siècles de l'église* (Paris, 1913); H. Preisker, *Christentum und Ehe in den ersten drei Jahrhunderten* (Berlin, 1927); P. Resch, *La Doctrine ascétique des premiers maîtres égyptiens du quatrième siècle* (Paris, 1931); R. Reitzenstein, *Historia Monachorum und historia Lausiaca* (Göttingen, 1916); J. Ribet, *L'Ascétique chrétienne* (Paris, 1888); H. Schumacher, *Das Ehe-Ideal des Apostels Paulus* (München, 1932); H. Strathmann, *Geschichte der frühchristlichen Askese* (Leipzig, 1914); J. Wilpert, "Die gottgeweihten Jungfrauen," *Zeitschrift für katholische Theologie*, Vol. XIII (1889); O. Zöckler, *Askese und Mönchtum* (Frankfort, 1897).

ment of that goal of character which should lead to perfection, for which no sacrifice could be too great. Later, this renunciation would be seen as the way of the cross (Matt. 10:38; Mark 8:34; Luke 9:23).

The disciples' faith and ecstatic expectation produced a temporary cohesion, which voiced an appeal to all who would hear their story, and produced a practical social expression of their brotherliness in some attempt to help the less fortunate of the group (Acts 2:44–45). Moreover, in the light of the earthly life of their Messiah, the calls to self-denial and possible sacrifice of life itself in preparation for the new age were not softened but rather the sense of urgency was increased.

Bursting upon this enthusiastic early Christian group came the ardent Hellenistic Jew, Paul, with his confidence that he, also, had seen the Lord, and therefore had right to apostleship, and with his surety that the Christ-possessed believer would emerge triumphant in the fierce struggle against this present world. This titanic conflict was very real to Paul, who not only practiced self-restraint but also mauled and mastered his body (I Cor. 9:25–26) to bring it into subjection and to defeat the messenger of Satan, his thorn in the flesh (II Cor. 6:4–10). Were Paul alone, disaster might result; but, when he is weakest, Christ within him makes him strong. With Paul, then, it is not a metaphysical discussion of flesh versus spirit,[2] nor merely the Jewish idea of the keeping of Torah in order to rise above the evil *yeṣer*, or inclination,[3] but a cosmic contest between Christ and the believer on one side and Satan and the flesh on the other.

Paul was entirely in accord with late Judaic and Greco-Roman ideology in regarding the world as demonic. Judaism had its good and evil spirits as well as its good and evil inclinations, or *yeṣers*. Thus within later Judaism there was a modified dualism. To be sure, God made both *yeṣers*, and, according to Ezek. 36:26, he will ultimately remove the evil inclination. The mischievous demons of Stoicism were vexatious rather than

---

[2] E. Burton, *Spirit, Soul and Flesh* (Chicago, 1918); Schumacher, *op. cit.*

[3] *Qiddusin 30b* on Gen. 4:7; cf. *Sir.* 21:11a.

wicked, but, later, Neo-Pythagoreans had good and evil demons.[4]

Fehrle[5] is correct in emphasizing ancient man's belief in evil demons, contact with which rendered man impure. On the other hand, before man could approach deity, not to mention the effecting of union with deity, he must be pure. But sexual intercourse robbed one of this necessary purity. This was early and generally accepted. Union with deity, to accomplish which one must free himself from bodily demands, was a familiar conception in ancient Greece, in cults of Pythia, Athene, Demeter, and others, and in the first century of the Christian Era the idea was widespread through the mystery religions. Doubtless, as Fehrle says, that purity which was originally demanded only of the priesthood in the cults came to be necessary for the laity; for anyone desiring blessedness must be pure. We know that in the Eleusinian-Demeter, Cybele-Attis, and Isis-Osiris cults, and in Mithraism, various practices of continence and of dietary abstinences were followed not only by the priests but by the initiates and members themselves.[6] The mysteries, with their emphasis upon blessed immortality, would tend to disparage the things of this world. But union with deity was the end sought, and purity of life the means. Therefore, the explanation of their prohibitions of foods and sexual intercourse during specified periods was to rid the body of all possible demonic infection and to prepare it for attainment to deity.

The dualism of Orphism (the body a drag upon the soul) persisted, and if this religious influence purified and drew near to the Dionysiac mystery cult, and had attraction for the Pythagoreans, the unity of these interests was disrupted by the Peloponnesian War. Plato deepened and spiritualized the tenets of Orphism, which continued its influence into Neo-Pythagoreanism and Neo-Platonism. The protest of the Cynics whose diet was limited and whose only possessions were a rough cloak, a

---

[4] Cf. Plutarch *Of Isis and Osiris* 26.   [5] *Op. cit.*, p. 35.

[6] H. Graillot, *Le Culte de Cybèle dans l'empire romain* (Paris, 1912); F. Cumont, *Textes et monuments figurés relatifs aux mystères de Mithra* (2 vols.; Brussels, 1895-99); J. G. Frazer, *Golden Bough* (London, 1920-22), Part IV, Vols. I and II.

begging-bag, and staff, manifested itself in a steeling of the will, through ἄσκησις, but, as Capelle[7] suggests, a deeper explanation would lie in the unrest in political and social affairs in contemporary Hellas. Their goal was ἐγκράτεια, which Socrates had urged, and which is found again in early Christianity (Acts 24:25; Gal. 5:23; II Pet. 1:6). The two types of asceticism, which Capelle has designated as the mystical-religious (Orphic, Pythagorean, Platonic) and the ethical-voluntary (Cynic, Stoic), did influence Christianity, but we find in addition to these philosophic ascetic streams, the highly emotional, sometimes ecstatic, experiences which were so common in the mystery religions induced by purificatory ascetic practices to insure union with the god.

It is quite possible that this demonic cosmology played a part in Paul's attitude toward marriage. To be sure in late Judaism, although marriage is normal and God-ordained and monogamy is emphasized, nevertheless woman is the origin of sin (Sir. 25:24), and Adam's sin caused the begetting of children (II Bar. 56:6). Moreover, the great majority of Essenes forbade marriage, and Jewish apocalypticism advocated fasting or continence as preparation for revelation (Dan. 10:3; En. 83:2; 85:3; Mart. Is. 2:11; IV Ezra 5:13, 20; 6:35). And from early times sexual continence was required for contact with deity.[8]

It is natural to suppose that after the dissolution of Alexander's empire some impress would be made by Hellenistic influences upon even the most intense expressions of Judaism. According to Preisker,[9] the asceticism of the Essenes is a combination of Pharisaic striving for purity with elements of Orphic and Pythagorean thought. In literature Sirach, with its philosophy of the *via media*, and the Wisdom of Solomon, reflecting the Platonic idea of the body weighing down the soul, show Greek philosophic touches. Philo in his dualism of the soul (a "fragment of divinity") and the body (a "heavy burden") was

---

[7] *Op. cit.*   [8] Strathmann, *op. cit.*

[9] H. Preisker, *Christentum und Ehe in den ersten drei Jahrhunderten* (Berlin, 1927); Haussleiter, *op. cit.*

more Greek than Jew, and he had high admiration for the contemplative ascetic Therapeutae living in the region of Lake Mareotis in Egypt. The asceticism of these Therapeutae differed from that of the Essenes in Palestine. To be sure, they, too, studied the Scriptures and fasted, some for three, others for six, days. The seventh day was a festival when a common meeting was held, to which women also came. But during the week the members of the group retired each to his own μοναστήριον. Philo praised this sort of life, doubtless believing that one pursuing it would more easily rid himself of pleasures, most mischievous of passions, which, adhering to the body, effect an obstacle to virtue. Pleasures and appetites are keepers of the prison, which is the body, and Philo would flee them. His asceticism arose from the dualism in Greek philosophy, and his goal was control of the body in order that the soul might contemplate God. Certainly, Philo was a forerunner of Plotinus, if not of Clement and Origen.

We have seen that in the Greco-Roman world the idea was widespread in the mysteries that sexual relationship induced demonic influence and that the act made anyone impure. This fear of impurity may have influenced Paul's viewpoint, as Dellung suggests.[10] Certainly, there is a taint in procreation (Rom. 5:12, 15), and it is better not to marry or, if married, to remain continent.[11] Why? Because the time is short before the return of Christ, and because the married person cannot give himself to the Lord as can the unmarried. Add to this eschatology an ecstatic and pneumatic Christ-possessed personality with its glorying in sufferings (II Cor. 6:4–10; 11:27, 28), and there results an enthusiasm which readily carried over to the Pauline communities, providing two strong appeals for a growing asceticism: first, the imminent new age and, second, the keeping of one's body inviolate that Christ might dwell within.

There seem to have been ascetic practices of Christians elsewhere. Some members of the Roman church practiced vegeta-

10 *Op. cit.*

11 For I. Cor. 7:29–31 see K. Müller, *Die Forderung der Ehelosigkeit für alle Getauften in der alten Kirche* (Tübingen, 1927).

rianism (Rom. 14:2, 20, 21), and widely circulated throughout the ancient world was the teaching that abstinence from meat, beans, eggs, wine, and some other foods was essential for purity of soul and revelation of deity. The later Pythagoreans, through whom Orphic religious teaching was transmitted, and the Neo-Platonists made much of these dietary rules. There were some at Colossae who lived by rules which included fasting and discipline of the body (Col. 2:23) and with which Paul was not wholly in sympathy, because they infringed upon the freedom of a Christ-possessed individual.

As time passed and the Messiah did not come, the basis of procedure of Christian living was sought in the words and life of Jesus, and it was a life of discipline, self-denial, and the cross (Matt. 5:11, 10:38; 16:24; Luke 6:22, 9:23; 14:27; Mark 8:34).

Fasting, already an important part of later Judaism, was increased by those intense souls who awaited the return of the Bridegroom (Matt. 9:15). Arbesmann has shown how abstinence from various foods such as eggs, beans, garlic, figs, pomegranates, certain kinds of meat, wine, even bread was required as religious ἄσκησις in Orphism, Pythagoreanism, with the Cynics and Stoics, the Essenes and Therapeutae, the Neo-Pythagoreans and Neo-Platonists, and also as preparation for initiation into the various mystery cults.[12] Beans were regarded by Pythagoreans (probably from Orphism) as inducing dreams; others thought that meat and eggs might contain the spirit of the dead. Swine, symbol of evil (Matt. 8:30; Mark 5:12; Luke 8:32), apparently played a role in the Eleusinian-Demeter cult and later were regarded by Clement of Alexandria as incentive to lust. With the Jews, fasting was also an aid to prayer, and in New Testament times it is quite probable that the followers of Jesus fasted four days a week rather than the Jewish two, although, as Zöckler says, the origin of the Wednesday (betrayal) and Friday (crucifixion) fasts is obscure.[13]

For the Christian, marriage is permissible, but chastity is better (Matt. 19:12), and riches greatly interfere with entrance

---

[12] Op. cit.   [13] O. Zöckler, *Askese und Mönchtum* (Frankfurt, 1897), p. 152.

into the Kingdom (Matt. 19:16–22; Mark 10:17–27, esp. v. 24; Luke 18:18–27). Luke, the Hellenist, is especially ascetic, and his attitude, as Jülicher[14] says, "can be traced back to the Cynical philosophy or to the dualistic ideas existing at the bottom of all forms of religion about the beginning of our era, with just as much probability as to certain special phenomena of late Judaism—such an attitude was characteristic of the whole of the post-Apostolic church, and was only suppressed by a sort of compromise at a later time."

Already in Paul's time virgins in some Christian communities were especially recognized, and their importance steadily grew, although as late as Tertullian and Cyprian the taking of the vow was still a private matter, from which it was not impossible, though not customary, to withdraw.[15] Widows also were held in esteem (Ignatius, "To the Smyrnaeans," chap. 12, salutes virgins who are called widows: καὶ τὰς παρθένους τὰς λεγομένας χήρας), but, as their numbers grew and they became an economic problem, the younger widows were encouraged to marry again, which certainly was not Pauline doctrine. Of spiritual marriage we have only very scattering references in early Christianity, but by the third century this sort of asceticism was common, and there were many "brothers" and "sisters" maintaining their virginity without forsaking their secular tasks.[16] This urge to present one's body to the deity free from contamination of any kind, or to keep it chaste for the sake of prophecy, is the natural carrying-over of a Hellenistic dualism—a dualism which had been deepened by political and social upheavals in the Greek world.[17]

Not only was Christian apocalypticism strong in this early period but the approach of the Christian to the world was pessimistic, if not negative, and every persecution increased his cer-

---

[14] An Introduction to the New Testament, Eng. trans. J. P. Ward (New York, 1904), p. 336.

[15] Achelis, op. cit.; H. Koch, "Virgines Christi," op. cit., and Virgo Eva-Virgo Maria.

[16] P. de Labriolle, "Le Mariage spirituel dans l'antiquité chrétienne," Révue historique, Vol. CXXXVII (1921).

[17] Capelle, op. cit., p. 698.

tainty not only that the world was demonic but also that the end was near. Moreover, suffering in the flesh rid one of sin; and, if the time had not arrived for the return of Christ, the martyr could go to him. This martyr psychology which the church had to curb was another means of effecting union with deity. The document known as I Peter reflects the sufferings which some Christian groups were being called upon to bear toward the end of the first century. Naturally the end of the age was regarded as near, and Christians ought to remain faithful, for, when they suffer for doing right, it is counted as a merit. At best they are sojourners and exiles, and, though free, they must not misuse this freedom for scandalous conduct. Although there is here no incentive for the Christian to seek martyrdom, that soon follows.

The ecstatic and persistent Ignatius is an excellent example of the zeal for martyrdom. Like Paul, he enjoyed his sufferings; unlike Paul, but in keeping with the trend toward organization, he magnified the place of the Spirit-possessed bishop. Not only was Ignatius an extraordinary Christian but he enthusiastically embraced martyrdom as did Polycarp, seeking the fulness of the sufferings of Christ. Certainly, the "martyr complex" gave an additional impetus for denial of the world and of life and provided almost instant attainment of a goal, which for less impetuous souls lay only in the future, either through natural death or through the prior return of Christ.

Meanwhile, the Christian lived in his world, but it was a disciplined life. He was *in* the world but not *of* it, and if in contrast to the championing of the cause of the poor by Luke and James[18] other communities found satisfactory solutions for the rich also (I Timothy, Hermas, and Clementine of Alexander), at all events the Christian must keep himself unspotted from the world. The Didache encouraging fasting, abstinence, and chastity is a further evidence of the stabilization of the Christian movement.[19] Together with this unemotional ac-

---

[18] M. Rostovtzeff, *Social and Economic History of the Roman Empire* (Oxford, 1926), esp. chap. iv.

[19] M. M. Deems, "The Place of Asceticism in the Stabilization of the Church," *Journal of Religion*, X (1930), 563–77.

commodation of the Christian to his world, there were ecstatic outbursts such as Revelation and the *Shepherd of Hermas*, emphasizing virginity and protesting against any regularity of life which, however disciplined, served to depart from the early apocalypticism. The number of virgins (144,000) mentioned in Rev. 14:3 (cf. 7:44), although not to be taken literally, nevertheless, as Dobschütz says, "presupposes the existence at this time of no small proportion of Christian ascetics." These chosen ones "follow the Lamb wherever he goes" and will have the preference of being "reaped" first. Furthermore, as in the environment out of which I Peter came, persecution and suffering are present, and the end is near. As Professor Case has pointed out, in times of stress the last woes were thought to be at hand.[20] But, in the letters to the churches, the writer hopes to blast out of their complacency, liberalism, and ineffectiveness those Christian communities which had lost their original enthusiasm and devotion and had now commenced making social and economic adjustments to life around them.

Later, Hermas is proud of his fasts for the purpose of revelation and his "much continence" (*Vis.* ii. 2.1; ii. 3.2; *Sim.* v. 3.6, the perfect fast). Both prepare the body for Spirit-possession. Moreover, he would arouse God's people from conformity to the world and would have them remember that they dwell in a strange land. Although he cries out against luxury and wealth, he nevertheless makes a place for mutuality between rich and poor. But this was about the time when commerce and industry were bringing forward a new class in the Roman Empire; and, with tradition still preventing the Roman patrician from trading, it is more than probable that in this new class were many Christians against whom Hermas felt bound to direct his criticism.[21] The night spent with the virgins is not easily explained except on the basis of the doctrine which the author wishes to impart, namely, that if a Christian is accompanied by Christian virtues, and gives himself continually to prayer, he will fall into no

[20] S. J. Case, *The Millennial Hope* (Chicago, 1918), p. 142.

[21] Rostovtzeff, *op. cit.*, chap. v; D. W. Riddle, "The Messages of the Shepherd of Hermas," *Journal of Religion*, Vol. VII (1927).

evil.[22] But it is Spirit-possession which assures victory. Should the Holy Spirit vacate the body, evil spirits will move in, and their works are to be feared. Chastity of body, however, makes a worthy dwelling-place for the Spirit. If Hermas' writing is a book of discipline, it is decidedly different from the Didache and is a protest against the evident, continued integration of the church in the world, and a potent appeal for the Christians of his day to become more otherworldly minded than they were.

In the transition period between the early apocalypticism and the era when Christianity became more stabilized in itself and in the world, both ascetic interests, the emotional-ecstatic, and the calmer, disciplined way, were in evidence. Furthermore, with the break between the old religion and the new the fervor of turning from the world was not decreased. Despite the wave of asceticism which swept over Palestinian Judaism upon the destruction of the temple, there is also evidence that the Talmudists resented the intense asceticism of the Christians.[23]

The early asceticism of the Christian groups, then, was caused by the central hope (the immediate return of the Messiah) which led to renunciation of the things of this world, and by the early implantation and adoption of a Hellenistic dualism, requiring a cosmic struggle between the Christian and the demonic powers (to conquer which no sacrifice, whether of food or sexual enjoyment, could be too great), and heightened by the social conflict between rich and poor. The chiliastic urgency did not disappear but in a very definite way received an impetus from martyrs and "martyrologies."

It was with the "Apologists," however, that Christianity became permeated with Hellenistic philosophic interest. The Christian life was not only self-controlled but conformable to reason. Already an additional life of the Messiah had appeared (John), which had declared him to be the Logos, and which commended to his followers a life of purity and separation from the things of the world, even though they lived in it. And for

[22] Buonaiuti, op. cit.

[23] K. Kohler, art. "Ascetics," Jewish Encyclopedia.

one who had Christ within, eternal life had begun. Then, too, Jesus in this Gospel was the voluntary martyr.

When, a little later, Christians like Justin and Athenagoras felt called upon to defend their religion, they claimed for it antiquity[24] and respectability in the matter of their adherents living a life of self-restraint and high moral value, the equal of any produced by philosophy. Justin asserts that Christians marry only for the sake of procreation and that many within the group, including men, keep themselves virgins. Marriage thus becomes a matter of self-control. In this position he is supported by Athenagoras and Tatian. The latter, while admitting that demons bring woes upon the world and must be subdued, nevertheless charges the lack of mastery over the passions as being responsible for many evils including care of the body, with which the securing of property and marriage are directly related. Christians also are wary of the spectacles and shows. Yet, in the *Epistle to Diognetus*, it is clearly affirmed that Christians are not a peculiar people, but live according to discipline and reason.

To Minucius Felix Christians are the best philosophers. They are temperate and chaste and marry only once, if at all. The poverty of the Christian is an aid to freedom, for it prevents his dependence upon externals.

Clement of Alexandria stresses this principle, and yet he is the outstanding example of the union of several streams of ascetic interest.[25] Indeed, Clement's objective, *apatheia*, is in contrast to the Montanist Tertullian's eschatologic fervor and the stringent asceticism of Marcion and other Gnostics[26] whose dualism was more thorough than Clement and the main body of Christians could approve. However, both of those outlawed excrescences carried their influence ascetically into the very midst of the orthodox faithful.

[24] According to Justin, Plato derived his laws from the Decalogue!

[25] Preisker, *op. cit.*: "Bei Clemens von Alexandrien verbinden sich jüdische, urchristliche, und hellenistische und nicht zuletzt speziell philosophische Gedanken bei der Beurteilung der Ehe" (p. 210; cf. p. 200 also).

[26] E. de Faye, *Gnostiques et gnosticisme* (Paris, 1913; 2d ed., 1925).

Montanism, out of Phrygia, noted for its fanaticism, with its special fasts and continence as prerequisites for ecstatic prophecy, stressed the imminent end of the world. It was a call to a more rigid Christian life and, though permitting marriage, discouraged it and designated second marriage adultery. Naturally it encountered opposition, which Hobhouse credits to its asceticism rather than to its theological differences.[27] It spread throughout the Mediterranean world and made its most famous convert, Tertullian, at Carthage.

Tertullian was already an ascetic and a rigorist. To him demons infested the world, seeking to destroy the Christian and residing in pagan religious places, and hence Christians should not attend the shows. Their shows are contests with unchastity, *their* spectacle will be the coming of the Lord! Although the Christians sojourn in the world, their joys are in the world to come, and Tertullian himself would "depart and be with Christ."[28] Women should not adorn themselves, and men detract from modesty and sobriety if they attempt to improve on nature. Martyrdom may be expected at any time. Should he die first, he asks his wife to remain unmarried, for celibacy and continence are better than even a first marriage, which, however, is lawful. A widow, knowing what she renounces, therefore sacrifices more than a virgin. Many who are married, voluntarily and by mutual consent, make themselves eunuchs, following the words of Jesus. No philosophic ascetic, but emotional, ecstatic, apocalyptic, Tertullian was merely strengthened by the Montanist oracles to seek to direct the church back to its primitive enthusiasm. Although the Montanists do not repudiate marriage, they do not indulge it. Paul's reason for his position on marriage (because the time is shortened) supersedes the earlier Jewish command to increase and multiply, and sanctification may be won through virginity from one's birth, from baptism, or through continent monogamy, that is, renunciation of sexual connection. But Tertullian by this discipline would

[27] W. Hobhouse, *The Church and the World in Idea and in History* (London, 1916).

[28] References are too numerous to give (see Koch, *Quellen zur Geschichte der Askese und des Mönchtums in der alten Kirche*).

remove the gaze of the Spirit-possessed Christian from this world and have him fasten it upon the world to come!

The early leaders of Gnostic groups were as sincere and as fervid and more religious than philosophic. Basilides opposed marriage on the basis of Jesus' words in Matt. 19:12 and also on those of Paul. Valentinus and his followers were vegetarians and also renounced marriage and magnified the conflict of spirit with flesh, soul with body. Marcion, a worthy successor to Hermas in protesting against adjusting the church to the world, was such an extreme ascetic that he was accused of being a Cynic.[29] He renounced marriage, limiting baptism to virgins, celibates, eunuchs, and widows. He would eat no flesh but fish and used water rather than wine in the Eucharist. His intense asceticism—and there were many who followed his leadership—drove him into a modified dualism as a result of which he discarded the Old Testament and kept, of the New, only parts of Luke and ten Pauline letters. It does not fall within our province to follow the course of Gnosticism, but it owed its Christian beginnings to certain zealously ascetic souls who believed in living a life of self-denial and renunciation here, for the benefit of the life to come.

To Clement of Alexandria it is possible for the true Gnostic to be united with God here,[30] but the way of the Christian in the world is philosophically determined toward self-control. By Clement's time the church had grown in numbers and influence. Now even the rich might be saved,[31] if they used wisely their wealth, and especially if they kept beside them a man of God as a "trainer and governor." Besides, the distribution of wealth is an aid to salvation, but it is better discipline (*askesis*) to avoid luxury.

Evidently the environment of Clement was one of luxury. "Luxury has deranged all things, it has disgraced man. A lux-

---

[29] De Faye, *op. cit.*, p. 147.

[30] Heussi, *op. cit.*: "Clemens ist vor allem, obwohl er selbst kein 'Mystiker' gewesen ist, deutlich bereits eine Vorstufe zu der Form des späteren Mönchtums, die mit der sog. 'mystischen Theologie' verbunden war" (p. 43).

[31] "Who Is the Rich Man That May Be Saved?"

urious niceness seeks everything, attempts everything, forces everything, coerces nature. . . . . To such an extent, then, has luxury advanced that not only are the female sex deranged about this frivolous pursuit, but men also are infected with the disease." Accordingly, Clement would direct minutely the activity of the Christian in this world and prescribe even in detail his dress. Marriage is for the procreation of children but not for inordinate satisfaction. It affords an opportunity for self-control, and the philosophic, Christian marriage is in accordance with reason and self-restraint.

But Clement, in addition to his philosophical interests, uses Scripture and tradition to substantiate the disciplined way of the Christian in this world. The examples of Jesus and Paul and the apostles as having followed ascetic practices increased in importance as time passed. Indeed, the fervid but learned Origen took literally the announcement by Jesus in Matt. 19:12 and emasculated himself. He advised abstinence from certain foods to prevent sexual passion, for salvation would be found through nonsensuality. Origen, like his predecessor, incorporated Hellenistic dualism and mysticism. The Christian fights not only against the inner emotions but against demons, and only the "pneumatic" are the real church and therefore deserve a place above the clergy! Asceticism is a daily martyrdom. In Origen, as successor to Clement of Alexandria, we are conscious of the ecstatic type of asceticism of early Christianity in addition to the worthy place of philosophy, and Origen, according to Heussi, had direct influence upon Egyptian monasticism.[32]

Gnosticism, in its various phases, was not simply a protest against the stabilization of the Christian life in this world, but also, and chiefly, an expression of religious syncretism, so evident throughout the Roman world in the second century, especially in the reigns of the Severii. At the same time the mystery religions enjoyed a brief renaissance, stressing their ascetic demands. Philosophy, in its religious expression, was also experi-

[32] Heussi, *op. cit.*, pp. 45 ff., who quotes W. Volker, *Das Vollkommenheitsideal des Origenes* (Tübingen, 1931), who terms Origen the strongest connection between the pneumatic, early Christian teachers and monasticism!

encing a resurgence of faith in the ascetic Neo-Pythagoreanism, so well lived by Apollonius of Tyana, and in the ascetic-ecstatic Neo-Platonism, soon to follow.

With Paul's language not easily understood, and in the light of the virgin life (as well as birth) of Jesus, and of Paul, and with the heightened value already attached to virginity, it is not surprising that about the middle of the third century there appear two "Epistles concerning Virginity." The ascetic urge and the emphasis upon the Virgin and virginity are further to be noted in the writings known as apocryphal, including gospels, acts, passions, and apocalypses, and in which not only Mary but all female followers of Jesus are reported as being virgins. In addition to continence, fasting and otherworldliness are common evidences of the Christian life. One of the most interesting of these apocryphal books is the *Acts of Paul*, containing other "beatitudes": "Blessed are the pure in heart for they shall see God. . . . . Blessed are they that keep the flesh chaste. . . . . Blessed are they that abstain (or the continent). . . . . Blessed are they that have renounced the world. . . . . Blessed are they that possess their wives as though they had them not. . . . . Blessed are they that have kept their baptism *pure*. . . . . Blessed are they that for love of God have departed from the fashion of the world. . . . . Blessed are the bodies of the virgins" (ii. 5, 6). The increased urgency toward complete chastity in these "beatitudes" in contrast to those in Matthew needs no further emphasis. The idea of considering wives as "sisters," familiar since Hermas' day, is advocated here. If these apocryphal writings were indeed the popular devotional literature of the time, as Preisker has said, then the appeals for hyperstringency in Christian life were far more extensive than is sometimes supposed. To be sure, these writings, based largely upon a fundamental Hellenistic dualism of spirit versus flesh, and incorporating a personal mysticism, also from Hellenism, reveal their affinity to Gnosticism and to Neo-Pythagoreanism and Neo-Platonism.

Cyprian's treatise "On the Dress of Virgins" recognizes the very special place which the institution of virginity had at this time in the Christian communities. It is impossible to estimate fairly the number of those who were dedicating themselves as brides of Christ, but, from Cyprian's plea that they remember their calling and forsake the ornamented dress and usual recreations of other women and hold to simplicity and virginity, the impression is created that there were many and that their place was definitely set off from the usual Christian discipline. Many of the restrictions which Cyprian throws around the virgins may be compared with those advocated by Clement of Alexandria for *all* Christians, or at least, for all those who would follow the Christian philosophic discipline toward *apatheia*. It is probable that with the continual adjustment of average Christians to the world, that even those who had voluntarily set themselves aside as dedicated to Christ had commenced to pursue the freer life. This would not do, certainly—above all for those who had renounced the world.

Already under Cyprian's leadership the church was moving against the abuses naturally arising from too much daring in the matter of virginity. In the famous letter to Pomponius[33] the Church Father insists upon virgins dedicated to Christ, living separately from men. Now this writing is evidence not only of a definitely honored institution within the Christian groups, but also that in certain areas the gift of chastity was being presumed upon, and abuses were resulting. Let those who have carried too far the testing of their physical restraints repent, if they have sinned, and then let them be restored to the church, provided they effect an immediate separation from those among whom they have been living. If they can continue their virginity, well. Let them remember they are "brides of Christ." However, if they cannot stand the strain, then let them marry. (Later, councils, Elvira and others, had by canons to attempt to check an abuse not easily curbed.) In any event, let them be found *obedient* to bishops and priests, who hold the key to salvation, and who have the power to cast out of the church. In other words, the spirit-filled and honored ascetics

[33] *Ep.* lxi (Oxford ed., iv).

or virgins, formerly in a category of their own, are now being brought more directly under the authority of the established clergy. How successful was this method? We do not know, but not many years after arose the monastic movement which was later regularized. On the other hand, the practice of celibacy in the clergy increased, and finally came to be the rule, in the West.

It was natural now that Christian professional asceticism should take some definite form. However else monasticism may have arisen, we know that its central roots run far back into the self-denial and world-renunciatory attitude of Christian communities. Already by the end of the third century the way was open and direct to regularization of the ascetic life. Although the Christian philosophic school in Alexandria over which Clement and then Origen presided was no monastery, it would be inevitable that teachers (and pupils) would uphold in their own lives the very discipline which they advocated for all true "Gnostics." That this school had its counterparts elsewhere may be derived from Eusebius' account of the martyr Apphianus (*Mar. of Pal.* 4). Far more important, however, than the schools were the traditions of Christian asceticism, including the ecstatic, apocalyptic, Spirit-possessed, and, later, martyr type, and the rigidly disciplined, self-controlled way by which the Christian could live in the world without being of it. Then, too, as we have seen, there were those who had uniquely dedicated themselves as virgins to the head of the movement, and who, therefore, enjoyed an honored place. Preceding the organization which Pachomius seems to have brought to bear upon the developing institution, there were desert anchorites, stressing bodily asceticism, magnifying meditation and concentration on God's will, observing silence and humility, and engaged in strife against the ever present and thoroughly real demons.[34] Egypt was the natural territory for the development of monasticism. Here were many ascetics, and here the one important city was close to desert silences. Here, too, had been

---

[34] Heussi, *op. cit.*: "An den Ort, sagt Poimen, an den der Satan geworfen wird, werde auch ich geworfen" (p. 262).

the Therapeutae and here were the κάταχοι of Serapis.[35] Furthermore, in the syncretistic Greco-Roman world of the last quarter of the third century, with the renaissance of the mysteries, and the extension of the popular Neo-Pythagoreanism and Neo-Platonism, the discipline of the body for the good of the soul, or for union with deity was entirely familiar apart from Christianity. Furthermore, the Corpus Hermeticum, assigned by Reitzenstein to this period, and Manichaeism, whose founder was said to have visited India, had ascetic disciplines, although the influence of the latter upon Christianity, at this time, was probably little more than that of stimulating emulation.

Some of the emphasis upon asceticism by the Christians was as a protest against the paganism and immorality of the Greco-Roman world, but at the beginning of the fourth century, following the period of comparative peace from Gallienus to Diocletian, during which time considerable numbers were added to the membership of the church, it is probable that many felt bound to express disapproval of regularized Christianity, or desired to live a more intense life than the church could provide, and these retired to the desert districts. This inclination toward more formal expression of asceticism, now separated from the Christian groups in the world, would be strengthened as the church became more lenient in its treatment of the lapsed. With the economic disintegration of the Empire already begun, many Christians would seek solution of their problems in voluntary exile from the things of this world.

Thus, Christianity from its beginnings harbored within it the germ of that which was to become a formal institution guided by rules. But, as the organism developed, it was inevitable that it should partake of the environment so favorable to its growth.

[35] See Gobillot, *op. cit.*, Vol. X (1920), Vol. XI (1921), Vol. XII (1922).

THE EFFECT OF THE BARBARIAN INVASIONS UPON THE LITURGY

MASSEY HAMILTON SHEPHERD, JR.

Divinity School, University of Chicago

THE liturgy of the Mass is a signal part of that religious and institutional structure of Catholicism which has remained to the present day as the most enduring creation of Greco-Roman culture. When under Constantine the church emerged from the catacombs into the clear sun of imperial favor, the pattern of its Eucharistic worship and the ideology supporting it were already formulated in essential principles. During the fourth century development was largely confined to amplifications in the details of ritual and doctrine and elaboration of artistic adornments in newly erected or renovated basilicas. With the death of Theodosius I in 395 paganism was no longer a vital factor in Greco-Roman religious life. The role which the liturgy played in the triumph of Christianity may be judged by reference to the instructions delivered to newly baptized converts which have come down to us from two pre-eminent fourth-century bishops, Cyril of Jerusalem, representing the Greek East, and Ambrose of Milan, the Latin West. In their respective lectures "On the Mysteries," each bishop characterizes the Eucharist in terms redolent of the sentiments and aspirations of Christianity's religious environment.

On the one hand, the Eucharist is "the spiritual sacrifice, the bloodless service," a "sacrifice of propitiation" which not only supersedes the old covenant given to Israel but gathers into itself as well the functions and values of the official state cultus of paganism. For the Christian sacrifice of the body and blood of Christ is an offering to God not only "for the common peace of the churches" but also "for the welfare of the world, for kings, for armies and allies, for the sick, for the afflicted, and in short for all who need help."[1] At the same time the Eucharist is a sacramental mystery whereby. those regenerated unto eternal life in the waters of baptism are fed with the heavenly and life-giving food of the Lord's flesh. As in the contemporary "mystery religions" the sacrament establishes a mystical fellowship in the experience of the Lord's victory over death among those who have voluntarily sought initiation. It is a mystery which must "remain sealed" and "not be profaned by evil living" or "divulged to those for whom it is not meet."[2]

Christianity was still predominantly urban in membership at the close of the fourth century, especially in the western part of the Empire. The Christian gospel had made its greatest appeal to those underprivileged, oppressed, and dissatisfied elements of society who found in the community life of the churches a satisfaction for their social needs. At the head of these Christian communities stood the bishops, whose choice was usually that of the entire membership in their several localities. By imperial legislation as well as by the growing prestige of Christianity during the fourth century the bishops became the dominant personages in the cities of the Empire. They not only received civil and judicial powers as magistrates but, by virtue of the immunities and sanctity inhering in their office, they were regarded as the chief protectors and defenders of the people against the oppression of the governmental bureaucracy or the unscrupulous rich. The bishops organized and administered the charities and relief of the poor; superintended hospitals, orphanages, and hostels; and, if necessary, melted down the church plate to redeem captives taken in the ever increasing barbarian incursions and raids. With the final collapse of Roman imperial authority in the West during the fifth century the bishops served as the chief advocates of the old Roman population before the new Germanic overlords and the leading representatives of the old culture in the formation of a new social order.

[1] Cyril of Jerusalem *Catecheses mystagogicae* v. 8. (The lectures were in fact delivered by Cyril before he became bishop.)

[2] Ambrose *De mysteriis* ix. 55.

This Christian appropriation of Greco-Roman civic community ideals was concretely exhibited in the conduct of public worship. The bishop presided at all services, assisted by his clergy. In Rome, where the Christian population was too numerous to be gathered in one congregation, the unity of the worshiping body about the bishop was symbolized in the *fermentum*. The pope would send a particle of the host consecrated at the altar where he was celebrating mass to each of the presbyters who represented him in the titular churches to be included in their celebrations of the Eucharist.[3] The bishop did not confine his liturgical presidency to his cathedral but visited different basilicas on successive Sundays and festivals of saints and martyrs, the people following him from church to church as announced. The Roman *Missal* has retained to the present day at the head of each mass the notices of the ancient "stations," as they were called, where the pope was accustomed to officiate.

The first part of the Eucharistic liturgy was open to the public. It consisted mainly of chants, lections, and a sermon. In the churches of the West it was customary for the bishop only to preach. Augustine's commission to preach while still a presbyter was an exceptional case, granted by his bishop in recognition of his peculiar fitness for the task.[4] At the conclusion of the sermon all nonbaptized persons as well as Christians undergoing penance were dismissed: for only those initiated and in good standing were permitted to be present at the offering and consecration of the holy mysteries. All the faithful received the sacrament at each celebration; anyone who failed to commune was liable to discipline.[5]

The social and cultural changes brought about in western Europe as a result of the barbarian invasion and settlement begun in the early fifth century were reflected in modifications of

[3] Innocent I *Epistola* 25, ad Decentium (Migne, *Patrologia Latina*, XX, 551 ff.).

[4] Bishop Valerius received no little criticism from his colleagues for this infringement of custom (Possidius *Vita Augustini* 5).

[5] Council of Antioch (341), canon 2; I Council of Toledo (400), canons 13–14. Cf. Jerome *Epistolae* xlviii. 15, lxxi. 6; Augustine *De sermone Domini in monte* ii. 7.

the church's institutional structure, and particularly in the liturgy both in regard to the outward circumstances of its performance and also in regard to its inner spirit and meaning. The Mass lost its character of a corporate act performed in the name of a worshiping community by ministers of its own choice and requiring the active participation of all those present. Instead it became a rite celebrated in behalf of the people by an appointed clergy who alone understood its formularies, and could be performed whether a congregation was present or not. The sacramental-mystical aspect of the Eucharist gave way almost entirely to a preponderant emphasis upon its sacrificial character. We turn now to an examination of the forces which brought about this change.

The permanent settlement of the Germanic peoples and their social and political amalgamation with the older racial stock in the western territories of the Roman Empire extended over a period of some three centuries or more. Broadly speaking, it resulted in a change from an urban mode of social organization with municipalities as the basic units of government to one which was agrarian and feudal. This transformation was not a conscious creation of the new peoples, for the barbarians had no thought of destroying the institutions of the Empire. Their desire was simply to plunder and take for themselves a share of its property and riches. Economically the cities of the Empire were already in a state of decline. Repressive taxation and decrease in commerce caused the middle class almost to vanish. The aristocracy, who enjoyed or took to themselves exemptions from expensive public services, moved to their country estates, where they succeeded in making themselves well-nigh autonomous. Smaller landholders, in order to escape the exactions of the imperial government, sought the protection of these powerful patrons by leasing their property to them for life. Their heirs were seldom able, if desirous, to get the lands back. The barbarians themselves, being accustomed to a pastoral or agricultural economy, settled on the landed estates rather than in the cities. As "guests" of the proprietors they appropriated anywhere from one-third, as in Italy, to two-thirds, as in Gaul, of the lands and the *coloni* or serfs who worked them. The cities, reduced to fortresses, became the butt of frequent siege and massacres. Famine and pestilence combined with intermittent warfare depopulated them to mere shadows of their former strength.

Amid the general disorder of the times there was a steady cultural decay. Monuments of the older civilization disappeared either through wanton destruction by barbarians unable to appreciate them or through neglect of Romans no longer able to maintain them. Learning passed from schools and libraries supported by the state into the cloistered walls of monasteries or episcopal palaces, there to be restricted to ecclesiastical subjects.[6] The attitude of the barbarians toward education is well exemplified in the complaint which the Goths made when the grandson of King Theodoric was compelled by his mother to attend the school of a teacher of letters so that he might "resemble the Roman princes in his manner of life." They reminded Queen Amalasuntha that "even Theodoric would never allow any of the Goths to send their children to school; for he used to say to them all that, if the fear of the strap once came over them, they would never have the resolution to despise sword or spear."[7] Among the Roman population itself, particularly the laity, the decline of letters was marked. Boethius (d. 524) was the last writer of significance who was not an ecclesiastic. By the beginning of the sixth century the gap must have been large between the vulgar Latin spoken by the people and the written language of literature, including the liturgy. In southern Gaul, where the Catholic population was predominantly Gallo-Roman, Caesarius, bishop of Arles (502–42), comforted his episcopal colleagues who complained of being too ill-versed in rhetoric to preach with a reminder that eloquent speech would be understood by very few of the Lord's flock, and that it would be far more to the point to preach in "a

[6] Cf. II Council of Vaison (529), canon 1, requiring presbyters constituted in parishes to follow the custom in Italy of taking into their homes young unmarried men and training them in psalmody, the lectionary, and the Scriptures and thus preparing them as their successors.

[7] Procopius *De bello Gothico* i. 2. 6–17 (trans. Dewing).

simple and pedestrian language which all the people can understand."[8] Only with the revival of learning under Charlemagne
at the close of the eighth century does Latin "again become correct because," as F. Lot neatly remarks, "now it is a dead language."[9]

The countryside was gradually Christianized during these
centuries of invasion and turmoil. There the indigenous paganism, dressed in the nomenclature of Roman mythology, persisted longest.[10] The oriental mystery religions, so popular in
the cosmopolitan cities of the Empire, had made little impression in rural districts. Of mystic inwardness, sacramental communion, and intense longing for individual redemption coupled
with communal solidarity the folk paganism of the country
knew little or nothing. The rustics were attached to local nature
divinities of springs, trees, and stones, who could be made
kindly and helpful in the ordinary concerns of daily living by
sacrifices and honorific festivals. The large attention paid to
magic and divination showed their solicitude for divine favor
toward human enterprises by fulfilling earthly wishes and turning away misfortune. Offerings to the dead were expressive of
a strong belief in life after death.

The paganism of the Germanic peoples was not essentially different in character from that of their Roman and Celtic neighbors.[11] However, a significant number of the barbarians had accepted Christianity, though in its Arian form, before their entrance into the western Empire. Through the apostolic labors of
Bishop Ulfilas (d. 383) the Goths had received baptism. Largely
through their example Arianism became likewise the religion
of the Burgundians, Swabians, Vandals, and Lombards. These
peoples vested Christianity in tribal and national forms with

[8] *Sermo* i. 20 (ed. G. Morin, *Sancti Caesarii episcopi Arelatensis opera omnia* [Ma-
redsous, 1937], I, 18–19).

[9] *The End of the Ancient World and the Beginning of the Middle Ages* (New York,
1931), p. 379.

[10] The principal sources for late pagan survivals are the sermons of Caesarius of
Arles and Eligius of Noyon (640–85), the *De correctione rusticorum* of Martin of Braga
(d. 580), canons of church councils, and the early Penitentials.

[11] Cf. Tacitus *Germania* 9–10; Gregory of Tours *Historia Francorum* ii. 9 (10).

a native ministry and a vernacular Bible and liturgy. The Vandals, for example, had their own "patriarch," who was closely associated with the court of their king rather than any fixed see.[12] Their bishops also seem to have moved with the tribes and only settled in sees as long as the peoples themselves were settled. The prominence the king enjoyed in their religious life is illustrated by Gregory of Tours's notice of the custom in the Arian churches of the barbarians "for the kings to communicate from one cup and the lesser people from another," when they approached the altar for the Eucharist.[13] Conversions of barbarian kings to Christianity were usually followed by mass conversions of their peoples; as is witnessed by the conversions to Catholicism of the Frankish pagan Clovis (496), the Arian Visigoth Recared (589), and the pagan Jute Ethelbert (597).

The Catholic bishops continued to reside in the old Roman cities, whence they sought to extend their authority over the newly forming rural churches of their dioceses. These village parishes, which might be as small as ten families,[14] were most often located on the great estates. Landlords who furnished the means for their erection and endowment considered them private property and claimed the right to hire and fire at their own will the clergy who ministered in them and to share in the oblations of the parishioners. The general disorder of the times bred numerous clergymen unattached to any church, who had received orders from deposed bishops or through other irregular means, and who wandered about seeking such temporary employments as they might obtain in rural parishes. The bishops strenuously resisted these encroachments upon their ancient prerogatives.[15] Roman law recognized only a single community in each city as having the right of holding and disposing of church property, and churches in outlying districts had no

---

[12] Victor of Vita *Historia persecutionis Africanae provinciae* ii. 13, 54.

[13] *Historia Francorum* iii. 31.   [14] XVI Council of Toledo (693), canon 5.

[15] Episcopal councils during the period were constantly occupied with the problem. See I Council of Orleans (511), canon 7; IV Council of Orleans (541), canons 7, 26, 33; II Council of Braga (572), canons 5 and 6; III Council of Toledo (589), canon 19; Council of Chalon (644), canon 14; etc.

rights apart from the bishop's church. Private chapels of ease for the convenience of wealthy families had been allowed only under the express stipulation that mass was not to be celebrated in them on the major festivals, when everyone should repair to the city or parish church.[16] Translation of clergy from one church (i.e., community) to another was contrary to ancient custom and the written law of the church.[17] The bishops ultimately won their case. In the reforms of the eighth century, instigated by Boniface and carried through by the co-operation of the pope and the Carolingian Frankish kings, the bishops secured a control over both the property donated by the lords to the church and the tenure of the clergy. Yet the bishops themselves became great landowners through purchase, gifts, or bequests, as distant from the people as the great nobles. They were required to visit each parish once a year; but otherwise their contacts with them were through the archpresbyters or archdeacons. Often they despoiled the rural parishes of their revenues to the point where their clergy were in want and the buildings in bad repair. Canons had to be passed repeatedly limiting them to one-third or less of the offerings and oblations of the rural churches.[18] When the Germanic kings accepted Catholicism, the bishops took a place of first rank at court. In Gaul the people and clergy lost any voice in their selection; they became appointive officers of the crown. Even the cathedral churches saw them seldom. Canons were passed requiring their attendance in them at least on major festivals, as Christmas, Easter, and Pentecost.[19] If the king desired their presence at court, they could be excused from even this slight require-

[16] Council of Agde (506), canon 21; I Council of Orleans (511), canon 25; Council of Clermont (535), canon 15; IV Council of Orleans (541), canon 13.

[17] I Council of Nicaea (325), canon 15; cf. I Council of Arles (314), canons 2 and 21; II Council of Arles (452), canon 13; etc.

[18] I Council of Orleans (511), canons 14 and 15; Council of Tarragona (516), canon 8; III Council of Orleans (538), canon 5; I Council of Braga (563), canon 7; II Council of Braga (572), canon 2; IV Council of Toledo (633), canon 33; cf. VII Council of Toledo (646), canon 4; Council of Merida (666), canons 14 and 16; XVI Council of Toledo (693), canon 5.

[19] III Council of Orleans (538), canon 14; Council of Lyons (583), canon 5; Council of Latona (670/71), canon 8.

ment. The old Roman civic community ideal was gone. One can illustrate the change by reference to the rite of baptism. No longer was it observed only at the seasons of Easter and Pentecost in the presence of the bishop in the baptistry of his cathedral church; but it was performed at any time in the local parishes. The bishop's sealing with chrism and laying on of hands in confirmation thus became a distinct sacrament, divorced from baptism, and reserved for the bishop's annual visitations.

The liturgy reflected almost at once the social, cultural, and ecclesiastical changes which set in during the fifth century. Most noticeable was the loss of congregational participation in the Eucharist, and particularly the substitution of occasional for regular reception of communion by the people at all celebrations. Despite the laxity and indifference on the part of many which one would expect to accompany the great increase in the church's membership when it gained imperial favor,[20] there are abundant notices of the prevalence of daily communion throughout the churches of the West at the end of the fourth century.[21] Yet within a century's time a council at Agde (506) legislated that it was necessary to commune at least on Christmas, Easter, and Pentecost if one desired to be considered a Catholic;[22] and a writer in northern Italy complained of many who received communion only once a year.[23] Only at Rome, where old traditions remained strongest, does it appear that lay people continued to commune every Sunday and holy day.[24] There was no requirement of it, however; and many must have left the church after the consecration and immediately before

[20] Cf. above, n. 5, and especially references in Chrysostom *Homilia* xxviii. 1 in I Corinthians; *Homilia* iii. 4 in Ephesians; *Homilia* xvii. 7 in Hebrews, where many commune only once or twice a year.

[21] References in F. Cabrol and H. Leclercq (eds.), *Dictionnaire d'archéologie chrétienne et de liturgie* (hereinafter cited as *DACL*), III, 2459 ff.

[22] Canon 18. The emphasis in this canon on the word "Catholic" leads one to wonder if the Arian Visigoths, who then controlled southern Gaul, communed any less frequently (cf. above, n. 13).

[23] Pseudo-Ambrose *De sacramentis* v. 25.

[24] Gregory the Great *Dialogi* iv. 58; Bede *Epistolae* 2.

the communion, for at that point the archdeacon announced the place of the next "station."[25]

The Roman custom of frequent communion was also characteristic of the churches in the British Isles. The Celtic Christianity of Ireland and Scotland had its roots in old Gallo-Roman traditions and customs of the early fifth century, brought by the mission of Patrick (*ca.* 432) before the barbarian invasions cut off the Celtic peoples from contact with Continental Christianity for a hundred and fifty years or more. Regular communion of the laity on Sundays and saints' days was one of the few old customs (like their dating of Easter) which the Celts kept unmodified.[26] As for the Anglo-Saxons, they received the Roman practice from the Benedictine monks whom Pope Gregory the Great sent to evangelize them in 596–97.[27] Both Roman and Greek traditions of frequent lay communions were known to Theodore of Tarsus, archbishop of Canterbury (668–93), whose rare administrative gifts did much to bring together the Celtic and Anglo-Saxon missions in Britain.[28] Not long after he died, however, the English church fell on evil days. A picture of the state of affairs is afforded by Bede's letter to Archbishop Egbert of York (734). Among other things, the saintly monk complains that few receive communion more often than at Christmas, Epiphany, and Easter. He himself would counsel a daily communion, as of old; but at least the Roman custom of communion on Sundays and holy days should be a minimum for unmarried youths and aged folk, and for married people, too, if they would be continent for a brief period beforehand.[29] These recommendations were incorporated into a canon

[25] *Ordo Romanus* I, 20. The Greek churches, unlike the Roman, enforced the old canons which excommunicated those who did not receive communion for three successive Sundays. See Council of Sardica (343/44), canon 11; Council *in Trullo* (or Quinisext, 692), canon 80; *Penitential of Theodore* i. 12, 1–2; *Confessional of Egbert* 35.

[26] References in W. A. Phillips (ed.), *History of the Church of Ireland from the Earliest Times to the Present Day* (London, 1933), I, 353.

[27] Cf. Bede *Historia ecclesiastica* ii. 5.   [28] *Penitential of Theodore* i. 1⸳, 1–2.

[29] *Epistolae* 2. It is difficult to determine to what extent requirements of precommunion continence, and also fasting, may have affected the frequency of lay communion. Recommendations of such sort go back to the fourth century (cf. Jerome *Epistolae* xlviii. 15); and the custom of fasting communion is quite primitive. Yet there are no canons making such requirements of laymen before the eighth century.

by the Council of Cloveshoe in 747.[30] Similar injunctions were later passed by councils across the channel in the time of Charlemagne; but the minimum requirement of thrice annual communion became the normal custom.[31]

When people no longer received communion regularly, they no longer continued the ancient practice of bringing their oblations of bread and wine to church each Sunday.[32] In the Gallican churches this was more likely to happen than at Rome, for in the Gallican liturgy the Eucharistic elements were collected and prepared before the service proper began. At the offertory a ceremony similar to the Great Entrance in the Greek liturgies took place. When later the Roman rite superseded the Gallican, numerous capitularies of the Carolingian sovereigns were ineffective in getting the people to offer their oblations every Sunday at the offertory. Besides, a new notion was gaining prevalence, that the people's gifts were not fit to be used and preparation of the bread and wine for the mass was better done by the priests.[33]

In southern Gaul in Caesarius' day the theaters and public games drew many Catholics away from church. Many, if they came to mass at all, hurried away before the sermon, and sometimes before the reading of the Gospel lection.[34] Salvian, with characteristic pessimism, viewed this situation as a proof of the ruinous corruption of the Roman civic character in contrast to the noble virtues of the new barbarian peoples.[35] The Gallo-Roman populace probably surmised that it was their last chance at free public entertainments before they ceased because of barbarian destruction or an empty public purse. Bishop Caesar-

---

[30] Canons 22–23.

[31] Council of Salzburg (or Ratisbon, ca. 800), canon 6; Council of Chalon-sur-Saône (813), canon 46; Council of Tours (813), canon 50.

[32] II Council of Mâcon (585), canon 4.

[33] Theodulf of Orleans Capitula ad presbyteros parochiae suae 5 (Migne, Patr. Lat., CV, 193).

[34] Council of Agde (506), canon 47; I Council of Orleans (511), canon 26; Council of Valencia (524), canon 1; Statuta ecclesiae antiquae 24, 88 (a sixth-century Gallican collection, probably from time of Caesarius of Arles); III Council of Orleans (538), canon 29; cf. Council of Carthage (401), canon 5.

[35] De gubernatione Dei vi. 2 ff.; cf. Augustine De civitate Dei i. 32.

ius at Arles admonished his flock repeatedly for their lack of devotion and respect to the holy mysteries.[36] Even if one did not care to receive communion, one should not depart before the Lord's Prayer was said (at the close of the consecration) and the benediction of the bishop given immediately before communion.[37] Otherwise there would be no profit to one's soul from the mass. No one could accuse Caesarius of not being prompt about beginning and ending the services. Nor were they unduly long; mass lasted from one to two hours, vigils only a half-hour.

If the Gallo-Roman city people were not addicted to a Puritan view of the Lord's Day, the country folk were hardly more diligent. Synods continually passed canons forbidding work in the fields and vineyards on Sundays and holy days under pain of heavy penalties.[38] But, whereas Bishop Caesarius dwelt upon the spiritual benefits to be derived from church attendance, the episcopal fathers at the Council of Mâcon (585) induced the farmers to come to mass by promising that God would reward them by keeping away deadly plagues and sterility from the soil and domestic animals. The behavior of the lay folk during service was a further indication of the extent to which they lost any sense of vital participation or responsibility with regard to the Eucharist. Caesarius complained of people chattering and joking aloud while the lections were being read. The pages of Gregory of Tours (d. 594) are full of tales of violence committed during divine worship. Canons were passed prohibiting people from coming to mass in arms or otherwise raising disturbances.[39]

A more fundamental factor in the decline of lay communion was the dissociation of the liturgy from ideas current in the mystery religions. The passing of these cults at the end of the

[36] *Sermones* lxxiii, lxxiv, lxxvi (ed. Morin, I, 293–99, 302–4).

[37] A peculiarity of the Gallican liturgies, unknown at Rome.

[38] III Council of Orleans (538), canon 28; II Council of Mâcon (585), canon 1; Council of Auxerre (578), canon 16; Council of Narbonne (589), canon 4; Council of Chalon (644), canon 18; Council of Rouen (650), canons 14 and 15.

[39] III Council of Orleans (538), canon 29; Council of Chalon (644), canons 17 and 19.

fourth century left Christianity at least nominally the only organized religion of consequence in the West. There was, therefore, a decreasing emphasis upon a cultic distinction between the initiated and the noninitiated. The decline of the catechumenate, as well as of the public penitential discipline, was marked during the course of the fifth century. The church commenced to baptize first and instruct afterward. Infant baptism became the normal practice in Christian families—influenced partly, no doubt, by the Augustinian doctrine of original sin—and barbarian tribes were taken into the church en masse. The old custom of conferring baptism only at Easter and Pentecost to a prepared class of catechumens was obsolete in many places in the sixth century.[40] In the liturgy the dismissals of the catechumens (and penitents) dropped out; and the old distinction between the "Mass of the Catechumens" and the "Mass of the Faithful" vanished. In Rome they survived at least until the pontificate of Gregory the Great (590–604).[41] In Spain they disappeared about the same time, for Isidore of Seville makes no mention of them in his exposition of the Spanish liturgy, written about 620.[42] They existed in southern Gaul and Burgundy in the early sixth century[43] and are mentioned as still in use, though the explanation shows them to be vestigial, in the neighborhood of Autun by the late seventh-century writer on the Gallican liturgy.[44]

A pertinent question might be raised as to whether the sacramental character of the Eucharist (i.e., communion) would have been so impaired if the liturgy had been translated into

[40] Council of Girona (517), canon 4; Council of Auxerre (578), canon 18; II Council of Mâcon (585), canon 3, where it appears that many parents preferred to have their children baptised on some saint's day, probably with a view to winning thereby the saint's patronage.

[41] *Dialogi* ii. 23.

[42] This fact is the more striking when one is reminded that the *De ecclesiasticis officiis* is but a compendium of extracts from earlier writers. That Isidore knew about the dismissals is certain from his reference in *Etymologiae* vi. 19. 4.

[43] Council of Epaone (517), canon 29; *Statuta ecclesiae antiquae* 84.

[44] *Expositio brevis antiquae liturgiae Gallicanae* i (ed. J. Quasten, pp. 16–17). As to date and locale of this work I have adopted the opinion of Quasten and of A. Wilmart, in *DACL*, VI, 1102.

the vernacular, especially after Latin ceased to be understood by the people generally. We have already noted that the Arian barbarians enjoyed a vernacular liturgy; nor was there anything contrary to the ancient customs of the church in thus naturalizing the Gospel.[45] It is particularly strange that the Celtic Christians in Ireland and Scotland did not produce a vernacular liturgy, in view both of the fact that they had a native literature and also of the singular way in which they modified the institutions of the church during their period of isolation from Continental Christianity.[46] Two factors may account for this. The indigenous peoples of the West, whether Celtic, Iberian, or Punic, unlike the native peoples of the East, latinized their institutions, religious and otherwise, when they became incorporated in the Roman imperium. When Christianity reached them, it was already a part of Roman imperial culture. Acceptance of Catholicism meant also an acceptance of the Roman imperial traditions which they so admired.[47] This fact holds good also for the Germanic invaders. In Gaul and Spain they even gave up their own language for secular purposes as well (probably due also to the fact that the Latin population greatly outnumbered them, which was not the case in Britain or Germany). Leclercq has suggested that the Celtic Christians did not produce a vernacular liturgy because their Christianity was for the most part a monastic and scholarly movement.[48] Certainly the Irish monasteries played a major role in the preservation of much of the Latin literature that has come down to modern times. Knowledge of Latin declined gradually and imperceptibly as well as unevenly in areas that had been thorough-

[45] Even the Catholic Goths in Constantinople were allowed to conduct services in their own language. Chrysostom gave them the Church of St. Paul and, with the aid of an interpreter, often preached to them himself (Theodoret *Historia ecclesiastica* v. 30; cf. also Victor of Vita *Historia persecutionis Africanae provinciae* ii. 4).

[46] The *Stowe Missal* contains only a few rubrics in Irish.

[47] This is the theory of F. Cumont, "Pourquoi le latin fut la seule langue liturgique de l'Occident," *Mélanges Paul Fredericq* (Bruxelles, 1904), pp. 63–66. Ante-Nicene missions among the Celtic people in Gaul were in the vernacular (see Irenaeus *Adversus haereses* i praef.).

[48] *DACL*, VIII, 1312.

ly Romanized. In southern and western Gaul the people were still able to make the simple Latin responses required of them by the liturgy as late as the latter part of the sixth century.[49] Canons and capitularies of the eighth-century reform movement in Britain and Gaul required parish priests to explain the formularies of the liturgy and teach the Creed and the Lord's Prayer to the people in their own tongue.[50]

A negative factor so far as translating the liturgy is concerned was undoubtedly the fact that the German liturgy of the barbarians was unorthodox. Little is known about this Arian rite.[51] In form it probably followed closely the liturgy used in Constantinople, for Bishop Ulfilas had received his episcopal consecration and missionary commission from that see in 341.[52] The many similarities in detail between the Gallican rites in the West and the Greek liturgies of the East (such as the Trisagion, the Great Entrance, the position of the diptychs and kiss of peace, etc.), were not transmitted by the barbarians. Many of them antedate the conversion of the barbarians to Catholicism.[53] When the Visigoths in Spain accepted Catholicism (589), the Nicene Creed was introduced into the liturgy at the suggestion of King Recared.[54] From Spain its liturgical use spread slowly into Gaul; Rome only adopted it in 1014.

[49] The evidence is chiefly from Caesarius of Arles and Gregory of Tours. See the study of G. Nickl, *Der Anteil des Volkes an der Messliturgie im Frankenreiche von Chlodwig bis Karl den Grossen* (Innsbruck, 1930).

[50] *Statuta quaedam S. Bonifacti* 26 (Mansi, XII, 385); Council of Cloveshoe (747), canon 10; Council of Chelsea (787), canon 2; Councils of Aix-la-Chapelle (789), canon 69; (801), canon 5; (809), canon 3; (813), canon 14; Council of Frankfort (794), canons 33 and 52; Council of Reims (813), canon 2; Council of Mainz (813), canon 45.

[51] For sources see H. von Schubert, *Geschichte der christlichen Kirche im Frühmittelalter* (Tübingen, 1921), pp. 23–24.

[52] The liturgy was not a point of contention between Catholics and Arians. Differences in phraseology of their prayers were slight, if one may judge from the rite contained in the *Apostolic Constitutions*, compiled in latter half of the fourth century by a divine of Arian tendencies (see F. E. Brightman, *Liturgies Eastern and Western* [Oxford, 1896], pp. xxv, xxviii–xxix).

[53] Cf. Innocent I *Epistola* 25, ad Decentium (416); II Council of Vaison (529), canon 3.

[54] III Council of Toledo (589), canon 2; the rite of Constantinople was cited as a precedent.

Since the laity no longer understood or participated actively in the mass, sacerdotal control of the liturgy was greatly enhanced. To this state of affairs the Germanic and Celtic peoples were not averse. Their cultural and religious background favored a class of priests who alone knew the secret of letters and symbols as carriers of divine and wonder-working powers. The respect which even the most violent barbarians frequently (though by no means invariably) showed toward the clergy, church buildings, and sacred rites was remarkable. The clergy became a distinct caste, marked by a special dress and a tonsure.[55] In the conduct of worship they continued to wear Roman dress. But fashions changed with the new society. By the end of the seventh century the old Roman civil dress had become stylized into ecclesiastical vestments with symbolical meanings.[56] So completely did the clergy control the liturgy that they began to charge fees for performing baptism and chrism, a practice condemned by the synods.[57] During mass the lay folk were excluded from the sanctuary inclosed by the chancel; and in Spain they could not even enter it to receive communion.[58] Deacons and subdeacons ceased to be intermediaries between the celebrant and the congregation to become simply assistants of the priests. They disappeared altogether in small rural parishes unable to support more than one minister. A seventh-century Spanish council recommended that a priest always have an assistant at mass or the divine office, if possible— but in order that he might have someone to take his place should he suddenly take sick![59]

[55] Isidore of Seville *De ecclesiasticis officiis* ii. 4; IV Council of Toledo (633), canon 41; contrast with canon 20 of Council of Agde (506).

[56] *Expositio brevis antiquae liturgiae Gallicanae* ii. Isidore of Seville knew only the stole (IV Council of Toledo [633], canon 40). For earlier canons on vestments see *Statuta ecclesiae antiquae* 41; I Council of Braga (563), canons 9 and 11; I Council of Mâcon (583), canon 6; Council of Narbonne (589), canon 1.

[57] II Council of Braga (572), canon 7; Council of Merida (666), canon 9; XI Council of Toledo (675), canon 8.

[58] I Council of Braga (563), canon 13; IV Council of Toledo (633), canon 18. The latter rule did not obtain in Gaul; Council of Tours (567), canon 4. See Nickl, *op. cit.* pp. 61 ff.

[59] XI Council of Toledo (675), canon 14.

The enhancement of sacerdotal control in matters liturgical was definitely correlated with the notable extension of the sacrificial conception of the Eucharist. To the period under discussion belongs the development of votive masses, i.e., private masses offered for individual personal advantage or particular intentions.[60] The stages of this development are somewhat obscure. There is no evidence before the fifth century that private or special intercessions and thanksgivings were liturgically solemnized other than in connection with the regular, common mass of a Christian community, except in the case of requiem masses at funerals or on anniversaries of the departed.[61] Augustine taught that these masses for the dead were thank offerings for the good, propitiatory offerings for the "not very bad," and in the case of the "very bad, even though they do not assist the dead, they are a species of consolation to the living."[62] Pope Gregory the Great (590–604) greatly extended this doctrine and the practice of requiem masses by his development of the belief in purgatory. He was also the first theologian clearly to teach that the celebration of masses obtained for those who offered them temporal goods and benefits and warded off earthly dangers.[63] It is a fact not without significance that Pope Gregory presented this teaching in story form in his *Dialogues*, a method well adapted for the instruction of the half-civilized barbarians. He sent the work, when completed, to Queen Theudelinda of the Lombards.[64] The earliest surviving Roman service-book, the so-called Leonine Sacramentary (sixth century), contains masses "in time of drought," and "after illness," as well as nuptial, requiem, ordination, and anniversary masses. The seventh century saw a much richer development. The Gelasian Sacramentary, a Roman Mass-book brought to Gaul and considerably enriched there with Gallican formularies, contains

---

[60] The best account of the votive mass is in A. Franz, *Die Messe im deutschen Mittelalter* (Freiburg im Breisgau, 1902), pp. 115 ff.

[61] The earliest instance of a private mass of which I know is that recorded by Augustine *De civitate Dei* xxii. 8, celebrated to rid a house of demons.

[62] *Enchiridion* 110.   [63] *Dialogi* ii. 23; iii. 3; iv. 55, 57.

[64] Paul the Deacon *Historia Langobardorum* iv. 5.

some sixty votive masses, including such items as: when taking a journey, for charity, in a time of mortality, because of sterility, for demanding rain, for peace, in time of war, for kings,[65] against evil judges, for the irreligious, for the sick, for a deceased priest, etc.[66] There is even evidence of some grave abuses and superstition in connection with this form of devotion, such as the practice of saying a requiem mass for a living person so as to make him die.[67] Votive and private masses led to the custom of saying mass more than once in a single day. Priests argued that the more the saving sacrifices were offered, so much the more would their fruits be enjoyed. Ecclesiastical authorities were cautious about allowing it, however, for the weight of long tradition was against it. The Council of Auxerre (578) prohibited two masses in one day at the *same* altar.[68] Church reformers in the eighth century, like Boniface, influenced by conservative Roman practice, favored the ancient custom of one mass a day. The question was debated into the ninth century.[69]

There remains to say a word concerning the development of the ideal of liturgical uniformity in the Latin church. Ancient custom allowed bishops in local churches to enjoy a wide liberty in liturgical expression, limited only by a more or less traditional arrangement of the order of worship and by the literary talents of the bishops themselves. Fourth-century developments of rigid standards of orthodoxy made such liturgical freedom vulnerable from a doctrinal standpoint.[70] This fact, coupled with

[65] Cf. Council of Merida (666), canon 3, ordering daily mass for the safety of the king and army whenever King Receswinthe went to war.

[66] It is not possible to distinguish always those votive masses which originated at Rome from those which were composed elsewhere. Rome was probably conservative in the matter. The sacramentary sent to Charlemagne by Pope Hadrian I between 784 and 791 contains very few votive masses. But this was the *pope's* service-book. The sacramentaries used by the Roman clergy doubtless contained more.

[67] XVII Council of Toledo (694), canon 5.

[68] Canon 10.

[69] Walafrid Strabo *De ecclesiasticarum rerum exordiis et incrementis* 21 (Migne, *Patr. Lat.*, CXIV, 943). Cf. *Statuta quaedam S. Bonifacti* 23 (Mansi, XII, 385).

[70] Cf. XI Council of Carthage (407), canon 9.

the deterioration in the Latin language which set in during the fifth century, led to the production of a number of approved sacramentaries by learned bishops or presbyters. The divisive political situation created in western Europe by the barbarian invasions retarded any movement toward liturgical conformity over wide areas following the rite of great sees, as took place in the East in the fifth and sixth century. The best that could be done under the circumstances was an endeavor to establish the same *order* of liturgy within a single province according to the usage of the metropolitan church.[71] In Gaul the constantly shifting political boundaries caused by the Frankish customs of royal succession and the ceaseless warfare of the Merovingian rulers made even this ideal impossible.   In Spain, however, something approaching national liturgies was achieved; first among the Sueves in Galicia,[72] and later among the Visigoths after their conversion to Catholicism.[73] The growing prestige of the papacy caused some dissemination of Roman service-books in Italy and Gaul. When the Benedictine monks became missionary, they carried the Roman use with them to the British Isles; from there Boniface and his associates brought it back to the Continent in the eighth century in their missionary and reform work in Germany and the western Frankish territories.[74] With the rise of the Carolingian house to a place of dominance among the Franks, a new era dawned in western Europe. The Gallican church was reformed, an alliance was struck with the papacy, and dormant Roman imperial ideals were reawakened. As a part of this revival the Frankish sovereigns introduced the Roman rite throughout their domains to supersede the hetero-

[71] Council of Vannes (465), canon 15; Council of Agde (506), canon 30; Council of Girona (517), canon 1; Council of Epaone (517), canon 27.

[72] Council of Braga (563), canons 1, 4, 5; they adopted the liturgy of the Roman church sent by Pope Vigilius to Bishop Profuturus of Braga in 538.

[73] IV Council of Toledo (633), canon 2; XI Council of Toledo (675), canon 3. This is the so-called Mozarabic liturgy. It should be noted that the uniformity had only to do with the order and not with the texts of the services. Leading bishops continued to compose texts and formularies throughout the seventh century. The bishops in turn furnished parish priests with an "official book" (IV Council of Toledo [633], canon 26).

[74] Cf. Boniface *Epistolae* 42, 111.

geneous Gallican liturgies, which had suffered by the general decay of church life in Gaul under the later Merovingians. We do not know whether the idea was originally the pope's or Pepin's, but Charlemagne's legislation made it an actuality. Thus the local liturgy of the church in Rome was extended over most of Western Christendom and made a principal agent in the formation of the medieval Christian synthesis.[75]

[75] Details may be found in H. Netzer, *L'Introduction de la Messe romaine en France sous les Carolingiens* (Paris, 1910).

THE FEUDALIZATION OF THE CHURCH

JOHN T. McNEILL

Divinity School, University of Chicago

FEUDALISM was a political, social, and economic *modus vivendi* which came into operation in western ·Europe during the eclipse of the state in the century after Charlemagne. The causes of the development of feudalism do not lie in the field of religion. Religion always craves a peaceably ordered society, and churchmen were vocal against the anarchic drift of the ninth century for which they sometimes severely and perhaps unduly blamed the policies of kings. Feudal society differed from complete anarchy mainly by virtue of an infinite series of personal contracts formed between men of power. While these contracts were frequently violated, their sanctity was generally defended by the church. The church helped to prevent the extinction of culture and order and to humanize the life of those barbarous times. It is not our purpose, however, to examine the social influence of Christianity in the feudal age. We are concerned instead with the other side of the picture: the impression made by feudal upon Christian institutions.

The church entered the feudal era in a well-developed state of organization, and its structure was always capable of relatively easy territorial expansion or local division. In detail, the inception of new units of organization was indeed often hotly contested. Friction was generated both on the question of authority in the erection of parishes and on that of the wisdom in given instances of erecting them. In general, the bishops asserted freedom of action in this matter, though their decisions on occasion called forth censure from the archbishops. Such objections were not idle or baseless. It was the calculated policy of some bishops to multiply churches in order to increase the

episcopal revenues from consecrations and visitations.[1] Whatever the motives of those responsible for the development, a
great increase in the number of parishes is a prominent feature
of the history of the Carolingian age; and most of the new
churches apparently justified their creation by service to a growing population.

I

When a church building was erected for a new parish, it was
the bishop's function to consecrate the edifice and to mark the
parish bounds. At the consecration he solemnly invested the
priest with the church keys, the bell rope, and a copy of the
gospel. The church relied for maintenance not upon free gifts
but upon landed property provided for that purpose. The
donor of the property was ordinarily required to subscribe to a
deed of gift (*libellus dotis*) which contained a list of the lands
bestowed, a statement of the number of the serfs upon them,
and a pledge binding himself and his heirs not to repossess the
estates.[2] Had these contracts been uniformly subscribed and
kept, the medieval church would have escaped some trouble-
some problems. But in many cases no such engagements were
made by the donors; in others they were made but not kept.

The decentralization of society in the feudal world was reflected in the structure of the church. One of the factors making
at once for decentralization and secularization was the existence
of a vast number of private or proprietary churches. On the
origin of the *Eigenkirche* (*ecclesia privata*) there exists some difference of opinion. Stutz thinks it traceable to "the priesthood
of the Germanic *Hausvater*."[3] Werminghoff states that "the

---

[1] Imbart de la Tour, *Les Paroisses rurales du IVe au XIe siècle* (Paris, 1900), pp.
103 f.; cf. H. Leclercq, "Paroisses rurales," in F. Cabrol, *Dictionnaire d'archéologie
chrétienne et de liturgie* (2d ed.), XIII, Part II, 2198–2235.

[2] De la Tour, *op. cit.*, pp. 100 f.

[3] U. Stutz, *Die Verwaltung und Nutzung des kirchlichen Vermögens in den Gebieten
des weströmischen Reichs* . . . . (Berlin, 1892), pp. 66 ff.; *Die Eigenkirche als Element des
mittelalterlich-germanischen Kirchenrechtes* (Berlin, 1895), p. 17. H. von Schubert in
Das älteste germanische Christentum (Tübingen, 1909), pp. 24 f., and *Geschichte der christlichen Kirche im Frü:mittelalter* (Tübingen, 1921), pp. 10, 27, has called special attention
to the pagan background of the *Eigenkirche* in the Arian Germanic kingdoms.

conception of the *Eigenkirche* is to be explained only from Germanic ideas of law: it arises from the pagan house sanctuary in which the German practices priestly functions for his family and domestics."[4] But it has been pointed out by Imbart de la Tour and others that the institution appears in late Roman as well as in Germanic society. Apparently in the Roman environment it sometimes replaced the pagan domestic altar. Pöschl finds lay possession of churches in the eastern empire in the third and fourth centuries but holds that the private church in Italy, France, and Spain became widespread under the influence of the invading Germanic peoples; and much evidence favors this view.[5]

It is worth noting that in one of the *Novellae* of Justinian the lay founder of the church is expressly given the right of presentation to it. The passage reads in part as follows: "If any man has erected an oratory and he himself, or his heirs, has desired to present a cleric to it, if they furnish a competency for his [the cleric's] livelihood and nominate to the bishop such as are worthy, those nominated shall be ordained."[6] Thus the private church had a position in Roman law. It was not a product of feudalism, but it was through the favorable conditions of feudal life that it became prevalent in the West.

Private churches were founded on the initiative of persons who had the means of building, protecting, and sustaining them, and they remained the property of the founders and their heirs. Not all the *fundatores* were laymen. Bishops possessed and controlled many such churches, and in numerous instances these were situated within dioceses other than their own. While the lands held by monasteries were becoming populous, many churches were founded on them. These were controlled by the abbots. Such relationships were decidedly unfavorable to the

---

[4] A. Werminghoff, *Geschichte der Kirchenverfassung Deutschlands im Mittelalter* (Leipzig, 1905), I, 84.

[5] De la Tour, *op. cit.*, pp. 176 ff.; A. Pöschl, *Bischofsgut und Mensa Episcopalis* (Bonn, 1908), pp. 32 ff.; cf. P. Thomas, *Le Droit des laïques sur les églises et la patronage laïque au moyen âge* (Paris, 1906), pp. 2 ff., 28 ff.

[6] *Novellae* cxxiii. 18; text in *Codex juris civilis*, ed. D. Gothofred (Frankfort, 1688), col. 257.

maintenance of unity in the diocese. But more serious were the effects of the increasing number of lay proprietorships with rights and claims that challenged the authority of bishops.

The proprietary church receives mention in numerous conciliar decisions from the fifth to the twelfth century. These canons of councils are chiefly aimed against infringement by the founders or their heirs of episcopal spiritual control. In the assumptions on both sides there is obviously a marked change from the pagan concept of a private sanctuary in which the father of the family officiated as priest of the household. The lay lord was not the priest and could not, without the clergy, dedicate the church or instal the priest. But the bishop's spiritual authority might be infringed by undue influence on the part of the seigneur in the appointment of the priest or upon his conduct in office.

The councils attempted to reduce to a minimum the damage to unity and order. According to their provisions, a layman who builds a church may not invite to dedicate it "any other bishop than he of the city (*civitas*) in which the church is built."[7] Proprietors may not "introduce foreign (*peregrinos*) clerics into their oratories."[8] The possessions of the church are by conciliar decisions placed under the defense of the founder and his heirs; but, if members of the founder's family fall into distress through no fault of their own, they may receive a maintenance from the property. The founder or his heirs are to denounce to the bishop, or to a judge, any priest who destroys or removes the property of the church. Similarly an offending bishop is to be denounced to his metropolitan and an offending metropolitan to the king. The patron, however, is enjoined against all rapine and violence in his own activities in this connection. It is provided that the founders shall, while they live, take care of the church and present suitable clerics to the bishop for ordination. If such are not presented, the bishop shall institute those of his own choice with the consent

[7] Council of Orange (441), canon 10 (Mansi, *Concilia*, VI, 437 f.).

[8] Council of Orleans (541), canon 7 (Mansi, *Concilia*, IX, 114; *Mon. Ger. Hist.*, *Concilia*, I, 89).

of the founder; but, if the bishop presumes to ordain rectors for these churches against the founders' wishes, he shall be obliged to institute others to the satisfaction of the founders.[9] When a candidate was presented by the patron to the bishop, it was the latter's duty to examine him for learning, faith, and morals. The ecclesiastics insisted that the fitness of the presentee was to remain in the judgment of the bishop; yet the bishop might not reject the candidate *sine ratione,* and preference on the part of the bishop for another person went unrecognized.[10]

II

The early villa evolved into a community, and the oratory originally intended for the villa was formed into a parish church without interference with the proprietary rights. Through these conditions there came to exist a situation of somewhat serious import for church order and a trend toward decentralization which the hierarchy were long unable to check. The reply of Pope Zachary to Pippin's inquiry, in which the founder's right of presentation is denied,[11] can hardly be thought of as a serious effort to cancel the whole pattern of the relationship already widely established between priests and powerful laymen. The Council of Frankfort (794) permits the proprietor to alienate the property, provided the church is retained in daily cult use,[12] and the Council of Rome held in 826 declares that a founder's oratory or monastery is not to be taken from his *dominium* and that he may nominate to it the priest of his choice with the bishop's consent and saving obedience to the latter.[13]

[9] Council of Orleans (541), canon 33 (Mansi, *Concilia,* IX, 119); Council of Toledo (655), canons 1 and 2 (Mansi, *Concilia,* XI, 25 f.).

[10] Council of Riesbach (799), canons 2 and 5 (*Mon. Ger. Hist., Concilia,* II, 213); Council of Paris (829), canon 22 (*Mon. Ger. Hist., Concilia,* II, 627).

[11] *Mon. Ger. Hist., Epistolae,* III, 484: "ab episcopo noverit presbyterum postulandum."

[12] "De ecclesiis, quae ab ingenuis hominibus construuntur: liceat eos tradere, vendere, tantummodo ut ecclesia non destruatur, sed serviuntur cotidie honores" (Council of Frankfort [794], canon 54 [*Mon. Ger. Hist., Concilia,* II, 171]).

[13] *Mon. Ger. Hist., Concilia,* II, 576, canon 21; cf. Werminghoff, *op. cit.,* p. 86. Mansi gives the canons of this council under date of 853 (*Concilia,* XIV, 1001 ff.).

The admission of private property rights in churches and their supporting estates was in fact bound to entail the subjection of these properties to exchange through all manner of private transactions. When an estate was divided among heirs or passed from the founder's family, right of presentation, regarded as appendant to the manor, was either alienated to a single owner or shared by more than one inheritor. The possessor of the right of patronage, or of a share in that right, was free to dispose of it as he wished. It could be bought and sold, bequeathed and inherited; and it could be divided between any number of persons. In many cases the private church was actually transferred from the founder's family and from later proprietors of the domain on which it stood, and by a commercial transaction came into the patronage of persons who lived at a distance from it and had no special reason to take an interest in the worshipers.[14] It was not until the twelfth century that the reformers of the church were able to retrieve in a measure the loss of unity and vigor she had suffered through the admission of the proprietary church. The canonist Gratian, as Stutz has repeatedly noted, took from the patrons of these churches their right to sell or bestow them. Pope Alexander III did his utmost to abolish these practices and to reduce the patron's right to that of presentation alone.[15]

Meanwhile, in general, the feudality, by a policy of aggression in their relations with their owned churches and through them with the ecclesiastical world, had extended their local influence and power. Since the effects of this secular pressure were not different from those which occurred where aggression was not based on founder's rights, we shall meanwhile note the more general aspects of the gravitation toward secularism

[14] For numerous examples see Thomas, *op. cit.*, pp. 20 ff.; E. Lesne, *Histoire de la propriété ecclésiastique en France* (2 vols.; Paris, 1910 and 1926), I, 74 f.; cf. E. Gibson, *Codex juris ecclesiastici Anglicani* (2d ed.; Oxford, 1761), II, 757 ff.

[15] U. Stutz, "Papst Alexander III gegen die Freiung langobardischer Eigenkirchen," *Abhandlungen der preussischen Akademie der Wissenschaften, Phil.-hist. Kl.*, VI (Berlin, 1936), 35, and the writer's earlier studies there cited. Gratian states: "[Fundatores] habent jus providendi et consulendi et sacerdotem inveniendi; sed non habent jus vendendi, vel donandi, vel utendi tamquam propriis" (*Decreti, secunda pars*, Causa XVI, Questio VII, cxxx [*Corpus juris canonici*, ed. Richter-Friedberg (1879), col. 809]).

which not only characterized proprietary churches but assailed all others likewise. The conditions which gave rise to feudalism tended to place each man's life and property in the *patrocinium* or protection of another. "The lordless man," says Freeman, "became a kind of outlaw." Every church had property and every priest his life to be defended against greed and violence. When laymen found it necessary to seek the patronage of the mighty, the rural clergy had in most cases no recourse but to do likewise. It was at a price of spiritual independence that they placed themselves and their churches under the protection of powerful possessors. The tendency was for the feudal aristocracy to make the most of the obligations to them of their clerical vassals, and practically to interpret *patrocinium*, or protective patronage, as *dominium*, or ordinary feudal lordship.[16] The outcome was thus to place the parish churches generally in substantially the same position with respect to property as the private churches were. In the ninth and tenth centuries this feudalization of churches became all but universal. The absorption of the churches in feudalism may be symbolized to our minds by the fact that in many places church buildings were fortified and munitioned for war.[17] While the private church was, under conditions, recognized in canon law, many councils of the Merovingian age adopted regulations penalizing priest and layman who formed contracts for the enfeoffment of other parish churches. But such prohibitions were apparently ineffective from the first, and the trend toward universal feudalization of church property went on unchecked in the Carolingian and Saxon periods.

III

The feudalization of the episcopate kept pace with that of the lower clergy. The bishop, however, was in a much more favorable social and political position than the ordinary priest. As the proprietor of a vast domain, he was in a position to compete

[16] A. Luchaire, "Patronage," in Cabrol, *Dictionnaire*, XIII, Part II, 2565 f.; De la Tour, *op. cit.*, p. 212; Thomas, *op. cit.*, p. 20.

[17] See especially R. Rey, *Les vieilles églises fortifiées du midi de la France* (Paris, 1925), pp. 11–31.

with the great lay feudatories. The bishop's domain was called the *mensa episcopalis*. The *mensa* included an area about the cathedral together with estates in various parts of the diocese and even, in some cases, beyond it. Some of these lands were managed directly by the bishop and his appointed officials (mayors, provosts, etc.).[18] Other portions of the episcopal lands were held by lay vassals who looked to the bishop as their lord and did him homage. Still others were the lands of churches, abbeys, and priories of which he was patron by right of foundation. In addition to fiefs in land, the bishop possessed a class of incorporeal fiefs,[19] which consisted of such salaried offices as those of the cathedral deans, the cantor, the chancellor, and the servitors of the episcopal *familia* or private household. In the latter were commonly included by the twelfth century a chaplain or chaplains, an equerry, a smith, a chamberlain, a carpenter, a porter, and the pantryman, butler, and cook, who constituted the department of cuisine.[20] These offices were all regarded as fiefs. For them, the holders did homage to the bishop. Certain of the vassals of the bishops of Paris had the duty of attending the bishop to bear his throne when he was carried in procession in his consecration.[21] But the bishop was a vassal as well as a suzerain. His feudal superior might be a king, duke, count, or archbishop. In this relationship, the bishop took the ordinary obligations of feudalism: homage, fealty, payments, and military services.

It was the policy of kings, notably of Otto I, to play the bishops against the secular feudality in order to strengthen the throne. Under Otto, numerous bishops became counts, each receiving the grant of a *gau* from the king and becoming his direct vassal for this territory. Otto's liberal policy, according to Thompson, made the bishops "the pillars of the throne,"[22] even

[18] A. Luchaire, *Manuel des institutions françaises: période des capétiens directs* (Paris, 1892).

[19] A. Luchaire, *Social France in the Time of Philip Augustus*, trans. E. Krehbiel (New York, 1912), p. 144.

[20] J. Mortet, *Maurice de Sully, évêque de Paris (1160–1196)* (Paris, 1890), p. 89.

[21] Luchaire, *Manuel des institutions françaises*, p. 46.

[22] J. W. Thompson, *Feudal Germany* (Chicago, 1928), p. 44.

if it increased the chronic tension between them and the lay feudality. The feudal bishop indeed paid for his wealth and eminence. At the best amid onerous spiritual duties he ruled and developed his lands and yielded taxes and military and other services to the king, despite the contrary provisions of the canon law. At the worst he was a ruthless baron with poor pretensions to piety or Latin. Thompson observes that Otto the Great" fought his wars in large part with church vassals."[23] The bishops were usually selected with some discernment by kings, and they proved themselves generally more efficient leaders than the hereditary dukes and counts. Their lands became productive. Wise kings saw the expediency of advancing them in temporal power and wealth, much as some later rulers encouraged town life and merchandise that they might have at their disposal increased taxable wealth and man-power in time of need.

Their control of episcopal elections thus became a matter of primary importance for kings. Everywhere such control was a feature of the rise of royal power. Under the Saxon kings, permission to elect canonically was a privilege accorded to a few sees only. Though Burchard of Worms, in his *Decretum* (*ca.* 1008–12), solemnly records the canonical requirements for episcopal elections, his contemporary, Thietmar, bishop of Merseburg (1009–18), coolly resigns the disposition of bishoprics to kings and emperors.[24] In France the rise of feudalism drew the episcopal elections away from the late Carolingian kings into the hands of the great seigneurs. Even in the days of Charles the Bald, a count of Rouen or of Cambray could secure the election of his nominees and a count of Auvergne could temporarily expel a bishop of Clermont. In later decades such interference was virtually normal. The bishoprics of Brittany, Normandy, and Burgundy fell a prey to the great dukes or to the less mighty but not less greedy aristocracy. Their appointees were

[23] *Ibid.*, pp. 32 and 39; A. Hauck, *Kirchengeschichte Deutschlands* (Leipzig, 1890), II, 653.

[24] E. N. Johnson, *The Secular Activities of the German Episcopate, 919–1024* (Chicago, 1932), p. 68. Johnson cites numerous parallel observations by writers of the time.

often men like themselves, warriors of indifferent morals.[25] But the theoretic position of the kings was better than their actual control, and the more influential of the clergy had good reason to desire an efficient kingship to check the violence of the baronage. Pope John X, intervening in an episcopal election at Liége, wrote: "We conserve the ancient principle by which none can confer the episcopate on a cleric except the king to whom the scepter has been divinely given."[26]

The recovery of royal power was attended by the resumption of royal appointments to the bishoprics. Already Louis the German and Charles the Fat had introduced the practice of royal investiture with the crozier;[27] this became the common procedure in the late tenth century. According to F. Lot, Hugh Capet secured the nomination of from twenty to twenty-five of the seventy-six or seventy-seven sees in France. The secular character of the episcopate was scarcely altered by the fact of royal versus seigneurial nomination. Philip I of France favored as bishops those who were "not the most religious" in order to make as complete as possible his politically and financially profitable control of the church. Through the claim of *droit de régale*, he secured incomes from vacant sees. The custom of *spolia*, the plunder of a deceased bishop's goods (the wills of clerics were not held valid), had passed from the people to the lords and' was now a right asserted by the kings. Louis VI's maintenance of this "barbarous right of spoil" is cited by Thompson as evidence against the assumption that Louis with

[25] Imbart de la Tour, *Les Elections épiscopales dans l'église de France du IXe au XIIe siècle (Etude sur la décadence du principe électif) 814-1150* (Paris, 1891), pp. 214 ff.; G. Weise, *Königtum und Bischofswahl im fränkischen und deutschen Reich vor dem Investiturstreit* (Berlin, 1912), pp. 23 ff., 37 ff., 56 f.

[26] J. P. Migne, *Patrologia Latina*, CXXXII, 806 f.

[27] The earliest recorded royal investitures are that of Rimbert for Hamburg-Bremen by Louis the German (865) and that of Herifrid for Auxerre by Charles the Fat (887). Louis in full assembly solemnly bestowed on Rimbert the episcopal staff (". . . . cum pontificalis baculi juxta morem commendatione") (*Vita Rimberti*, cap. 11, *Mon. Ger. Hist.*, *Scriptores*, II, 770). The *De gestis episcoporum Autissiodorensium* (i, xli) states that Charles the Fat conferred on Herifrid the pastoral staff ("pastoralem confert baculum") (Migne, *Patr. Lat.*, CXXXVIII, 255); cf. De la Tour, *Les Elections épiscopales* ... , p. 345; H. von Schubert, *Geschichte der christlichen Kirche im Frühmittelalter*, p. 565.

all his benefactions to the church had other than self-interested motives toward it.[28]

But while time favored the kings, a number of the great feudatories long maintained the privilege of nomination to one or more bishoprics. The dukes of Normandy, whose duchy was coextensive with the archdiocese of Rouen and contained seven dioceses, adopted a vigorous policy toward the episcopate. In 1049 Duke William appointed his fourteen-year-old half-brother Odo to the rich see of Bayeux. Odo's services at Hastings were immortalized in the Bayeux tapestry and rewarded by the earldom of Kent and some hundreds of parcels of English land. When by his complicity in a conspiracy against William Rufus he lost these English holdings, Odo gave himself energetically to his episcopal duties. But the crusade attracted him with promise both of piety and of adventure, and he died at Palermo in 1097. The see of Bayeux, as Gleason's recent study has shown, furnishes an excellent example of the baronial episcopate through several generations. In the twelfth century the bishop's vassals included great and small barons, vavasors, and free peasants. They owed military aid to the Norman dukes and to the kings of France.[29]

The military aspect of a bishop's activities in the feudal age varied considerably with his circumstances and his disposition. Even a high-minded and saintly man had no option but to supply soldiers to his lord in warfare. The peace-loving St. Wulstan, bishop of Worcester in the days of William the Conqueror, on occasion "showed himself a skilled military leader."[30] One of the offenses of St. Anselm in the eyes of William Rufus was the fact that the knights he dispatched to the king's aid against

[28] F. Lot, *Etudes sur le règne de Hugues Capet* (Paris, 1903), p. 223; Lesne, *op. cit.*, II, 2, 102 ff.; A. Fliche, *Le Règne de Philippe I, Roi de France, 1060–1108* (Paris, 1912), pp. 337 ff.; J. W. Thompson, *The Development of the French Monarchy under Louis VI: Le Gros, 1108–1137* (Chicago, 1895), pp. 73 f.

[29] S. E. Gleason, *An Ecclesiastical Barony of the Middle Ages: The Bishopric of Bayeux, 1066–1204* (Cambridge, Mass., 1936), pp. 9 f., 49 ff., 72.

[30] J. W. Lamb, *St. Wulstan, Prelate and Patriot* (London, 1933), p. 172.

the Welsh in 1097 proved a scurvy lot of ill-equipped men.[31] Burchard of Worms had to dislodge from his city by force of arms a horde of insolent bandits, and during a visit to Italy his attendant knights fought a battle near Lucca.[32] Many feudal bishops fought and bled in the cause of their king, which was often that of public order, and most of them gave much time, money, and effort to military engineering, preparation of troops, and a variety of matters of secular administration. In some cases the military phase was dissociated from constructive purpose, and the bishop was an adventurer or a conscienceless marauder. "The hierarchy tended more and more to become a military caste like the feudality."[33] Numerous laymen obtained episcopal appointments. Athanasius II of Naples (872–94) was consecrated only four years after his accession to the see and later succeeded his brother as *magister militum*, took a wife, and pursued a ruthless and ambitious secular policy.[34]

Popular legend treated the worldly bishop sometimes with frank admiration, sometimes with vindictive resentment. The *Chanson de Roland* names Archbishop Turpin of Reims among the *baruns* of Charlemagne. He harangues and blesses the Franks before battle and is also a hero in the fight. At his death, he is celebrated "par granz batailles e par mult bels sermons."[35] On the other hand, Hatto of Mainz, a shrewd and probably unscrupulous supporter of monarchy in King Arnulf's time, emerges in legend as a blasphemer and an oppressor and an awful example. A fifteenth-century romancer states that, because he used to say, "If I lie may mice devour me," he was indeed devoured by these rodents.[36]

[31] Eadmer, *Historia novorum in Anglia et opuscula duo de vita S. Anselmi et quibusdem miraculis ejus* ("Rolls Series," Vol. LXXXI [London, 1884]), p. 78; F. M. Stenton, *The First Century of English Feudalism* (Oxford, 1932), pp. 147 f.

[32] *Vita Burchardi* 7, 8 (*Mon. Ger. Hist., Scriptores*, IV, 835 f.).

[33] Johnson, *op. cit.*, pp. 206 ff.; J. W. Thompson, *Economic and Social History of the Middle Ages* (New York, 1928), p. 657.

[34] Pöschl, *op. cit.*, III, 171.

[35] *Chanson de Roland*, secs. xii, lxxxix, xcv, cxiv, and clxv. I have consulted the edition of G. Bertoni, *La Chanson de Roland* (Florence, 1935).

[36] "Devoratus est a muribus," says Engelhusius (d. 1434), quoted by M. Beheim-Schwarzback, *Die Mäuseturmsage von Popiel und Hatto* (Posen, 1888), p. 39.

The feudal bishop exhibited little concern for the rule of clerical celibacy. Many were publicly married; many had numerous illegitimate children for whose worldly prosperity they were prepared to play fast and loose with church rules. Bishop Thébaud (Tetbaldus) of Rennes (990+) was the son of a priest, Loscoran. He married Oirelan, the daughter of an archdeacon, Alveus of Nantes, and after her death remarried. He retired from the bishopric, securing it to his son, Gaultier, who after his episcopal consecration married Oidelina. While Thébaud was still alive, and an abbot, Gaultier passed on the office to his son Guérin (Garinus). At the latter's death (1037) the see went to Gaultier's half-brother, Tristan (Triscannus).[37] This is a celebrated and extreme instance of a common phenomenon. The synod of Westminster (1102) legislates against the succession of sons to the churches of their fathers, and Eadmer quotes a letter from Paschal II to Anselm (1107) in which it is taken as an assumed fact that "almost the greater and better part of the clergy of England are the sons of priests."[38]

IV

The necessity of the protection of church property and the desire to avoid making bishops responsible for "worldly business"[39] called into existence a class of official known as the *advocatus*, sometimes called *vocatus* (whence German *Vogt*) or *defensor*. Kings and lords had also their *advocati*, and the policy of the Carolingians was to have an *advocatus* appointed for every bishop and abbot and to use these functionaries as agents of the king rather than protectors of the church. Counts and *missi* participated in and largely controlled their appointments.

---

[37] For these bishops I adopt the dates given by P. B. Gams, *Series episcoporum ecclesiae Catholicae* (2d ed.; Leipzig, 1931), p. 606. For the record see *Gallia Christiana*, XIV, 743 ff.; A. Houtin, *Histoire du célibat ecclésiastique* (Paris, 1929), p. 111.

[38] Synod of Westminster (1102), canon 7; D. Wilkins, *Concilia Magnae Britanniae et Hiberniae* (London, 1737), I, 382; Eadmer, *op. cit.*, p. 185. H. C. Lea has shown the prevalence of this state of things in England a generation after Hildebrand's efforts at reform (*History of Sacerdotal Celibacy* [3d ed.; London, 1907], I, 330 ff.).

[39] "Negotia secularia," II Tim. 2:4, an oft-quoted expression in the canons. In Mansi, *Concilia*, XIV, 1005, and XVII, 229, however, we find: "ne cum humana lucra attendunt aeterna praemia perdant."

Sometimes an ecclesiastical *advocatus* was simply nominated by the king himself. The advocate received for his services a fief in ecclesiastical property. The functions of the office were in time enlarged from those arising from the representation of the bishop or abbot before the law, to include a wide range of administrative duties. The office declined with the empire but came into prominence again in the role of defender of ecclesiastical establishments, especially of monasteries, amid the welter of feudal violence. The advocate was now a servant of the abbey. Since his duties might involve war and capital punishment, he was normally a layman.[40] The similar lay functionary for the bishop was now usually called *vicedominus*.[41] Where the monastery had free choice, it selected a mighty man of valor and resources who dwelt near enough to bring prompt aid to the house if it should be menaced. The founder of the monastery, or a generous donor, often became *advocatus;* and in many foundation charters the office is attached permanently to the founder's heirs. By the eleventh century its hereditary character was widely recognized; it was also freely bought and sold. It came to be held by clerics and by women, often, indeed, by ruffians and despoilers who behaved, as Senn observes, "with the legendary brutality of the feudal barons." These men snatched the possessions they were appointed to protect and from the fortresses erected for defense issued with their men at arms to terrorize monks and peasants.[42] A diploma of Robert I (1013) is directed against those who ought to be *advocati* and *defensores* but who are on the contrary "praedetores et raptores"[43] and they are similarly described by Abbo of Fleury ("quorum defensores esse debuerant eos vastant").[44]

Monastic wealth abounded. Lesne aptly remarks that the

[40] F. Senn, *L'Institution des avoueries ecclésiastiques en France* (Paris, 1903), pp. 2 ff., 21, 26 ff., 40 ff.

[41] Senn, *L'Institution des vidamies en France* (Paris, 1907), pp. 60 ff.

[42] Senn, *Institution des avoueries*, pp. 112, 150 ff.

[43] Senn quotes the document (*Institution des avoueries*, pp. 214 f.). It appears in E. Martène, *Veterum scriptorum . . . . amplissima collectio* (2d ed.; Paris, 1724), I, 379.

[44] *S. Abbonis abbatis Floriacensis collectio canonum* ii (Migne, *Patr. Lat.*, CXXXIX, 476).

personal poverty of monks helped to create their corporate wealth.[45] Conforming in large measure to the prescribed limitations of their personal needs, corporately the monks joined field to field. These ascetics welcomed, without ascetic scruple, pious gifts of land. If this was wilderness land, they knew better than all others how to make it productive. The abbey estates in favorable circumstances became not only of vast extent but also prosperous and populous. The institution of an abbey meant something parallel to the establishment of a chain of industrial plants in a capitalistic society. Their proprietors, kings, prelates, or barons looked upon them as revenue-producing investments whose value the gifts of later donors could be counted on to enhance. The functions of the abbots were no less political and economic than religious, and royal and feudal control of abbatial elections was inevitable.[46]

The ninth and tenth centuries witnessed widespread secularization of the abbatial office. Not only were the royal abbeys placed under the rule of monks who would use their resources in support of the king but many secular canons and laymen were made abbots on action of the ruler.[47] Even kings credited with piety resorted to this practice, a fact which Pöschl would explain by the necessity of having the vast monastic estates with their reservoirs of man-power under the control of soldiers. To require the religious abbot to lead troops was directly to violate monastic principles.[48] In any case, whether by the intrusion of laymen into the abbey or by the military behavior of abbots who were regular monks, monastic principles were habitually

---

[45] *Op. cit.*, I, 106.

[46] H. Lévy-Bruhl, *Les Elections abbatiales en France*, Vol. I: *Epoque franque* (Paris, 1913), pp. 49 ff.; Werminghoff, *op. cit.*, pp. 96 ff.; K. Voigt, *Die karolingische Klosterpolitik und der Niedergang des westfränkischen Königtums: Laienäbte und Klosterinhaber* (Stuttgart, 1917), pp. 3 ff.; U. Berlière, *Les Elections abbatiales au moyen âge* ("Académie royale de Belgique, Classe des lettres, etc.," Vol. XX, Fasc. 3 [2d ser., 1924]), pp. 13 ff.

[47] Lévy-Bruhl, *op. cit.*, pp. 113 ff., 129 ff.; Voigt, *op. cit.*, pp. 163 ff. On the origin of the royal abbeys see Lesne, *op. cit.*, II, 15 ff. Episcopal complaint against Charles the Bald's policy in this matter was voiced in 858, Council of Quierzy, canon 8 (*Mon. Ger. Hist., Capitularia*, II, 4, 34; Mansi, *Concilia*, XVIII, 303; Voigt, *op. cit.*, p. 88).

[48] Pöschl, *op. cit.*, II, 55.

violated. The Council of Trosly (909) protests against lay abbots who settle with their families in the monasteries and require accommodations for their knights and dogs.[49] We have evidence, too, that in many cases the office became hereditary. In Ireland this abuse became exceedingly prevalent; St. Bernard in his *Life of St. Malachy of Armagh* notes its occurrence through fifteen generations.[50] Many of the lay abbots were members of royal families. Nunneries were bestowed by French rulers on queens and the sisters of kings.[51] Other appointees were counts who were in a position to obtain what they demanded from the king or otherwise to procure, by force or guile, control of the monastery. German margraves and dukes in certain instances figure as lay abbots.[52]

Coulton supposes that it is with reference to the royal abbey of St. Denis that St. Bernard wrote in 1125 to William of St. Thierry of an abbot riding with more than sixty in his train and appearing like a prince rather than a ruler of souls. A few years later, commending Suger for his reform of St. Denis, Bernard refers to the bad old days when the cloister was frequented by knights and even entered by women.[53] If, in his description of the princely abbot, Bernard had in mind Ives I (1075–94), the train of horsemen may have been needed for protection from the abbot's enemies, by whom, in fact, he was finally slain. Ives obtained a laudatory epitaph but left a bad

[49] Council of Trosly (909), canon 3 (Mansi, *Concilia*, XVIII, 270). In the *Capitula* of Rudolf of Bourges (*ca.* 850), cap. ix, lay *seniores* of churches are warned that they are not to lodge in the houses of priests "with their wives or other women, and their dogs" (Mansi, *Concilia*, XIV, 948). Adso (*ca.* 980) connects the same two offending species, women and dogs, in an incident related in his *Translatio S. Baseoli* xii. He records the miraculous deliverance of that sixth-century saint from the annoyance of laymen's dogs that had frequented the church of Vierzy and violated the font. The animals went mad and died (J. Mabillon, *Acta sanctorum ordinis S. Benedicti*, saec. IV, pars ii [=Tomus VI] [Venice, 1738], p. 148).

[50] *S. Bernardi Vita S. Malachiae* xix. Bernard's statement refers to "bishops," an error for "coarbs" or hereditary abbots, and requires further correction (see H. J. Lawlor, *St. Bernard of Clairvaux's Life of St. Malachy of Armagh* [London, 1920], pp. xv, 45, 164 ff.).

[51] Lesne, *op. cit.*, II, 157 ff., 166 ff.

[52] Voigt, *op. cit.*, pp. 91 ff.; Berlière, *op. cit.*, pp. 14 ff.; Pöschl, *op. cit.*, III, 167 ff.

[53] G. G. Coulton, *Life in the Middle Ages* (New York, 1931), IV, 155 ff.

reputation.[54] Equally deserving of remembrance is Thurstan, the Cluniac monk of Caen whom William the Conqueror made abbot of Glastonbury in 1077. He climaxed many foolish acts by commanding the substitution for the old Gregorian chant of new forms devised by William of Fécamp, and brought Norman soldiers into the chapter house to assure the new harmony (1083). Far from raising their holy song at his bidding, the monks hastily sought asylum in the church. The Norman archers followed and, shooting from an elevated perch, slew three and wounded eighteen of the brethren as they clung about the altar. Thurstan was deprived by the king, but he recovered his post under William Rufus by a payment of five hundred silver pounds.[55]

Many of the great abbots lived and died under severe criticism of the worldliness of their lives. It has been observed that in the medieval animal tales, the abbot is often identified with crafty and destructive beasts—the wolf, the hedgehog, the otter, the fox, and the bear.[56]

V

There is, in fact, nothing to surprise the student in the data we have here reviewed. As the price of its survival, organized Christianity has always had to adapt itself to environmental conditions. Critics of the feudal clergy have habitually contrasted their wealth and worldly show with the simplicity and poverty of Jesus and the Apostles. The doctrine of apostolic poverty for the ministry of the church presupposes that it is possible to gain spiritual influence without gaining temporal power. But every spiritual movement induces social, political, and economic change and forces upon the spiritual leaders re-

[54] *Gallia Christiana* VII, 365 f. Two Latin verse epitaphs are given. "Vita fuit clara sed mors vehementer amara," says one of these.

[55] *Anglo-Saxon Chronicle*, trans. J. Stevenson, *Church Historians of England*, II (1853), 130; *Chronicle of Florence of Worcester, ibid.*, pp. 305 f.; Henry of Huntington, *Historia Anglorum*, ed. T. Arnold ("Rolls Series," Vol. LXXIV [London, 1879]), p. 207; William of Malmesbury, *Gesta pontificum Anglorum*, ed. N. E. S. A. Hamilton ("Rolls Series," Vol. LII [London, 1870]), p. 197. These accounts vary in detail.

[56] G. Grupp, *Kulturgeschichte des Mittelalters* (Paderborn, 1923), II, 213.

sponsibilities of a secular sort. St. Paul was carried up into the third heaven; but he also took a collection for the necessity of the saints. Bishops were early intrusted with church funds, and, in an age in which wealth was mainly in land, bishops would of necessity have to administer landed estates and to expose themselves to all the entanglements involved in that function. If prelates of feudal times had been as propertyless as the Apostles, the church might have perished as a folk institution. Monasticism, the special nursery of sainthood, was not less inevitably caught in the feudal network. The monastery, however spiritual the motives on which it rose, represented so many mouths to feed. "We are Gauls and not angels," said Martin's monks in protest against his overascetic regime. Those responsible for a monastery were bound to seek for it guaranties of economic security. Such guaranties could only be sought in feudal contracts and royal privileges. It was hardly to be expected that kings and barons would enter upon contracts framed primarily for the spiritual advantage of the monastery.

The damage suffered by the church was grave and almost irreparable. Yet, beneath the worldliness and the barbarity, the splendor and the shame of the feudal church, real Christianity survived. Monks with a conscience often sought escape from cloister conditions intolerable to spiritual men. Cluny gave new vigor to the ascetic life and challenged the forces of secularism in the church; and Cluny was only the most successful of many fresh starts in monastic religion. The torch of learning burned low; but there were a few who cherished the works of the Church Fathers and sought even beyond them the classical writings on which the minds of the Fathers were nourished. Misguided men attempted to support the faith by fraud. The very framers of the Forged Decretals, on any tenable theory of the origin of these fabrications, must have had beyond their own special interests some deep concern for the deliverance of the church from secular domination and all its attendant abuses. One interesting phase of the situation is the lofty note often struck in the decisions of church councils. These good resolutions were, as a rule, pathetically far from all possibility of fulfilment; and they received assent from prelates and abbots who were deeply involved in the practices they denounced. They constitute a record of those ideals for the church to which all inertly subscribed; and a more sincere and aggressive generation of churchmen would utilize them as a basis of action. The social implications of Christianity were stressed by numerous writers. The peace movement of the eleventh century was regarded both by its clerical leaders and by its lay supporters as a natural expression of their religion. Some there were, indeed, who with a sort of spiritual utopianism, anticipated a fundamental renewal of humanity (*renovatio mundi*) under the leadership of Rome.[57]

The Roman see long disappointed these wistful hopes. Under the sway of a greedy and depraved aristocracy it descended into an abyss of corruption. At length, however, after its restoration to decency through the intervention of a German king, the spirit of reform found incarnation in a pope. The accumulated resentment of the church for a long series of outrages found vent in the wrath of Hildebrand.[58]

[57] J. T. McNeill, *Christian Hope for World Society* (Chicago, 1937), pp. 31–48.

[58] Considerations of space exclude discussion of royal immunities and of papal exemptions. See H. Leclercq's articles, "Exemption monastique" and "Immunité," in Cabrol, *Dictionnaire*, V, 952–62, and VI, i, 323–90, respectively; and H. Claus, *Untersuchung der Wahlprivilegien der deutschen Könige und Kaiser für die Klosterwahl . . . . bis zum Jahre 1024* (Greifswald, 1911), pp. 14 ff., 102.

ARISTOTELIANISM IN WESTERN CHRISTIANITY

University of Chicago

THE influence of Aristotle, like that of other philosophers whose works have been the subject of prolonged discussion, has had a varied history. Sometimes it consists in the positive effect of doctrines Aristotle held or of doctrines attributed to him, sometimes in the reaction against his peculiar methods and conclusions, sometimes in a general disapprobation of philosophy and of his doctrines as examples of philosophic error. The issues, moreover, to which the methods of the Aristotelian philosophy are applied are often problems to which Aristotle gave no consideration or which he mentioned only in passing; the statements quoted from him are often interpreted in applications far removed from the contexts in which they originally appeared; and, conversely, his position is sometimes restated by writers who make no mention of his name or who profess to oppose his philosophy. The complexity of the disputes that attended the introduction of the principles, methods, and conclusions of the Aristotelian philosophy into the discussion of Christian tenets and doctrines in the West discloses the wide variety of meanings and associations attached to that philosophy at different times and by different men: these diversifications are due in part to the varying information concerning the character and contents of Aristotle's works, slight until the thirteenth century, at which time the concentrated labors of a hundred years of translation had rendered the major part of the writings of Aristotle into intelligible Latin; in part they are due to the different settings in which his influence was exerted and which determined the interpretation of such of his doctrines as were available.

206

The judgment of Aristotle which was at once the earliest and most persistent marked him, together with other philosophers, for blanket condemnation in the name of the Christian religion: this denunciation, made by the Apologists and the writers of the Patristic period, appeared recurrently during the course of the Middle Ages, emerged as one of the dominant notes of the reaction against scholasticism during the Renaissance and Reformation, and is rediscovered in the religious writers of every century thereafter. On the other hand, during the fourth and fifth centuries after Christ the main lines of a religious philosophy had been constituted, largely through the powerful influence of Augustine, out of materials of a Platonic or Neo-Platonic origin or on which a Platonic stamp had been set; in that systematization Aristotle figured as a philosopher secondary to Plato, with whom, however, he was in fundamental agreement, and a single true philosophy was shown to emerge from the joint efforts of the two philosophers. Finally in the thirteenth century the suspicion that had been voiced from time to time in the preceding centuries, that Aristotle was in radical disagreement with Plato, received convincing documentation, and the strenuous efforts to recover the truth of his position were also turned to the constitution of a philosophy not only distinct from that of Plato but independent of, though not contrary to, theology. Three strands of the shifting significances may thus be separated in the medieval discussions of the Aristotelian philosophy: (1) the Aristotle who figures in the tradition in which philosophy is opposed as such to religion; (2) the Aristotle of the tradition in which the Platonic philosophy is thought to be in substantial agreement with, or useful preparation for, the whole of Christian thought and Aristotle to be in agreement with Plato; and (3) the Aristotle whose philosophy is thought to be in fundamental opposition to Plato though, according to his defenders, consistent with Christianity. The controversies that arise in the first tradition involve the opposition of a religion to philosophy; those of the second turn on the reduction of one philosophy to another; those, finally, of the third revive an opposition of arguments reminiscent of the refu-

tations used by Aristotle himself against Plato or those used by
Plotinus against Aristotle in his re-estimations of the relation
between Plato and Aristotle.

Aristotle was one of the frequent examples in the primitive
Christian criticism of the vanity and arrogance of intellectual
inquiry. Distrust of Aristotle and other philosophers went back
for authoritative justification to the warnings in the New Testament against philosophy and vain deceit after the tradition of
men and not after Christ,[1] against questionings and disputes of
words,[2] against the profane babblings and oppositions of the
knowledge which is falsely so called,[3] against wordy and profit-
less disputations that subvert them that hear.[4] Many of the
Apologists, Greek and Latin, had taken the hint from these
passages to seek the source of heresies in the doctrines of the
pagan philosophers.[5] The resultant disapprobation is directed

---

[1] Col. 2:8.   [2] I Tim. 6:4.   [3] *Ibid.* 20.   [4] II Tim. 2:14.

[5] Cf. Irenaeus (who distinguishes Aristotelians from the rest only by their interest in
minute and subtle questions) *Contra haereses* ii. 14. 2–6 (*Patrologia Graeca* [henceforth
cited as *PG*], VII, 750–54) (cf. Aristotle's doctrine concerning the use of demons by men
[*PG*, VII, 1272]); Hippolytus of Rome (who derives the error of Basilides from Aristotle)
Refutatio omnium haeresium vii. 15–19 (ed. P. Wendland [Leipzig, 1916], pp. 191–95);
Epiphanius (who associates the Peripatetics with the Pythagoreans as the source of a
single heresy) *Adversus haereses* i. 1. haeres. VII, and *Rescriptum ad Acacium et Paulum*
(*PG*, XLI, 205 and 168); Gregory of Nyssa (who derives the impiety of Aetius from
Aristotle's κακοτεχνία) *Contra Eunomium* i (*PG*, XLV, 265). Sometimes the attack was
not upon all philosophy but upon certain of the doctrines of some philosophers: thus
Clement of Alexandria thought that philosophy was divinely given and might properly
be used by a Christian (*Stromata* i. 4 [*PG*, VIII, 716–17]), that it is a preparation for
Christ and a handmaiden of theology (*ibid.* i. 5 [*PG*, VIII, 717–28]), provided no one philosophy is followed but an eclectic choice is made from all (*ibid.* i. 7 [*PG*, VIII, 732–36]),
that Paul's warnings are not against all philosophies, but against those according to the
tradition of men, particularly the Epicurean and the Stoic, and that philosophers are
children unless made men by Christ (*ibid.* i. 11 [*PG*, VIII, 748–52]). By an ironic trick
of history these attempts to associate all or some specified philosophic sects with early
heresies have become valuable sources of information concerning the doctrines held by
or attributed to Greek philosophers. The doctrines attributed to Aristotle assumed
in repetition a fixed form. According to Hippolytus of Rome, Aristotle thought the
elements of all things were substance and accident; he differed from Plato in considering
the soul to be mortal and to be constituted of the fifth body (more subtle than earth, air,
fire, or water); he held that there are three kinds of goods (not one, as Plato thought):
external goods, goods of the body, and goods of the soul; that evils exist only below the
moon; that the world-soul and the world itself are eternal (*Refutatio omnium haeresium*
i. 20 [pp. 24–25]). On the other hand, Aristotle's influence on the heresy of Basilides
reduces almost entirely to the fact that he divided substance into three kinds: genus,
species, and individual (*ibid.* vii. 1. 15 [pp. 191 ff.]). Irenaeus introduces the three

largely against the method of philosophy, and Aristotle is criticized primarily for his logic long before the fifth century after Christ, when philosophers who read Greek became rare in the West and the *Organon* came to be the only work of Aristotle which could be consulted even in part. Tertullian, who had written in Greek before he turned to Latin, thought philosophy the cause of heresies and distinguished Aristotle from other philosophers in that he taught the heretics dialectic and furnished them with the instrument for constructing and destroying conjectures, contentions, arguments, sophisms.[6] Ambrose, who read Greek, argued that it had not pleased God to save his people by dialectic, which is suited to destroy, not to construct:[7] all the force of impiety is derived from philosophy, but

"principles" that were long to be attributed to Plato, matter, "exemplum," and God, but in the context of a discussion of matter in the philosophies of Epicurus, Democritus, Anaxagoras, Empedocles, and the Stoics, without explicit differentiation from the "principles" of Aristotle (*Contra haereses* ii. 14. 3–5 [*PG*, VII, 751–52]). Clement of Alexandria lists Aristotle with other philosophers, the Stoics, Plato, Pythagoras, who thought there was more than one principle and who included matter among the principles (*Stromata* v. 14 [*PG*, IX, 132]). Origen repeats the criticism of Aristotle's doctrine concerning Providence, adding, however, that to restrict the extent of providence is less irreligious than to deny it entirely as did Epicurus (*Contra Celsum* i. 21 [*PG*, XI, 696–97]); moreover, Aristotle thought the soul was made of ether, a doctrine that the Platonists and Stoics combatted (*ibid.* iv. 56 [*PG*, XI, 1122]). Eusebius, quoting in great detail from Atticus the Platonist and also from Plotinus and Porphyry, repeats arguments derived from Plato and Moses against the Aristotelian analysis of morals, providence, the origin of the world, the fifth body, astronomy, the immortality of the soul, the world-soul, and Ideas (*Praeparatio evangelica* xv. 3–13 [*PG*, XXI, 1301–41]). Epiphanius criticizes Aristotle for setting up two principles: God and matter; for thinking that divine providence governs things above the moon but does not extend to sublunar things, which were made without reason; for distinguishing two worlds, a superior incorruptible and a lower corruptible; for defining the soul as the entelechy of the body, that is, "continuous and perpetual motion" (*Adversus haereses* iii. 2. 10 [*PG*, XLII, 796]). Cyril of Alexandria quotes Plutarch to show that Aristotle thought Providence extended only to the moon and that God was not the principle of the universe, notwithstanding that Plato thought there were three principles: God, matter, and Ideas (*Contra Julianum* ii [*PG*, LXXVI, 572–73]). Theodoret is careful to contrast the three "principles" of Plato—God, matter, and Ideas—with the three "principles" of Aristotle— matter, form, and privation (*Graecarum affectionum curatio* iv [*PG*, LXXXIII, 901]); moreover, according to Aristotle, providence extends only to the moon (*ibid.* v and vi [*PG*, LXXXIII, 940–41 and 957]) and the soul is mortal (*ibid.* v [*PG*, LXXXIII, 940]). Much the same doctrines are attached to the name of Aristotle when philosophers of the West discuss his relation to Christianity; see below, nn. 67 and 68.

[6] *Liber de praescriptionibus adversus haereticos* 7 (*Patrologia Latina* [cited henceforth as *PL*], II, 22–23).

[7] *De fide* i. 5. 42 (*PL*, XVI, 559).

its arguments have become ineffective since fishermen are believed rather than philosophers, publicans rather than dialecticians;[8] there is a fundamental opposition between the words of
philosophers and the simple truths of fishermen.[9] Jerome, with
wider erudition and greater linguistic powers, treats Aristotle
as the prince of dialecticians who are engaged in syllogistic disputations which Christians should flee;[10] he contrasts Aristotle
in that role of prince to Paul, the prince of the Apostles;[11]
Aristotle is the source of the arguments of the Arians,[12] but
fortunately neither Plato nor Aristotle is any longer read, for
the words of simple fishermen have drowned out the disputes
of dialecticians, and the wisdom of the world has resulted only
in heresies.[13] St. Bernard, in the twelfth century, contrasts the
subtleties and ingenuities of Plato and Aristotle to the science
of life and rejoices in the example of the Apostles who were
ignorant of the liberal arts;[14] Martin Luther in the sixteenth
century is convinced not merely that the metaphysics, physics,
and morals of Aristotle are false but that logic is inconsistent
with theology and that the syllogistic form does not hold in
divine matters;[15] and it would be possible to fill in the centuries

[8] *Ibid.* i. 13. 84–85 (*PL*, XVI, 570–71).

[9] *De incarnationis dominicae sacramento* 9. 89 (*PL*, XVI, 876). Cf. *De officiis minis-
trorum* i. 13. 48–50 (*PL*, XVI, 41–42) for a criticism of the doctrine of providence
ascribed to Aristotle.

[10] *Commentariorum in epistolam ad Titum liber* iii (*PL*, XXVI, 631).

[11] *Dialogus contra Pelagianos* i. 14 (*PL*, XXIII, 529).

[12] *Dialogus contra Luciferianos* 11 (*PL*, XXIII, 174).

[13] *Commentariorum in epistolam ad Galatas liber* iii. 5 (*PL*, XXVI, 428).

[14] *Sermo III in festo Pentecostes* 5 (*PL*, CLXXXIII, 332); *Sermo I in festo SS. Petri
et Pauli Apostolorum* 3 (*PL*, CLXXXIII, 407); *Sermo XXXVI in Cantica Canticorum*
(*PL*, CLXXXIII, 967). Cf. G. de Ghellinck, "Dialectique et dogme au Xe–XIIe
siècles," in *Beiträge zur Geschichte der Philosophie des Mittelalters* (cited henceforth as
BGPM) (Münster, 1913), Supplement Band I, pp. 79–99. J. A. Endres cites many
such antidialectical pronouncements in "Forschungen zur Geschichte der frühmittel-
alterlichen Philosophie," *BGPM*, Band XVII, Heft 2–3.

[15] *Disputatio contra scholasticam theologiam* (*D. Martin Luthers Werke* [Weimar,
1883], I, 221 ff.). Propositions 41–53 (p. 226) are directed specifically against Aristotle
and the Scholastic understanding of Aristotle: "45. Theologus non-logicus est mon-
strosus haereticus, Est monstrosa et haeretica oratio. Contra dictum commune.
46. Nulla forma syllogistica tenet in terminis divinis. Contra recen. Dialect . . . ."

with the numerous writers who are suspicious of dialectic, most of whom illustrate its errors by reference to the name of Aristotle.

If scriptural authority could be found for abandoning the philosophy of the world and the works of the Gentiles, no less urgent directions could be cited from the same source by writers who thought it necessary that Christians render reason for the faith that was in them[16] and proper that they make use of the implements provided them by the work of the pagans, much as the chosen people had appropriated the possessions of the Egyptians,[17] or as Moses was instructed in all the wisdom of the Egyptians,[18] and Daniel had knowledge and skill in all learning and wisdom including that of the Chaldeans.[19] Augustine urged on such grounds the appropriation as from unjust possessors of all statements of the philosophers, particularly of the Platonists, that were true and suited to the Christian faith.[20] Aristotle was included in that judgment, although he was not Plato's equal in eloquence and although the glory of Plato obscured that of other philosophers,[21] for in all important points, in erudition, in doctrine, and in the morals counseled in their philosophies, Plato and Aristotle were in agreement, notwithstanding that they might seem at variance to the unlearned or the inattentive, since their works have led after centuries of disputes among

---

50. Breviter, Totus Aristoteles ad theologiam est tenebrae ad lucem. Contra schol.
51. Dubium est vehemens, An sententia Aristotelis sit apud latinos." Cf. Luther's letter to John Lang of November 11, 1517 (*D. Martin Luthers Werke. Briefwechsel* [Weimar, 1930], I, 121–22), which was sent with the theses and which comments upon them. "Cur enim Christus et omnes martyres occisi sunt? cur doctores passi invidiam? nisi scilicet, quia superbi et contemptores veteris et inclytae sapientiae seu prudentiae visi sunt, aut quod talia nova sine consilio illorum protulerint, qui vetera sapiebant." For the criticisms directed by Erasmus and Luther against syllogistic philosophy, see R. McKeon, "Renaissance and Method," in *Studies in the History of Ideas*, III (New York, 1935), 71 ff.

[16] I Pet. 3:15.   [18] Acts 7:22.

[17] Exod. 3:22; 12:35–36.   [19] Dan. 1:4, 17.

[20] *De doctrina Christiana* ii. 40. 60–61 (*PL*, XXXIV, 63). The argument used by Augustine appears in the works of many Christian writers, among others Jerome, Cassiodorus, Isidore of Seville, Alcuin.

[21] *De civitate Dei* viii. 4 and 12 (*PL*, XLI, 227–28 and 237).

wise and acute men to the single discipline of the most true philosophy.[22] Dialectic, furthermore, was useful for the understanding of the Scriptures and for the refutation of heretics.[23] The philosophy of Plato was not far removed from the Christian truth, since Plato had contended that truth is perceived not by the eyes of the body but by the pure mind,[24] and he had distinguished the intelligible from the sensible world, the world of being from the world of change.[25] Yet Augustine, adapting that Platonic distinction, could make use of scriptural citation to reverse the proportion between knowledge and belief. Since the invisible things of God are made manifest and are perceived through the things that are made,[26] and faith is the substance of things hoped for, the argument of things unseen,[27] the invisible and changeless things of God, are in this life the object of belief, whereas Plato on the contrary thought the changing to be the object of belief and the eternal to be intelligible.[28] For Augustine faith is the beginning of knowledge: we believe in order that we may understand, and truth consists in seeing what was previously believed.[29]

Secondary information and simple or imaginative popularizations were long the sources of many of the doctrines referred to Plato and Aristotle and the bases of most of the generalizations and judgments pronounced on those philosophers. Throughout the Middle Ages Cicero, Seneca, Apuleius, Macrobius, Chalcidius, and Augustine were the chief sources of Platonism until a more learned tradition returned, not at first to Plato himself

[22] Contra academicos iii. 19. 42 (PL, XXXII, 956).

[23] De doctrina Christiana ii. 31, 48 to 47, 55 (PL, XXXIV, 57–61).

[24] De vera religione iii. 3 (PL, XXXIV, 124). Cf. De civitate Dei viii. 5 (PL, XLI, 229–30).

[25] De civitate Dei viii. 6 (PL, XLI, 231).   [27] Heb. 11:1.

[26] Rom. 1:19–20.   [28] Timaeus 29C; Republic vi. 508C.

[29] De trinitate ix. 1 (PL, XLII, 961): "Certa enim fides utcumque incohat cognitionem: cognitio vero certa non perficietur, nisi post hanc vitam, cum videbimus facie ad faciem." In Joannis evangelium: "Non quia cognoverunt crediderint, sed ut cognoscerent crediderunt. Credimus enim ut cognoscamus, non cognoscimus ut credamus. Quod enim cognituri sumus, nec oculus vidit, nec auris audivit, nec in cor hominis ascendi (Isai. 64:4; I Cor. 2:9). Quid est enim fides nisi credere quod non vides? Fides ergo est, quod non vides credere; veritas, quod credidisti videre."

but to the works of the Greek Christian Neo-Platonists. Similarly at the time of the Carolingian Renaissance the "Aristotelian" logic seems to have been studied primarily in the *Dialectica* and the *Ten Categories* wrongly attributed to Augustine or in the section descriptive of dialectic in the *Marriage of Mercury and Philology* of Martianus Capella. But even the small portion of Aristotle's work that became part of the Western intellectual tradition was placed in a Platonic setting. It had been the plan of Boethius to translate all the works of Aristotle and prepare commentaries on them, to translate all the dialogues of Plato and furnish them with commentaries; moreover, he "would not disdain to recall the doctrines of Aristotle and Plato into some sort of single concord," and he would show that "they did not disagree in all doctrines as they did in many, but that they were in accord in many doctrines of the greatest importance in philosophy."[30] "Philosophy" herself, in the pages of Boethius, refers to both "our Plato" and "my Aristotle,"[31] but notwithstanding his detailed use of distinctions drawn from the *Organon*, as in the *De trinitate*, the theological works of Boethius no less than the *Consolation of Philosophy* belong in the tradition of Platonism. Although there is a persistent report in the thirteenth century that Boethius had translated the whole of the logic of Aristotle as well as the *Physics*, *Metaphysics*, and *De anima*, only the first two books of the *Organon* seem to have been known prior to the twelfth century.[32] The *Categories* and the *De interpretatione*, together with the *Isagoge* or *Introduction* which Porphyry had prepared for the *Categories*, constituted the "Old Logic," and these together with Boethius' commentary on the *Topics* of Cicero, and his essays on division, on topical differences, and on categorical and hypothetical syllo-

---

[30] *In librum de interpretatione*, editio secunda II (*PL*, LXIV, 433).

[31] *De consolatione philosophiae* i, prosa 3; v, prosa 1 (*PL*, LXIII, 606, 831).

[32] For the discussion of the translations of Boethius see P. Mandonnet, *Siger de Brabant et l'averroïsme latin au xiiime siècle* (2me ed.; Louvain, 1911), Ire Partie, pp. 7–11. C. H. Haskins argues that Boethius' translation of the *Posterior Analytics* has been preserved, although it did not return to use until the twelfth century ("Versions of Aristotle's *Posterior Analytics*," in *Studies in the History of Mediaeval Science* [Cambridge, Mass., 1924], pp. 231 ff.).

gisms constituted the basic erudition in dialectic. As Plato is modified in subordination to the new faith, the Aristotelian logic is modified by the Neo-Platonic *Introduction* of Porphyry, which became an inseparable part of the *Organon* during the Middle Ages, for whereas Aristotle thought that dialectical demonstration, which he treated in the *Topics*, is subordinate to scientific demonstration, Porphyry took the materials of his introduction from the *Topics*, and the dialectical formulation which resulted had the effect of restating the Aristotelian logic in terms that resembled the dialectic of Plato. Boethius recognized the existence of a difference between Plato and Aristotle, but even in considering Porphyry's questions concerning universals, his justification for what he considered an Aristotelian answer, which was to be repeated often in the Middle Ages, was simply that Aristotle had written the book from which the problem arose.

> Plato, however, thinks that genera and species and the rest not only are understood as universals, but also are and subsist without bodies; whereas Aristotle thinks that they are understood as incorporeal and universal, but subsist in sensibles; we have not considered it proper to determine between their opinions, for that is of more lofty philosophy. But we have followed out the opinion of Aristotle very diligently for this reason, not in the least because we approve of it, but because this book has been written for the *Categories*, of which Aristotle is the author.[33]

The influence of Aristotle and that of Plato was only slowly, even in the case of writers who esteemed them, brought to a form that can be traced directly to the works of those philosophers. John Scotus Eriugena, although he considered Plato "the greatest philosopher in the world,"[34] and although his philosophic discrimination was acute enough to earn him an important place in the history of Neo-Platonism and his knowledge of Greek good enough to enable him to translate the works of the pseudo-Dionysius the Areopagite and Maximus the Con-

---

[33] *Commentaria in Porphyrium a se translatum* i (*PL*, LXIV, 86). Cf. R. McKeon, *Selections from Medieval Philosophers* (New York, 1929), I, 98; Boethius, *In topica Ciceronis commentaria* iii (*PL*, LXIV, 1106).

[34] "Plato . . . . philosophantium de mundo maximus" (*De divisione naturae* i. 31 [*PL*, CXXII, 476C]); "Plato . . . . philosophorum summus" (*ibid*. iii. 36 [*PL*, CXXII, 728A]).

fessor and to amass a considerable erudition in the works of
Gregory of Nyssa, seems to have known none of the works of
Plato except the fifty-three "chapters" of the *Timaeus* available
in the fourth-century translation of Chalcidius. Likewise, although he thought Aristotle "the most acute discoverer of the
distinctions of natural things,"[35] he reduced the categories,
which Aristotle considered irreducible *summa genera,* first to
"superior genera,"[36] and then, in good Neo-Platonic fashion, to
each other.[37] Gerbert in the tenth century revolutionized the
curriculum of the schools by returning to the works of earlier
writers, in dialectic to the translations and essays of Boethius.
As late as the twelfth century, Peter Abailard, known to his
contemporaries as the "Palatine Peripatetic,"[38] seems to have
the traditional conception of the relation of Aristotle to Plato
and to have little erudition in Aristotle's works beyond the
contents of the Old Logic. He speaks of Plato as the greatest
of philosophers[39] and seems to have considered Aristotle primarily as a logician, "the prince of peripatetics, that is of dialecticians."[40] He professes to have read the *Sophisticis elenchis*

[35] "Aristoteles acutissimus apud Graecos, ut aiunt, naturalium rerum discretionis
repertor" (*ibid.* i. 14 [*PL*, CXXII, 462D–463A]). Although Eriugena seems to describe
Aristotle as a physical philosopher, the distinctions referred to are those of the ten
categories.

[36] "Ut scias plane, decem genera praedicta aliis duobus superioribus generalioribus-
que comprehendi, motu scilicet atque statu, quae iterum generalissimo colliguntur
genere, quod a Graecis τὸ πᾶν, a nostris vero universitas appellari consuevit" (*ibid.*i.22
[*PL*, CXXII, 469B]).

[37] "Et quoniam video, omnes fere categorias inter se invicem concatenatas, ut vix
a se invicem certa ratione discerni possint; omnes enim omnibus, ut video, insertae
sunt: in qua proprietate singula quaeque inveniri valeant, aperias flagito" (*ibid.* i. 26
[*PL*, CXXII, 472C]).

[38] "Peripateticus Palatinus Abaelardus noster . . . ." (John of Salisbury *Metalogicon*
ii. 17 [ed. C. C. J. Webb (Oxford, 1929)], p. 92 [874c]). "Peripateticus Palatinus, qui
logice opinionem preripuit omnibus coetaneis suis, adeo ut solus Aristotilis crederetur
usus colloquio" (*ibid.* i. 5 [p. 17 (832B)]). Cf. *ibid.*, pp. 78, 120, 136, 144.

[39] ". . . . ille maximus philosophorum Plato . . . . qui testimonio sanctorum Patrum
prae caeteris gentium philosophis fidei Christianae accedentes . . . ." (*Introductio ad
theologiam* i. 17 [*PL*, CLXXVIII, 1012]).

[40] ". . . . Peripateticorum, id est dialecticorum princeps . . . ." (*ibid.* iii. 7 [*PL*,
CLXXVIII, 1112]). Cf. "Peripateticos autem dialecticos seu quoslibet argumentatores
appellat [*sc.* Porphyrius]," *Glossae super Porphyrium*, Vol. I: *Die Logica "Ingredienti-
bus" (Peter Abaelards philosophische Schriften*, ed. B. Geyer, *BGPM*, Band XXI [1919]),
p. 8; McKeon, *Selections from Medieval Philosophers*, I, 220.

and he quotes from the *Prior Analytics*, but his conception of Aristotelianism and of logic is derived almost wholly from Boethius[41] and from the first two books of the *Organon*. He has little difficulty reconciling Plato and Aristotle on the problem of the universal, for what "Aristotle denies with respect to actuality, Plato, the investigator of physics, assigns to natural aptitude, and thus there is no disagreement between them."[42] Throughout the twelfth and the early thirteenth centuries when the works of Aristotle, first the *Organon*, then one by one other works, were translated and interpreted, the fortune of Aristotle continued to be advanced by men whose philosophic doctrines were Platonic. John of Salisbury, a pupil of Peter Abailard, who makes use of the whole of the *Organon*, although he finds the *Posterior Analytics* too difficult for all except a few minds,[43] reports that Bernard of Chartres, whom he calls the most per-

---

[41] "Memini tamen quendam libellum vidisse et diligenter relegisse, qui sub nomine Aristotelis de sophisticis elenchis intitulatus erat, et cum inter cetera sophismatum genera de univocatione requirerem, nil de ea scriptum inveni" (*Glossae super Periermenias, BGPM*, XXI, 400). Yet the only explicit citations he makes from that work (*ibid.*, pp. 400 and 489) would not require either wide or frequent reading, and he is not accurately informed concerning the contents of the *Prior* and *Posterior Analytics*, although he quotes occasionally from the former. For Abailard's knowledge of the New Logic see B. Geyer, "Die alten lateinischen Uebersetzungen der Aristotelischen Analytik, Topik und Elenchik," in *Philosophisches Jahrbuch*, XXX (1917), 25-43; J. C. Sikes, *Peter Abailard* (Cambridge, 1932), Appen. II: "The Aristotelian Translations Known to Abailard," pp. 272-75. Whether or not his own familiarity with Aristotle extended further, Abailard reports that his contemporaries knew only the *Categories* and the *De interpretatione*. "Sunt autem tres quorum septem codicibus omnis in hac arte eloquentia latina armatur, Aristotelis enim duos tantum, Praedicamentorum scilicet et Peri ermenias libros usus adhuc latinorum cognovit; Porphyrii vero unum, quid videlicet de Quinque vocibus conscriptus, genere scilicet, specie, differentia, proprio et accidente, introductionem ad ipsa praeparat praedicamenta; Boethii autem quatuor in consuetudinem duximus libros, videlicet Divisionum et Topicorum cum syllogismis tam Categoricis quam Hypotheticis" (*Dialectica*, pars secunda, analytica prior i [*Ouvrages inédits d'Abélard*, ed. V. Cousin (Paris, 1836)], pp. 228-29; cf. p. xxviii.)—". . . . de Ubi quidem ac Quando, ipso attestante Boethio, in Physicis, de omnibusque altius subtiliusque in his libris quos Metaphysica vocat, exequitur. Quae quidem opera ipsius nullus adhuc translator latinae linguae aptavit; ideoque minus natura horum nobis est cognita" (*ibid.*, pars. prima, lib. ii *in praedicamenta*, p. 22; cf. p. xlvi).

[42] *Glossae super Porphyrium, BGPM*, XXI, 24; McKeon, *Selections from Medieval Philosophers*, I, 244.

[43] *Metalogicon* iv. 6 (pp. 170-71 [919C-20A]).

fect Platonist of his times,[44] and his followers tried to bring Aristotle and Plato together, but John adds that in his judgment they came too late and labored in vain to reconcile men, when dead, who had disagreed as long as they were alive.[45] Gilbert de la Porrée held "almost the same doctrine" of Platonic Ideas,[46] but seems to have invented, "to express Aristotle," the term *forma nativa* to distinguish the *exemplum* existing in things from the idea in God's mind which it reflects.[47] This same Chartrain Platonism enters subtly into the *Book of the Six Principles*, in which Gilbert treats the last six categories, since to his mind Aristotle dealt adequately with only the first four. That work, together with the *Isagoge* of Porphyry, became an integral part of the *Organon* in medieval manuscripts and was frequently the subject of commentary by medieval philosophers. Thierry of Chartres, the younger brother of Bernard, author of the *De sex dierum operibus* which combines the cosmological ideas of Genesis with those of the *Timaeus*, made early use of the New Logic, for he included the first book of the *Prior Analytics*, the *Topics* and the *De sophisticis elenchis* in the preparation of his *Heptateuchon* about 1141.[48] John of Salisbury satirizes these attempts of his contemporaries to interpret Aristotle in Platonic

---

[44] "Bernardus quoque Carnotenis, perfectissimus inter Platonicos seculi nostri . . . ." (*ibid.* iv. 35 [p. 205 (9380)]). "Ille [Guaterus de Mauretania] ideas ponit, Platonem emulatus et imitans Bernardum Carnotensem . . . ." (*ibid.* ii. 17 [p. 93 (875A)]). Some indication of the source of the Platonism of the century is furnished by his definition of Ideas in Seneca's words: "Est autem idea, sicut Seneca diffinit, eorum que natura fiunt exemplar eternum," and Augustine is cited to clarify the concept.

[45] Egerunt operosius Bernardus Carnotensis et auditores eius ut componerent inter Aristotilem et Platonem, sed eos tarde uenisse arbitror et laborasse in uanam ut reconciliarent mortuos qui, quamdiu in uita licuit, dissenserunt" (*ibid.* ii. 17 [p. 94 (875D)]). Cf. *ibid.* iv. 35 (p. 206 [939A]) for an example of Bernard's Platonism derived from his "exposition of Porphyry." For medieval judgments of Aristotle and of the relation between Plato and Aristotle see M. Grabmann, "Der Einfluss des heiligen Augustinus auf die Verwertung und Bewertung der Antike im Mittelalter" and "Aristoteles im Werturteil des Mittelalters," in *Mittelalterliches Geistesleben* II (Munich, 1936), 20 ff. and 71 ff. See also A. Schneider, *Die abendländische Spekulation des zwölften Jahrhunderts in ihrem Verhältnis zur Aristotelischen und jüdisch-arabischen Philosophie*, BGPM, Band XVII, Heft 4 (Münster, 1915).

[46] *Metalogicon* iv. 35 (p. 205 [938B–C]).   [47] *Ibid.* ii. 17 (pp. 94–95 [875D]).

[48] A. Clerval, *Les Ecoles de Chartres au moyen âge du ve au xvie siècle* (Chartres, 1895), pp. 222–23.

terms: all profess to follow Aristotle, but in an effort to make him clearer, they teach the doctrine of Plato or an erroneous opinion which deviates with equal error from the doctrines of Aristotle and those of Plato;[49] what these Platonizing thinkers promise is well known to philosophers who contemplate lofty things, but, as Boethius and many others attest, wholly alien to the doctrine of Aristotle.[50] Yet John repeats as his own the old judgments of the relative positions of the two philosophers in almost the words in which they had previously been expressed,[51] and he thinks of Aristotle primarily as a dialectician, though pre-eminent, to be sure, so that all dialecticians—

[49] "Postremo quod, quasi ab aduerso pectentes, ueniunt contra mentem auctoris et, ut Aristotiles planior sit, Platonis sententiam docent aut erroneam opinionem, que equo errore deuiat a sententia Aristotilis et Platonis; siquidem omnes Aristotilem profitentur" (Metalogicon ii. 19 [p. 97 (877A)]). Cf. "Qui autem ea [sc. universalia] esse statuit, Aristotili aduersatur" (ibid. 20 [p. 98 (877C)]).

[50] "Magnum profecto est et notum philosophis contemplantibus altiora quod isti pollicentur; sed, sicut Boetius et alii multi testantur auctores, a sententia Aristotilis penitus alienum est" (ibid. 17 [p. 94 (875D)]). Yet John's insistence on holding to the Aristotelian rather than the Platonic interpretation is, somewhat like the similar insistence of Boethius, based not on the truth of the doctrine but on the relation of the peripatetic tradition to logic. "Unde licet Plato cetum philosophorum grandem et tam Augustinum quam alios plures nostrorum in statuendis ideis habet assertores, ipsius tamen dogma in scrutinio uniuersalium nequaquam sequimur; eo quod hic Peripateticorum principem Aristotilem dogmatis huius principem profitemur. Magnum quidem est et, quod Boetius in secundo commento super Porphirium nimis arduum fatetur tantorum uirorum diiudicare sententias; sed ei qui Peripateticorum libros aggreditur, magis Aristotilis sententia sequenda est; forte non quia uerior, sed plane quia his disciplinis magis accomoda est. Ab hac autem longissime uidentur abcedere tam illi qui genera et species uoces esse constituunt aut sermones, quam alii qui premissis de rerum inuestigatione opinionibus distrahuntur. Et quidem omnes ab Aristotile puerilius aut stolidius euagantur quam Platonici, cuius sententiam agnoscere dedignantur" (ibid. 20 [pp. 115-16 (888B-C)]).

[51] "Sed cum ei [sc. Platoni, principi philosophorum] Aristotiles discipulus, uir excellentis ingenii et Platoni impar eloquio sed multos facile superans, in docendi officium successisset . . . ." (Policraticus vii. 6 [ed. C. C. J. Webb (Oxford, 1909)], II, 111-12 [647C]). Cf. ". . . . ut cum Aristoteles, Platonis discipulus, vir excellentis ingenii, et eloquio quidem Platoni impar, sed multos facile superans, sectam Peripateticam condidisset" (Augustine De civitate Dei viii. 12 [PL, XLI, 237]). "Licet autem nominum et uerborum turbator habeatur, non modo subtilitate, qua cunctis celebris est, sed et mira suauitate dicendi eualui, adeo quidem ut Platoni merito proximus fuisse uideatur" (Policraticus vii. 6 [II, 113 (648B)]). Cf. ". . . . si quid suo more Aristoteles nominum verborumque turbavit . . . ." (Boethius, De syllogismo categorico i [PL, LXIV, 783]). "Aristoteles longe omnibus—Platonem semper excipio—praestans et ingenio et diligentia . . . ." (Cicero Tusculan disputations i. 10. 22). ". . . . Aristoteles, quem excepto Platone haud scio an recte dixerim principem philosophorum" (Cicero De finibus v. 3. 7).

Apuleius, Cicero, Porphyry, Boethius, Augustine, Eudemus, Alexander of Aphrodisias, Theophrastus—glorify themselves by adoring his footsteps, and *Philosopher,* the common name of them all, is made proper to him.[52]

In the thirteenth century, as translations of Aristotle's works appeared in increasing numbers,[53] disputes arose concerning problems of two fundamentally different kinds. In the first place the increased knowledge of Aristotle gave vastly greater scope to the differences that were suspected between his philosophy and that of Plato; part of the disputation was to the end of distinguishing two philosophies. But in the second place the new Aristotle had come into the West already incased in a Neo-Platonic interpretation which was not always in accord with the Christian Neo-Platonism, since it had been acquired from the labors of Arabic and Hebrew philosophers: part of the disputation was to the end of reducing the new Aristotelianism to a familiar Platonic form. These Neo-Platonic "errors" were often and in various ways incorporated into the Aristotelian philosophy: the translations of Aristotle were difficult and imperfect and frequently contained Platonizing intrusions; inauthentic works like the *Liber de causis* and the *Theologia Aristotelis,* which passed under the name of Aristotle, were excuse for mingling the ideas of Proclus and Plotinus with those of Aristotle; because of the obscurity and defects of the translations there was a tendency to go to secondary sources, like the *Fons vitae* of Avicebron or the *De divisione philosophiae* and the *De immortalitate animae* of Gundissalinus, whence were derived Platonic conceptions of matter, of the soul, of creation, or of the organization of the parts of philosophy; finally a great many

---

[52] *Metalogicon* ii. 16 (p. 90 [873C]); cf. *ibid.* iv. 7 (p. 171 [920A]); *Policraticus* vii. 6 (II, 112 [648A]); *Entheticus de dogmate philosophorum* 827–28 (*PL*, CXCIX, 983B).

[53] For the history of the translation of the works of Aristotle during the twelfth and thirteenth centuries see A. Jourdain, *Recherches critiques sur l'âge et l'origine des traductions latines d'Aristote* (2d ed.; Paris, 1843); Mandonnet, *op. cit.;* M. Grabmann, *Forschungen über die lateinischen Aristotelesübersetzungen des xiii. Jahrhunderts, BGPM,* XVII, Heft 5–6 (Münster, 1916); Haskins, *op. cit.;* Ueberweg-Geyer, *Die patristische und scholastische Philosophie* (11th ed.; Berlin, 1928), pp. 343–51; E. Franceschini, "Aristotele nel mediaevo latino," in *Atti del IX congresso nazionale di filosofia* (Padua, 1935).

philosophic writings, the books of Hebrew philosophers like Avicebron and Maimonides, of Arab philosophers like Alfarabi, Algazeli, Avicenna, and Averroes, of Greek commentators like Eustratius, Michael of Ephesus, Aspasius, Simplicius, Alexander of Aphrodisias, John Philoponos, were translated at the same time as the works of Aristotle and were used to interpret his philosophy and to reconcile it with the Christian religion. Two lines of defense and attack were possible in the disputes that resulted: the Augustinian philosophy might be defended as in accord with faith and Aristotelianism attacked on all points in which it departed from the Augustinian statement, or the Aristotelian philosophy might be defended and Augustinism attacked on some points indifferent to faith, but derived from Plato and so inconsistent with the Aristotelian truth.

This opposition appears equally in the condemnations pronounced on the Aristotelian writings and doctrines during the thirteenth century and in the philosophic disputations which preceded and accompanied those condemnations: on the one hand, an effort was made to involve peripateticism as such in the condemnation of erroneous doctrines, and there was, on the other hand, an effort to dissociate the errors attributed to peripateticism, frequently by showing their Platonic origin, from the doctrines found in the works of Aristotle. When the "reading" of the physical and metaphysical works of Aristotle was first banned at the University of Paris in 1210 and in 1215, those prohibitions were associated with the condemnation of the doctrines of the heretics Amalric of Bène and David of Dinant.[54] In 1270 thirteen propositions were listed for condemnation at the University of Paris without specification of author,[55] but they included doctrines of Aristotle and doctrines which Averroes and other commentators seemed to have derived from Aristotle; and, according to the testimony of Giles of Lessines,

---

[54] *Chartularium universitatis Parisiensis*, Nos. 11 and 20 (ed. H. Denifle and A. Chatelain [Paris, 1889], I, 70–71 and 78–79). For the reception of the writings of Aristotle at the University of Paris see J. Launoy, *De varia Aristotelis in academica Parisiensi fortuna* (3d ed.; Paris, 1662; 4th ed.; Wittemberg, 1722); Mandonnet, *op. cit.*, I, 1–63, and *passim*; Ueberweg-Geyer, *op. cit.*, pp. 350–51.

[55] *Chartularium universitatis Parisiensis*, No. 432 (I, 486–87).

the fifteen propositions of the original list had also included two theses of Thomas Aquinas which had been removed before judgment was pronounced.[56] The 219 propositions condemned in 1277, three years after the death of Thomas Aquinas, were specifically attributed to the Latin Averroists,[57] yet they seem to have been directed against all forms of the peripatetic philosophy, not merely against its Averroistic interpretation.[58] This tendency to combine all new philosophic doctrines in a single condemnation was, however, opposed by equally persistent efforts to separate the various strands. An anonymous treatise once attributed to Giles of Rome lists in detail the errors of various philosophers, and, if these doctrines are compared with the propositions of the condemnation of 1270, only those errors concerning the immortality of the soul and concerning the beginnings of the world and the human race would seem in the judgment of this critic to be attributed properly to Aristotle, while the error concerning the unity of intellect figures on the list of the errors of Averroes.[59]

Both problems, the eternity of the world and the unity of the intellect, are treated frequently in the writings that precede these condemnations. Thomas Aquinas recognized that Aristotle had advanced the doctrine that neither the world nor time had a beginning, but he defended Aristotle against the contemporary Augustinians on the grounds that no demonstrative reasons are conclusive for or against the eternity of the world, and creation is an article of faith; this position Aquinas supports with reasons drawn alike from Gregory the Great, Boethius, Aristotle, Algazeli, Avicenna, and Maimonides.[60] With respect to the doctrine of the unity of the active intellect or that of the unity of the intellective soul, Aquinas argues that

---

[56] Mandonnet, *op. cit.*, Vol. I, chap. v, pp. 106 ff.

[57] *Chartularium universitatis Parisiensis*, No. 472 (I, 542–55).

[58] Mandonnet, *op. cit.*, Vol. I, chap. ix, pp. 218 ff.

[59] *Tractatus de erroribus philosophorum Aristotelis, Averrois, Avicennae, Algazelis, Alkindi et Rabbi Moysis* (Mandonnet, *op. cit.*), ii, 3–10. Cf. M. M. Gorce, *L'Essor de la pensée au moyen âge* (Paris, 1933), pp. 158 ff.

[60] *Scriptum super libros sententiarum* ii, dist. i, q. 1, a. 5. Cf. *Summa theologica* I, q. 46, a. 2, and the opuscule, *De aeternitate mundi contra murmurantes*.

neither thesis is true nor correctly attributable to Aristotle.[61] Moreover, the two heretics who were joined with Aristotle in the condemnations of 1210 and 1215 are related in the analysis of Aquinas not to any part of the Aristotelian philosophy properly understood, but to the doctrine of the world-soul which Aquinas knows as attributed to Varro by Augustine: there are three possible errors concerning the relation of God to the world: (1) that God is the soul of the world (*anima mundi*), (2) that God is, as those who follow Amalric think, the formal principle of all things, and (3) that God was prime matter, as David of Dinant thought.[62] Roger Bacon, who participated in the Franciscan defense of the orthodox Augustinian philosophy, took precisely the opposite position to that of Aquinas, defending the doctrine of the unity of the active intellect but condemning the doctrine of the eternity of the world. According to Bacon, the natural philosophy and metaphysics of Aristotle were condemned at Paris before 1237 because of the doctrine of the eternity of the world and of time and also because the books were erroneously translated,[63] but Bacon held, as he tells us all wise and learned men did, that the active intellect is God.[64]

[61] *Scriptum super libros sententiarum*, ii. dist. 17, q. 2, a. 1. Cf. *Summa theologica* i, q. 76, a. 2 and q. 79, a. 5; *Contra gentiles* ii, cc. 76 and 78; *Quaestiones disputatae de animaa*. 4; *De unitate intellectus contra averroistas parisienses*.

[62] *Summa theologica* i, q. 3, a. 8 concl.

[63] *Fratris Rogeri Bacon compendium studii theologiae* i. 2 (ed. H. Rashdall [Aberdeen, 1911], p. 23). Elsewhere Bacon says that both Aristotle and Avicenna had taught not that the world was eternal without beginning but that it was created *ex nihilo*, although the obscurity of the text of Aristotle, the difficulty of his doctrines, and the imperfection of the translations have introduced contradictions into his doctrine of the eternity of the world (*Metaphysica fratris Rogeri ordinis fratrum minorum, de viciis contractis in studio theologie*, ed. R. Steele [Oxford, n.d.], pp. 10–11). Again in the *Opus majus*, vii. 1 (ed. J. H. Bridges [Oxford, 1897], II, 235) Bacon writes that Aristotle, in common with Albumazar, Avicenna, Ethicus, and Hermes Trismegistus, mentions Adam and Eve in his *De regimine regnorum*, and therefore understood that there was a first man and a beginning to the world.

[64] *Opus majus* ii. 5 (I, 39). Cf. R. McKeon, *Selections from Medieval Philosophers*, II, 29–31. This doctrine of the unity of the active intellect is associated in the thirteenth century with the name of Averroes, but Bacon derives it from Alfarabi, Avicenna, and Aristotle, and cites Augustine to show that it is in accordance with Christian doctrine. Elsewhere (*Communium naturalium fratris Rogeri liber* i, pars iv, dist. 3, c. 3 [ed. Steele (Oxford, 1911), pp. 286–90]) he distinguishes this doctrine of the unity of the active intellect from the Averroistic doctrine of the unity of the intellective soul, and in still another place he explicitly contrasts the statements of Alfarabi and Avicenna to the

According to Bacon, the "moderns" approve of Avicenna, who was the outstanding expositor and the greatest imitator of Aristotle, and of Averroes, whose every statement has obtained the grace of wise men in these times, notwithstanding that Averroes treats some subjects less well than others (*licet in aliquibus dixit minus bene*) and notwithstanding the excommunication, "because of dense ignorance," of the works of both.[65] Avicenna and Averroes have corrected Aristotle on many points, Averroes has confuted Avicenna, and our wise men have removed errors from them all.[66]

What was at issue in the disputes of the thirteenth century was clearly not the simple enunciation or denial of propositions which all Christian philosophers were agreed to defend but rather a fundamental difference of interpretation of all philosophic propositions. Much the same errors concerning the relation of God to the world or concerning creation had been attributed to the ancients before the translation of the works of Aristotle. John of Salisbury, in the twelfth century, derives the erroneous doctrine of the soul of the world from Seneca, who is one of his accustomed sources of Platonism, and advises students of the nature of the soul to avoid the philosophers and confine their studies to the Fathers who express the truth more faithfully.[67] Boethius writes that Aristotle thought the world

---

error of Averroes ("licet Averroës somniet hic et vacillet in verbis, nunc unum, nunc aliud balbutiendo . . . . *Opus tertium*" [*Fr. Rogeri Bacon opera quaedam hactenus inedita* (ed. J. S. Brewer [London, 1859], p. 77)]), further attributing the error of supposing the active intellect to be part of the human soul to the bad translation of Aristotle (*ibid.*, p. 75).

[65] *Opus majus* i. 9 (I, 20).

[66] *Ibid.* i. 6 (p. 14); cf. ii. 13 (pp. 55-56); v. 1. 5 (II, 11).

[67] "Porro ratio transcendit omnem sensum, et iudicium suum etiam in corporalibus et in spiritualibus rebus immergit. Contemplatur omnia inferiora et ad superiora prospectum intendit. Rationi Hebreorum consentit Senece diffinitio, etsi ille aliud senserit. Ait enim: Ratio est quedam pars diuini Spiritus humanis immersa corporibus. Quod tamen aut errori Gentilium accommodandum est, qui Animam Mundi in animas singulas discerptam opinabantur, ipsamque mentiebatur esse Spiritum sanctum; aut benignius interpretandum est ut pars non in quantitate, sed in uirtute dicta credatur" (*Metalogicon* iv. 17 [p. 182 (925D-26A)]). "Qui vero naturam anime diligentius inuestigare uoluerint non modo Platonis, Aristotilis, Ciceronis, et ueterum philosophorum scripta reuoluant, sed Patrum qui ueritatem fidelius expresserunt" (*ibid.* iv. 20 [p. 187 (928B)]).

had never begun and would never come to an end, its life extending to an infinity of time, and Boethius argues therefrom that the world is not eternal but only perpetual.[68] In the thirteenth century these same errors and many others related to them continued to be discussed, but they had become instances in the formulation of opposed philosophic positions: either they were assembled into a single body and associated with the name of Aristotle as his doctrines or as consequences derived from them, illustrative of the dangers of the use of reason beyond its proper limits and without the control of theology, or some portion of them was assigned to the influence of Plato and the effort was to distinguish between a proper and an improper philosophic language.

The defenders of Aristotelianism had many ways of stating the inferiority of Platonism, among which two recur frequently in their criticisms: Plato expressed his physical doctrines in metaphorical language which was open to misinterpretation and likely to lead to error, and Plato derived his principles from eternal separated species rather than from the inspection of the nature of things. Augustinians, on the other hand, were convinced that the language of wisdom and of philosophy must be analogical, and, while they were willing to grant that Aristotle repaired a defect in the method of Plato, they contended that

---

[68] De consolatione philosophiae, v, prosa 6 (PL, LXIII, 859–60). According to St. Ambrose the difference between Aristotle and Plato on this point was that Aristotle held that the world had always been and would always be, whereas Plato held that it would always be although it had not always been (Hexaemeron i. 1. 3 [PL, XIV, 135]). These and other similarly well-known passages were easily available sources of information concerning the bare doctrine prior to the translation of Aristotle. St. Ambrose is likewise the source of a distinction between the principles of Plato and Aristotle much repeated in the Middle Ages, even after the translation of Aristotle, since the passage is used in the Sentences of Peter Lombard, which was a fundamental work in the curriculums of universities of the thirteenth and fourteenth centuries (ibid. i. 1. 1; cf. Lombard, Sententiarum liber ii, dist. 1, c. 3). The three principles of Plato are God, exemplar, and matter; those of Aristotle are matter, species, and "operatorium." According to John of Salisbury, it was Plato's doctrine that there are three true existences, God, matter, and idea, which are the principles of things and themselves immutable in nature (cf. Apuleius De Platone et eius dogmate i. 5. 190 [De philosophia libri, ed. P. Thomas (Leipzig, 1921), p. 86]); the Stoics fell into the error of supposing matter and idea coeternal with God, the Epicureans dispensed entirely with idea, but the Fathers, as Augustine testifies, proved that only God is eternal (Metalogicon iv. 35 [pp. 204–6 (937D–939B)]; cf. ibid. ii. 20 [pp. 97 ff. (876B ff.)]).

he added a corresponding defect in his own method, whereas Augustine combined the virtues of the two in such fashion as to construct for the first time a complete philosophy. Albertus Magnus still engaged in the task of reconciling Plato and Aristotle, while objecting to the poetic language of the former: no man is perfected in philosophy except by the knowledge of the two philosophies of Plato and Aristotle;[69] the controversies between them arose from the tendency of Plato to seek principles in the reasons of universals, whereas Aristotle sought them in the natures of things;[70] moreover, Plato expressed his physical doctrines in metaphorical language.[71] In the work of Albertus' pupil the lineaments of Platonism and Aristotelianism are marked more sharply. Aquinas is careful to remark repeatedly in his commentaries on Aristotle that the criticisms which Aristotle directs against Plato assume a literal meaning where Plato intends to be metaphorical, but he adds that such refutation is justified in philosophic questions, since the language of Plato is faulty and may lead to error.[72] But he is even more

---

[69] *Metaphysicorum liber* i, t. 5, c. 15 (ed. A. Borgnet [Paris, 1890], VI, 113*a*).

[70] *Commentarii in II Sententiarum* dist. I, a. 4 (XXVII, 15*a*).

[71] *De anima* iii, t. 2, c. 10 (V, 347*b*). Cf. *Metaphysicorum liber* iii, t. 2, c. 10 (VI, 157*b*–161*b*).

[72] "Ubi notandum est, quod plerumque quando reprobat opiniones Platonis, non reprobat eas quantum ad intentionem Platonis, sed quantum ad sonum verborum ejus. Quod ideo facit, quia Plato habuit malum modum docendi. Omnia enim figurate dicit, et per symbola docet: intendens aliud per verba, quam sonent ipsa verba, sicut quod dixit animam esse circulum. Et ideo ne aliquis propter ipsa verba incidat in errorem, Aristoteles disputat contra eum quantum ad id quod verba ejus sonant" (*In Aristotelis librum de anima commentarium*, i, lect. 8). "Dicunt autem quidam quod isti poetae et philosophi, et praecipue Plato, non sic intellexerunt secundum quod sonat secundum superficiem verborum; sed suam sapientiam volebant quibusdam fabulis et aenigmaticis locutionibus occultare; et quod Aristotelis consuetudo fuit in pluribus non obiicere contra intellectum eorum, qui erat sanus, sed contra verba eorum, ne aliquis ex tali modo loquendi errorem incurreret, sicut dicit Simplicius in commento. Alexander tamen voluit quod Plato et alii antiqui philosophi hoc intellexerunt quod verba eorum exterius sonant; et sic Aristoteles non solum contra verba, sed contra intellectum eorum conatus est argumentari. Quidquid autem horum sit, non est nobis multum curandum: quia studium philosophiae non est ad hoc quod sciatur quid homines senserint, sed qualiter se habeat veritas rerum" (*In libros Aristotelis de caelo et mundo expositio*, i, lect. 22). "Hoc autem videtur dicere contra Platonem . . . . ; quamvis quidam dicunt hoc Platonem non sic intellexisse sicut sonant verba ejus, contra quae hic Aristoteles disputat. . . . . Sed quicumque fuerit intellectus Platonis non refert ad propositum, quia Aristoteles obiicit contra verba ipsius" (*ibid.*, i, lect. 29). "Et secundum hoc

careful to emphasize the inadequacy of the principles of the Platonic philosophy and he carries that criticism even against Augustine where the Augustinian philosophy follows the Platonic manner in philosophic questions that have no religious implications.

The difference between Aristotelians and Augustinians in the thirteenth century may be stated succinctly in the relative positions they assigned to Plato, Aristotle, and Augustine, for the Aristotelians tend to criticize Augustine when he is led astray by Plato, and the Augustinians to criticize Aristotle when he is not in accord with Augustine. According to the analysis of Aquinas, the difference lies in their conceptions of the sources of certainty: some philosophers posited no cognoscitive power except the sense and therefore denied that certainty and truth were humanly attainable; Plato placed mind above sensation and held that knowledge was possible of immobile species which were separate from sensible things; Aristotle showed that something stable can be found in sensibles and held that the judgment of the senses is certain concerning sensibles and that beyond the senses there is an intellective power which judges of truth not by independently existent intelligibles but by the light of the active intellect which constructs its intelligibles. Augustine followed Plato as far as the Catholic faith permitted, and posited not subsistent ideas but reasons of things in the divine mind.[73] According to Bonaventura, on the other hand, the deficiencies of Aristotle can be explained by the fact that he was concerned exclusively with science, those of Plato by the fact that he spoke only the word of wisdom, while Augustine, through the gift of the Holy Ghost, united the word of science with the word of wisdom.[74] The errors of those who follow

---

Aristoteles non obiicit hic contra sensum Platonis, sed contra Platonicorum verba, ne ab eis aliquis in errorem inducatur" (*ibid.*, iii, lect. 6). Cf. *In metaphysicam Aristotelis commentaria*, i, lect. 15; iii, lect. 11; vii, lect. 11.

[73] *De spiritualibus creaturis quaestio unica*, a. 10, ad 8. Cf. *Quaestiones disputatae de veritate* q. 21, a. 4, ad 3: "Augustinus in multis opinionem Platonis sequitur, quantum fieri potest secundum fidei veritatem. . . . ."

[74] "Unde quia Plato totam cognitionem certitudinalem convertit ad mundum intelligibilem sive idealem, ideo merito reprehensus fuit ab Aristotele; non quia male diceret,

Plato, according to Aquinas, arise from Plato's metaphorical use of words, leading the unwary in most cases to set up independent entities and powers not justified by examination of things; the errors of Aristotle, according to Bonaventura, arise from denying the Platonic ideas. To be sure, Aquinas is cautious in the statement of his criticism of the doctrines of a saint as revered as Augustine. Avicebron and Avicenna were led into erroneous views concerning the activity of matter by following Plato,[75] whereas Augustine sometimes merely recites the doctrine without asserting it,[76] sometimes modifies it when contrary to Christianity to a better interpretation,[77] sometimes states the doctrine, as that God is charity, in a form that may lead the incautious into error,[78] sometimes goes so far astray as to approximate in his manner of expression that of Averroes,[79] and sometimes even falls into error in matters indifferent to faith.[80] According to Bonaventura, on the other hand, Aris-

---

ideas esse et aeterna rationes, cum eum in hoc laudet Augustinus; sed quia despecto mundo sensibili, totam certitudinem cognitionis reducere voluit ad illas ideas; et hoc ponendo, licet videretur stabilire viam *sapientiae*, quae procedit secundum rationes aeternas, destruebat tamen viam *scientiae*, quae procedet secundum rationes creatas; quam viam Aristoteles e contrario stabiliebat, illa superiore neglecta. Et ideo videtur, quod inter philosophos datus sit Platoni sermo *sapientiae*, Aristoteli vero sermo *scientiae*. Ille enim principaliter aspiciebat ad superiora, hic vero principaliter ad inferiora. Uterque autem sermo, scilicet sapientiae et scientiae, per Spiritum sanctum datus est Augustino, tanquam praecipuo expositori totius Scripturae, satis excellenter, sicut ex scriptis apparet" (*Sermo* iv. 18-19 [*Doctoris seraphici S. Bonaventurae opera omnia*, ed. Patres collegii a S. Bonaventurae (Quaracchi, 1891)], V, 572).

[75] *Summa theologica* i, q. 115, a. 1 concl.

[76] *Ibid.* i, q. 77, a. 5, ad 3: "In multis autem quae ad philosophiam pertinent Augustinus utitur opinionibus Platonis, non asserendo, sed recitando."

[77] *Ibid.* q. 84, a. 5 concl.: "Et ideo Augustinus, qui doctrinis Platonicorum imbutus fuerat, si qua invenit fidei accommoda in eorum dictis, assumpsit; quae vero invenit fidei nostrae adversa, in melius commutavit."

[78] *Ibid.* iia–iiae, q. 23, a. 2, ad 1: "Hic enim modus loquendi consuetus est apud Platonicos, quorum doctrinis imbutus fuit Augustinus; quod quidam non advertentes, ex verbis ejus sumpserunt occasionem errandi."

[79] *Scriptum in libros sententiarum* ii, dist. 13, q. 1, a. 3, ad 1: ". . . . et sic potest intelligi quod Augustinus lucem aliis corporibus connumerat per modum loquendi, quo etiam Commentator in II *De anima*, calorem naturalem corpus esse probat. Nihilominus Augustinus non intendit hoc asserere quasi fidei conveniens, sed sicut utens his quae philosophiam addiscens audierat. Et ideo illae auctoritates parum cogunt."

[80] *Ibid.* ii, dist. 14, q. 1, a. 3 sol.: "Similiter etiam expositores sacrae Scripturae in hoc diversificati sunt, secundum quod diversorum philosophorum sectatores fuerunt, a

totle considered all things, as a natural philosopher, in terms of motion,[81] and from his denial of the Platonic ideas a triple error arose with respect to exemplar ideas, divine providence, and the disposition of the world according to penalties and glory; and from this triple error there followed a threefold blindness, concerning the eternity of the world, the unity of the intellect, and future rewards and punishments.[82] Aristotle can be excused for such blindness, since he spoke as a natural philosopher of things that could not be understood through nature, but other illuminated philosophers, like Plotinus of the sect of Plato and Tully of the academic sect, posited ideas and so avoided such errors.[83]

The old opposition of Plato and Aristotle thus lies behind the philosophic movements that led to the condemnations of 1270 and 1277. The opposition was to lead to a twofold resolution, the distinction of one philosophy from another faulty philosophy and the reduction of one philosophy to another in the name of theology. The Latin Averroists were the object of a double attack—an attack by Aristotelians intent on refuting in the name of philosophy the philosophic errors which Averroism had introduced and had attached to the name of Aristotle,[84] and an attack of orthodox Augustinians impatient of distinctions between Averroistic and Thomistic Aristotelianism and concerned to destroy in the name of the true doctrine the

---

quibus in philosophicis eruditi sunt. Basilius enim et Augustinus et plures sanctorum sequuntur in philosophicis quae ad fidem non spectant opiniones Platonis: et ideo ponunt caelum de natura quatuor elementorum." Cf. *Summa theologica* i, q. 66, a. 2, ad 1: "Augustinus sequitur in hoc opinionem Platonis, non ponentis quintam essentiam."

[81] *In hexaemeron collatio* iv. 17 (*Opera omnia*, V, 352).

[82] *Ibid.* (*Collatio*, vi, 204, 360-61).   [83] *Ibid.* (*Collatio*, vii, 2-3, 365).

[84] Cf. Thomas Aquinas *De unitate intellectus contra averroistas parisienses:* "Nec id nunc agendum est ut positionem praedictam ostendamus erroneam, quia repugnet veritati fidei christianae: hoc enim cuique satis in promptu apparere potest. . . . . Intendimus autem ostendere positionem praedictam non minus contra philosophiae principia esse quam contra fidei documenta. Et quia quibusdam in hac materia verba latinorum non sapiunt, sed Peripateticorum verba sectari se dicunt, quorum libros in hac materia nunquam viderunt, nisi Aristotelis, qui fuit sectae institutor, ostendemus positionem praedictam ejus verbis et sententiae repugnare omnino."

errors of a philosophy that does not spring uniquely from a concern with that doctrine. What is involved is the possibility of a philosophy independent of faith, concerned with different properties of things, proceeding in a different order from different principles,[85] and as Platonism had entered the Christian tradition so altered that faith had ceased to be concerned primarily with matters of opinion, but furnished instead the subject matter on which reason was to be exercised, so the doctrine of Aristotle, who had held that all argumentation, even the demonstrations and principles of science, was a matter of faith, entered the Christian tradition as the fundamental authority in a movement to set up a sharp separation of knowledge from faith.[86]

The errors that followed the introduction of the body of the Aristotelian works and their attendant commentaries into the West were therefore viewed in two ways: (1) as errors of a philosophy that is without guidance or check of theology, and in this view the method of Peripateticism was suspect though the doctrines of Aristotle might with proper precaution and modification be used, or (2) as errors of a mistaken philosophic analysis and imperfect method, and in this view such philosophic statements of Augustine or even of Aristotle as required to be modified were open to criticism, not because of a conflict with theology, but for philosophic reasons and on grounds derived from consideration of the nature of things. The Augustinians therefore tried to free Aristotelianism of errors, satisfied that, if Aristotle did not himself commit them, they followed from his doctrine, by adapting philosophy to the Christian Platonism of Augustine; the Christian Peripatetics, particularly Aquinas, separated theology from philosophy, distinguished the philosophy of Aristotle from the subsequent doctrines, inconsistent with that philosophy although derived from it by commenta-

[85] For Aquinas' conception of the relation of philosophy to faith see *Contra Gentiles* ii. 4; *Scriptum super libros sententiarum* ii (prol.).

[86] *Scriptum super libros sententiarum* iii. dist. 24, a. 2, q. 2: "Fides non potest esse de scitis." Cf. *Summa theologica* iia–iiae, q. 1, a. 5. Aristotle, on the other hand, constantly used belief of sciences, principles and syllogisms; cf. *Posterior Analytics* i. 2. 72a25; *ibid.* 10. 76b22.

tors, and divested Augustine of the suspicions of Averroism and Avicennism.[87] That opposition of fundamental attitude has continued since the thirteenth century, sometimes within what purports to be an Aristotelian tradition, sometimes with explicit recognition of historical affiliations, but more frequently in indifference or hostility to one or both of the ancient traditions. Duns Scotus, in the fourteenth century, was to develop his subtle philosophy from beginnings that Aquinas would have thought Platonic,[88] while William of Ockham labored to return to an Aristotelianism freed of Platonic additions. The opposition survives in the revival of Aristotelianism in Spain in the sixteenth century. Aristotelianism was to return with such Platonic admixtures after Luther.[89] The opposition to the strands of Platonism that emerged in the seventeenth century in writers like Malebranche might be shown to have Aristotelian elements for all the opposition professed in the same context to scholasticism, and many of the arguments of Aquinas survive for the defense of revealed religion in the controversy with the Deists. Finally the revival of Thomism in the nineteenth and twentieth centuries in Belgium and France seems in some of its exponents to tie philosophy to theology so closely in a "Christian philosophy" as to suggest that the Aristotelian search for an independent philosophy had yielded once more to Augustinism. The history of Aristotelianism in the West has continued to represent the Aristotelian philosophy in many guises: Aris-

[87] See E. Gilson's penetrating analysis of Avicennizing Augustinism in the thirteenth century, "Pourquoi Saint Thomas a critiqué Saint Augustin," *Archives d'histoire doctrinale et littéraire du moyen âge*, I (1926–27), 5–127. Cf. F. Ehrle, "John Peckham über den Kampf des Augustinismus und Aristotelismus in der zweiten hälfte des 13. Jahrhundert," *Zeitschrift für katholische Theologie*, XIII (1889), 172–93; "Der Augustinismus und der Aristotelismus in der Scholastic gegen Ende des 13 Jahrhunderts," *Archiv für Literatur- und Kirchengeschichte des Mittelalters*, V (1889), 603–35. C. Baeumker argues that Thomas Aquinas was himself early under the influence of the Arabic interpretation of Aristotle ("Petrus de Hibernia der Jugendlehre des Thomas von Aquino und seine Disputation vor König Manfred," *Sitzungsberichte der bayerischen Akademie der Wissenschaften* [Philosophisch-philologische und historische Klasse (1920)], Abhandlung 8).

[88] E. Gilson, "Avicenne et le point de départ de Duns Scot," *Archives d'histoire doctrinale et littéraire du moyen âge*, II (1927), 89–149.

[89] Cf. P. Petersen, *Geschichte der Aristotelischen Philosophie im protestantischen Deutschland* (Leipzig, 1921).

totelianism consists sometimes in vain and useless logic-chopping, inimical to the spirit and ends of religion; it is sometimes a useful supplement to the true doctrine, insufficient in itself and requiring purgation of errors, many of which Aristotle never committed, but which were labeled errors by the theologians or by practical philosophers who had not in all cases read far in the works of Aristotle; it is sometimes the path of natural reason to philosophic or religious truth, but in this form the doctrines and methods that have such Aristotelian derivation are not always called by his name, for they are often useful to refute "Aristotelian" errors which were not part of the philosophy of Aristotle.

THE INFLUENCE OF MEDIEVAL JUDAISM ON CHRISTIANITY

A. EUSTACE HAYDON

University of Chicago

F AR more fundamental than any later influence of Judaism upon Christianity was the dominant control of the Jewish heritage of religious ideas which formed the ground pattern of Christian thought through all the centuries. The concept of history as the unfolding of the plan of one supreme, personal God whose purposive will marshals all the events of time toward a perfect goal was a creation of the people of Israel. It stands in sharp contrast with the basic world-views of other great religions. Judaism set the pattern; Christianity and Islam inherited it and embroidered it with the colorings of their cultural histories. Another gift from Israel was the idea that God revealed his will to man—a revelation preserved in Scripture and elaborated by tradition. By a device of interpretation, Christianity took over the Old Testament, added the New, and developed a tradition of its own. Christian theology through the centuries was firmly fettered by this inherited Jewish concept of an authoritative divine revelation. As an integral phase of this sense of special relationship with God came the attitude of intolerance natural to those who alone possess the divine truth necessary for salvation. Nothing that Jewish genius contributed to influence Christianity in later ages could compare in importance with this original heritage which has dominated Christian history from the beginning until modern times.

After gentile Christianity was launched on an independent career, with a consciousness of its divine selection to supersede the religion of Israel, the church began to build barricades to insulate Christians from Jewish influences.[1] These restrictions increased through the centuries. The Jew was branded as reprobate and "perfidious." He was forbidden to have Christian slaves or Christian nurses and servants. Intermarriage was prohibited. Efforts were repeatedly made to keep Jews out of official positions in which they would have authority over Christians. Laymen and unskilled clerics were forbidden to engage in religious disputes with them. All criticism of Christian dogmas or ridicule of the sacred symbols and ceremonies was condemned as blasphemy. Under the watchful eye of a church, confident of its truth and sure of its divine authority, Judaism as a religion and culture had little opportunity to exert an influence through the untrammeled free play of social interaction.

For a brief period, under the Carolingians, the Jews were freed from restraint and given privileges in violation of canon laws and conciliar decrees.[2] Then Jewish cultural influences were powerful on court and commons. Even the clergy were affected. In wrathful protest, Agobard of Lyons jeopardized his career. This ninth-century episode was unique and soon ended. The Jews came down the medieval centuries treasuring their religious heritage, but walking with careful steps. The church had no power to suppress Judaism, but the threat of excommunication could compel good Christians to restrain Jews from actions distasteful to the church, and all too easily the secular arm could be enlisted to exploit, persecute, or expel members of the Jewish community. The popes, with notable exceptions, protected them for "reasons of piety": the Jews were the guardians of the Scriptures, their degraded state was a living proof of the triumph of Christianity, and prophecy promised that a remnant would at last be saved. It is not surprising that Judaism was rarely aggressive as a cultural influence. Even when Jewish scholars were forced to justify their faith in public discussion, they responded hesitantly, fearful of

[1] Details, to the Middle Ages, are in James William Parkes, *The Conflict of the Church and the Synagogue* (London, 1934), Appendix; for the thirteenth century, in Solomon Grayzel, *The Church and the Jews in the XIIIth Century* (Philadelphia, 1933).

[2] H. Graetz, *The History of the Jews* (London, 1892), III, 164–71.

the fruits of victory. Yet, throughout the Middle Ages, Judaism was always present as a leaven—a continually enriched cultural heritage—from which great individual Jews arose to make contributions to the religious development of the West.

The influence of Judaism upon medieval culture was certainly more pervasive than the bare records of history show. Jews of distinction who served Christian princes as physicians or financiers and who were also poets, scientists, and philosophers could hardly fail to exert some influence from their high station. There must have been some results from the many close friendships recorded between Jewish and Christian scholars. Unfortunately, a veil is drawn over all these most intimate relationships of Jewish members of the medieval communities with their Christian neighbors and friends. We know that at the times and places where the Jews were most favored and free, there the cause of liberalism advanced and the smoldering fires of revolt against social and ecclesiastical abuses burst into flame. But which was cause and which effect, no one can surely determine. The Jews with their devout difference were a universal leaven. They were amazingly mobile. Hardly one of the great Jewish scholars who have left their mark died in the place of his birth. They moved about Europe and from Europe to the East as physicians, travelers, men of business, ministers of state, teachers, and diplomats. They were friends and counselors of kings, popes, and cardinals. They collaborated with Christian scholars in the translation of works in all branches of science and religion. They helped the fumbling fingers of Christian biblical scholars as they tried to unlock the treasuries of the old Scriptures, or to correct their Latin version, or to find their way through the tangled maze of futility of medieval scholastic exegesis. They were almost the sole masters of Hebrew. When a Christian scholar wanted to learn that language, he became a pupil of a Jewish teacher. When he sought the explanation of a text, he was forced to drink from the cup of rabbinical wisdom. Much of this influence appears only as a bare record of contacts. The ban of disapproval fell upon any deference to the heritage of Judaism. From Jerome to Reuchlin, the Christian scholar felt the necessity of apologizing for seeking guidance from the Jews. Yet much help was necessary since Christian Hebrew scholarship could not walk alone until the dawn of the Reformation. In the friendly atmosphere of scholarly collaboration Jew and Christian met with the best chance of influencing each other, but over this area the shadows lie darkly. It would be futile to estimate the extent of the Jewish contribution where the evidence is so uncertain and intangible, the influence unacknowledged or unknown.

The cultural heritage of the Greco-Roman world, mediated to the Moslems through Syrian Christians and enriched by the Arabs, was brought to the door of European Christianity in the form of Arabic culture. The Jews belonged to both the Moslem East and the Christian West. Their brethren of the East were linguistically assimilated to the Moslem culture. Through Hebrew as a channel all the wealth of Arabic science and philosophy could be transmitted to the Jews of Europe. By the middle of the twelfth century the Spanish Jews were prepared to help turn into Latin, for the scholars of Christendom, Eastern science, Greek philosophy, and its Arabic and Hebrew commentaries to join the stream of Greek translations flowing in by way of Sicily and Italy.[3]

The period from the eighth to the close of the thirteenth century was the golden age of Jewish culture in Europe. During that time the streams of influence which affected Christianity most significantly had their origin. Before the eighth century the Jews were present in Europe as traders and intermediaries between the Orient and the West, but the center of Jewish learning was still in Babylonia. In Visigothic Spain they were subjected to deadly repression, and, while their services made them welcome to the ruling classes in France and central Europe, there is no tangible evidence of their contribution to Christian cultural life. The rise of the Carolingians and the Moslem conquest of Spain prepared the way for a brilliant era of Jewish scholarship which had far-reaching effects on the West.

[3] George Sarton, *Introduction to the History of Science* (Baltimore, 1931), II, 113–16, 282–84, 338–48.

The Jew was equipped by religious heritage and training to serve as a stimulating influence upon his Christian environment. In spite of the restrictions placed upon him, there was no organized anti-Jewish antagonism until the thirteenth century to bar friendly contacts. Jewish scholars of the medieval period show a remarkable versatility and breadth of knowledge. They were especially distinguished as linguists. Although they commonly avoided the Latin, as the language of the church, Jewish scholars of Spain knew Arabic and Hebrew and could communicate the resources of these languages in the vernacular. In twelfth-century Spain at least, the educational program included languages, Bible, Talmud, poetry, the relation of philosophy to revelation, mathematics, logic, astronomy, music, mechanics, optics, medicine, natural science, and metaphysics.[4] Moreover, they had behind them centuries of achievement in the age-old specialty of the Hebrew scholar—biblical and talmudic exegesis. During the eleventh and twelfth centuries Spanish and French Jews built the structures of grammar, lexicography, and exegetical method which were to be a powerful ferment in the later history of Christianity. Long before Christian thinkers were seriously troubled by the problem of reconciling a naïve theism based on revelation with the claims of reason and philosophy based on science, the Moslems and Jews had found the way of compromise. Medieval Judaism had much to offer to Christianity, not only from the treasury of its past but from new creations in science and philosophy. Although the Jews were relatively few in number, they were able to contribute much more than their share to the new learning under extreme difficulties. If there had been no artificial barriers between Jew and Christian, if the high wall of intolerance had not been so difficult to surmount, if the two religions had been free to work out their common problems by mutual stimulus and interaction, the influence of Jewish culture and learning upon Christianity could have been vastly greater than it was.

4 Jacob R. Marcus, *The Jew in the Medieval World* (Cincinnati, 1938); cf. M. Maimonides, *Guide of the Perplexed*, trans. M. Friedländer (London, 1885), Vol. I, chap. 34.

In some phases of the development of Christian culture Jewish influence is unmistakably clear. It flowed from two main sources: first, from the work of Jewish scholars as linguists and exegetes, transmitting the cultural wealth of the Moslems and their own through translations, developing the science of grammar and the method of interpretation for the new and revolutionary opening of the sacred Scriptures; second, from the achievement of Jewish thinkers in reconciling biblical theology with the two continuing currents of Greek philosophy.

The amazing activity of the Jews of Spain as translators during the twelfth and early thirteenth centuries made available to the Jewish scholars of Europe the most important works of science and philosophy written in Arabic. Included were the writings of Moslem and Jewish mediators of the philosophy of Greece—Ibn Gabirol, Maimonides, Ibn Rushd, Ibn Sina—the works of Aristotle, scientific treatises on mathematics, astrology, astronomy, and medicine, as well as on philology, grammar, lexicography, and biblical interpretation. The translations were made into Hebrew by Jews for Jews. This Greek-Arabic learning mediated to European Jews through the writings of their own scholars who had been immersed for centuries in Arabic culture came to them in Hebrew dress almost as a native heritage. They began at once to do creative work, especially in medicine, mathematics, astronomy, and biblical exegesis. A disturbing intellectual ferment began to penetrate the peaceful Christian traditionalism. In the twelfth century the Christian scholars of western Europe turned longing eyes toward Spain as the fountainhead of the new learning, but the Hebrew language brought it no nearer to them than the Arabic. It was necessary to present the Greek, Moslem, and Jewish authors in Latin or vernacular dress. Christian scholars found their own way to the original Greek texts. In opening the door to the rich and disturbing library of Arabic and Hebrew works, the Jews gave valuable help as collaborators. The translations of the converted Jew, John of Seville, who worked with Dominicus Gundisalvi, at Toledo, had a far-reaching influence upon Christian thought. Made in the twelfth century, they opened fresh and startling vistas. To the scientific and Aristotelian works being translated at the same time by Gerard of Cremona, they added the philosophic writings of significant Jewish and Moslem thinkers—Ibn Sina, al-Farabi, Ibn Gabirol, and al-Ghazzali. Gerard translated Isaac Israeli. Of the non-Christian religious philosophers whose influence carried through the Scholastic era only Maimonides and Ibn Rushd were missing. They became available in Latin early in the thirteenth century to weight the scales in favor of Aristotle.

A large number of Jewish scholars collaborated in the transfer of the scientific writings of Moslems and Jews to the languages of the West. Abraham bar Ḥiyya, one of the greatest mathematicians of the twelfth century, worked with Plato of Tivoli in the translation of mathematical works, including his own influential treatise on practical geometry.[5] The Christian Simon Cordo of Genoa had the help of Abraham ben Shem-Tob in translating two important medical works.[6] Many Jewish translators worked in the service of royal patrons. Alfonso X, of Castille, gathered together a group of scholars to turn into Castillian the astronomical works of the ancients and the Moslems.[7] In this company were the Jews Isaac Ibn Sid, Samuel ha-Levi, Abraham Alfaquin of Toledo, and Judah ben Moses. With their Christian associates they translated a long list of physical and astronomical treatises. The famous Alfonsine Tables were compiled by Judah and Isaac. The court of Anjou also employed Jewish translators. There Faraj ben Salim (Moses Faragut) translated al-Razi's monumental encyclopedia of Greco-Arabic medicine,[8] and a generation later (1328), Kalonymus ben Kalonymus translated the reply of Averroes to al-Ghazzali's *Destruction of Philosophy*.[9] Jacob ben Maḥir ibn Tibbon (d. 1304), of the family famous for translations into Hebrew, not only translated scientific texts but produced original astronomical works which were soon turned into Latin and used

[5] Sarton, *op. cit.*, II, 206–7.   [7] *Ibid.*, pp. 835–38.

[6] *Ibid.*, p. 1096.   [8] *Ibid.*, p. 833.

[9] E. R. Bevan and Charles Singer, *The Legacy of Israel* (Oxford, 1927), p. 222.

later by Copernicus, Erasmus, and Kepler.[10] The record is not complete. Behind the well-known individuals there are glimpses of other Jewish workers who helped Christians to turn Arabic and Hebrew works into Latin.

Jewish translators performed a double task. They made the Greek and Arabic wisdom available to their own people in the West and shared with Christian scholars the labor of ushering in the dawn of the new learning to Christian Europe. Without the Jews, Christianity would have recovered the forgotten heritage of Greek thought and attained a knowledge of the philosophy and science of the Greco-Arabic world, but later, more slowly, and with greater difficulty. The presence of Arabic-speaking Jews in Spain as translators speeded up the process of transmission, and the creative work of European Jews who were imbued with the culture of the East gave pioneer leadership in the new orientation of Christian culture.

Since both Jews and Christians revered the Old Testament as a sacred deposit of divine revelation and by interpretation sought guidance for life from the sacred book, it would be natural to expect a fruitful interaction of Judaism and Christianity on this common ground, with the Jews, as masters of the Hebrew and with long training in the art of interpretation, making generous gifts to the younger religion. In reality, the Middle Ages were already yielding to the Renaissance before the Jewish achievement in Hebrew scholarship made any significant impact upon Christianity. When the gentile Christians threw off the bondage of the Jewish law, contact with the Hebrew language was lost. The early Fathers used the Septuagint; the medieval Schoolmen, the Vulgate. After the time of Charlemagne there was an occasional Christian scholar who knew a little Hebrew, but through all the Middle Ages an effective mastery of Hebrew scholarship was demonstrated by only one known Christian writer, Nicholas of Lyra, who worked at the dawn of the fourteenth century. Christian scholars were dependent upon Jewish guidance when they consulted the Hebrew texts. Jerome set the example when he cut across church preju-

[10] Sarton, *op. cit.*, II, 850–53.

dices by enlisting Jewish help in making his Vulgate translation. Rabanus Maurus gave credit to a "modern Jew" for helpful passages inserted in his commentary on the Book of Kings.[11] With Jewish assistance Stephen Harding made his revision of the Vulgate,[12] and Peter the Venerable ventured into the maze of the Talmud.[13] Even in the medieval controversies with the Jews regarding the teaching of their books, it was necessary to call upon Jewish apostates to champion the Christian cause.

In the thirteenth century training in Hebrew was urged by several scholars for purposes of translation, for anti-Jewish propaganda, for the censorship of Hebrew books, and, by Roger Bacon, for the understanding of the Old Testament and to provide a missionary medium more reasonable than force for the conversion of the Jews. Little was done until, in 1311, the Council of Vienne, under the leadership of Pope Clement V, ordered teaching in Hebrew at the papal court and at the universities of Paris, Salamanca, Bologna, and Oxford.[14] But still Hebrew learning languished.

Meanwhile, the Jews were perfecting the tools and method which were to exert an important influence on the work of the early Protestant reformers. The interpretation of the Torah had been a central interest of Jewish scholarship since pre-Christian times. In the eight century the rabbinical mode of interpretation was challenged by the Karaites. From that time until the twelfth century Jewish scholars labored in Babylonia, Africa, Spain, France, and Italy to forge effective instruments for Bible study—Hebrew philology, grammar, lexicography—and to achieve an exact method of exegesis. That work came to fruition in the grammatical and exegetical writings of Rashi (d. 1105), Abraham ben Ezra (d. 1167), Moses, and David Kimchi (in the twelfth century). These men were the most influential of the large number of scholars who emancipated scriptural interpretation from the subjective vagaries of the past by insistence upon the primary importance of the literal sense. Un-

---

[11] Bevan and Singer, op. cit., p. 288.

[12] Sarton, op. cit., II, 154–55.   [13] Ibid., p. 161.

[14] Corpus juris canonici, Clementis Papae V. Constitutiones v, tit. I, c. I.

fortunately, the immense library of linguistic knowledge, the brilliant achievements of the Jews in biblical scholarship, were ignored by the medieval Schoolmen. They were content with the Vulgate version and continued to torture the Scriptures in search of their fourfold sense until Nicholas of Lyra, the one great Christian exegete of the Middle Ages, appropriated the method and materials of the Jewish masters and laid the founda- tion of the biblical interpretation which was to play such an important role in Protestantism.

Lyra went beyond the Vulgate to the original Hebrew. He acknowledged his debt to Rashi, who, "of the Hebrew teachers, is said to be more rational in elucidating the literal sense."[15] Rashi often yielded to the lure of the Midrash and Lyra to the mystical interpretation of the Schoolmen,[16] but for both the literal meaning of Scripture was primary. Reuchlin commented upon Lyra's indebtedness in the extravagant statement that all Lyra's commentaries could be included in a few pages if every- thing borrowed from Rashi were excised.[17] At the least he was a bridge between the centuries of Jewish achievement and the pioneering period of Protestant exegesis. More than a century passed before his influence became significant. Then his empha- sis upon the fundamental importance of discovering the exact, literal sense from the original text was continued by the Refor- mation leaders. Huss, Melanchthon, Luther, Servetus, Zwingli, Calvin—all made use of his work. Lyra's system of interpreta- tion was being taught at Erfurt when Luther was a student there. There is no evidence of his influence in Luther's early interpretation of Scripture where he copied the Scholastic method of seeking for the fourfold sense, but the later Luther praised Lyra highly and followed him step by step in his com- mentary on Genesis.[18]

[15] *Patrologia Latina*, ed. J. P. Migne (Paris, 1878), CXIII, 30.

[16] ". . . . cum Dei adjutorio intendo circa litteralem sensum insistere: et paucas valde et breves expositiones mysticas aliquando interponere, licet raro" (*ibid.*).

[17] Graetz, *op. cit.*, IV, 442.

[18] C. Siegfried, "Rashis Einfluss auf Nicolaus von Lira und Luther in der Auslegung der Genesis," *Archiv für wissenschaftliche Erforschung des Alten Testamentes*, I, 428 ff., II, 36 ff.

During the century and a half which separated Lyra from the Reformation, while the Renaissance was diffusing its humanistic light over Europe, the study of Hebrew became increasingly important. The Jewish academies of Italy rendered an international service in the teaching of the language. Scores of converted Jews had a new career opened for them as instructors in Hebrew for Christians, especially in Germany.[19] Reuchlin learned the language in Italy from Jacob Loans and Obadiah Sforno. Of the converted Jews the most influential were Mathew Adrian, teacher of Conrad Pellican, the first Christian writer on Hebrew grammar, and Elias Levita, who taught Johannes Eck, Cardinal Egidio de Viterbo, General of the Augustinians, and Sebastian Münster. These Jewish teachers introduced their pupils not only to the language but, more important, to the rich storehouse of biblical scholarship of medieval Jews. Levita lifted Moses Kimchi's Hebrew grammar out of the twelfth century and made it the handbook of Protestants. Reuchlin's writing on Hebrew philology and grammar drew heavily upon the Kimchis. In his commentaries he could use Saadia, Rashi, Ibn Ezra, Maimonides, and Gersonides. Münster did his great work on Hebrew grammar in appreciative dependence upon Levita. After all the centuries of separation Jew and Christian worked with the same exegetical tools on the common heritage of sacred texts.

This fresh approach to the Scriptures was surcharged with menace to the peace of the church. The attitude of the authorities was reflected in Melanchthon's report: "The Italians say, 'He is a good grammarian; therefore he is a heretic.' "[20] Since the thirteenth century laymen had been forbidden to interpret the Bible, while Scholastic exegesis was a bond slave in the service of authority. The literal sense of Scripture presented by scholarly Christian Hebraists was vastly more dangerous than it had been in the mouths of the lay preachers of the thirteenth century. When reinforced by the commentaries of Rashi, David

[19] D. de Sola Pool, "The Influence of Some Jewish Apostates on the Reformation," *Jewish Review*, II, 327–51.

[20] "Postill. III," *Corpus Reformatorum* (Braunschweig, 1853), XIX, col. 365.

Kimchi, and Maimonides, men whose works had been banned by the Inquisition, the ground was prepared for the harvest of revolt. The old authority was doomed when Luther could say, "Because they were without languages the dear Fathers at times belabored a text with many words and yet caught barely an inkling of its meaning; their comment is half guess work, half error."[21]

Reuchlin's Hebrew knowledge and his appreciation of the great Jewish commentators inadvertently strengthened the gathering forces of reform. When the apostate Jew, Pfefferkorn, received imperial authority to burn the Hebrew books of the Jews of Cologne and Frankfurt, Reuchlin was consulted. He advised the emperor that the Talmud, Zohar, the commentaries of Rashi, the Kimchis, Ibn Ezra, Gersonides, and Nachmanides should not be burned. There followed the long-drawn-out "battle of the books," which began as a struggle of Reuchlin against the Dominicans but spread to an alignment of the humanists against the clerics and at last blended in the broader battle of the reformers against the church.

An inconclusive argument might be made for the influence of medieval Jews upon the heretical movements which preceded this final revolt from the medieval church. Lea has noted that the first antisacerdotal movements occurred in those sections of France where the Jews were favored and flourishing. The return to the Bible and its interpretation in freedom from clerical control characterized those heretical groups in South France, the center of Jewish biblical exegesis, where the most rational and literal of all interpreters, David Kimchi, was so highly revered. During the thirteenth century royal mandates, canons of councils, and papal bulls reiterated their warnings against the influence of Jews upon Christians.[22] That there were intimate and friendly relations between Jew and Christian both in high places and on the level of the lowly folk is abundantly

[21] "To the Councilmen of All Cities in Germany That They Establish and Maintain Christian Schools," *Works of Martin Luther* (Philadelphia, 1931), IV, 118.

[22] See Grayzel, *op. cit.*, pp. 22–36; and also L. I. Newman, *Jewish Influence on Christian Reform Movements* (New York, 1925), pp. 360–426.

clear. Educated and efficient Jewish officials were too valuable
to be displaced. Through the thirteenth and fourteenth centuries Jewish physicians dominated the medical profession in
Europe by sheer merit. Banned by the church, they continued
to be the personal attendants of kings, aristocrats, popes, and
cardinals. When the common people found a voice to protest
against the exactions, neglect, and abuses of the church, they
were allied in sympathy with a people who through the Christian centuries had been forced to be perpetually protestant.
Moreover, the very things attacked by the rebels—the divine
mythologies, the teaching regarding Mary and the saints, the
use of images, reverence for the cross, and the magic of the
Sacraments—were exactly the things that repelled the Jews
from Christianity. The growing apprehension of the church during the twelfth and thirteenth centuries in regard to Jewish
proselytizing and the activities of Jews only superficially converted to Christianity may indicate a pervasive, intangible,
Jewish influence through personal contacts. On the other hand,
ecclesiastical condemnation of the heretical leaders for "judaiz-
ing" and "consorting with Jews" may mean nothing, for these
were accusations hurled back and forth between rival camps
since the early centuries. The fact that Jews were usually included with the heretics when the engines of suppression began
to move is no indication of their share in the heresies, for, whenever there was trouble—during the social disturbances of the
Crusades, during the Black Death, in the conflict of kings with
popes, in times of economic distress or the threat of foreign
invasion—the Jews were always the scapegoat and the foil for
propaganda. It is almost certain that what influence there was
flowed through the hidden channels of personal relations.
Judaism was a legal religion, although branded by the church
as a "perfidy," and loyal Jews who embodied it were always in
contact with Christians. During the centuries of the heresies
Jewish scholars were writing books in response to Christian
polemics, but for Jews only. Such works were carefully hidden
from Christians. The inquisition in the hands of the Dominicans
helped to keep them hidden. That the medieval Jews had a

significant part in nourishing the spirit of revolt against the church is a plausible conjecture but not a clearly documented conclusion.

Early in the thirteenth century Christian thinkers were shocked out of their complacent dependence upon traditional authorities by the translation of the complete writings of Aristotle on science and philosophy. The apprehension of the church in regard to his teachings is expressed in the efforts to suppress them by the Provincial Synod of Paris in 1210, by the University of Paris through Cardinal Legate Robert Courcon in 1215, and in the appointment of a commission by Pope Gregory IX in 1231 to edit Aristotle so that he might be safe for Christianity. But "the philosopher" was too deeply revered to be either suppressed or ignored. It was necessary to find a way of reconciling Christian theism with the truth of Aristotle. Long before, Judaism had been faced with the same problem. In the system of Moses Maimonides the Jews had a religious philosophy which embodied the thought of Aristotle within the pattern of an intellectually defensible theism. In addition, the more familiar and more comfortable Neo-Platonism had been modernized into a composite religious philosophy by Ibn Gabirol. Christian theologians were able to find suggestions for their own work of synthesis in both of these men. Those who preferred the Augustinian tradition and a warmer, more intuitive view of God found support in Ibn Gabirol. Those who felt compelled to follow the Stagyrite were glad to have the guidance of Maimonides through the more thorny thickets on the way.

In the reconciliation of the fundamentals of religious thought common to Judaism, Christianity, and Islam with the philosophy of Greece, the three religions pooled their intelligence. Thinkers of Islam and Judaism shared solutions worked out together in the milieu of Moslem culture. Christian theologians of the West later inherited their findings and added to them. A satisfactory solution of a common problem might be shared, regardless of source, by all three groups. The cross-fertilization of thought, coupled with the similarity of problems, makes it difficult to be sure of the dependence of a Christian thinker upon

a Jewish predecessor unless direct indebtedness is acknowledged, or the doctrine formulated is distinctive of a particular
author, or the borrowing is done in a word-by-word, idea-by-
idea sequence. While the influence of other Jewish scholars may
be questionable, it is generally recognized that the Scholastic
theologians made large use of the thought of Ibn Gabirol and
Moses Maimonides in the solution of their own theological
problems.[23] To these two should be added Isaac Israeli (845–
940).

The reputation of Isaac Israeli in the history of culture rests
especially upon his medical works, but his *De definitionibus* and
De elementis were the books used by the Schoolmen. Albertus
Magnus quoted from both. Vincent of Beauvais used him extensively in his *Speculum naturale*. Isaac's definitions often
offered suggestive insights. Thomas Aquinas quoted his definition of truth—"Veritas est adaequatio rei et intellectus."[24] The
amount of quotation from Isaac's writings in the Scholastics is
all out of proportion to his importance as a philosophic thinker
and may be merely the result of the inclusion of his works
among the earliest Latin translations from the Arabic when all
light from the East was welcomed.

A pervasive influence upon Christian thought flowed from
Ibn Gabirol's *Fons vitae*. There was nothing in the work to
indicate to which of the three religions the author belonged.
The Scholastics thought he was either a Moslem or a Christian.
His philosophic system was a synthesis of elements drawn from
the intellectual milieu of Arabic-Greek culture. The ground
pattern was Neo-Platonism altered so as to give at least a
verbal importance to the theistic doctrine of creation. It evaded

[23] J. Guttmann, "Einfluss der jüdischen Philosophie auf die christlichen Philosophen
des Mittelalters und der beginnenden Neuzeit," *Die Lehren des Judentums* (Leipzig,
1929), III, Teil 5, 378 ff.; "Guillaume d'Auvergne et la littérature juive," *Revue des
études juives*, XVIII, 243 ff.; "Alexander de Hales et la Judaisme," *ibid.*, XIX, 224 ff.;
*Die Scholastik des dreizehnten Jahrhunderts in ihren Beziehungen zum Judentum und
zur jüdischen Literatur* (Breslau, 1902); M. Joël, *Verhältniss Albert des Grossen zu Moses
Maimonides* (Breslau, 1876); "Etwas über den Einfluss der jüdischen Philosophie auf die
christliche Scholastik," *Beiträge zur Geschichte der Philosophie* (Breslau, 1876); M. Witt-
mann, *Die Stellung des Hl. Thomas von Aquin zu Avencebrol* (Münster i. W., 1899);
E. Gilson, *The Philosophy of St. Thomas Aquinas* (Cambridge, 1929).

[24] *De veritate* q. 1., a. 1.

the threat of pantheism in the Neo-Platonic emanation theory by interposing the creative divine will or word between the ineffable, original source and the created universe. At the same time the immanent divine presence flowing down through all levels of existence preserved a vital, emotional contact with the traditional God of religion who was in danger of being purified by the fires of the new philosophy into a remote abstraction.

William of Auvergne was especially impressed by Ibn Gabirol's theory of the word or will of God which acted as the creative mediator between the divine unity and the plurality of the world of matter and form, and by his teaching that God is the sole cause at work everywhere, for whose superabundance all lesser causes are merely channels of transmission.[25] Gabirol's distinctive doctrine that all existences, both spiritual and corporeal, are composed of matter and form was taken over by Dominicus Gundisalvi, Alexander of Hales, Bonaventura, Duns Scotus, Roger Bacon, and other Franciscans. Through the Franciscans it became a well-differentiated trend of medieval Christian thought. Duns Scotus went farther than the others in accepting Ibn Gabirol's unique idea that one universal matter underlies all forms from the highest to the lowest, with the exception of God alone.[26]

Both Albertus Magnus and Thomas Aquinas combatted Ibn Gabirol's teaching that spiritual existences are composed of matter and form. This attitude would naturally follow from their dependence on Aristotle. Yet Thomas devotes an unusual amount of attention to the ideas of the Jewish thinker. The explanation probably lies in the support drawn from him by the Franciscans. On this account the Dominicans were compelled not only to sharpen their teaching in regard to matter and form as over against their rivals but to meet, as Aristotelians, the reinforcement given by Ibn Gabirol to the Augustinian-Platonic tradition of realism in the Franciscan order.

Of all medieval Jewish writers, Moses Maimonides made the deepest impress upon Christian religious thinking. He was a convinced Aristotelian and a loyal Jew. In his *Guide of the Per-*

---

[25] *De universo* i, pars 1, c. 25, 26.   [26] *De rerum principio*, q. 8, a. 4.

plexed he reconciled the traditional doctrine of God and the Jewish scriptural heritage with the teaching of Aristotle. His rationalizing of Scripture and his success in ironing out the conflicts between philosophy and theology appealed to the Scholastics. They freely borrowed not only Maimonides' ideas but often his arguments and identical materials. He offered stimulating suggestions for the treatment of theological themes common to Judaism and Christianity, such as the relation of revelation to reason, proofs of God's existence, the nature of God, divine providence and foreknowledge, the conflict between the doctrine of creation out of nothing and Aristotle's theory of the eternity of the world, the mechanism of prophecy, the relation of miracles to natural law, and the interpretation of the legal system of the Old Testament. Many of the Christian writers of the thirteenth century drew materials from Maimonides on one or several of these topics.

The Schoolmen found it necessary to define the separate functions of the two sources of truth—revelation and reason. To justify the acceptance of revelation, Maimonides[27] stressed the limitations of human reason, the intellectual laziness of most men, the liability of the human mind to error. Where man's reason fails or errs, Scripture gives truth which reason finds acceptable. Aquinas[28] and Duns Scotus[29] stated this relationship of revelation and reason more tersely but followed the same line.

In proving the existence of God, Aquinas agreed with Maimonides that the most effective way is "from the supposition of the eternity of the world, which being supposed it seems less manifest that God exists."[30] Both scholars took three proofs from Aristotle, each elaborating in his own way the arguments from motion, from efficient cause, and from degrees of truth and being. The proof from necessary existence Aquinas adapted from Maimonides.[31]

[27] *Guide* i, c. 33; ii, c. 16.

[28] *Summa contra Gentiles* i, c. 3, 4, 5.   [29] *Sent.* i, dist. 2, q. 3, 7.

[30] *Summa contra Gentiles* i, c. 13; *Guide* ii (Introd.).

[31] *Summa theologica* i, q. 2, a. 3. *Guide* ii, c. 1.

The three great theistic religions were challenged by Aristotle to define the nature of the God of religion in a philosophically respectable manner. Their personal God, resplendent in his robe of colorful attributes, was too anthropomorphic to fit into the new philosophic scheme. Maimonides found the philosophically correct solution without sacrificing the religious value of God.[32] He asserted that the true nature of God could not be defined; that "he has no positive attribute whatever." Qualities descriptive of men cannot have the same meaning when applied to God. Yet God can be known through his activity, and all attributes commonly ascribed to God are really attributes of his acts. He may also be described by negative attributes. With varying degrees of reluctance the Scholastics agreed with Maimonides. There was little objection to the assertion that the essence of God could not be known. Albert[33] and Aquinas[34] agreed that no attributes could be used univocally for God and man, although Thomas argued that some human qualities may not be purely equivocal[35] when applied to God, and Albert protested against robbing God of positive attributes. Aquinas criticized Maimonides' method of saving religious values by positing knowledge of God by way of negation and through his activities,[36] and yet, because the divine substance is beyond the reach of human intellect and nothing positive can be predicated of it,[37] he began his own demonstration by the negative way.[38] Duns Scotus followed Maimonides.[39]

Aristotle's doctrine of the eternity of the world made trouble for theologians who were expected to believe in creation out of nothing. Maimonides assembled the arguments used to support both positions and decided that neither the eternity of the world nor creation out of nothing could be proved by human reason. Only through revelation, by faith, can we know that the world was created or had a temporal beginning. Such belief is reasonable and accounts, better than the rival theory, for the multi-

[32] *Guide* i, c. 51, 53–58.

[33] *De causis et processu* i, tr. 3, c. 6.

[34] *Summa contra Gentiles* i, c. 32.

[35] *Ibid.* i, c. 33.

[36] *De potentia*, q. 7, a. 5.

[37] *Summa theologica* iii, q. 1, a. 2.

[38] *Summa contra Gentiles* i, c. 14.

[39] *Sent.* i, dist. 8, q. 4. 2.

plicity of the world we know. Bonaventura,[40] Albertus Magnus,[41] and Thomas Aquinas[42] used Maimonides' collection of proofs[43] as a starting-point for their own discussions of the problem. In dealing with creation in his *Physics*, Albert followed Maimonides closely; in his theology he went his own way. Both Albert and Aquinas agreed with Maimonides that the eternity of the world cannot be proved and that its temporal beginning must be accepted by faith. Albert followed Maimonides in saying that only through revelation could we know that the world was created out of nothing; Aquinas thought it could be rationally demonstrated. As to whether a created world could be eternally created, Maimonides and Aquinas were not positive; Albert said it was impossible. On this issue the two great Dominicans found in Maimonides a very comforting collaborator.[44]

Maimonides'[45] rational interpretation of the legal system of the Pentateuch influenced the Scholastics. Materials were drawn from him, often with objections and criticisms, by William of Auvergne,[46] Alexander of Hales,[47] Thomas Aquinas,[48] and Duns Scotus.[49] His division of the law into judicial and ceremonial and the explanation of the latter as a defense of the Israelites against the allurements of the pagan world won their approval. They drew help and stimulus also from his skilful allegorical evasion of biblical difficulties and the rational tone of his treatment of miracles and prophecy.

Similarity of thought, however, does not necessarily imply borrowing or even mutual influence. Aquinas and Maimonides give the same interpretation of evil, but it is evident that Thomas followed Pseudo-Dionysius, and Maimonides the Moslems. Christian scholars recognized in the great Jewish thinker

---

[40] *Lib. sent.* ii, dist. 1, a. 1, q. 2.   [42] *Summa contra Gentiles* ii, c. 32–37.

[41] *Physics* viii, tr. 1, c. 11, 13, 14, 15.   [43] *Guide* ii, c. 13–22.

[44] Anselm Rohner, *Das Schöpfungsproblem bei Moses Maimonides, Albertus Magnus und Thomas von Aquin* (Münster i. W., 1913).

[45] *Guide* iii, c. 27–49.   [47] *Summa* ii, q. 42; iii, q. 28, 54, 55, 58.

[46] *De legibus.* c. 1–4, 16.   [48] *Summa theologica* ii, pars 1, q. 101, 102.

[49] *Sent.* iii, dist. 40.

a man devoted to the same religious fundamentals that they were anxious to preserve. They welcomed him as an ally, built upon his materials, often adopted his conclusions, and just as often opposed him. Thomas Aquinas, the greatest of them all, agreed with him more frequently than the others until Eckhart, who apparently found no fault in him at all.

Beyond the boundaries of Christianity as doctrine and institution was the so-called secular, social life moving, during the later Middle Ages, toward a new orientation in which Jewish influence played its part. After the shock of the spread of Islam the Jews laid the foundations for a new commerce, developed money-lending, and created the techniques of later capitalism. Christians had taken full possession of these achievements when they began to crowd the Jews toward the ghettos in the fourteenth century. In the development of the sciences which broke the mold of medieval living, Jewish scholars made significant contributions. They excelled especially in mathematics, astronomy, and medicine. As a counterpoise the spirit of intolerance which Christianity took over from Judaism continued through the centuries in both camps. Jewish apostates must bear a large share of the blame for the increase of Christian intolerance after the twelfth century which bore such bitter fruit for the half-Christianized Jews in the Inquisition. As a protestant minority, the Jews, beyond the limitations of their stubborn religious loyalties, were a factor for change and enlightenment in the general culture. While both Jewish and Catholic writers give them too much credit for dissolving the medieval religious synthesis and ushering in the modern age, there can be no doubt that they contributed more than their share toward that event.

THE EFFECT OF THE CRUSADES UPON EASTERN CHRISTIANITY

MATTHEW SPINKA

Chicago Theological Seminary
Chicago, Illinois

I

AMONG the most important events affecting the fundamental character of the ecclesiastical settlements of the territories conquered by the Crusaders in Palestine and Syria was the repudiation of the oath exacted from all Crusading leaders by Emperor Alexius I. In accordance with the terms of this oath, which the Crusaders did not deny,[1] the conquered territories, formerly a part of the Empire, were to be restored to the emperor. This arrangement would have undoubtedly resulted in the recovery of hegemony by the Greek church. By renouncing allegiance to the emperor, the Crusaders made the Latin church supreme. Into the story of the Latin ecclesiastical settlements it is not possible to go by reason of the limitation of space;[2] accordingly, this study is concerned only with the relations with, and the effect upon, the Eastern Christian communions. Specifically, this category includes the Jacobites, the Maronites, the Armenians, and the Greeks.

In the kingdom of Jerusalem these relations were at first not greatly complicated because of the relatively small number of the native Christians who survived the siege. We do not have exact information concerning their respective strength; nevertheless, we may get a fairly clear idea of the general situation. Before the conquest of the city, the Turks had greatly reduced the Christian population: alarmed by the actively helpful atti-

---

[1] Raimondi de Aguilers, *Historia Francorum*, in *Recueil des historiens des croisades, historiens occidentaux* (Paris, 1866), III, 267.

[2] For this phase of the subject see my article, "Latin Church of the Early Crusades," *Church History*, Vol. VIII, No. 2 (June, 1939).

tude of the Christians of Edessa and Antioch toward the Crusaders, they formed the plan, *more Turcico*, of putting the Christians of Jerusalem to death.[3] Fortunately, prior to the massacre, a large number of these doomed people had saved themselves by flight.

Nevertheless, a remnant of the Christian population managed to survive. William of Tyre, the chief historian of the period, reports that, when Jerusalem was taken by the Crusading contingent under Godfrey of Bouillon, the native Christians met them in a procession headed by their clergy. They carried crosses and relics and, singing hymns, led the Crusaders to the Church of the Holy Sepulcher.[4] When shortly after the taking of the city the Crusaders sallied forth to the Battle of Ascalon, "Peter the Hermit remained in Jerusalem, ordering and commanding Greeks and Latins, as well as the clergy, faithfully to hold a procession to God, and to offer prayers and alms that God might give victory to His people."[5] There is no indication that the Greeks refused to comply.

It is interesting to speculate what might have happened had the Greek patriarch of Jerusalem, Simeon, lived to witness the conquest of the city. During his life he had been most helpful to the Crusaders and fully co-operated with them. When the Crusaders embarked upon their perilous undertaking, Simeon took a leading part in an effort to insure its success. Before the capture of Antioch he, together with the papal legate, Adhemar du Puy, sent in October, 1097, an urgent appeal to the West for reinforcements.[6] It is indicative of the honor in which he was held that Simeon's name preceded that of the papal legate. Later, writing from the camp at Antioch in January, 1098, "the Patriarch of Jerusalem and the bishops, Greek as well as Latin," issued another eloquent and urgent call for more men.[7] The

[3] William of Tyre, *Historia Francorum,* in *Recueil des historiens des croisades, histo riens occidentaux* (Paris, 1859), I, 501.

[4] *Ibid.,* pp. 356–57.

[5] L. Bréhier (ed.), *Histoire anonyme de la première croisade* (Paris, 1924), p. 210.

[6] H. Hagenmeyer (ed.), *Epistulae et chartae ad historiam primi belli sacri spectantes* (Innsbruck, 1901), pp. 141–42.

[7] *Ibid.,* pp. 146 ff.

letter was addressed "to our very dear brethren" in the West. Shortly before the siege of Jerusalem, Simeon left the city and went to Cyprus to collect alms for the relief of his flock[8] but did not live to return to his see. With the radically changed relation of the Crusaders toward Emperor Alexius I resulting in the repudiation of their oath to him, it was unthinkable that the Latin clergy would consider any other course than that of electing their own patriarch. They chose for that position Arnulf Malecorne, who, however, upon the arrival of the new papal legate, Archbishop Dagobert of Pisa, was forced to give place to the latter.

From the scattered and incidental notices of the treatment of the native Christians by the Latin conquerors it is possible to conclude that at first the situation was fairly satisfactory. At the time of the conquest the surviving Armenian, Greek, and Syrian Christians had taken refuge in the Church of the Holy Sepulcher. Tancred found them there and promised them full protection under a detachment of two hundred soldiers detailed to guard the holy place. The native Christians freely showed the Latins the sacred objects of the sanctuary and later themselves revealed the location of the holy cross. On the other hand, the Latins admitted the Greeks to their services and left them in possession of many monasteries and churches, although some were, of course, assigned to their own clergy and monks.

Most of the Jacobite clergy of Jerusalem, including their metropolitan, Cyril, had fled to Egypt before the Turkish fury. Consequently, when the Latins took possession of the city, they found many Jacobite ecclesiastical properties vacant or unclaimed. Such, for instance, were two villages, Adesia and Beit Arif, which were thereupon granted to a certain knight, Gauffier by name. But when Metropolitan Cyril returned from Egypt, and the Jacobite patriarch, Athanasius III, himself appealed to King Baldwin I for restitution of these possessions, the villages were returned to the Jacobite community. This, however, did not end the matter: the case was settled with comparative ease only because in the meantime Gauffier had

---

[8] William of Tyre, *op. cit.*, p. 350.

been taken prisoner by the Turks. But thirty-three years later he returned from his captivity and drove the unfortunate Jacobites from what he regarded as his property. It was only by the intervention of the Jacobite metropolitan, Ignatius, who secured the good will of Queen Melisenda, the wife of King Fulk, that the villages were returned to the Jacobites and Gauffier was compensated by a payment of two hundred dinars. All this tended to pacify the Syrians.

The Armenian catholicos, Gregory II Vahram (1065–1105), also was in the city at the time of the conquest. The Turks intended to kill him, but "God saved him from their hands."[9]

That the treatment of the native Christians by the Latins soon produced deep resentment may be readily inferred from the domineering conduct of the latter. The newly restored sees were filled by Latins; the Holy Sepulcher was placed in the care of a Latin monk, Gerard; a Latin patriarch was elected without any reference to the views of the Greeks; and the native Christians were deprived of their monasteries and were scandalized by the fact that women servitors had been installed in the various holy places and that relics had been appropriated by the Latins. This disaffection was manifested on the occasion of a curious event which helped to secure comparative relief for the wronged communities. When the populace gathered in the Church of the Holy Sepulcher on Saturday of the Holy Week of 1101 in expectation of the usual miraculous descent of the holy fire from heaven, this phenomenon failed to materialize. It was not until the dispossessed Christian communities were reinstated in their properties and women servants were removed from the Church of the Holy Sepulcher and the monasteries that the light appeared again.[10] Fulcher of Chartres, who as chaplain of King Baldwin I was probably an eyewitness of this event, adds some details to this account, without fundamentally altering it.

Since at the time of the conquest of Jerusalem the Moham-

---

[9] Matthew of Edessa, *Armenian Chronicle*, in *Recueil des historiens des croisades, documents arméniens* (Paris, 1869), I, 54–55.

[10] *Ibid.*

medan population had been almost completely wiped out, and the few survivors had later been expelled from the city,[11] Jerusalem was very sparsely populated during the first years of the Latin kingdom. In fact, King Baldwin I found the scarcity of inhabitants a serious problem, not only because the garrison was insufficient to man the defenses of the city but because he needed workers and merchants. After taking counsel with his nobles, he decided upon a policy of inviting the native Christian population to settle in the city. Accordingly, he made surreptitious tempting offers to Greek and Syrian Christians living in Transjordania and Hauran. Large numbers of these people accepted the invitation and removed to Jerusalem. According to the royal promise, they received concessions and privileges.[12] We are not told specifically what religious concessions were granted, but presumably the non-Latin Christians were free to conduct their ecclesiastical affairs in freedom.

II

In Antioch and Edessa the attitude of the Latin church toward the native Christians, such as the Greeks, the Jacobites, the Maronites, and the Armenians, stood out with greater clearness than in the case of the kingdom of Jerusalem, for these people comprised the majority of the population. Antioch had been a Greek stronghold even during the Seljuq period of domination (1084–98) and remained an important Greek settlement after its conquest by the Crusaders. In a letter written by the leaders to Urban II on September 11, 1098, they reported that "the Turks and pagans" had been expelled; "the heretics, however, Greeks and Armenians, Syrians and Jacobites, we cannot expel."[13] Nevertheless, they confirmed the Greek patriarch of Antioch, John IV, in his office and submitted to him as the head of the Greek-Latin Christian community. William of Tyre asserts that this was done for the sake of observing canonical rules.[14] Moreover, the Latins restored the basilica of St. Peter which had been desecrated by the Turks, who had

[11] William of Tyre, op. cit., p. 500.

[12] Ibid., p. 501.

[13] Hagenmeyer, op. cit., p. 164.

[14] Op. cit., p. 274.

used it as a stable. They provided it with icons embellished with gold and silver taken from the spoils. The clergy installed in the newly consecrated basilica comprised both Greeks and Latins. Moreover, the Latins refrained from deposing the Greek bishops in actual possession of any of the 153 episcopal sees subject to John IV, and filled only the vacant sees by Latin ecclesiastics. Nevertheless, within two years the attitude toward the Greek church changed so radically that John found it impossible to retain his post. William of Tyre, describing the event with studied understatement, says, "Videns ipse quod non satis utiliter praeesset Graecus Latinis, urbe cedens, Constantinopolim abiit."[15] Thereupon, a Latin was elected to the patriarchal office.

John's withdrawal was passed over by William of Tyre with a noncommittal phrase. But the matter is treated in greater detail by another historian, Ordericus Vitalis.[16] According to this writer, Bohemond soon determined to make the Latin influence in the ecclesiastical affairs supreme, for the Greek dominance was inimical to his anti-imperial policy. John, however, remained faithful to the emperor and the Byzantine rite. When Bohemond was taken captive on August 15, 1100, his party instantly spread the rumor that the patriarch was plotting to deliver Antioch to the emperor. John indignantly repudiated the charge but retired to a hermitage and later left Syria altogether.

As for the Armenians, they had been settling the territory round about Antioch throughout the eleventh century. Furthermore, the Armenian church was not treated as if it were a monophysite, i.e., a heretical body, but was generally regarded and dealt with as if it differed from the Roman church only in certain usages. Accordingly, a certain amount of friendly intercourse characterized the relation of the Latins to the Armenians.

Despite this general situation, however, it was with a Syrian group that the Latin church attained its most lasting success.

---

[15] *Ibid.*

[16] *Historia ecclesiastica* (Migne, *Patrologia Latina*, CLXXXVIII, 775).

These were the Maronites, occupying Mount Lebanon. For lack of space, the story cannot be fully treated, but it may be found in the work of Pierre Dib.[17] William of Tyre asserts that,

after having followed for almost five hundred years the error of a certain heresiarch, Maron (hence their name Maronites), and having separated from the church of the faithful, and having practiced their sacraments, these Syrians, under a divine inspiration, shook off their languor and . . . . having abjured their error by which they had been held so long a time and so dangerously, they returned to the unity of the church catholic, and adhering to the orthodox faith, were ready to accept and observe with great veneration the traditions of the Roman church.[18]

It is not possible here to enter into an extended discussion of this difficult problem. Suffice it to say that for our purpose it is enough to accept the fact of union between the Maronites and the Latins which has continued to our day. Because of this, the Maronites were accorded all the privileges of the Latins—both ecclesiastical and civil. They likewise enjoyed the juridical rights of the Latin bourgeoisie.[19] They retained their own patriarch who received his pallium from the pope.

The Syrian Jacobites, however, remained faithful to their ancient monophysite creed, although with some exceptions. They were quite numerous. Michael the Syrian, their patriarch of Antioch from 1166 to 1199, affords us some idea of the extent of their ecclesiastical establishment by listing the episcopal appointees from the ninth to the twelfth centuries.[20] The highest number of bishops consecrated by any one patriarch was ninety-nine. In his garrulous *Chronicle* Michael describes with abundant details the vicissitudes of the political and ecclesiastical life of his people, widely dispersed as they were throughout Syria, Mesopotamia, and Palestine, but mentions no serious interference or persecution of them on the part of the Franks. Instead, he praises their tolerance in almost exaggerated terms:

[17] *L'Eglise Maronite* (Paris, 1930), Vol. I, chap. iii.

[18] *Op. cit.*, II, 1076–77.

[19] R. Grousset, *Histoire des croisades et du Royaume Franc de Jerusalem* (Paris, 1934), II, 157–58.

[20] J. B. Chabot (ed.), *Chronique de Michel le Syrien, patriarche jacobite d'Antioche (1166–1199)* (4 vols.; Paris, 1899–1910), III, 448–82.

The Franks . . . . who occupied Antioch and Jerusalem had, as we have already mentioned, bishops in their states. Pontiffs of our church lived in their midst without persecution or molestation. For although the Franks are in accord with the Greeks about the duality of natures, yet they differ from them on many points of the faith, and are greatly estranged from them in their usages. . . . . At present we wish to show that the Franks, who at this time occupy territories in Palestine and Syria, ... never raise any difficulty on the subject of faith, nor concerning the adoption of one sole formula among all Christian peoples and tongues. But they consider as a Christian anyone who adores the cross, without further inquiry or examination.[21]

This generous witness to the tolerance of the Latins toward the Syriac population is somewhat marred by an incident which the doughty Syrian patriarch himself narrates, and which indicates that the virtue was dictated more by political than by purely religious considerations. This was the long-drawn-out and stubborn struggle between the somewhat obstinate Jacobite patriarch, Mar Athanasius VII (1090–1129), and the metropolitan of Edessa, Bar Sabuni. For some reason, the latter had been deposed and excommunicated by the patriarch. Count Baldwin II du Bourg came to the aid of the metropolitan of his capital and interceded with the patriarch on his behalf.

When these measures proved unavailing, Bar Sabuni appealed to the Latin patriarch of Antioch, Bernard of Valence. This worthy summoned Mar Athanasius to Antioch and, failing to persuade him, finally imprisoned him.[22] When the matter reached the ears of the prince, the Jacobite patriarch was ordered released. The prince likewise sharply rebuked Patriarch Bernard, saying: "You should not have judged the Syrians; that authority does not belong to you."[23]

A further proof of the cordial relations which existed between the Latin and the Jacobite churches not only in Edessa but even in Antioch is furnished by Michael in narrating some incidents which occurred during his own term of office as patriarch. Michael visited the Latin patriarch of Antioch, Amalric of Limoges, at a time when the latter had left that city in a protest against the introduction of a Greek patriarch, Athanasius. The restoration of a Greek patriarch to Antioch had been agreed to

[21] *Ibid.*, p. 222.   [22] *Ibid.*, p. 209.   [23] *Ibid.*, p. 210.

as far back as 1144, whem Emperor Manuel had defeated Prince Raymond, and was reaffirmed in the reign of Reginald of Châtillon. It had been imposed upon the latter by Emperor Manuel as a part of the penalty for Reginald's unprovoked and brutally conducted invasion of Cyprus during which he had carried off bishops and archimandrites as well as civil officials to Antioch for ransom. In order to retain his possession of the city, the defeated Reginald was obliged to concede the emperor's request that the patriarchs of Antioch *must* be chosen from among the Byzantine prelates.[24] Accordingly, when Prince Bohemond III of Antioch had brought a certain Athanasius from Constantinople (1164),[25] Amalric resented this action and in protest left the city, "hurling anathemas against the Franks of Antioch."[26]

As a sequel to this quarrel between the two patriarchs, Michael recounts the story of an earthquake (probably in 1170) which caused the collapse of the church of St. Peter. The priests and worshipers, with the Greek patriarch Athanasius, were buried under the debris. When the prince heard of the disaster, he instantly concluded that the earthquake had been brought about by Amalric's anathema and implored the latter to put a stop to the calamity. The patriarch replied: "Chase out the Greek patriarch with ignominy, for he is an interloper!" The prince ordered it done, but the unfortunate Greek prelate was found dying, having been struck by a falling pillar in the church. Nevertheless, he was put in a litter "and thrown outside the city."[27] There he died. Thereupon, Amalric made his triumphal entry into Antioch, after a voluntary exile lasting some four years.

Since such friendly relations existed between these two communions, it is not strange that in the end they led to a strong

[24] Joannis Cinnami, *Historiarum Libri VII* (Migne, *Patrologia Graeca*, CXXXIII, 528).

[25] E. A. W. Budge, *The Chronography of Gregory Abû'l Faraj* (London, 1932), I, 289.

[26] Chabot, *op. cit.*, p. 326.

[27] Michel le Syrien, "Chronique" in *Recueil des historiens des croisades, documents arméniens*), I, 371.

pro-Roman sentiment and desire for union. Had the Latins retained their hold upon the Holy Land, it is quite possible that this *rapprochement* might have produced some lasting results. At any rate, in 1237 the Jacobite patriarch, Ignatius II (1222–53), visited Jerusalem during the Easter season and there in the presence of the Dominican provincial, Philip, made his submission to Rome. He repeated his profession in a letter to Pope Innocent IV in 1247.[28] But he was not followed by the Syrian church as a whole.

Similarly friendly contacts existed between the Latins and the Armenians. Catholicos Gregory II (1065–1105) firmly believed that his church differed in no essential tenet from the Latin or the Greek communions and consequently undertook negotiations with Pope Gregory VII and Alexius Comnenos for recognition. The pope actually acknowledged the profession sent him by Gregory as essentially orthodox, although he advised the latter to omit the "Trisagion" from the liturgy and to reform certain usages. In recognition of the communion between the two churches he conferred the pallium on the Armenian catholicos.[29] The negotiations with the Greek church were not equally successful, for the Greeks demanded a change in the symbol of faith, which Gregory refused to make on the ground that the objectionable terms were held by the Armenians in an orthodox sense.[30] Accordingly, the latter consistently represented themselves, in their intercourse with the Latins and the Greeks, as opponents of monophysitism, and expressly condemned Eutyches equally with Nestorius, professing to adhere to the Cyrillian definition of the two natures in Christ. Their position to this day may be described as "pre-Chalcedonian." But they were equally cordial in their relations with the Jacobites and were unambiguously regarded by them as fellow-monophysites, since they rejected the decisions of the Council of Chalcedon, holding them to be pro-Nestorian.

[28] E. Rey, "Les Dignitaires de la Principauté d'Antioche," *Revue de l'orient latin* (Paris, 1900–1901), VIII, 155.

[29] Fr. Tournebize, *Histoire politique et religieuse de l'Arménie* (Paris, n.d.), p. 164.

[30] B. Leib, *Rome, Kiev et Byzance* (Paris, 1924), pp. 263–64, n. 2.

Armenians constituted the majority of the Christian population of the principality of Antioch. They were therefore treated with consideration. Catholicos Basil of Ani (1105–13) was received by Baldwin II in Edessa "with all regards due to his high ecclesiastical dignity"; the latter "gave him villages and many presents and showed him much friendship."[31]

Similar good will was shown by the Edessan rulers to the successor of Basil, Gregory III Bahlavuni (1113–66). It was during the term of office of this illustrious prelate that the patriarchal see was transferred to the castle of Hromgla (probably Rumkala, on the Euphrates, east of Edessa), within the borders of the county of Edessa. This fortified place formerly belongèd to Count Joscelin II. When this prince died (1144), his widow, Beatrice, leaving for Europe, granted the fortress to Catholicos Gregory and his brother. This incident is reported by Bar Hebraeus in a manifestly perverted form to the effect that the Armenian catholicos usurped the possession by force.[32] Beatrice in turn received properties in Cilicia from the Armenian ruler, Thoros II. This generosity on the part of Joscelin's widow may have been more apparent than real, for Edessa had already fallen into the hands of the Turks.

Gregory built at his new patriarchal see a magnificent church and transferred to the new sanctuary many famous relics. The prestige he enjoyed is attested by the honor with which he was received on his pilgrimage to Antioch and Jerusalem. Guiragos relates that, when the catholicos, who "was loved by all peoples," reached Antioch on his way to visit the holy places in Jerusalem, "all the inhabitants went out to meet him . . . . and conducted him with solemn pomp to the throne of the Apostle Peter, where they seated him."[33] It was at this time that Gregory took part in the synod (held at Antioch, November 30, 1139), under the presidency of the papal legate, Alberic of Ostia, which deposed Patriarch Raoul of Domfront.[34] When

---

[31] Matthew of Edessa, op. cit., p. 75.　　　　[32] Budge, op. cit., p. 277.

[33] Guiragos, "Extrait de l'histoire d'arménic," in Recueil des historiens des croisades, documents arméniens, I, 418.

[34] Tournebize, op. cit., pp. 235–39. But this author dates the Jerusalem council as of April 21, 1142 (p. 237).

the catholicos reached Jerusalem, he was received with equal honor by the patriarch. "He renewed on that occasion the ancient treaties of Tiridates and St. Gregory with Emperor Constantine and of the patriarch [pope] Sylvester."[35] Catholicos Gregory is said also to have sent an embassy to Pope Eugenius III (in 1145), and the latter accepted the Armenian profession of faith as essentially orthodox.[36]

It was during Gregory's term of office that Edessa fell, on December 23, 1144, under the attacks of Zangi. The Mohammedan leader mercifully spared the inhabitants, and only about two thousand perished on this occasion. Among them was the Latin patriarch, Hugh. But, according to Bar Hebraeus, the Jacobite metropolitan, Basil, was dragged naked before Zangi, although he was released later. The author remarks further: "Wherever the Turks found a Frank they killed him; but they left alive our people [Jacobites] and the Armenians."[37] This statement fits better the circumstances of the second fall of Edessa, although the author definitely places it during the first. Three years later, Baldwin of Marash and Joscelin retook the city, although they were able to hold it only five or six days. It was quickly recaptured by the Turks, who then wreaked a terrible vengeance upon the unhappy city. The Franks were put to death on sight, but the Syrians and the Armenians were spared. The Jacobite metropolitan was seized. Baldwin lost his life during the fearful struggle. He was greatly beloved by the Armenians, whom he is said to have preferred to his own people.[38] He had an Armenian confessor, Basil, who composed in his memory a fulsome funeral oration, replete with highly ornate figures of speech and hyperbolic flights of imagination. Nevertheless, it is an eloquent witness to the deep regard which Armenians entertained for the count.

Catholicos Gregory III was succeeded by one of the most

[35] Guiragos, *op. cit.*, p. 418. According to an Armenian tradition, when Tiridates II embraced Christianity, he went to Rome accompanied by St. Gregory, and there Tiridates and Constantine, and Gregory and Sylvester, concluded treaties of friendship.

[36] Tournebize, *op. cit.*, p. 238.   [37] Budge, *op. cit.*, p. 270.

[38] Gregory the Priest, "Chronique," in *Recueil des historiens des croisades, documents arméniens* I, 161.

illustrious figures in the history of the Armenian church—St. Narses IV the Gracious (Shnorhali, 1166–73), a theologian, poet, eloquent orator, as well as a great soul. Under him there was inaugurated a unionistic policy of which he was a sincere proponent, and which had for its objective the reunion of the Armenian and the Greek churches. He held two conferences with the Byzantine theologian, Theorianus (1170 and 1172), who was sent by Emperor Manuel Comnenos. The two negotiators came to mutual understanding regarding the fundamental objections, namely, that the Armenians were no more monophysites than the Greeks were Nestorians.[39] But before the formal recognition could be secured, the catholicos died, and negotiations were dropped for the time being.

But the policy of reunion was zealously and enthusiastically supported by Gregory's nephew and successor, Gregory IV (1173–93). He resumed the negotiations with Emperor Manuel, and in 1179 convened a council at Hromgla to consider the terms offered by the Greeks. The Fathers freely condemned Eutyches and Nestorius and professed to adhere to the Cyrillian definition of the two natures in Christ but were silent on the Council of Chalcedon. Besides, a violent opposition to the unionistic policy of the catholicos was offered by the clergy of Greater Armenia, who refused to attend the council and fought any suggestion of concessions to the Greeks and the Latins.

Gregory IV was likewise in friendly relations with the Latin church. When the Greeks of Cilicia disseminated charges of Eutychianism against the Armenians with a view to instigating a discord between them and the Latins, Gregory sent (1184) to Pope Lucius III the Armenian bishop of Philippopolis to assure the pope of the orthodoxy of his church. Lucius received the bishop with great honor and affirmed that no dogmatic differences separated the two communions.[40] But he counseled the catholicos to introduce certain liturgical changes.

The acknowledged leader of the unionist party within the Armenian church during the terms of office of Gregory IV, V, and VI (1195–1202) was St. Nerses of Lampros, archbishop of

---

[39] Tournebize, *op. cit.*, p. 246.   [40] *Ibid.*, p. 270.

Tarsus (d. 1198). He aimed at reunion with both the Latin and the Greek communions. The negotiations with the Greeks conducted at the Council of Tarsus in 1196 led to no positive results. Thereupon, negotiations with the Latins came to the fore. Nerses' writings depicted the rather low state of the Armenian church, and he endeavored to reform the situation by adopting the Latin standards. In his *Reflections* he compared the two communions as they existed at the time of the conquest, and his conclusions were clearly in favor of the Latins.[41] This quite naturally excited a storm of opposition from the nationalistic, anti-unionist party. He was accused before the ruler, Leon II, of heresy and innovations. In a courageous defense presented to Leon,[42] Nerses clearly revealed the character of the reforms advocated by the unionist party. Making a skilful use of the adoption, on the part of the ruler, of certain Western social customs, Nerses argued:

If now you no longer plait your hair, if you no longer let your beard grow, and if you have ceased to wear the ample garments, it would be even more blameworthy for us to reject with contempt the perfected institutions which we have borrowed from the Franks. . . . . In fact, having found the Armenian churches without sacerdotal garments, we adopted those of the Latins, and with their help we have restored the ancient usages. We saw that our ecclesiastics united the third, the sixth, and the ninth hours of the common prayer; fortified by the example of the Latins, we now celebrate each office at its assigned hour and chant the praises of God seven times a day. . . . .[43]

He continues to enumerate other borrowings from Latin usages, none of which, however, approximates any fundamental or dogmatic innovation.

This vigorous reformatory program would not have been possible had not Leon II (1187–1219) favored it. His support was motivated by political considerations: he had long desired to obtain a royal crown. This he wished to secure from the West rather than from the Byzantine Empire, for the obvious advantage of not having one's overlord inconveniently too near at hand. He attempted to secure his objective on the occasion

---

[41] Nerses of Lampros, *Reflections upon the Institutions of the Church*, in *Recueil des historiens des croisades, documents arméniens*, I, 576 ff.

[42] *Ibid.*, pp. 579–603.   [43] *Ibid.*, pp. 599–600.

of Emperor Frederick Barbarossa's presence in Asia Minor at the head of the Third Crusade. But the latter's death frustrated Leon's plans. Nevertheless, what he failed to secure from Barbarossa he obtained from his son, Emperor Henry VI. The latter, in conjunction with the pope, granted Leon the coveted royal title and sent him a splendid crown. Pope Celestine III commissioned the archbishop of Mainz, Cardinal Conrad of Wittelsbach, chancellor of Germany, who was then at Acre, to perform the coronation ceremony in his own behalf. But before this could take place, the pope demanded that Leon accept the program of the reforming party in the Armenian church. Leon convened a synod at which the papal conditions were presented. There was considerable opposition by the conservative party to the acceptance, but Leon quieted them by assuring the Fathers that his submission would be merely nominal; thus the value of the act was vitiated from the start by the conscious insincerity of Leon. Accordingly, this event does not warrant the conclusion sometimes drawn that the Armenian church accepted the papal supremacy. At any rate, Leon gained his objective and was crowned king at the Cathedral of St. Sophia in Tarsus, on January 6, 1198 (the Armenian New Year); both the papal legate and the Armenian catholicos participated.

Had the Crusaders retained their conquest of Syria, it is possible that the political success would have influenced the ecclesiastical situation in the direction of a permanent union between the Latins and the Armenians. But, with the collapse of the Latin power even long before the ultimate surrender of Acre, the unionistic impulse spent itself.

III

The most important subject for our consideration is the treatment accorded by the Latins to the Byzantine Orthodox church. The relation of these two communions comes to the fore predominantly only during the Third and the Fourth Crusades.

As far as the Third Crusade is concerned, the case of the church of Cyprus is of particular importance. King Richard Coeur de Lion seized the island in 1191. A few years later he bestowed it upon Guy de Lusignan, in whose family it remained for almost three centuries. Guy's successor, Amalric (1194–1205), adopted a policy of latinization of the Cypriote church. Pope Celestine III appointed, in 1196, two commissioners, under whose direction a Latin archbishop with three bishops were set up. This action is even less excusable than the intrusion of the Latins into the spheres of the autocephalous patriarchates of Jerusalem and Antioch, for in the case of Cyprus the Latin archbishop was actually set up alongside the Greek archbishop. Accordingly, this action constituted an open breach of the canons, particularly of the eighth canon of the Third Ecumenical Council which acknowledged the Cypriote church as autocephalous. The policy of complete subjection of Orthodox Greeks to the papacy was then ruthlessly pursued. By the convention of Famagusta of 1222, only four sees out of fourteen remained to the Greeks. Even this was a modification of the papal order demanding the entire suppression of all of them.[44] The Greek archbishop, Neophytos, was forced to flee, and the remaining bishops were deprived of all real power, for no Greek could assume any ecclesiastical office without the permission of the Latin ordinary. The situation led to a defiance on the part of the Greeks and resulted in a number of deaths which were looked upon as martyrdoms (1231).

The persecution was resumed in 1240 by Pope Gregory IX and was so severe that the Greek archbishop and his bishops, after stripping the churches of their treasures, secretly left the island. In 1251 the Latin metropolitan, Hugo Fagiano, ordered all Greeks who had been married with Latin rites to attend none but Latin churches and threatened to excommunicate Greek priests who should refuse to submit to him.[45] Finally, Pope Alexander IV in 1260 issued a bull abolishing the Orthodox Cypriote archiepiscopal see, and subjecting the Greek community altogether to the Latin hierarchy.

With the capture of Constantinople by the Crusaders in 1204, the Latin church was confronted with the opportunity of deal-

[44] J. Hackett, *A History of the Orthodox Church of Cyprus* (London, 1901), pp. 84–85.

[45] Raynaldus Odoricus, *Annales ecclesiastici* (Cologne, 1733), No. 37.

ing with the Byzantine church in its own stronghold and on a far vaster scale than ever before. Pope Innocent III was opposed to a permanent occupation of the city and wanted the Crusaders to proceed on to their goal—Egypt. But that was to expect too much of these "all too human" Crusaders. The spoils seized were too great. It is true that the rank and file of the army at first looked with serious misgivings upon this despoiling of fellow-Christians. According to the description of one of the simple knights, the bishops preached that it was "a righteous deed" to assault the city. They promised to "assoil all those who should attack them [the Greeks], in the name of God and by the authority of the apostolic," for the Greeks were "the enemies of God."[46]

The plunder of Constantinople, in which the Crusaders made no distinction between churches and private property, and despoiled and grossly desecrated even the Cathedral of St. Sophia, has often been described and needs no further mention. But it was a rather unfortunate prelude to the papal attempt to secure union of the two churches—East and West. Nor did the flight of Patriarch John X Kamateros from Constantinople predispose his flock to look upon the Latin patriarch, the Venetian Thomas Morosini, with favor. John had been invited by Emperor Theodore Lascaris to Nicaea but refused the offer and resigned his post in February, 1206. A few months later he died at Didymateichos. Upon his resignation, Michael IV Autoreianos (1206–12) was elected at Nicaea. The Greek clergy and monks, who had remained loyal to John, after his death regarded the patriarchal office as vacant, for they dared not acknowledge the Nicaean patriarch for political reasons. Many of the higher clergy had likewise fled before the Latins, finding refuge in the realms of Emperor Theodore Lascaris, or the other newly established Greek states of Epirus and Trebizond. At the time of the conquest, the number of clergy and monks was estimated at "a good thirty thousand."[47] Many of these remained.

[46] Robert of Clari, *The Conquest of Constantinople* (New York, 1936), p. 94.
[47] *Ibid.*, p. 112.

In the meantime, Thomas Morosini was created Latin patriarch in 1205. This was contrary to canons, for the lawful patriarch was actually living. The Byzantine historian who wrote *Concerning the Statues Destroyed by the Franks in Constantinople*[48] describes the Latin patriarch as excessively fat, shaven, wearing clothes "which were as if sewed to his body," and wearing leather gloves. He had to promise Venice to place only Venetians in the archiepiscopal sees. He died in 1211, and the see then remained vacant for four years. Innocent's triumph over Constantinople was complete when in 1215 the two rival candidates for the see appealed to him for decision, and he, setting both aside, appointed his own nominee, Gervasius.

The situation in the other newly created feudal territories— the kingdom of Salonica, the lordship of Athens, the principality of Achaia, the triarchies of Euboea, the Palatine county of Cephalonia, and the duchy of the Archipelago—although in general resembling the ecclesiastical arrangements in the empire of Romania, yet bore an individual character of its own. Many of the higher Greek clergy fled before the invaders. The revered and distinguished Athenian metropolitan, Michael Acominatus, brother of Nicetas Choniates, had left his beloved city shortly after it was taken. He retired to the island of Khios, where he stayed for the rest of his life. Metropolitan Manuel of Thebes went to the island of Andros into a voluntary exile. The archbishop of Crete found refuge at Nicaea. Corinth was not taken by the Latins until 1210. At the time of Corinth's capture, there was no Greek metropolitan. Only the Greek bishop of Negroponte, Theodore, made his submission and was permitted to retain his see.

Pope Innocent III desired to utilize the conquest of Byzantium for the realization of the age-long dream of reunion of the churches. With that aim in mind, he sent Cardinal Benedict of St. Susanna to Romania and Nicaea to win the Greeks for union on a dogmatic basis. The cardinal labored for two years

---

[48] This is usually ascribed to Nicetas Choniates and is included among his works by Migne (*Patr. Graeca*, CXXXIX, 1041 ff.); but there is some doubt as to his authorship.

(1205–7), but in vain. A dogmatic union proved an impossible goal.

Innocent required from the Greek clergy, whose orders he otherwise acknowledged, canonical obedience to himself and the Latin hierarch of Romania and the acknowledgment of the papal supremacy. But the oath of obedience was administered in a form objectionable to the Greeks: they were required to place their hands in the hands of the Latin prelates and to become their vassals, as the Greeks understood the meaning of the ceremony. Moreover, they had to inscribe the names of the pope and the Latin patriarch in the diptychs. In case they refused, they were deprived of office. It was more difficult to secure acknowledgment of the Latin patriarch than of the pope. The Greeks regarded Thomas Morosini as an intruder and the see of Constantinople, after Patriarch John's resignation, as vacant.

The newly created feudal lords were not particularly interested in furthering the aims of the papacy. Indeed, in the majority of cases, they freely despoiled the church. In northern Greece, Thessaly, and Euboea the barons subjected the Latin church to unjust exactions, seized monasteries and churches, and maltreated the monks. The same situation prevailed in Achaia, where Aleman, the lord of Patras, imprisoned the archbishop, Antelm of Cluny, and Villehardouin of Achaia refused to pay all ecclesiastical tithes. His subjects, both Greek and Latin, gladly followed his example.[49] He likewise forbade his subjects to make bequests to the church. In Athens, which had for its archbishop a Frenchman, Bérard, the ruler of the duchy, the Burgundian Othon de la Roche, repeatedly infringed upon the privileges of the Latin church, levying contribution upon the clergy and refusing to pay the tithes. At Thebes the greater part of the revenue of the archbishop was seized by its rapacious feudal lord. It must be confessed that in some instances the hierarchy was no better, robbing and plundering their sees just like the feudal lords.

Under these circumstances the Latin church had many griev-

[49] W. Miller, *The Latins in the Levant* (London, 1908), p. 64.

ances, although the Greek was in a still worse situation. By 1210 almost all ecclesiastical property had been secularized.[50] To correct these abuses, Emperor Henry (1205–16) convened a synod at Ravennika in 1210, at which a concordat was adopted: the feudal lords promised to pay ecclesiastical tithes, but, on the other hand, the clergy—Greek and Latin—had to pay them the ancient land tax. Nevertheless, the concordat remained largely a dead letter. It was not until 1223 that the papal legate, John, was able to secure a new treaty, which worked a little better.

In 1213 Pope Innocent III sent Cardinal Pelagius of Albano to secure the submission of the Greek clergy in Romania and to win the hierarchs of Nicaea for union. He was not at all suited for his task: he conducted himself in the most high-handed fashion and drove the Greeks to the verge of an open revolt. George Acropolete says of him: "He forced all to submit to the rule of old Rome. For that reason, he imprisoned monks, bound priests with chains, and closed all churches. He gave them the choice of one of two things: either to acknowledge the primacy of the pope among all the hierarchs, and to mention his name in the liturgy, or else death for refusing to do so."[51] Such tyranny drove the Greeks to appeal to Henry. They professed their loyalty to him in civil matters: "We who are of another race, and have a pontiff of our own, have submitted to your rule with our bodies, but not with our souls and spirits. We cannot repudiate our rites and ceremonies."[52] Accordingly, they requested that he either free them from the cardinal's demands or permit them to join their compatriots elsewhere. Henry, not wishing to lose so many valuable citizens, "against the will of the above mentioned legate opened the churches, freed the imprisoned monks and priests, and in such manner quieted the storm which overtook Constantinople." He only stipulated that the Greeks must acknowledge papal supremacy. Nevertheless, many of the monks and some priests left the city and took refuge with Theodore Lascaris. Pelagius'

---

[50] W. Norden, *Das Papsttum und Byzanz* (Berlin, 1903), p. 241.

[51] Georgii Acropolitae, *Annales* (Migne, *Patr. Graeca*, CXL, 1030).   [52] *Ibid.*

negotiations with that monarch likewise led to no positive result.

In conclusion it may be said that the Crusades as envisaged by Pope Urban II had for one of their goals the union of the Christian communions of the East and the West. But neither side was ready to surrender its interpretation of the dogmatic differences, such as the procession of the Holy Spirit, the use of leavened or unleavened bread, and the diversity in customs and usages. Moreover, the Crusading leaders turned the expeditions into private dynastic enterprises in which their greed and avarice, their bad faith, and later the flagrant rapacity of the leaders of the Fourth Crusade, the consequent disregard of the rights of the Greek church, and the establishment of the Latin ecclesiastical domination, made union of the two churches impossible. All this deeply embittered the future relations of the Eastern and Western churches. In the end, Crusades became a phase of the *Drang nach Osten* politics and an economic expansion and lost most of the original religious character. In their treatment of the other native Christians of the East, the Latin policies gained no permanent result except in the case of the Maronites. Although the Armenian and even the Jacobite communions for a short time showed themselves willing to court closer relations with the Latin church, the ultimate downfall of the Crusading venture cut short the development of a possible ecclesiastical *rapprochement* between these communions and Rome.

RENAISSANCE CULTURE AND CHRISTIANITY

WINFRED ERNEST GARRISON
Disciples Divinity House, University of Chicago

THE immediate influences of Renaissance culture upon the religious life of both clergy and laity were conspicuous, spectacular, and, in many cases, devastating. It produced notable changes in the visible characteristics of the church as an operating institution. It radically altered the attitudes of the intellectual classes and of vast numbers of persons who could not be called intellectuals by even the most elastic use of the term but who received its impact at second hand, and it popularized a new body of interests, a new conception of the social and even of the cosmic order and of man's place in it, and a different evaluation of religion as a factor in the social structure and in the life of the individual. But it did not immediately and directly affect the character of official, orthodox, institutional Christianity.

The Renaissance may be considered as a period, about a century and a half, ending at approximately 1525. It may also be considered as a body of thought and culture, an impulse, and a spirit. But since this cultural movement, originating for the most part in Italy, moved like a wave across Europe and arrived in other countries at different and later times and after it had largely spent its force in Italy, the chronological definition must be modified accordingly. The "when" of the Renaissance cannot be defined without reference to the "where."

But even when freed from too rigid bondage to dates, the Renaissance remains a fairly recognizable period in history. Within that period, whatever limits are assigned to it in any particular area, the effect of the cultural movement upon religion was upon the attitudes of men toward religion as it had previously been formulated and organized rather than upon the formulation and organization. The deeper influence of Renaissance culture upon the thought of Christian leaders and upon the church itself appeared only later. It is not too much to say that this influence is a much more potent and constructive factor in serious religious thought in the twentieth century than it was in the sixteenth.

Yet the immediate manifestations of the Renaissance spirit in the field of religion were far from negligible. Without them, the later and greater consequences could scarcely have occurred. It was the change in the attitudes of laymen toward religion, the rise of new intellectual interests, the development of techniques for the discovery of truth independent of revelation and not amenable to ecclesiastical authority, and the reassertion of the forgotten value and rights of the individual man, that ultimately forced the church—or some of the churches—to adopt what we have come to think of as a modern outlook. These are in great part heritages from the Renaissance. That body of inheritance included liabilities as well as assets from the standpoint of religion.

Even in the period of the high Renaissance, and in Italy, where it reached its most colorful and brilliant expression, the church received into itself certain products of the movement which affected its externals and to some degree modified its mood and its manners without modifying its faith or its organization. The most conspicuous contributions came from the arts.

Architecture is, of all the arts, the one most indispensable to any religion whose social scope extends beyond the family. If worshipers are to assemble, there must be, in most climates, a roof over their heads. Even in Greece, where the cult of the ancient gods and the mildness of the climate together rendered shelter for a worshiping assembly unnecessary, the dignity of the gods and the importance of the cultus required temples as impressive symbols of this interest and as places *at* which, if not *in* which, to worship. The Greek architect's problem was to design a structure beautiful and big enough externally to be commensurate with the status of his gods, but small enough internally to fit the ritual needs—which were nothing more than housing for an image and the paraphernalia of sacrifice—and to be within the limits of the only known method of carrying a roof load across the width of a room, namely, by a stone slab or architrave. That problem was solved by surrounding a small cella with a peristyle, thus gaining internal adaptation of structure to function, impressive external dimensions, structural solidity, and beauty. The Greeks felt no need of large public edifices of any other sort.

Rome inherited the architectural elements which Greece had created, but, with a more complex social life on an expanded scale, there came the need for buildings that were large inside as well as outside—basilicas, courts of law, public baths, palaces. It was not necessary that these should have the austere beauty of a Doric temple, but it was necessary that they mirror the magnificence and wealth of imperial Rome, that they be big enough to hold the throngs that were to frequent them, and— a basic matter to the practical builder—that a method be devised for carrying a roof across a wide and unobstructed area. The arch and the barrel-vaulted roof were the solution of this problem. As the arch prolonged horizontally became a barrel-vaulting, sometimes on an enormous scale, as in the still standing ruins of the Baths of Caracalla, so the arch revolved upon its vertical axis produced the dome, as in the Pantheon. Dome construction was neither fully learned nor much used, but there was enough of it to furnish a fruitful suggestion in that revival and adaptation of Greco-Roman architecture which is called the Renaissance style.

The church received directly the heritage of the basilica and through centuries built according to the Roman method, with such modifications as produced the Romanesque and with such diversification of design as suited her varied purposes. Out of the north, but certainly not from the Goths, came the radically different Gothic with its pointed and aspiring arches, its long-drawn lofty nave, its slender or clustered columns, its traceried windows, its pervading sense of mystery and elevation. Structurally, its characteristic was a method of counteracting the lateral thrust of a steep roof by external buttresses and the reduction of walls to little more than these buttresses and the windows between them. Spiritually, it became the world's most successful artistic expression of all that is mysterious and wonderful in religion, and of humility and adoration in the heart of man. Neither architects nor builders nor donors attached their names to Gothic churches. They cost untold labor and embodied exquisite artistry. But in the anonymity of their designers and promoters, no less than of their craftsmen in stone and glass, and in the upward sweep of all their lines, they refused to advertise the power and resources of man and were content to speak of the grace and the power of God.

Renaissance architecture came in with Brunelleschi (1377–1446), as definitely as full-blown humanism came in with Petrarch. There were palaces to be built for the newly powerful and the newly rich. There were also churches to be built, to satisfy the civic pride of thriving towns and to exhibit, to the eyes of men who were beginning to pride themselves on their emancipation from cultural traditions, the splendor and glory of the church, its opulence and power, and its leadership in the new cult of beauty. Sometimes churches were built to minister to the pride of a prince—or a *condottiere* turned prince —as when Sigismondo Malatesta threw around the Gothic church at Rimini a Renaissance shell and "did over" the interior with a liberal sprinkling of the monogram of himself and his beloved Isotta.

It is not specially significant that an occasional prince or city built a church to the glory of themselves. That is done even yet. More important is the fact that they found ready at hand an architectural style which lent itself so thoroughly to that use, and that this style was so prevalent that the glorification of man became, almost automatically, the leading motif in every church built during the period. First Brunelleschi, then Alberti (who did the Malatesta job), then all the other architects, went back to the Roman ruins for their models and to the extant works of Vitruvius for their instruction in the art of constructing buildings which would be, above all, magnificent and elegant. As ancient Rome had built with an eye to luxury, splendor, and an exhibition of the power of imperial Rome, so now the church, reviving the Roman style and developing it into Renaissance, erected arrogant and pretentious buildings displaying the magnificence of the imperial church.

Medieval art dealt rather with symbols of what was deemed the highest reality than with representations of specific realities. Its theme was not the particular person or object or situation but the supersensible mystery which eye cannot see and which brush or chisel may suggest but cannot represent. Architecture, which shares with music the quality of being nonrepresentative, was therefore the characteristic art of the Middle Ages. It outclassed music in that respect because the technique of tonal structure developed more slowly than that of building construction; and that was true partly because the remains of ancient architecture were easily accessible and supplied useful models, while the remains of ancient music were fragmentary, inaccessible, and unsatisfactory as models even when found. So in the field of nonrepresentative art, the main tradition was that of architecture. In this, and in the associated arts which used stained glass and mosaic as their materials, medieval art was at its best because it was least pictorial, most symbolic, and most adequately expressive of the prevailing interest in mystery and dogma.

Medieval painting and sculpture also tended toward the symbolic rather than the representative. In Byzantine painting, in the miniatures with which manuscripts were adorned, in pictorial mosaics, which have an unbroken and magnificent tradition from the fourth century to the thirteenth, and in the highly individualized capitals of columns in many Romanesque cloisters, there are illustration and representation of a high order, but of such sort that their high artistic value can be appreciated only if one realizes that the pictorial quality is subordinate to the symbolic.

The mood of the Renaissance reversed the order of value of these qualities. With the rise of a new sense of the beauty and value of this present world came the development of more adequate techniques for its pictorial and plastic representation. There had been two reasons why Byzantine painters and sculptors had not represented the human figure with realistic accuracy: first, they did not want to; second, they did not know how. After about the middle of the fifteenth century, artists had both the desire and the resources for such representation, and art began "to dignify the mundane life of man."

Yet art and religion remained in mutual dependence. The church needed the visual enrichment that only art could give. Artists needed the patronage which only the church could supply. The result was a compromise. In spite of a rising tide of secular interest, painters and sculptors continued to employ religious subjects to please the ecclesiastical customers, as well as secular subjects to please the growing class of secular-minded customers, but for both alike they employed methods which, instead of enforcing the ideals of mysticism and asceticism, glorified the natural man and brought glad tidings of great joy touching the life that now is.

Thus the church took into its bosom the influences against which it had warred in its creeds, and by a process of "visual education," through the medium of the pictures above its altars, the sculpture in its aisles, and the very architecture of the edifices that housed its services, inculcated the humanistic doctrine that its dogmas denied. It is not wonderful that, during the century in which every successive pope from Pius II (1458) until the election of Paul IV (1555) was a thoroughgoing man of the Renaissance, the apparatus and accessories of worship took on the coloration of the times. If this matched the people's mood in an age when, as in Boccaccio's dream of the two ways, men were turning from the arduous pursuit of otherworldly felicity—or from the admiration, if not the emulation, of those who sought that goal—and were setting their hearts upon the sight of the eyes, the joys of the flesh, and the pride of life, this Renaissance transformation of the visible church was an influence that marshaled them the way that they were going. And yet, let it be repeated, the dogmas, the sacraments, the basic ritual, and the organization of the church remained unaltered.

Only a passing and parenthetical reference can be made to music and the reciprocal influences of the Renaissance and the church in that area of culture. Most of the important developments in music during the Middle Ages had been the contributions of the church or of churchmen, though there had been a parallel (but narrower) stream of secular music in the troubadours of France and the minnesingers of Germany. Plain-song had been embellished by polyphony. Franco of Cologne transcended the canons of Pythagoras, which had been accepted as immutable principles, and declared that the true judge of consonance and dissonance was the ear. He meant *his* ear, but his example emboldened others to use their own. Elaborations of descant and the "new organum" followed. With the growth of secular inventiveness in musical form, church music began to get out of hand. In 1322 Pope John XXII issued reproof and instructions. He criticized the

disciples of the new school [who] display their probation in notes which are new to us, preferring to devise methods of their own rather than to continue singing in the old way; the music therefore of the divine office is now performed with semi-breves and minims [i.e., quarter and eighth notes] and with these notes of small value every composition is pestered. . . . . Their voices are incessantly running to and fro, intoxicating the ear, not soothing it.

He would eliminate the short notes and would permit no harmonies except the intervals of the octave, the fifth and the fourth, and these only on special occasions.

The injunctions of the pope were not literally obeyed, or not for long. Clever evasions were practiced even while his regulations were nominally in force. New elaborations were devised, partly in the royal chapels and partly in the secular schools of music which had great importance in England, the Netherlands, and Italy in the fifteenth century. Secular music was again in full tide, with Italy in the lead after about 1550, and again the music of the church was in danger of losing its distinctive and devotional character. That it did not do so was largely due to the work of Palestrina (b. 1526), who, as choirmaster of the Sistine Chapel, undertook in a conservative spirit (which contrasted with that of the novelty-loving progressives of the

Venetian school) to utilize for the church such modern ideas as seemed to him adaptable to religious uses and to discard the rest. He accepted the commission, given him by Gregory XII, to make a complete revision of plain-song. The counter-reformation in Roman Catholic music was due largely to the genius and industry of Palestrina. In music, as in no other art, the church absorbed and adapted as much of the contribution of the Renaissance as was consistent with its spiritual purposes and rejected what was not.

Protestant music, with Luther in the lead, was of an entirely different order. By its emphasis upon participation by the congregation, it led to a characteristic development of hymns, chorals, and choral singing. The Reformation influenced music quite as much as music influenced the Reformation.

In the ways that have been mentioned, the spirit of the Renaissance penetrated the church, producing conspicuous changes in its externals through the acceptance of the new methods and products of art and altering the interests and attitudes of churchmen even if it did not directly affect the doctrines or structure of the church itself.

But more important was the influence of Renaissance culture upon the attitudes of the great body of intelligent laity toward the church, or—to state it more broadly—upon the place of religion in the life of man. A shift was occurring in the center of gravity of man's interests. From being central and determinative for the whole range of thought and behavior, religion as represented by the church became a secondary, often a marginal, sometimes a negligible, consideration. To be sure, the institutions and ceremonials of religion continued to be the most conspicuous objects in the social landscape, but the spiritual life, the means of grace, and the hope of heaven were no longer the dominant interests. There was a secularization both of thought and conduct and of the standards by which both were evaluated.

It was, then, not so much that the official expressions of religion were changed by the Renaissance, or even that there was any general and immediate repudiation of them, as that those who still professed to hold them relegated them to a lower level of interest than they had hitherto occupied. What specifically happened was the development of impressive quantities of essentially secular scholarship, literature, art, and science. The great impetus for this came from an intense devotion to the cultural products of classical antiquity and a vastly increased knowledge of them. With this came an implicit, sometimes even an explicit, acceptance of the Greco-Roman conception of the dignity and possibilities of man, and, as Symonds has put it, "the further perception that classic literature alone displays human nature in the plenitude of intellectual and moral freedom." The Augustinian views of both man and society—"original sin" and "the City of God"—passed definitely into eclipse. Michelet defined the Renaissance as "the discovery of the world and of man." With newly opened and almost dazzled eyes, men looked upon these discoveries and found that they were good.

The novelty of appreciation of the beauty of the world must not be exaggerated or oversimplified. The familiar statement that Petrarch was the first man who ever climbed a mountain to admire the view lacks both convincing documentation and inherent credibility. Even saints were not oblivious to the beauties of nature. In the fourth century Basil, writing to his student-friend Gregory of Nazianzus in Athens, praised the scenic charm of a location in Pontus where he proposed that they should together retire to monastic seclusion. No one can deny that Francis was keenly sensitive to the haunting loveliness of the Umbrian hills, and an almost Buddhistic reverence for life led him to claim kinship with every creature. But Francis loved wind and sun and the blue shadows on the hills, and birds and mice and men, not for what they were in their own right or for what they might mean to him in his own right but because they were *creatures*—manifestations of God's thought and objects of his providence, and therefore fitting objects for the love of their fellow-creatures, his children.

The transition from this to the Renaissance man's appreciation of the beauty of nature and of the human body, and his delight in either making or contemplating their representations through the mediums of art, and his new-found (and more rarely experienced) joy in exploring for himself the secrets of nature and of life, was a very real transition. What it would lead to was yet to be determined. What it led to in the period of the Renaissance was the setting-aside of religion as a major and controlling interest by those who were in the full current of the new movement and the exaltation of secular interests. The ideals and values of the Renaissance tended, for better or worse, to become those of Greco-Roman paganism.

As some of these ideals and values were better and some were worse, the practical results were various and contradictory. For fine spirits, preoccupation with the visible aspects of things and the acceptance of unaccustomed liberty for the individual did not exclude a sense of spiritual realities and a moral order. We find, for example, Vittorino da Feltre, the teacher; Michelangelo, the artist; Castiglione, the courtier. For base spirits, the "discovery of the world and of man" meant release for indulgence in luxury, ruthless power, indecency, or the sins of the flesh. So we find Alexander VI, the pope; Ludovico Sforza, the usurper of Milan; Aretino, the foul-mouthed and blackmailing "scourge of princes"; and Filelfo, the racketeer of humanism. The recovery of freedom and the discovery of the values of the natural life were not accomplished without great cost to morals and religion. The Roman church itself was deeply corrupted and required subsequently a drastic house-cleaning which had to be more than once repeated. When that cleaning was reasonably complete, it was found that the important gains of the Renaissance had been swept out along with its immoral and irreligious liabilities. The tightening of discipline and of control over thought, which became effective in and after the Council of Trent, diminished even that degree of intellectual liberty which had been permitted in the medieval church. And meanwhile the abuses, which the Renaissance did not introduce but which it rendered more conspicuous, had furnished one reason for a wave of revolt which left Western Christianity permanently divided.

The Protestant Reformation began within the period which

is designated by the term "Renaissance" and was to no small degree a product of the forces which collectively bear that name. This was particularly true of the reforming movement in Italy, which owed much to the importation of Protestant ideas from northern Europe but more to indigenous impulses stemming directly from the characteristic Renaissance challenge to institutional authority, its critical spirit, and its insistence upon the intellectual and spiritual freedom of the individual. The Italian Reformation was crushed by the counter-reformation, which was also a counter-renaissance. Its methods were partly those of religious and moral reform within the church and partly those of police power and inquisition.

To the Reformation as a whole, the Renaissance furnished indispensable elements. It might be called "the Christian Renaissance," though that term has been applied, not altogether inappropriately, to fourteenth-century mysticism. Rejecting the pagan abuses of the Renaissance principle, and fully accepting the conception of religious individualism only in the revolutionary period of the movement when it was necessary for individuals to claim the right of revolt against ecclesiastical authority, the Protestant leaders made fruitful use of motives and methods which had been deeply implicit in the main stream of Renaissance culture.

First may be mentioned the interest in origins and a respect for ancient standards as possessing a validity superior to that of later ones. For humanists this meant an almost incredible enthusiasm for the Greek and Latin classics and a desire to attain the classical ideal of free and versatile personality; for reformers in religion, an equal enthusiasm for the Scriptures as the authoritative classics of the faith and a desire to restore primitive, and therefore perfect, Christianity.

The critical attitude toward contemporary institutions had led humanists to satirize ecclesiastics and flout the authority of the church, even while they remained within its membership and sometimes in its pay. Consider Lorenzo Valla's desolating critique of the "Donation of Constantine" and his no less desolating judgment upon papal misgovernment of the patrimony which

Constantine had not given to the successors of Peter; Petrarch's almost libelous descriptions of the court at Avignon; Boccaccio's hilarious and bawdy mockery of licentious monks and clerics; Guicciardini's caustic comments on Vatican politics and morals; Michelangelo's sonnet on the apostasy of Rome, where "the blood of Christ is sold, so much a quart"; Pomponazzi's general challenge of orthodox dogma and his specific denial of the immortality of the soul. The freedom these men and multitudes of others claimed, and could not be prevented from exercising in the confused state of Italy and the church from the fourteenth century to the sixteenth, was claimed and exercised also by those who, despairing of reformation within, cast off the authority that the others had only belittled or ignored, and undertook to build a new house on the ancient foundation and according to the original plans.

For the fulfilment of this purpose, the Renaissance had furnished to the Reformers the apparatus and the methodology of scholarship. Luther and Melanchthon knew their Greek. Zwingli and Calvin were linguistic humanists before they were religious reformers. Even the despised—unjustly despised— Anabaptists had their classical scholars who knew Hebrew as well as Greek.

In setting up new standards of orthodoxy no less rigid than the old, in forming alliances with the state wherever this was possible and utilizing the resources of the state to enforce uniformity of religious faith and practice, in setting up as its doctrinal basis a new Augustinianism which doomed the natural man to damnation and made even his good works bad except as supernatural grace redeemed him and sanctified them, orthodox Protestantism departed radically from the central principle of Renaissance culture. The recovery of that principle—the theologically unconditioned value of the natural life at its best and the essential validity of human processes of knowledge— remained for other agencies.

The tracing of that recovery would carry us far beyond the limits of our period and would involve following the course of philosophy and science from the sixteenth century to the twentieth, with consideration also of political and economic changes and social philosophies. In all these fields the major contributions have been made neither in the name of religion nor by professional religious leaders. But their effect upon religion has been profound.

Specifically, the whole modern movement toward religious liberty, the toleration of divergent opinions, and the belief that social stability is consistent with individual freedom of thought and utterance and is not conditioned upon religious homogeneity, is a development of ideas which gained currency in the Renaissance. These ideas for a time greatly modified the attitudes of Roman Catholics toward their church, but were decisively rejected by that church as alien to its system and not to be tolerated except when expediency requires. They were first partially utilized by the Reformers as a basis of revolt, then rejected by those Protestant churches which became national or were otherwise dominant in a given area. Their recovery and application—in so far as they have been recovered and applied—have been due more to "secular" than to religious thought. But liberal thought, growing out of the Renaissance and developing through the agencies of science, philosophy, and social progress, has penetrated modern religion.

The most significant influence of Renaissance culture upon religion is not that which was manifest in the period which is called the Renaissance but that which has colored and molded religious thought and practice from the eighteenth century to the twentieth.

NATIONALISM AND EUROPEAN CHRISTIANITY

WILHELM PAUCK

Chicago Theological Seminary
Chicago, Illinois

NATIONAL consciousness developed only during the late Middle Ages. The factors which brought it to the fore cannot be easily isolated. For a long time the feeling of natural community, which prevailed among men and which determined their actions, arose from their membership in tribal or clannish groups and from local and dynastic associations. Until this day, the people of the great unified national states of Europe think of themselves not only in terms of nationality but also in clannish, sectional, or territorial categories of loyalty. The place where a person lived and worked was cherished by him as his fatherland. So a citizen of the free German city of Cologne prized it as "his beloved fatherland."[1] In Italy it was customary to speak of a *natione senese* or of a *natione florentina,* and one meant thereby the people of Siena and of Florence.[2] The great medieval battles, which in the light of history are celebrated today as national achievements, were at their time estimated by the participants as dynastic or regional events. They had then no national significance. In the Battle of Legnano (1176), in which the Lombardian League defeated the Emperor Barbarossa, Italians fought on both sides. And in the Battle of Bouvines (1214), in which Philip Augustus of France triumphed over his English and German enemies, Frenchmen stood against Frenchmen.[3]

To be sure, some of the medieval wars led to the rise of a genuine national consciousness. The claim of the German emperors for universal rule caused an Englishman of the twelfth

---

[1] W. Mitscherlich, *Nationalismus* (2d ed.; Leipzig, 1929), p. 74.
[2] *Ibid.*   [3] *Ibid.*

286

century to ask: "Who has put the Germans as judges over the peoples?"[4] The Italians expressed their resentment against the Empire by calling the Germans barbarians, and the French compared "Gallic devotion" with German impertinence.

One of the chief contributing factors making for national consciousness was the international enterprise of the Crusades. In the frequent frictions among the various participants, traits which were deemed national came to the fore. The French learned to despise the undisciplined Germans, and the Germans felt an aversion against the *levitas Gallorum*.[5] The more the medieval people got in touch with one another, first by the life of the universal church, then especially in connection with the political ambitions of their rulers, and finally by the quickly increasing flow of commerce, the more they began to distinguish themselves from one another according to national characteristics. At the end of the medieval period the Germans knew that the Italians called them the "German beasts"[6] and that all over the world they were laughed at as the *vollen, tollen Deutschen*. Shakespeare, for example, voiced the international opinion through the mouth of Portia.[7] She liked a German "very vilely in the morning, when he is sober, and most vilely in the afternoon when he is drunk. When he is best, he is a little worse than a man, and when he is worst, he is little better than a beast." The English were known for their self-sufficient pride and their insular provincialism. They appeared foolish because of their oft-observed habit of exclaiming, at sight of a handsome foreigner: "It is a pity that he should not be an Englishman,"[8] or of voicing astonishment at a beautiful article manufactured outside of England. "Philip is a Spaniard," remarks one of the characters of the Elizabethan drama, *Sir Thomas Wyatt*, "and

[4] Paul Joachimsen, *Vom deutschen Volk zum deutschen Staat* (Leipzig, 1920), pp. 19 f.

[5] Joachimsen, *Geschichtsauffassung und Geschichtsschreibung in Deutschland unter dem Einfluss des Humanismus* (Leipzig, 1910), p. 5.

[6] E. G. Oskar Schade, *Satiren und Pasquille aus der Reformationszeit* (Hannover, 1863), III, 191, 20.

[7] *Merchant of Venice*, Act I, scene 2.

[8] Heinrich Spiess, *England im Spiegel des Auslandes* (Berlin, 1911), pp. 10 f.

what is a Spaniard?"[9] The French were criticized for their deceitfulness and instability. To the northern Europeans all Italy appeared as

> .... full of them that snarle,
> And bay and barke at other men's abuse
> Yet live themselves like beasts in all abuse.[10]

The awareness of these national traits and the animosity that accompanied them had very little practical effect as long as no national political or cultural units existed in which they could be incorporated. When the medieval order of universal ecclesiastical control was disrupted by the rise of strong monarchical states and by the development of humanism, conditions were given for the first time in which nationalism could be an effective force. To be sure, the historical process of the growth of political and cultural nationalism was very slow; it was to reach its climax only in the nineteenth and twentieth centuries. But even in its beginnings it was powerful enough to contribute to the downfall of the unified Christian civilization of the medieval church. When the medieval feudal states were transformed into governmental military units, centralized in increasingly powerful and sovereign monarchies, the feelings of national patriotism got a frame. Such lands as France, England, and Spain in which the centralization of political power in the monarchy developed most strongly along national lines thus became national states. As early as 1302 the whole French people represented by the spokesmen of the barons, cities, and prelates stood unanimously behind the king in his protest against the claims of Boniface VIII. In a similar way, Edward III of England and the parliament made efforts to achieve some emancipation from the papal influence upon England. It would be wrong to understand these events as intentional nationalist protests against the international supremacy of the papacy or even against the universal character of the church. They must rather be seen as indications of the political self-assertion of the dynastic monarchies

[9] Richard V. Lindabury, *A Study of Patriotism in the Elizabethan Drama* (Oxford, 1930), p. 87.

[10] *Ibid.*, p. 94.

tending toward a political absolutism in their dominions on the basis of their conquest of the diversified feudal forces of nobles, prelates, and bishops. This conquest was largely made possible by the rivalry of feudal powers against one another which caused them to turn one by one to the royal power with their desires and complaints, thus enabling the arbiter to assume control over their affairs. The motives of the new central political powers did not thereby become national or even nationalistic. They were and remained dynastic. Even the wars which in the light of modern history we are accustomed to judge as conflicts between the nations were centered around dynastic interests and ambitions, for which the people as nations had very little concern. But it was natural that some of these conflicts had the effect of eliciting national feelings. Such was the case during the Hundred Years' War between France and England. Also the Italians experienced a wave of national enthusiasm of defense against the French invaders during some stages of the French-Spanish struggle for the domination of Italy, beginning in 1494. But nationalism as such still played no significant role. It represented merely a possibility which had to be reckoned with.

That this whole development must be understood in terms of the achievement of territorial sovereignty on the part of the princes is best illustrated by the conditions of Germany. The rise of royal power in western European lands was paralleled in Germany by the emergence of the sovereignty of territorial princes. They had appropriated royal rights for themselves and established their superiority in victorious struggles with the feudal estates. The weakness of the imperial power which had lain prostrate since the defeat of the Hohenstaufen had called forth this strength of the territorial states. To be sure, the public life of Germany was still represented and dominated by the Empire. But the emperors never succeeded in affirming themselves as full central authorities. The unification of Germany which could correspond to the unification of the western states thus never became a fact. Shortly before the Reformation this situation produced a consciousness of a conflict between emperor and Empire, the former represented by the Hapsburg dynasty and the latter by the estates among which the territorial princes played the dominating role. The diets were the scenes of this conflict. Under such circumstances, the sense of a national unity never became a political reality. But, in contrast to the actual divisiveness of Germany, the longing for unity was so strong that, as we shall see, a German nationalism developed, which, although it was merely a dream or an attitude, had no exact parallels in other lands.

How important these changes were in the political life of Europe is indicated by the fact that the church was drawn into them and especially that the papacy was compelled officially to recognize them. The achievement of national or territorial sovereignty by the princes implied also their control over the affairs of the church in their dominions. The national and territorial churches which thus came into being were the result of a co-operation between the papacy and the princes—a co-operation which is all the more remarkable because it continued to be characterized by the mutual resentment between popes and princes that had arisen from the medieval investiture struggles. In the interest of the maintenance of their ecclesiastical supremacy which had been deeply hurt (1) by their humiliation on the part of the French national crown during the Babylonian captivity at Avignon, (2) by the papal schisms resulting therefrom, and (3) by the effects of the change of fiscal policy forced upon them by new economic circumstances, the popes often became the allies of the princes in their attempts to subject the clergy to their territorial jurisdiction. The policy of the Curia, definitely begun at the Council of Constance, of negotiating concordats with the territorial rulers amounted not only to a tacit recognition by the papacy of the existence of national and territorial churches within Christendom, but it was also dictated by the papal desire to keep the clergy and laity under control, when they demanded the right of assuming a direct responsibility for the affairs of the church. The immediate beneficiaries of this policy were the princes who, on the one hand, cleverly loosened the clergy from papal control only so far that it could not be used by the papacy against them and, on the other hand, sufficiently recognized the papal authority that they could rely on it for support in their efforts to dominate the clergy.[11]

It is one of the ironies of history that this development benefited both the Reformation and the counter-reformation. Certainly it is an oversimplified, if not mistaken, interpretation of these processes to say that the Reformation was also caused by the late medieval development of territorial churches. To be sure, the Reformation assumed an ecclesiastical organization by its alliance with the domination of the territorial princes over the church, but it must be recognized that what happened in England under Henry VIII did not take place in France or Spain, where strong national churches had come into being, and that in Germany some of the territorial princes whose ecclesiastical policy had been no different from those who furthered the Reformation chose to remain loyal to the papacy and Roman Catholicism without surrendering their territorial ecclesiastical sovereignty.[12]

In the struggles which produced these territorial and national churches the national sentiment only rarely came to the fore, although it was always latently present. It was significant that the Reform Councils were constituted in "national" voting units according to the pattern of the organization of the universities. But just as the "nations" of the universities represented geographical divisions, the "national" groups of the councils were not strict folkic units. At Constance the English "nation," representing the North, included also Ireland, Scotland, and Scandinavia, and the German "nation," representing the East, comprised Hungary and the Slavic countries. The hottest nationalist feelings which were aroused during the negotiations were caused by the Spaniards when they demanded that in the interest of maintaining the division of four nations the small English delegation be attached to the German nation. But this Spaniard-English conflict, which was ultimately settled by the seating of the Spaniards as a fifth "nation," called forth much less nationalist fervor than the rivalry of the Spaniards from

[11] Justus Hashagen, *Staat und Kirche vor der Reformation* (Essen, 1931), p. 231.
[12] *Ibid.*

Aragon, Castile, Navarre, and also Portugal among themselves.[13]

Nationalism, however, was always a threat to the church. This is proved by the fact that, after the condemnation and execution of Huss, his Czech followers expressed their loyalty to their leader in the Hussite schism dominated by high national fervor. It was of similar importance that, after the Council of Basel, the Germans expressed their desire for imperial and ecclesiastical reform in the terms of the *Grievances of the German Nation*. During the second half of the fifteenth century these grievances represented a permanent item on the agenda of the German diets. They not only contained the complaints of the German (ecclesiastical and secular) estates directed against the financial and administrative exploitation of the German Empire by the Curia but they also included the demands for the restoration of imperial unity. This combination of ecclesiastical and political concerns resulted in the development of nationalist sentiments which, with ever increasing hostility, were directed against the foreign ecclesiastical rule of Rome. The less realistic these sentiments were, the stronger they became. For they did not take into account the actual character of the dynastic ambitions of the emperors (especially Maximilian I) and of the princes and city magistrates, all of whom desired a political and ecclesiastical reform primarily for their own advantage. While other lands laid the foundations of a strong national unity, from which aggressive nationalisms arose in a slow, but steady, growth, the Germans suffered from the political disunity which the legacy of the medieval empire had bestowed upon them, and they expressed their suffering and dissatisfaction in a fervent nationalism that corresponded little to actual facts and achievements.

The content of this nationalism was expressed not only in the *Grievances of the German Nation* but also in the new awareness of German history which was one of the chief fruits of the transplantation of humanism from Italy to Germany. The fig-

[13] George C. Powers, *Nationalism at the Council of Constance* (Washington, D.C., 1927), p. 101.

ure of Ulrich von Hutten symbolizes the combination of the longing for ecclesiastical and political reform and of a nationalistic German historical consciousness.

All over Europe humanism had the effect of releasing patriotic feelings among its members. Particularly in Italy, since the days of Petrarch, it was a national movement, instilling into the minds of its followers a youthful, exuberant feeling of patriotic strength and promise. More slowly and gradually, it assumed similar characteristics also in France, Spain, and England. But in Germany, where almost from the beginning its scholarly ideals assumed rather philistine, pedestrian, conservative forms, it called forth a historiographic scholarship which was unique in its patriotic fervor. The stimulator of this peculiar interest had been the Italian humanist and papal legate, Aeneas Silvius Piccolomini.[14] In Frankfort, in 1454, he told the Germans, in order to persuade them to assume the leadership in a crusade against the Turks, that they should be mindful of the glory of their ancestors who had proved invincible even to Caesar and Augustus. And in 1459 he undertook to refute the complaints of Martin Meyr, the chancellor of the archbishop of Mainz, concerning the exploitation and impoverishment of the Germans by the Curia. He compared the Germany of his day with that of Roman times. He not only wanted to prove the growth of civilization among the Germans under the impetus of the Christian religion but he also desired to glorify the perennial power of the German virtues by directing attention to what the ancient historians, Caesar, Strabo, and Tacitus, had written about them. After his *Descriptio de situ, moribus et conditione Germaniae* had been first printed in 1496 in Leipzig, it furnished the incentive to the German humanists, among whom I name here particularly Bebel, Althamer, Aventinus, C. Celtis, Nauklerus, Sebastian Münster, Sebastian Franck, Jacob Wimpfeling, and Beatus Rhenanus, to concern themselves with the German past and present. In numerous writings of varying

[14] Paul Ulrich, *Studien zur Geschichte des deutschen Nationalbewusstseins im Zeitalter des Humanismus und der Reformation* (Berlin, 1936), pp. 32 f., 56 f.; Joachimsen, *Geschichtsauffassung und Geschichtsschreibung . . . . ,* p. 32.

quality they undertook to furnish the first geographical and historical descriptions of Germany. Relying upon Caesar and particularly upon Tacitus'[15] *Germania* and soon also upon the medieval historical traditions, they showed the glory of German achievements and praised the merits of the German character. For the first time in German history they unfolded a picture of German cultural unity. As they contrasted it with the actual particularistic divisiveness of their country, they pleaded for a restoration of the Empire on a national basis. While they were still bound to the ideological pattern of medieval Christian universalism, they began, nevertheless, to dissolve the Roman character of this universalism by appealing to the national character of the German Empire. They lifted the figure of Charlemagne as the first great German emperor from historical memory and gave to the struggles of the medieval emperors against Rome a national significance. The Alsatian humanists under the leadership of Jacob Wimpfeling[16] permitted a resentment against the French to color their patriotism. Others were under the influence of the feelings aroused by the demands for ecclesiastical and imperial reforms or by the dramatic figure of Emperor Maximilian or by the ideas of a crusade against the Turks or by the comparison between German and Italian scholarship or by the enthusiasm for local, sectional, or tribal traditions. But all of them, each in his own way, glorified the strength of the German historical character and tried to prove the justice of the German claim for leadership in the world.[17] They pointed to the scholarship of the German universities, which just at that time came into being. They praised the wealth and the civilization of the German cities. And they de-

[15] Hans Tiedemann, *Tacitus und das Nationalbewusstsein der deutschen Humanisten am Ende des 15. und am Anfang des 16. Jahrhunderts* (Berlin, 1913).

[16] Joseph Knepper, *Nationaler Gedanke und Kaiseridee bei den elsässischen Humanisten* (Freiburg, 1898).

[17] Walther Köhler, "Die deutsche Kaiseridee am Anfang des 16. Jahrhunderts," *Historische Zeitschrift*, CXLIX (1934), 47 ff.; Gerhard Ritter, "Die geschichtliche Bedeutung des deutschen Humanismus," *Historische Zeitschrift*, CXXVII (1922), 430 f.

rived an especially proud satisfaction from the fact that the Germans had given to the world the art of printing.[18]

It was Ulrich von Hutten who added to this somewhat stodgy, mothy world-view, which in spite of its new perspectives was still firmly bound to the traditional medieval ideas and ideals, a new zest and vitality. Restless by nature and uprooted from his knightly environment by the changes within feudal civilization, he had been drawn into the humanistic world of Laurentius Valla and Erasmus. He had learned from them the historically relative character of the institutions of the Roman church. He sensed that a new age was dawning but only vaguely conceived its character. While he gave himself enthusiastically to the new learning, his passion was aroused by the hindrances which the old church laid in its path. From the beginnings of his career as a wandering poet, he had been influenced by the nationalist ideas of the German humanists. They appealed to his own strongly developed patriotism. More and more he combined his resentment against the papal church with these emotions and ideas. In 1517 and 1518, after his second journey to Italy, just when he rose to fame as an imperially crowned poet laureate, he burst forth against the papal tyranny over Germany, proclaiming German freedom as the liberation from Rome. His dreams of the independence of the nation from foreign influences made him discover the national basis of the Empire. The old Roman Empire, so he came to see, was not continued in the German medieval empire. The emperors had received their crowns by grace of German political power and not by transmission from the hands of the popes. Only the "empty name" of the fallen Roman Empire had been transmitted to the Germans.[19] The Constantinian "Donation" was a forgery, as Laurentius Valla, whose book Hutten published in Germany, proved.

In Italy he had become acquainted with the *Annals* of Tacitus, first printed in 1515 in Rome. While the *Germania*, "as

---

[18] Werner Fritzemeyer, *Christenheit und Europa: Zur Geschichte des europäischen Gemeinschaftsgefühls* (München, 1931), p. 44.

[19] Hajo Holborn, *Ulrich von Hutten* (New Haven, 1937), pp. 76 f.

interpreted generally by the humanists, had given him the conception of the distinctive entity of the German people and the ideal of a universal German moral purity,"[20] the *Annals* provided him with the individual figure of Arminius, whom he now proceeded to make the symbol of the German character. He held him up before the eyes of his people as the German liberator. He placed him at the head of the German leaders and made "the emperors his successors." He understood the medieval conflicts between Empire and papacy as national clashes. He saw the successors of Varus on the papal throne and interpreted his own fight against the Romanists as in line with the resistance of his champion Arminius against the ancient Rome.[21]

Just when these ideas of Hutten had matured and when he disseminated them to an ever greater circle of hearers, the German nation began to be aroused by the appearance of Martin Luther as the religious critic of Roman ecclesiasticism. As his protest assumed more and more the character of a reform movement, it was inevitably drawn into that world of national emotional conflicts which I have been describing.

Did Luther's cause become that of a German national movement? Was the character of the German Reformation determined by the national spirit? These are the questions to which we must now direct our attention.

Anyone who desires to understand the German Reformation and the character of Protestantism must clearly distinguish between two questions: (1) How must Luther be understood in the light of the religious situation of Christianity from which he arose? and (2) How must the Reformation be understood in the light of the political and social conditions of Germany, of which it became a part?[22]

In the light of these two questions it becomes immediately clear that Luther did not become a reformer for national, or any other secular, reasons. His rise as the critic first of the in-

---

[20] *Ibid.*

[21] Joachimsen, *Geschichtsauffassung und Geschichtsschreibung . . . . ,* p. 106.

[22] Joachimsen, "Vom Mittelalter zur Reformation," *Historische Vierteljahrsschrift,* XX (1920–21), 467 ff.

dulgence system and then of the sacramental-hierarchical insti-
tutionalism of the Roman church and its theology cannot be
explained by reference to the development of the national consciousness or on the basis of the social and political disintegration of the medieval *corpus Christianum*. His religious "experience" which culminated in the question, How can I get a merci-
ful God? and the answer, *Sola fide*, is unique and indigenous to
him. To be sure, it must be seen against the background of the
religiousness of the monastic life. It must also be understood in
terms of the influences of the Occamistic theology, of mysticism,
of Augustinism, and of Paulinist biblicism upon Luther. These
influences, however, do not explain the prophetic character of
his religion.

How did the impetus which inhered in this religion produce
the Reformation? That Luther became the founder of new
Christian churches and that he upset the foundations of me-
dieval-ecclesiastical culture as no one before him had done—
this was made possible: (1) by the opposition of the Curia
against him, which he had to resist for reasons of conscience,
and (2) by the fact that in the years of 1517–21 he was forced by
the circumstances of this opposition to connect his cause with
that of the German people. When, at this time, he became
gradually a national hero, he himself, true to the call of a
religious prophet, always remained loyal to his spiritual objective: to create room in the world for Christian freedom. These
two concerns, the national need and the religious one, could
actually not be kept apart, but according to Luther's own will
and intention they always remained distinct from each other.
When, at a later time, he once called himself "the prophet of the
Germans,"[23] he seems to have united them in a religious-nation-
al self-consciousness. But, nevertheless, it remains true that the
Reformation was always more than a national religious movement, although, when this is said, one must also add that, because of its national reference, it was always less than a universal movement.

However this may be, it happened during the indulgence con-

[23] *W.A.* XXX, 3, p. 290, 28.

troversy that Luther's awareness of his contrast against the Roman Catholic institutional system of salvation was connected with the popular German grievances against the foreign Roman fiscalism. And during the immediately following fight against the danger of ban and excommunication, it occurred that Luther's gradual reconstruction of the Christian church and its faith was met by the national German movement. He became the hero both of the humanistic nationalists who, under the leadership of Hutten, aspired to freedom from Romanism, and of the inchoate popular movement which resented the Roman church as an oppressive social-political order.

The Ninety-five theses of 1517 drew Luther from the cloister into the world; his trip to Augsburg in 1518 put him in touch with the political life of the German nation; the disputation at Leipzig in 1519 brought him the support of Hutten and of German humanism. In 1520 he drew the consequences from these encounters by publishing the *Manifesto to the Nobility of the German Nation on the Improvement of the Christian Estate*. He himself unfolded a national-ecclesiastical program, giving concrete expression to the cultural self-consciousness of the German nation within the limits of the church. How far this extraordinary pamphlet was directly influenced by the voices of nationalism cannot be definitely determined.[24]

But it is clear that all the national-political forces of his day, which tended to undermine the international domination of the Roman church, were effective upon his mind, the *Grievances of the German Nation*, the polemics of the humanists and the national hopes of the Germans, the ever more articulate voices of the popular mind and the pamphlets of Hutten, and particularly in all probability the *Dialogue against the Roman Trinity*, called the *Vadiscus*, Hutten's sharpest manifesto of his anti-Roman campaign for German liberty.[25]

For Luther the *Manifesto* was part of his Christian reform program, as is indicated by the fact that it cannot be read apart

[24] Holborn, *op. cit.*, p. 141. See particularly Walther Köhler, *Luthers Schrift an den Christlichen Adel deutscher Nation im Spiegel der Kultur- und Zeitgeschichte* (Halle, 1895).

[25] *Ibid.*, pp. 281 ff.

from the two other great Reformation pamphlets of 1520, *On the Babylonian Captivity* and *On the Freedom of a Christian Man*. The nationalistic propositions which he made, calling the Germans to a national decision in words which were no less sharp and radical than Hutten's,[26] were not the most significant aspect of his mission. But to Hutten and his friend Crotus Rubianus and to the knights under the leadership of Franz von Sickingen and Sylvester von Schaumburg, Luther's cause[27] and that of the nation were the same. Crotus described Luther as "the father of his country,"[28] and Hutten wrote: "Not Luther alone is attacked in this affair, but every one of us. The sword is not pointed at one only, but every one of us is menaced."[29] The more Hutten came under the spell of Luther, with whom he finally identified himself with all the passion of his heart, although he never fully understood Luther's religious concern,[30] the more his romantic patriotism was kindled. But the identification of German with Christian liberty could not become effective unless the Reformation of the church as Luther had envisaged it in his pamphlet received the support of an emperor who executed it. When it became evident that Charles V was not the man for such a task, Luther was not shaken in the foundations of his belief. His trust was in the word of God. But Hutten collapsed in his inner being when disappointed in the emperor. Then he turned to the nation for the defense of German liberty—and did not find it.[31]

Charles V, the heir of the vast dynastic empire which Maximilian had built by clever political strategy and by the grace of a beneficent providence, personified the universal tendencies of medieval history. Under his leadership these tendencies were once more to dominate the national ones. The possibility of the

[26] *W.A.*, VI, 416, 27 ff.; 417, 29 ff.; 464, 16 ff., 31 ff.

[27] Köhler, *Luthers Schrift an den Christlichen Adel* . . . . , pp. 268 ff.

[28] *W.A. Letters*, II, 87 ff.   [29] Holborn, *op. cit.*, p. 157.

[30] On April 17, 1521, he wrote to Luther (*W.A. Letters*, II, 21): ". . . . sed in eo differunt utriusque consilia, quod mea humana sunt, tu profectior iam totus ex divinis dependes."

[31] Joachimsen, *Das Zeitalter der Reformation*, in *Propyläen-Weltgeschichte*, ed. W. Goetz (Berlin, 1931), V, 98 f.

realization of the Reformation as a national-religious movement was thus undone. But the national implications of Luther's cause could never again disappear. The meeting between the evangelical faith and patriotism had been too intimate. The longing for a national fulfilment of the hopes for ecclesiastical and political reform had been so deep that, although it could be dashed, it could never be extinguished.

Seldom had an emperor been greeted by the whole German nation as young Charles was welcomed in 1520. Jubilant voices went out to him from everywhere, not only from patriots like Hutten.[32] This expectation reached its climax at the time of the Diet of Worms. In deference to it Charles had to agree to give Luther a hearing. Against his own intention, he thereby proved that the old order of the *respublica Christiana* was nearing its end, for, by calling Luther, he demonstrated that the co-operation of the spiritual and secular powers according to the principles of a universal spiritual law was no longer an immediate, unquestioned, even automatic possibility. "Nothing more important for the future of the Reformation as a national movement could have happened."[33] The heat of national excitement can be gauged by the words of the papal legate, Aleander, who reported to Rome: Nine-tenths (of the Germans) raise the slogan "Luther," and the war cry of the other tenth, who may be indifferent to Luther, is at least: "Death to the Roman Curia!"[34] When the reformer himself came to demonstrate the absolute freedom of his biblical faith before Empire and emperor, he was not unmindful of his German responsibility. Disloyalty against the eternal word of God meant to him also disobedience against Germany.[35]

When Charles finally laid the ban upon Luther, he also banned the German nation by rendering its nationalism the political death-stroke. So one must conclude when one reads some of the expressions of the disappointment which during the

[32] Paul Thierse, *Nationaler Gedanke und die Kaiseridee bei den schlesischen Humanisten* (Breslau, 1907), p. 104.

[33] Joachimsen, *Zeitalter der Reformation*, p. 77.

[34] *Ibid.*, p. 76. [35] *W.A.* VII, 14 ff., 835.

following years appeared in the numerous popular pamphlets that left the German printing presses.[36]

It was doubtless best for the Christian religion and for Protestantism in particular that, in these decisive years, the religious universalism which from the beginnings had lived in Luther's teaching was not tied to a concrete German nationalism led by an emperor who considered himself the head of a unified German state. But it was also a consequence of this separation of the evangelical movement from the nation as a whole that, for a long time to come, German nationalism remained an unrealized dream, that it became a spiritual, cultural attitude rather than a political achievement. This fact was to determine Germany's position in the concert of nations in many tragic ways.

It is often said that the Reformation caused that division of the German nation, which, until recent times, has been the chief determining factor in Germany's foreign and inner policies. But not Luther and the Reformation were responsible for Germany's disunity, but the Emperor Charles V. When he chose to renew the medieval Catholic imperialism in order to be loyal to the destiny which had made him the ruler of the far-flung Hapsburg dynasty, he did not act with a wilful disregard of the national demands of the Germans, but according to inevitable political necessities and in terms of unavoidable implications of his inheritance. In the end, his wholly admirable career was a failure, because, in political and religious respects, the days of the universal Roman imperialism had passed. France and England, his two main political counterparts, held the future, because they embarked upon policies of national power. The de-

[36] The opinions of Lazarus Spengler, the city clerk of Nürnberg, expressed during and after the Diet of Worms, may be considered as representative (see Hans von Schubert, *Lazarus Spengler und die Reformation in Nürnberg* [Leipzig, 1934], pp. 289 f., 298, 348; see also K. Krause, *Helius Eobanus Hessus* [Gotha, 1879], pp. 320 ff.). The popular sentiments voiced in the pamphlets can be found in Schade, *op. cit.*, I, 3, 63 ff.; II, 39, 20 ff., 42, 34 ff., 67, 23 ff.; III, 103, 24 ff.; also in O. Clemen, *Flugschriften aus den ersten Jahren der Reformation* (4 vols.; Leipzig, 1907–11), esp. II, 185, 11 ff. The writings of the most popular of the evangelical pamphleteers, Eberlin von Günzburg, are of particular interest (*Sämtliche Werke*, ed. Ludwig Enders [3 vols.; Halle, 1896–1902], I, 8, 13, 80 f., 91; III, 155, 159).

feat of the Spanish Armada at the end of the century by the English fleet justly stands high in historical memory, because it marked the end of medieval Catholic imperialism and the beginning of modern national imperialism. In this victory the Protestant-Catholic conflict played a significant role. The Spanish prisoners who are reported to have said after the destruction of the Armada that Christ himself had proved to be a Lutheran[37] had a correct awareness of world-historical issues; for the modern nationalism which had triumphed over them could not have arisen without the Luthern Reformation.

Nominally the Holy Roman Empire continued to cast its shadow over Europe until 1806, when Napoleon's French nationalism strode across Europe, but ideally and actually it had perished under the religious assault of Martin Luther. The reformer was aware of this achievement. The "Latin nation," in defense of which men like Thomas Murner attacked the Reformation, no longer fascinated his mind. While in the Empire the territorial, particularistic powers established themselves, primarily because of the Reformation, thus deepening the political division of Germany, and while the old imperial ideal was once more raised high, he thought of the emperor as a free German lord and king, and the concern for Germany as a free nation always was on his mind.[38] One cannot interpret Luther as an advocate of nationalism or as a champion of national policies, but it can well be understood why the Germans have made him the symbol[39] and the representative of what they call *das deutsche Wesen*. They not only see in Luther those features of mind and character which they identify as the specific essence of German personal culture but they also recognize him as a prophet of that nationalism which throughout modern history has been their achievement and their dream. He is to them the

[37] *Somers Tracts*, ed. Walter Scott (2d ed., London, 1809), pp. 434 f.

[38] Otto Scheel, *Evangelium, Kirche und Volk bei Luther* (Leipzig, 1934), p. 63; see also Köhler, "Die deutsche Kaiseridee am Anfang des 16. Jahrhunderts," *op. cit.*, p. 50. I give the following references to Luther's works: *W.A.*, VI, 292; 418, 25 ff., 419, 23 ff.; XXX, II, 107, 9 ff., 110, 18, 129, 25 ff.; 130, 7 ff., 130, 22 ff., 131, 32 ff., 143, 145, 27 ff., 180, 44; L, 75; *W.A. Table-Talk*, IV, 523.

[39] Gerhard Ritter, *Martin Luther, Gestalt und Symbol* (Leipzig, 1925).

embodiment of that cultural nationalism which, begun in humanism, was given a fresh impetus by the Lutheran social ethics and its expressions in home, school, and state.[40]

But he is held high by them also as one who voiced the ambitions for political national unity, freedom, and power, which, for so long a time, remained unfulfilled.[41] It is indeed significant that no picture of Luther can be complete unless the traits of his personality on which these interpretations of his national significance are based are fully recognized. No other Protestant reformer and no other religious leader of his time was a national figure, a representative of his nation in the way in which he was such a person.

However, in spite of the validity of all this, the observation is still to the point that Luther would have opposed the pope with no less violence if the pope had resided in Germany and not in Rome. For the Reformation was not primarily a national movement but a supernational religious revolt against the institutional humanization of the revelation of the sovereign God. But its gospel of the prophetic Christian freedom on the basis of faith in the word of God was naturally connected by its contemporaries with that political and social freedom from the bonds of medieval Roman Catholic civilization which, in the course of developments within the medieval system, they had come to demand for themselves. It was the tragedy of the German Reformation that it encountered a nationalism and a political situation in Germany which it could not liberate. But what Protestantism could not achieve in Germany was accomplished in other lands. Particularly Sweden and England became free nations with the help of the Reformation. There Protestantism entered a full union with the national spirit. Of what character this union was is another story which cannot here be told.

[40] Karl Holl, *Die Kulturbedeutung der Reformation*, in *Gesammelte Aufsätze* (2d ed.; Tübingen, 1923), I, 468–543).

[41] See, e.g., the various expressions of Luther's love and concern for Germany in *W.A.*, V, 379; VI, 415, 13 ff.; *W.A.*, *Letters*, II, 305, 9 ff., 397 ("Germanis meis natus sum, quibus et serviam"); XVI, 53, 5 ff.; XIX, 261; XXX, 3, 290, 28 ff., 291 ff.; LI, 259, 7 ff.

THE RELIGION OF EARLY FREEMASONRY

CHARLES H. LYTTLE

Meadville Theological School
Chicago, Illinois

A Mason is obliged, by his tenure, to obey the moral law; and if he rightly understand the art, he will never be a STUPID ATHEIST nor an IRRELIGIOUS LIBERTINE. But though in ancient times Masons were charged in every country to be of the religion of that Country or Nation, whatever it was, yet 'tis now thought more expedient only to oblige them to that Religion in which all men agree, leaving their particular opinion to themselves; that is, to be GOOD MEN AND TRUE, or men of Honour and Honesty, by whatever denominations or persuasions they may be distinguished; whereby Masonry becomes the CENTER OF UNION and the means of conciliating true friendship among persons that must otherwise have remained at a perpetual distance.

SIX years after its formation in 1717 out of four small lodges of Freemasons meeting sporadically in London taverns, the Grand Lodge of England caused to be compiled from manuscript records of the craft's medieval charges and regulations, as well as from other sources we shall treat of later, an official book of *Constitutions of the Right Worshipfull Fraternity of Accepted Freemasons.*[1] The text quoted above constitutes Article I, "Of God and Religion," which follows the "History of the Craft" in the book. Considering the immense prestige and influence of Freemasonry in the Western world during the two centuries that have passed since its reorganization, as well as the bitter religious and political opposition it then encountered and is still meeting in the totalitarian states, a new study, by a non-Masonic historian, of its original religious basis may not be without value.[2]

---

[1] "Accepted" Masons were in general honorary members of the old fraternity of working or operative Masons and certainly after 1646, when Ashmole was "accepted" into a lodge, represented an increasing "speculative" element, interested chiefly in the antiquarian and secret symbolic (architecture-geometry) aspects of the craft, its traditions and usages. The fraternity, more rural and itinerant in character than the city guild, was thus more easily taken over by the speculative or "accepted" members (R. F. Gould, *Collected Essays* [London, 1913], chap. iii).

[2] A. Singer, *Der Kampf Roms gegen die Freimaurerei* (Leipzig, 1925).

Within Masonry itself a vigorous difference of opinion has long existed, some interpreters insisting that Deism was that basis; others that, in spite of the indifferentist tone of the article, Christianity was the understood foundation of the idealism of the new as of the old Freemasonry.[3] Of late years a German Masonic historian, Ludwig Keller, has gone to great lengths in maintaining that the real, though cryptic, intention of the sponsors of the revival and ensuing metamorphosis of Freemasonry was the promulgation of a religion of humanity which, since Pythagoras, had been, under different names and forms, the secret credo of numerous esoteric groups of heterodox thinkers in Egypt, Greece, Judea, Rome, the Middle Ages, and the Renaissance.[4] Gathering strength through the philosophic ferment and sectarian conflicts of the sixteenth and seventeenth centuries, this tendency, he argued, finally found free expression and expansion under the Whig regime in England in the new Freemasonry.[5]

Though it is impossible within the limitations of space imposed on this article to expatiate and to adjudge this long controversy, it may be feasible and profitable to indicate certain facts and arguments which seem to have been underestimated. Article I and the earliest ritual were undoubtedly composed by the leaders of the renascence and the ensuing metamorphosis of the fraternity. The two documents imposed a religious character upon Freemasonry which it has never lost. It is to be presumed that they carefully weighed every phrase of the article and purposefully capitalized certain words. It is obvious, therefore, that they meant the world to understand that the fraternity was revised in order to serve as a unifying, conciliating "Center of Union" in a time of dissension; that it was committed to some form of Theism as against "stupid atheists" and

---

[3] G. Oliver, *Golden Remains of Early Masonic Writers* (London, 1847).

[4] *Die geistigen Grundlagen der Freimaurerei* (Berlin, 1922), summarizing his many books and articles in the publications of the Comenius Gesellschaft.

[5] The records of the fraternity for the period from 1717 to 1723 are very meager. We have nothing but the *Constitutions* of 1723 and a much challenged "enrichment" of the "History" (1714–23) in Anderson's revised *Constitutions* of 1738. The minutes of the Grand Lodge commence in 1723.

was intended to foster ethical living by the power and light of religion, in opposition to irreligious libertinism. But what religion? That "in which all men agree," whose duties are primarily the practice of morality. To hold fast to such essentials, even though professing special doctrines, is a sign of rightly understanding the "Royal Art," that is, the art of spiritual architecture, the building of the temple of God in the soul.[6]

It is at once noticed that Christianity is not stipulated as the religious basis of the renovated fraternity. Natural religion is the basis, as is wholly proper and consistent for a brotherhood which has traversed many centuries and countries, according to the "History" prefixed to the Constitutions, and presumably is to continue this course in the future. In European theology from the twelfth to the middle of the nineteenth century the universality of natural religion and its priority to revealed were unquestioningly conceded, and the five "common notions" of Lord Herbert of Cherbury were generally accepted as its content, though his intuitionism was doubted.[7] "The religion in which all men agree" was its current definition in the period we are studying, and the religion of nature was commonly regarded not as complete in itself but as a divine preface to Christian revelation.[8] Such is the plain purport of a subsequent charge in the Constitutions:

No private piques or quarrels must be brought within the door of the Lodge, far less any quarrels about Religion or State policy; we being only, as Masons, of the Catholic religion above mentioned. We are also of all nations and tongues and kindreds and languages.

[6] Masonic historiography is voluminous and largely subjective. The most factual and least doctrinaire versions in recent years are: A. Wolfstieg, Werden und Wesen der Freimaurerei (Ursprung und Philosophie) (2 vols.; Berlin, 1923); Bibliographie der freimaurerischen Literatur (4 vols.; Leipzig, 1923–26); A. G. Mackay, Encyclopedia of Freemasonry (Clegg-Hughan revision; New York, 1921); A. E. Waite, A New Encyclopedia of Freemasonry (London, 1921); R. F. Gould, A Library of Freemasonry (Philadelphia, 1911). The Transactions of the Quatuor Coronati Lodge of London contain a series of valuable monographs (A.Q.C.).

[7] See his De veritate, trans. M. H. Carré (Bristol, 1937); C. H. Lyttle, "Lord Herbert of Cherbury, Apostle of Ethical Theism," Church History, December, 1935; C. C. J. Webb, Studies in the History of Natural Theology (Oxford, 1915), chap. vii.

[8] J. Toland, Tetradymus (London, 1720), p. 94; W. Wollaston, The Religion of Nature Delineated (London, 1722), p. 211; Wolfstieg, Ursprung, II, 182. A Scotch Lodge MS, Old Charges, of about 1690 contains the phrase, "the religion in which all men agree."

That is, "constructive" not "critical" Deism was the vital nucleus which British Masons might supplement, if they desired, by Anglican or Protestant or even Roman Catholic Christianity; Mohammedan Masons (if any) by Islam, etc. Thus only could Freemasonry be at once a "Center of Union" in the present and also claim a consistent lineage from Jewish, Egyptian, Greek, and Roman mysteries. It is patent, therefore, that Anderson, Desaguliers (whom we shall presently describe), and the other leaders of the revival believed sincerely that, in adapting the medieval *Old Charges* to the needs of the new age, they were preserving the essential religious spirit and faith of the old craft, as well as promoting the cause of true Christianity and its message of love, purity, and righteousness. Did they not place upon the altar of the lodge room a Bible opened at the first chapter of John's Gospel? Did not the "History" of 1723 refer frequently to the Messiah, "the Grand Architect of the Christian Church"? Did they not continue to hold the chief meetings of the Grand Lodge on the holy days of St. John the Baptist (June 24) and St. John the Evangelist (December 27)? Not Deism alone, or natural religion, its virtual synonym, but ethical Theism enriched by the "rational Christianity"[9] of the day, as well as the "love" ethic and Logos philosophy of the Johannine writings, was the religious basis of early Freemasonry and to a greater or less degree, except for the Grand Orient Lodge of France, has always remained such.

But we should gravely err if we deemed the propagation of Christian Deism, as such, the objective of the new aspect of Freemasonry. We should be equally wrong in surmising that its coryphees deliberately intended to break with the ancient beliefs and usages of the craft. On the contrary, their objectives were very practical and reverent, and they sincerely sought to carry on the principal features of the old brotherhood. They

[9] For "rational Christianity" of this period (Tillotson, Locke, Calamy, etc.) see N. Sykes, *Church and State in England in the Eighteenth Century* (Cambridge, 1934), p. 255; E. C. Mossner, *Bishop Butler and the Age of Reason* (New York, 1936), pp. 20 ff., and the same authority for Deism, Natural Religion, and the New Philosophy and Science; for critical Deism, N. L. Torrey, *Voltaire and the English Deists* (New Haven, 1930), chap. iii; for "Newtonianism" as a religious philosophy, E. A. Burtt, *Metaphysics of Modern Physics* (New York, 1925), p. 282.

explicitly provided by the article of 1723, as well as in its revision of 1738,[10] that the orthodox Christianity of the medieval fraternity might be sincerely adhered to by those Masons who chose to do so. Indeed, in all that we have in print of official and unofficial information concerning the renascence of the fraternity, there are but three utterances which might be construed as in anywise critical of orthodox Christianity. The first is Anderson's narrative of the events of the revival prior to 1723, when the minutes of the Grand Lodge begin: "The old Gothic Constitutions were examined and found faulty and James Anderson, M.A., was commanded to redact them in a new and better fashion." But there is certainly nothing anti-Christian in the term "Gothic" used for "medieval"! The second is in the "Master's Song" published at the end of the *Constitution* book of 1723:

> Thus, though in Italy the art
> From Gothic rubbish first was raised,
> And great Palladio did impart
> A style by Masons justly praised,
> Yet here his mighty rival, Jones,
> Of British architects the prime,
> Did raise such heaps of glorious stones
> As ne'er were matched since Caesar's time.

But this only expresses a preference for the Baroque style of architecture, which is not so strange, considering the magnificence of St. Paul's Cathedral, completed by the Masons of London in 1708; while the grand master and his wardens had just laid the cornerstone of the graceful new St. Martin's in the Fields (1722), a late Baroque masterpiece.

The third is of greater weight than the foregoing and occurs in an important publication of the year 1722, while the compilation of the *Constitutions* was in progress. The pamphlet is entitled *Long Livers*, by "Eugene Philalethes, F.R.S." It is ad-

---

[10] "In ancient times the Christian Masons were charged to comply with the Christian usages of each country where they traveled or worked; but Masonry being found in all nations, of divers religions, they are now only charged to adhere to that religion in which all men agree (leaving each Brother to his own particular opinion) . . . . for they all agree in the three great articles of Noah enough to preserve the Cement of the Lodge." J. Selden in his *De jure naturale* (London, 1640) refers to the "Three articles of Noah" as a basis for religious toleration: fear God, love the brotherhood, honor the king.

dressed to the "Most Ancient and Honorable Fraternity of Free Masons," whom it hails as "Men, Brothers":

. . . . the genuine language of the first Christian Brothers as we learn from the Holy Scriptures and an unbroken tradition. . . . .
  If the rejection of all heathen superstitious beliefs in gods and the belief in One God, the Almighty Father, Creator of heaven and earth, the greatest, most important, eternal, fundamental article of the most holy, universal, all-embracing faith makes anyone an atheist, then we are all such and boast of it. . . . . The religion that we acknowledge, which is the best which ever was and is and will be, and no one who lives by it can be forever lost, for it is the Law of Nature, which is the Law of God, for God is the Nature . . . . it says, love God above all and our neighbor as ourself; that is true, original, catholic, universal and comprehensive religion which all times and ages have acknowledged and which was confirmed by our Lord and Master Jesus Christ, who revived the old Brotherhood, whose Brothers we are. Our Confession is the Law of Nature, which through Jesus the Son of God is restored as the Law of Grace. *And it would have been better for the Christian world if it had held to this divine rule and not darkened his Holy Religion through senseless speculations.*
  . . . . Avoid all companies where religion is ridiculed, especially the mystery of the Holy Trinity, which is a Masonic teaching, taught by all sages, Socrates, Seneca. . . . .[11]

It is not beyond the range of possibility that this pamphlet, so strikingly analogous in many points to the views of Anderson and Desaguliers, as we shall see later, is the pseudonymous publication of the lost address of the latter on "Masons and Masonry," which was delivered before the fraternity at the Grand Lodge of June 24, 1721. In any case, its tenor is hardly anti-Christian, though manifestly the writer had a vehement dislike and distrust of dogmatic theology.

Christian Deism, like its parents, rational Christianity and natural religion, stressed conduct before faith, distinguished essential Christianity from orthodoxy, advocated tolerance as a corollary of the Christian ethic, and colligated in one lineage the gospel of Jesus Christ with the religious and moral philosophy of the noblest of the ancient sages, so that allegiance to the latter

---

[11] *Long Livers* is reprinted in the "Bain Reprints" by R. F. Gould (Sunderland, 1892), No. 2. (Italics ours.) For a discussion of the pamphlet see Wolfstieg, *Ursprung*, II, 183; W. Begemann, *Vorgeschichte und Anfänge der Freimaurerei in England* (2 vols.; Berlin, 1909), II, 60. It contains the merest trace of Rosicrucianism, in its reference to Christ as the "stone of the corner" (Aben). The author claims to be a "Masonic novice" and a "Christian Deist."

had saving efficacy and obviated the necessity for subservience to ecclesiasticism.[12] One would suppose that such an attitude found no support in the *Charges* of the fraternity in the medieval operative days, but that the latter, whenever it was relevant to speak of religion, would insist upon orthodox beliefs, with stringent injunctions against heresy. If such were the case, the protagonists of the revival, especially Anderson and Desaguliers, must have been guilty of brazen deception when they represented the new form of Freemasonry as the legitimate successor of the old, entitled to all its claims of venerable antiquity, dignity, and authority. Did the authors of the *Constitutions* deliberately falsify the old tradition, invent a preposterous history to provide authority for their "religion in which all men agree," and repudiate the orthodox piety of the cathedral builders?

By the testimony of the ancient records of the medieval craft, of which over seventy manuscripts have been recovered and analyzed, not one of these accusations is justified. It is impossible to repeat in this paper the painstaking analysis of the documents which has been carried on since 1860,[13] but certain conclusions may be briefly stated:

a) Strong emphasis is laid upon the moral conduct of the apprentice and fellow-craftsman (later Master Mason) and upon his fidelity to his calling and loyalty to his comrades under all circumstances.[14]

b) A history of the craft is offered which traces its pedigree back to Adam, Noah, Solomon, Hiram, the Egyptians, Euclid, etc., teachers and transmitters of the seven liberal arts, especially geometry.

c) The existence of craft secrets and lore is hinted at, to preseve the sanctity of which the initiate is strictly admonished. Traces of "speculative" Masonry appear.

---

[12] A. Plummer, *The Church of England in the Eighteenth Century* (Oxford, 1910), chap. iii; J. J. Tayler, *Retrospect of the Religious Life of England* (London, 1876), pp. 244 ff. M. Tindal in *Christianity as Old as Creation* (1730) and T. Morgan in *The Moral Philosopher* (1737) assumed the name. Addison and Shaftesbury deserved it.

[13] The documents may be found in R. F. Gould, *History of Freemasonry* (6 vols.; London, 1885); E. Conder, *Records of the Hole Craft and Felawship of Masons* (London, 1894). The oldest is probably the Regius MS of *ca.* A.D. 1390; next in importance is the Cooke MS of *ca.* 1425.

[14] The Regius MS was earlier supposed to be simply "A Poem of Moral Duties" owing to such strong emphasis. Its *primus punctus* is, "He who would thoroughly understand Masonry and come to authority must love God and Holy Church, love his Master as his comrades." A prayer to Mary was probably added by a clerical redactor.

d) The religious element is very slight, and theological doctrines are virtually nonexistent. The affinity of Masons for heretical tenets is more than once hinted at and rebuked.[15]

We do not know what manuscripts of the *Old Charges* Anderson used as the bases of the *Constitutions* of 1723; but one was publicly printed in 1722, at the time he was at work, and its charges to the candidate for the fellow-craft degree must have been under his eye.[16] What was their religious and moral import? Noting that the "History" traces the craft back to Lamech, Babylon, Euclid, Solomon, Charlemagne, and Athelstan, and that it begins with the benediction, "The Almighty Father of Heaven, in the Wisdom of His glorious Son, through the goodness of the Holy Ghost, three persons in one Godhead, be with our beginning and give us his grace to govern our lives that we shall come to his bliss that shall never have an end," we pass on to the charges, taken under oath, "So help me God and the contents of this Holy Book":

I am to admonish you to honor God in his Holy Church; that you use no heresy, schism or error in your undertakings or discredit men's teachings. . . . .[17]

[To be true to] our sovereign Lord, the King, his heirs and lawful successors, committing no treason. . . . .

Ye shall be true to your fellows and brethren of the science of Masonry and do to them as you would be done by. . . . .

Ye shall keep secret the obscure and intricate parts of the Science, not disclosing them to any but such as study and use the same. . . . .

Ye shall do your work truly and faithfully, endeavoring the profit and advantage of him that is the owner of said work.

Ye shall duly reverence your fellows, that the bond of charity and mutuall love may continue steadfast and stable amongst you.

Ye shall not frequent any houses of bawdery or be a pander to any of your fellows or others, which would be a great scandal to the Science.

[Other Charges prohibit drunkenness, gambling, adultery, evasion of debts, etc.]

[15] An excellent critical summary and appraisal of the *Old Charges* is given by R. F. Gould, *Concise History of Freemasonry* (London, 1903), pp. 201 and 273; *Collected Essays*, Vols. I and II; cf. Begemann, *op. cit.*, I, 68 ff.

[16] J. F. Newton, *The Old Constitutions of Freemasonry* (Anamosa, Iowa, 1917).

[17] The Cooke MS, with which the old *Constitution* of 1722 has much in common, stated the *primus punctus* as, "It becomes one who desires to attain the mastery of the art first and especially to love God, Holy Church and all Saints and his Master and fellows as his own brothers."

It is obvious that the main features and emphases of the old craft were continued in the revival, though with some modification. Legendary history, the participation of kings and ancient geometricians, the glorification and allegorization of that science, craft secrets, loyalty to king and church, avoidance of doctrinal and political dissension, fraternal unity and beneficence, and a strict moral discipline—all were in the tradition.[18]

But the new Arian form of the words introducing the "History" in the 1722 *Old Constitutions* as well as the alteration of the phrase "God and Holy Church" to "God *in* his Holy Church" indicate not only the nature and extent of the Christian Deist emendations which Anderson and Desaguliers were making but also the relative slightness of those changes—from a Latitudinarian point of view.[19]

With the best of logic they may have reasoned that, for an institution which had claimed and was to claim a lineage far antecedent to Christianity, the imposition of distinctive Christian dogmas upon Noah, Lamech, Solomon, and Euclid would be the height of historical inconsistency and absurdity. Was not Christian Deism the only possible compromise and consensus? Perhaps they felt that the paucity of theological content in the *Old Charges* indicated the tacit agreement of medieval Freemasons with this logic and this consensus!

The precise importance of their colleagues—Anthony Sayer, George Payne, John Beal, M.D., and the Duke of Montague—in the devising and effecting of the reconstruction of Masonry from 1717 to 1721–25 (when the development of the three de-

[18] It seems to the writer highly probable that the publications *Long Livers* and *The Old Constitutions of Freemasonry* were pseudonymously published in 1722 by Anderson and Desaguliers, respectively, or at their instigation, with the intention of serving advance notice of the changes they proposed to make to adapt the old fraternity. The leaders took pains to prepare the ground further by securing the full approval of Lord Townsend, then head of the government, and of publishing a specimen of the new catechism in the *Post Boy.*

[19] L. Vibert (*Anderson's Constitutions of 1723* [Washington, 1924]) asserts that these changes were responsible for the conflict in the Grand Lodge (1722–23). There is no explicit evidence of this, and the likelihood is that the trouble was due to Wharton's desertion of the Whigs and his participation in the notorious "Hell-fire Club." The enlarged emphasis on loyalty to "your lawful King, his heirs and successors" is quite as significant as the religious changes.

grees of the Blue Lodge was consolidated) we have no means of knowing.[20] There can be no doubt, however, that Anderson and Desaguliers were most responsible for the *Constitutions* of 1723, hence we may profitably direct our attention to exploring their individual religious views and possible motives for undertaking and guiding the revival.

Rev. James Anderson, M.A., was born and educated in Scotland (Marischal College, Aberdeen?) and may well have been acquainted with, if not a member of, a Scottish lodge, containing a number of "accepted," i.e., speculative Masons, before coming to London to occupy the ministry of the Scots' Presbyterian Church in Swallow Street, Piccadilly, close to the Huguenot church of which the refugee father of Desaguliers was then minister.[21] Tradition has it that he became chaplain of the London guild of Freemasons in 1710, that he suggested the admittance of wealthy "accepted" members in 1714, and that he had a hand in the rumored exclusion of operative Masons of the guild from the meetings of the Collateral Fraternity in 1715. Whether or not he actively participated in the union of the four London lodges in the Grand Lodge (1717) is uncertain, but it seems likely, since the various manuscript *Old Charges*, collected at the instance of Payne, were placed in his hands after he had been commissioned in 1721 to prepare the new *Constitutions*.

How much assistance Desaguliers gave him in preparing the new *Constitutions* cannot be exactly determined, but between them the History of the Craft was augmented by much material on Pythagoreanism (Jamblichus' works in that field had recently been published) and on the history of architecture, apparently from Adam Mirus. Anderson's archeological interests are patent, for he spends much time on the buildings of the Bible,

[20] Sayer was elected grand master of the Grand Lodge in 1717; George Payne, secretary of the Tax Office in Whitehall, in 1718 and 1720; Dr. Desaguliers in 1719; the Duke of Montague in 1721, with John Beal, M.D., as deputy; the unstable Duke of Wharton in 1722; the Whig Earl of Dalkeith, with Desaguliers as deputy, in 1723. After the struggle with the now Jacobite Wharton in 1723 and his invention of the Order of the Gormogons to rival Freemasonry, Desaguliers was again made deputy in 1725.

[21] Waite, *op. cit.*, I, 25; Gould, *Library*, II, 42; W. Robbins, *Transactions of the Quatuor Coronati Lodge*, XXIII, 56; Wolfstieg, *Ursprung*, II, 207.

particularly Solomon's Temple—a model of which was then on exhibition in London. Far from excising Christianity, he interjects into the old traditions frequent and inconsistent references to it; Noah is credited with preserving the "good old religion of the promised Messiah" along with the "Royal Art," while in Augustus' reign "God's Messiah, the Great Architect of the Church was born."[22]

This is, of course, Christian Deism after the fashion of Locke's *Reasonableness of Christianity*. It was not Socinianism, for we have a later sermon of Anderson against them and Deists.[23] Besides the revision of the *Constitutions* in 1738, we have from his pen a *Defence of Freemasonry*, published later than 1723. It is illuminating for its citations of the customs of the Pythagorean brotherhood, of the Essenes, Cabbalists, and Druids to justify the Mason's grisly oath of secrecy, the password and secret grip, the use of symbols of moral truth taken from geometry, the significance of the acacia carried in the ritual search for the body of the murdered Hiram Abif, Solomon's heroic master-architect, the white robe of the novice. Throughout the somewhat veiled disquisition one feels Anderson's strong sympathy for ethnic religions: "The conformity between the rites and principles of Masonry . . . . and the many customs and ceremonies of the ancients must give delight to a person of any taste and curiosity." His zealous antiquarianism appears in the plea that "Masonry, with all its blemishes and misfortunes, ought to be received with some candour and esteem from a veneration of its ANTIQUITY."[24] But the most positive and noteworthy of the guarded statements is that which concedes the "end, the moral,

[22] In the 1738 *Constitutions*, this was changed to: "The Word was made flesh, or the Lord Jesus Christ Immanuel was born, the Great Architect or Grand Master of the Christian Church . . . . who rose again from the dead for the justification of all who believe on him."

[23] See W. J. Chetwode-Crawley, *Transactions of the Quatuor Coronati Lodge*, Vol. XXIII.

[24] In 1721 Dr. William Stukely, Anglican priest, F.R.S., and one of the founders of the Antiquarian Society (1717), became a Mason, "suspecting it to be the remains of the mystery of the Ancients." In a later study of the Druids he says, "I was surprised to find them so near akin to Christian doctrine" (R. F. Gould, "Dr. William Stukely," *Transactions of the Quatuor Coronati Lodge*, VI, 127).

the purport and substance" of Masonry to be "to help men sub-
due their passions; not to do our own will, to make daily
progress in a laudable art; to promote morality, charity, good
fellowship, good nature and humanity."[25] In juxtaposition to
this, place his plea in the peroration of his most popular sermon
("No King-killers" [1715]):

As far as we are agreed, let us walk by the same rule and mind the same
things. So shall we be a happy people. Let us heartily join in prayer to the
God of all grace that He would be graciously pleased to heal all our divisions
and breaches by sending his Holy Spirit into our hearts and uniting them.

Does not the evidence justify the conclusion that, led by his
antiquarian interests to affiliate with an Aberdeen, then with a
London, lodge, composed chiefly of accepted or speculative
Masons, Mr. Anderson was further attracted to the fraternity by the strong emphasis of its traditions upon personal
morality and social harmony, infused with a simple and rational
Christian piety; and that, in a time when political and moral
anarchy, owing to Jacobite intrigue and religious skepticism,
was threatening the "freeborn English Nation" and its new
liberties won by the Whig party, he was foremost of several like-
minded brothers to perceive the advantage of adapting and
promoting Freemasonry as a means of restoring and fortifying
national unity, morality, and piety, especially among the aristocracy?

That Anderson and Rev. Joseph Theophilus Desaguliers
were well acquainted there can be little doubt, and this relation
may even include brotherhood, before the revival of 1717, in the
same lodge, the Old Horn in Westminster. But the activity and
eminence of the Anglican in Freemasonry far exceeded that of
his Presbyterian brother. From 1719, when Dr. Desaguliers was
made grand master of the two-year-old Grand Lodge, to 1744,
the date of his death, he was the presiding genius, rightly named
"the father of modern speculative Masonry." Whether he had a
hand in the union of the four old lodges in 1717 we do not know;
but that the revival moved rapidly, decisively, astutely, and

[25] The *Defence* is published by G. Oliver in *Golden Remains of Early Masonic
Writers*, Vol. I (London, 1847–50).

spaciously from the year of his grand-mastership is undeniable. His vision of a world-brotherhood dedicated to rational piety, scientific devotion, moral righteousness, and spiritual humanity seems not only to have been formed but to have been in the process of realization when he visited Edinburgh in 1721 and introduced that lodge to at least a modicum of the new principles and ritual.[26] In the flamboyant frontispiece of the *Constitutions* of 1723, for which he wrote the Dedication and Introduction, he is depicted, as deputy, standing behind the grand master, Wharton, to whom the Duke of Montague, who held the office in 1721, presents the book. The engraving is a perfect index of his role in the movement. By 1723 his leadership and program had gained such ascendancy that they became the salient issue in the crucial struggle between the politically and morally unstable Wharton and the resolute and steady Whigs, who had hitherto shaped and controlled the rise of the new Freemasonry. The result was a personal and spiritual victory for Desaguliers, who thereupon was given a free hand in completing the transformation, which attained virtual maturity in 1725. To it he had contributed not only his assistance with the *Constitutions* but the custom of toasts and speeches at the banquets, as well as the office of stewards who prepared them; he may have composed much of the new rituals and catechism and supervised their printing; he initiated the Benevolent Fund in 1724 for fraternal relief. To his influence and prestige was doubtless due the amazing influx of nobles of the highest rank, as well as of many members of the Royal Society.

Once the fraternity was well established and secure from political and religious attack, he turned his attention to promoting its spread among the élite of the Continent. During the apogee of his fame and popularity in Holland as a brilliant exponent of Newtonian physics and cosmology he paused to preside at the initiation of the later Emperor Francis I (1731). In 1737 he presided at the initiation of the Prince of Wales, whose chaplain he had been for many years; by the time of his death in

[26] D. H. Lyons, *History of the Grand Lodge at Edinburgh* (Edinburgh, 1900), p. 160.

1744, the emperor and the kings of Prussia and England were Freemasons![27]

His astonishing popularity as an eloquent exponent and vivid demonstrator of the new "experimental science," especially of the theories of Sir Isaac Newton, explains the facility of his entree and his influence with the upper classes. Nor was this success undeserved, for the great Newton himself sponsored his admittance to the Royal Society.[28] Oxford gave him an LL.D. On the other hand, he was jovial in temperament and genuinely interested in the skill and welfare of the artisans who aided him with the apparatus of his demonstrations.

Yet the greatest of his contrivings and services for science, freedom, and humanity was renovated Freemasonry, and the motive power of his devotion seems to have been a genuine zeal to retrieve the sinking cause of morality and religion by the appeal of Newtonian cosmology to the reason and the spell of the antique mysteries of geometry upon the imagination.

His inclination toward such a course and goal as well as his typically Latitudinarian espousal of Christian Deism to serve his purpose are already evident in his letter to Lord Chancellor Parker, F.R.S., following the Dedication, by the translator, of Nieuwentijdt's *The Religious Philosopher* (1718). The translator had claimed that he (Nieuwentijdt) has so well

proven the power, wisdom and goodness of God by the strongest arguments, observations, facts and demonstrations drawn from experiments . . . . it were to be wished that he had applied the texts of Scripture he quotes as properly as he has his philosophical considerations; but since he has not so well succeeded in what may be called his divinity, I have left several texts out of this translation . . . . but not his tautologies, in which he does so often call upon atheists and infidels . . . . if they shall still persist in the denial of a God after so many irrefragable arguments drawn from the wonderful struc-

---

[27] Sketches of his life are found in Mackay, *op. cit.*; E. Lennhoff, *The Freemason* (New York, 1934), p. 51; A. E. Calvert, *The Grand Lodge of England* (London, 1917), p. 21; Begemann, *Ursprung*, II, 115.

[28] Newton was president of the Royal Society until his death in 1727, and in 1728 Desaguliers published a pretentious poetical exposition of *The Newtonian System the Best Model Government*. It contains the significant stanza:

"What made the planets in such order move,
He saw, was harmony and mutual love."

Compatible with this is Newton's preoccupation with Johannine writings.

ture of human bodies and all the other glorious works of the universe. I
have, in these omissions, followed the advice of several learned friends, both
philosophers and divines.

The letter of Dr. Desaguliers indorses all the foregoing and adds
comments yet more revealing:

The proselytes of the scoffers of religion are gained among the weak and
ignorant or such conceited debauchees as are glad to be supplied with the
means of defending their immoralities, by attacking religion with a show of
wit and argument. I think I may say for the translation that it will perhaps
do more good than the original, because in giving us all his arguments for
natural religion, you have omitted those which his too eager zeal made him
draw from the modern philosophy for revealed religion, the weakness of
which latter might give those free-thinkers occasion to laugh who would be
struck dumb at convictions from the former.

Finally he declares against "so much academical disputings
about sacred subjects" and pleads that "questions about God,
the Great Architect of the Universe, should be handled in
private, after a prayer of humility and reverence."

Whether or not this passage shows that he was a Freemason
as early as 1718, it tells us clearly that he was concerned over
the prevalence of "academical disputings about religion," the
prevalence of atheistic or infidel skepticism associated with immoral debauchery, presumably in the ranks of society capable
of buying and reading such a book. Moreover, it discloses his
conviction that the way to salvage such souls is to present them
with proofs for the truths of natural religion, drawn from the
"modern philosophy" and that a private assembly, opened with
prayer, is the proper place to discuss such proofs—not, per-
chance, in the taprooms of taverns and coffee-houses.

That such atheism and immorality were flagrantly and increasingly prevalent among the nobility, Dr. Desaguliers had
the best opportunity for knowing because his drawing-room in
Westminster was filled with titled attendants upon his scientific demonstrations. But he was also curator and lecturer to the
Royal Society, an institution which, from its original dedication
to science and a "philosophy of humanity,"[29] had rested under

[29] T. Sprat, *History of the Royal Society* (London, 1667); Begemann, *Ursprung*, II, 21.

the suspicion of fostering and harboring infidelity.[30] That this suspicion was well founded in 1720 is manifest in the following journal entry of Dr. Stukeley, F.R.S., who became a Freemason the next year. Of Martin Foulkes, who was elected a deputy grand master in 1724, replacing Dr. Desaguliers, he says:

He has a good deal of learning, philosophy and astronomy . . . . in matters of religion an errant infidel and loud scoffer. Professes himself a god-father to all monkeys, believes nothing of a future state, of the Scriptures, of Revelation. He perverted the Duke of Montague, the Duke of Richmond, Lord Pembroke and many more of the nobility . . . . and this has done an infinite prejudice to religion in general, made the nobility throw off the mask and openly deride and discontinue even the appearance of religion, which has brought us to the deplorable situation we are now in, with thieves, murderers, perjury, forgers, etc. When I lived in Ormond St. in 1720 he set up an infidel club at his house on Sunday evenings . . . . he invited me earnestly to come hither but I always refused. From that time he has been propagating infidel opinions with great assiduity and made it even fashionable in the Royal Society so that when any mention is made of Moses, the Deluge, of religion, the Scriptures, etc., it is generally received with a loud laugh. I find that one-half our half-witted philosophers in London are infidels, ... So hard a matter it is to keep a golden medium, or to see the great beauty of the Church of England or of religion in general.

The fumigation of the Royal Society and British aristocracy from atheism and its attendant danger, licentiousness, was no hopeless task for the ingenuity of the scientist who could furnish the House of Commons with a satisfactory ventilating system! Dr. Desaguliers, who, for all his geniality, was a man of earnest resolution, arrived at the conviction, somewhere between 1718 and 1721, that in the ancient fraternity of Freemasons, about which his neighbor, Rev. James Anderson, was so enthusiastic, with its tradition of nontheological piety and practical morality, conveyed by allegorized geometry (architecture), provided with a Catholic pedigree running through Christianity back to Greece, Egypt, and Rome and including the Druids (a main interest of the antiquarians of those days), he had a providential device, as scientifically sound and as vividly didactic as the planetarium he had recently contrived for introducing his fellow-savants and his noble pupils to the objective knowledge of

[30] L. Keller, "Comenius und die Akademien der Natur-philosophie des 17. Jahrhunderts," *Monatshefte der Comenius-gesellschaft*, IV (1895), 1, 69, 133.

the heavens. By convincing them, in the emotional and mystical atmosphere of the lodge, of the subjective truths of natural religion, he might retrieve them from the skepticism and moral anarchy which, after the South Sea scandal, seemed about to engulf the national leaders and to imperil the new Whig-Hanoverian regime of political and religious freedom.[31] Moreover, Freemasonry, in doctrine and practice, was nonclerical, and the clergy were in deep disgrace in those days, owing to non-Juror disloyalty and Tory sympathies.

Desaguliers lost no time in developing the new Grand Lodge to suit his purpose. On June 24, 1721, at a Grand Lodge meeting over which the Duke of Montague presided as grand master, and which was attended by Lords Herbert and Stanhope (Wharton) and, in all probability, by Dr. Stukely and Martin Foulkes,[32] Dr. Desaguliers delivered a lecture on "Masons and Masonry"; and from the impetus of that meeting the fraternity moved swiftly on to provide itself with constitutions, ceremonial, regalia, beneficent fund, an illustrious membership of savants and princes—all under the tutelage of Dr. Desaguliers!

In almost every respect this metamorphosed Freemasonry practically paralleled the Church of England. It was "established," that is, it was assured of royal and government favor. The grand master and Grand Lodge were counterparts of the Archbishop of Canterbury and Convocation. Each separate lodge had its master (rector), wardens, and stewards (vestrymen). Catechism and liturgy were similarly provided for by ritual and lectures. The lodge room, with its blue, star-studded ceiling and longitudinally lined floor ("a temple of heaven and earth"), had its stone altar ("ashlar"), with the "three Lights" (candles) and tripillared canopy (Divine Strength, Wisdom, and Beauty upholding the universe). The square and compass on the open Bible, the all-seeing Eye above the altar, the G above

---

[31] Cf. Mandeville's offensive second edition of *The Fable of the Bees* (London, 1723) and the scandalous "Hell-fire Club" of the same period.

[32] The Duke of Richmond, mentioned by Dr. Stukely, was grand master in 1724–25, with Foulkes his deputy!

the Master's chair ("geometry")—what are these but the equivalents of cross, reredos, anagram of Christ, sedilia? Initiation was the analogue of Baptism; the banquets and its degree songs, of Communion with its hymns. For prophecies and miracles there were the mystery cults of the pagans and the marvels of science. But there was no substitute for sectarian intolerance, clerical place-hunting, and sedition![33]

Was such a development implicit in the vision of those who instigated the formation of the Grand Lodge in 1717—the year of the prorogation of Convocation over the Hoadley issue of freedom of conscience? At first they definitely envisaged an organ of co-operation between Latitudinarian and dissenting Whigs on the basis of Christian Deism. They appear to have become interested in Freemasonry as a useful instrumentality because of its antiquarian dignity and its features of mystery and secrecy; its claims of historical Catholicity far exceeding in breadth and length those of the Roman Catholic church—the ally of the Jacobites; and its emphasis on the moral and social teachings of primitive Christianity to the exclusion of sectarian doctrine and clericalism. That there were elements of Rosicrucianism in the speculations of the "accepted Masons" who were foremost in the revival of 1717 is entirely possible. Ashmole the antiquarian, accepted in 1646, was a Rosicrucian as well as a member of the Royal Society; the same is true of Fluud and Samber.[34] Yet it is doubtful that these first movers looked forward to any such revision and elaboration of Freemasonry as were effected by Desaguliers and his aristocratic friends shortly afterward.

Desaguliers, as we have seen, was interested chiefly in using the Newtonian version of natural religion as a means of saving the noble auditors of his lectures and his colleagues of the Royal Society from irreligious libertinism of the Hobbes and Mande-

---

[33] For illustrations of an early lodge room see Lennhoff, *op. cit.*; for anticlericalism *ca.* 1720 see Mossner, *op. cit.*, p. 37.

[34] See F. Katsch, *Die Entstehung der Freimaurerei* (Berlin, 1897); L. Keller, *Akademien, Logen und Kammer der XVIten und XVIIten Jahrhunderten* (Jena, 1912).

ville kind—a menace to themselves, to the new "experimental science," and to the Whig principles—as the Wharton episode plainly proved. Some antidote must be found to such societies as the Hell-fire Club, suppressed by royal decree in 1720, and the wholly classical liturgy of Toland's *Pantheisticon* (1720). Desaguliers, curator of the Royal Society, custodian, therefore, of its heritage of aspirations of Hartlib, Comenius, Haak, and Boyle for a select, tolerant, pansophical society, a cultured "temple of wisdom and humanity," felt a heavy responsibility. Following precedents and patterns which he had learned from the Redery-Kammers and singing societies of the Brotherhood of John in the Low Countries and the Rhineland, through correspondence with Dutch savants, he applied his astute and ingenious mind to adapting Freemasonry. He and his collaborators made it, in effect, the religious section of the Royal Society, élite yet fraternal, convivial yet solemn, an "established" church of natural religion for those who preferred such to Christian piety and moral sanctions.[35] Just enough Christianity was retained as would sanctify Masonry's claim to be the vestibule which the Grand Architect had designed for revelation. In the beginning, therefore, the emphasis was laid on the Christian aspect of Christian Deism; as the revival and transformation proceeded, the emphasis shifted to the Deistic elements of Christian Deism; the effect of such kinetic emphases, after 1725, was a surprisingly eclectic medium for the assimilation of pagan and Christian idealism and esotericism, of which modern Freemasonry, in its thirty-two degrees, is composed.[36] But the first three degrees of the Blue Lodge, with its primary teaching of personal piety and probity, brotherly love, and doctrinal toler-

[35] W. Stukely in his *Family Memoirs* (London, 1888), p. 373, notes that in 1750 "the Duke of Richmond and Mr. Foulkes, instead of going to church (a matter unfashionable with great folks), went to view a garden."

[36] In 1738 the semiofficial *Apology for the Freemasons* affirmed as its motto the old Greek formula "En kai Pan" ("All Things are One in All, and this One is in all things . . . . God, in whom we live and move and have our being") (G. Kloss, *Bibliographie der Freimaurerei* [Leipzig, 1845], No. 251).

ance, has never lost the character of a religion of humanity "in which all men agree."

Was the grand design of Anderson, Desaguliers, and their colleagues justified by its spiritual as well as institutional success? Are we entitled to trace the ebb of critical Deism, of skeptical libertinism, of attacks upon the Church of England and clericalism in general, of doubts concerning the religious and moral effects of science to the influence of Freemasonry in the eighteenth century? It is a well-founded surmise that we are.

CHRISTIANITY AND THE CULTURE OF INDIA

MARVIN HENRY HARPER

Leonard Theological College
Jubbulpore, C.P., India

I

THE modern expansion of Christianity in India, a nation of long history comprising more than one-sixth of the human race, must necessarily involve consequences of importance for Christianity as well as for the Indian people. Although the Christian church has existed in India for nearly two thousand years, it is only within the past few decades that it has had any large success in adjusting itself to its environment. This may be attributed, first, to the fact that until comparatively recent times very little was known about Indian culture, even by Indians, and, next, to the fact that those holding places of leadership in the Christian church have, with a few notable exceptions, been uninformed, indifferent, or even definitely hostile to India's cultural heritage. Nor did they give adequate consideration to the fact that Christianity is a social movement as well as a religion. The Christian church has begun to take root in Indian soil only since Christian leaders have become aware of the significance of India's cultural environment.

The cultural heritage of India is not only very rich and complex but also very ancient. Recent excavations at Harappa and Mohenjo-daro have revealed the fact that there existed in India five thousand years ago a civilization which was probably as advanced as that of contemporary Mesopotamia and Egypt. Since these early times, through invasion and trade contacts, India has felt the influence of almost all the significant cultures of the world. A great diversity of race and culture has resulted. At one end of India's social scale are those who are making valuable contributions to twentieth-century literature, art, and science, while at the other are whole tribes whose religious ideas, tools, weapons, and customs are those of the Stone Age.

One may say indeed that there are three Indias—the India of the great cities, the India of the hill and forest peoples, and, in between, the India of the village, in touch with both, yet distinct from both because of customs and beliefs which date back to antiquity. In many respects, it is this India of seven hundred thousand villages which is the true India. It is here that fully 85 per cent of Christian Indians now live.

Except in rather limited and sophisticated circles where Western civilization has largely replaced true Indian culture, the Indian spirit is characterized by a love of simplicity, a gracious modesty, a meditative or philosophical attitude of mind, an exaltation of the "passive virtues," such as patience, gentleness, and peaceableness, a disposition to place material resources in a secondary place and to look upon poverty with admiration, a respect for age and tradition, a deep love for music and art, and a desire to undergird the whole of life with religion.

Of recent years India's cultural environment has been made even more complex through her innumerable contacts with the West. The educated young Indian today is torn between a sense of loyalty to his native culture and the more alluring civilization of the West. Even towns and villages are now feeling the impact of such forces as Western education and science, the radio and cinema, industrialism, communism, and socialism. Many Western comforts and amenities of life are being enjoyed, on a simpler scale it is true, by the villager. The significance of the motorbus in bridging the gap between city and village is incalculable. India is being flooded with books, newspapers, and magazines, although her people are nearly 90 per cent illiterate! Unemployment, especially among educated youth, nationalism, uprisings of the depressed classes, secularism, and communalism (owing largely to the fact that representation in the various assemblies and legislatures is on the basis of the numerical strength of the religious communities) are contributing their share to the complexity of India's social environment.

By far the most prominent factor in Indian life, ancient or modern, is religion. The religious contribution of India to world-culture has been considerable. Four great religions—Hinduism, Buddhism, Sikhism, and Jainism—have been cradled here. India has given birth to some of the finest spiritual classics of the world, such as the *Vedas*, the *Upanishads*, the *Bhagavad Gita*, the *Bhagavata* and the *Dhammapada*. Her epics, such as the *Rāmāyana* and the *Mahābhārata*, have their place in the world's best literature. She has numbered among her sons such religious thinkers as Gautama, Mahāvīra, and Śankara. Yet our present concern is not so much with India's religious literature as with life. Religious activities in India are so very numerous, widespread, and diverse in character that only a cursory statement of those factors which have functional significance can be attempted here.

The masses of India live in a world which is controlled by spirits, most of whom are evil. These dominate every aspect of life, and their anger must be averted or their favor won through one's own religious acts or through the good services of a priest. Educated Indians themselves are often strongly under the spell of the supernatural, and philosophers have shaped their theories to fit the facts of experience. India's countless temples and shrines give evidence of the hope of her millions that, through the worship of divinities or spirits, supernatural aid may be secured or evil averted. There is a deity for almost every human experience from birth until death. Plague, earthquake, drought, prosperity, successful marriage, passing examinations, securing work, recovery from sickness—all these and many more affairs of daily life are in the control of supernatural powers. The priest, the wandering "holy man" (*sādhu*) or the world-renouncing ascetic (*sannyāsī*), the witch-doctor, and the scripture-reader are all to be feared and honored because of their powers over the supernatural. The popular cults of Krishna and Rāma, like the mystery religions of old, promise satisfaction to the religious quest of millions through their teaching that the Absolute assumed human form and lived among men, sharing with them their trials, temptations, and victories. Thus, according to popular thought, it is religion which furnishes the surest guaranties for the safety of the individual and the community in the manifold experiences of life.

The living religions of the Indian people are Hinduism, Islam, Sikhism, Jainism, the religion of the Parsis, and Christianity. In addition, there is the primitive Animism of the millions of hill and jungle people. Hinduism has been described by E. L. King as

an encyclopedia of religions, with caste as the only feature common to all its stages and adherents. The goal of existence is release from the round of rebirths based on deeds in past lives, and absorption into the immanent, impersonal Brahma. Both good and evil have their place, thus blurring the distinction between right and wrong. Human life is of no significance, and the individual is not responsible for his actions. Salvation is through knowledge, works or devotion. The ascetic ideal of saintliness prevails. Hinduism's quest for God and its permeating and cohesive powers are remarkable.

The influence of religion on the life of Hindus is not uniform. The popular Hinduism of the village folk, and of a large majority of city dwellers as well, regulates almost every act of their waking moments. Orthodox Hinduism, or Brahmanism, controls the social intercourse of a considerable number of educated caste Hindus in such matters as intermarriage, interdining, and touchability, and directs their religious practice and belief in a more or less formal way.[1] The liberal Hinduism of a great number of educated men and women requires only the observance of caste rules for the sake of membership in the Hindu social organization but permits perfect liberty as to belief.[2]

[1] Professor S. N. Das Gupta observes that "all orthodox Hindu schools of thought assume as their fundamental postulates the existence of the soul, the possibility of the liberation of the soul from matter, the infallible nature of the *Vedas*, the doctrine of *karma* and rebirth" (G. T. Garratt [ed.], *The Legacy of India* [Oxford: Clarendon Press, 1937], p. 114). The doctrine of *karma* holds that all events in the lives of men are predetermined by prior actions in former births. A person's wealth, caste, fortune, health, and all other aspects of life depend upon the quality and quantity of his deeds in former births.

[2] Sir S. Radhakrishnan, possibly India's most distinguished exponent of liberal Hinduism, declares that "Hinduism is bound not by a creed but by a quest, not by a common belief but by a common search for truth. Every one is a Hindu who strives for truth by study and reflection, by purity of life and conduct, by devotion and consecration to high ideals, who believes that religion rests not on authority but on experience" (*ibid.*, p. 277).

Since the great majority of Christian converts have come from among the depressed classes in rural areas, it is only natural that the practices and beliefs of popular Hinduism,[3] such as the worship of countless deities and spirits, obedience to caste rules, and belief in the doctrine of *karma*, transmigration, and rebirth, should be potent in influencing their lives. Many Christians, especially those who have been converted from the higher castes, have also been influenced by such philosophic concepts as the unity of the soul and all existence with the Absolute, the transmigration of souls (*samsāra*), the unreality of the phenomenal world (*māyā*), the inexorable moral law of the universe (*karma*), self-transcending activity free from the reward motive (*nishkamya karma*), detached contemplation (*dhyāna*), the seeking of union with the Absolute (*yoga*), and final absorption into the world-soul (*samādhi*).

It is not on the intellectual plane, however, that Hinduism has had its greatest influence on Christianity, or even upon Hindus themselves. Hinduism is primarily a socioreligious system. At the center of Hinduism is caste.[4] To caste, the centuries-old social structure of Hinduism probably owes its survival. Men can and have believed in many gods, or no gods, in future life, or the extinction of souls at death; they may be spiritualists or materialists; they may have many religious be-

---

[3] Space does not permit a detailed statement of the practices and beliefs of popular Hinduism, essential as is this subject to our study. Valuable material will be found in the "Religious Life of India Series," edited by J. N. Farquhar and Nicol Macnicol and published by Oxford University Press. Bishop Whitehead, *The Village Gods of South India*, and G. W. Briggs, *The Chamars*, both in this series, give excellent pictures of popular Hinduism in South India and North India, respectively. Nicol Macnicol, *Living Religions of the Indian People* (London: Student Christian Movement, 1936), gives valuable material on both popular and philosophic Hinduism.

[4] Religious sanction is given to caste first by a theory of the divine origin of the four great castes, based on a reference in the *Purushasūkta* (hymn of primordial man)—one of the late Vedic hymns—and next by a philosophy of caste based on the doctrines of *karma* and *dharma*. The status of every individual in life is determined by the *karma*, or actions, of his former birth. In the same way, his salvation depends on the fulfilment of his caste obligations (*dharma*).

Literature on the subject of caste is vast. Nontechnical treatments are found in R. P. Masani, "Caste and the Structure of Society," in Garratt, *op. cit.*; V. A. Smith, *Oxford History of India* (Oxford, 1928); W. E. S. Holland, *The Indian Outlook* (London: Edinburgh House Press, 1927); E. Senart, *Caste in India* (London: Methuen & Co., 1930).

liefs, or none, and yet remain within the Hindu fold provided they conform to the *dharma,* or customs, of their caste. But a man who breaks even the least of the caste laws may find himself an outcaste, debarred from the privileges of orthodox Hindu society. Caste rules have to do chiefly with what a man may eat and with whom he may eat, with whom he may marry, and within what occupation he may engage. Possibly no one factor in the culture of India has made the task of Christian missions more difficult than caste. Caste rules have forced many orthodox Hindu families to disinherit and outcaste members who have embraced Christianity. Fear of being driven from family, caste, and traditional occupation has undoubtedly caused many a convert to hesitate long before accepting Christian baptism. Had converts to Christianity been permitted to remain in ancestral homes after baptism, the history of Christianity in India might have been vastly different.

W. E. S. Holland well observes:

If Hindu caste divides India horizontally into thousands of isolated strata, Islam has caused a vertical division that has rent the entire fabric of society throughout the peninsula into two unequal parts. . . . . Though largely Indianized by blood, climate and contact, the Musalmans yet remain an absolutely separate entity.[5]

Islam has been characterized by one who has lived long in India as

an austere Faith of fatalistic submission to the arbitrary Will of one God, whose prophet is Muhammed and whose scripture the Koran. Its duties are belief in this God, prescribed prayers, almsgiving, fasting, the pilgrimage to Mecca. Among its strong points are brotherliness and missionary zeal, and among its weak, a low estimate of womanhood, a belief in a sensuous future life, and the lack of a theory of progress. In India Islam has been infected by both animism and Hindu pantheism.

Through the medium of the Persian language the best ethical thought of Islam influenced educated Hindus a few generations ago. One significant result of this influence was the gradual spread of a belief in the unity of God and the growth of indigenous monotheistic faiths. The second remarkable result was the production of a new vernacular, called Urdu, a mixture of

5 *Op. cit.,* pp. 27–28.

Persian and Hindi, which has become, after English, perhaps the most widely used language in India.

The cultural influence of Islam has been considerable. In addition to the concept of the unity of God and the Urdu language, already referred to, Professor Abdul Qadir mentions the significance of Islamic poetry, architecture (especially the domed mosque), painting (notably in the form of miniatures), the illumination of books, music and musical instruments, the *mughal* type of garden (such as the Shalimar in Kashmir), and libraries.[6]

Muslims form the second largest religious group in India today. Of the more than eighty million Muslims, who compose a quarter of the population, the great majority are descended from Hindu stock and retain many characteristics common to Indians as a whole. While it is true that no considerable number of Christian converts have come from Islam, it is, nevertheless, a fact, especially in the north of the peninsula, that the Christian community has taken on very much of the coloring of Muslim life.

Although Sikhism, Jainism, and the religion of the hill and forest tribes are extremely significant in the life of India, they have not, as yet, exerted an influence upon Christianity comparable to that of Hinduism and Islam. For this reason we pass them by in the present connection with mere mention.

II

Having now surveyed, in a most cursory manner it must be confessed, some of the more significant environing factors in the Indian cultural heritage, we are in a position to consider how, in certain specific details, Christianity as a socioreligious movement has interacted through the years with its environment.

Some centuries before the first Christian missionary entered India the culture of this land was known and appreciated in those countries which later were to become the home of early Christianity. It would seem that contacts between India and

[6] "Cultural Influences of Islam," in Garratt, *op. cit.*

the Mediterranean world in the pre-Christian Era were numerous and varied, and these, indirectly at least, played their part in shaping Christian life and thought in the early days of Christianity.[7]

In the Christian Era Apollonius of Tyana went to Taxila to study under Brahman preceptors. Plotinus was greatly interested in Hindu thought, and the resemblances between Neo-Platonism (which played so large a part in shaping the theology of Augustine and others) and the *Vedanta* system are very close. Clement of Alexandria is the first Greek writer to mention the Buddha by name (*Stromata* i. 15).[8] The points of similarity between Buddhist and Christian parables and miracles are startling. In *Jātaka* 90, for example, we read of a disciple of the Buddha who walks on the water while he is full of faith, but who begins to sink when his faith grows weak. *Jātaka* 78 records the fact that the Buddha fed five hundred of his brethren with a single cake and that much was left over. While there are undoubtedly textual problems involved in these similarities, it will be remembered that the *Jātaka* are centuries older than the Gospels. Some scholars believe that the rosary, the veneration of relics, and the exaggerated forms of asceticism, which were a striking feature of Alexandrian Christianity, may be traced to Indian influences.[9] Other possible influences might be traced,[10] but we must conclude with recalling the fact that Basilides, the Gnostic teacher, definitely borrowed from the East the phi-

[7] H. C. Rawlinson ("India in European Literature and Thought," in Garratt, *op. cit.*, pp. 3–20) notes the influence of the later Vedic hymns and the *Upanishads* upon the teaching of the Eleatic School, of the Hindu doctrine of transmigration upon Pythagoras, of Hindu pantheism upon the Orphites, and the resemblances between the Hindu *Varnas*, or castes, and the vision of the ideal polity in Plato's *Republic*. See also B. J. Urwick, *The Message of Plato* (London, 1920).

[8] J. W. McCrindle (*Ancient India*, pp. 184 ff.) quotes this and other references to Buddhism in Alexandrian writings.

[9] E.g., W. M. Flinders Petrie, in *Personal Religion in Egypt before Christianity* (New York and London, 1912), and I. C. Hannah, in *Christian Monasticism*. But this influence is denied by E. White, *History of the Monasteries of Nitria and Scetis*, and W. H. Mackean, *Christian Monasticism in Egypt* (London, 1920).

[10] An example of this is the interesting parallels traced by J. T. McNeill (*The Celtic Penitentials* [Paris, 1923]) between many of the practices of the early Celts and those of the Aryans of India.

losophy which he interweaves in an ingenious fashion into the framework of Christianity.[11]

III

The early history of Christianity in India is shrouded in obscurity and tradition. Yet it is fairly certain that the church has existed in this country from the very earliest period of our era. The first Christian missionary, according to tradition, was the Apostle Thomas. It is from him that the Syrian church in South India, the Mar Thomma, takes its name, for he is said to have made converts and to have built churches. It is not, however, until the close of the second century that we meet the first literary reference to the sending of missionaries. Clement of Alexandria records that Pantaenus was sent to India by Demetrius, the bishop of Alexandria. At various intervals during the next thirteen centuries groups of non-Roman Christians settled in the southern part of the peninsula. At the arrival of the Portuguese the condition of the church was far from healthy.[12] Nevertheless, the community seems to have retained the respect of non-Christian neighbors, and Syrian Christians were considered socially among the highest of the castes.

The outstanding figure of early Roman Catholic missions in India was Francis Xavier.[13] He worked with great zeal and baptized many converts. Methods adopted by him and his followers resulted in there being a quarter of a million Catholics at the end of the sixteenth century. But the Abbé Dubois, a fellow-Catholic, said pessimistically that very few were really Christian. After Xavier perhaps the most interesting Jesuit missionary of this period was Robert de Nobili,[14] who arrived in India in 1605. Whereas Xavier had worked largely among the outcaste fisherfolk, De Nobili determined to concentrate his efforts on the high-caste Brahmans. So cleverly did he embody the Christian

---

[11] J. Kennedy, "Buddhist Gnosticism," *Journal of the Royal Asiatic Society,* 1902, pp. 377 ff.

[12] See Julius Richter, *A History of Missions in India* (New York: Fleming H. Revell Co., 1908).

[13] *Ibid.*   [14] *Ibid.*

message in his *Fifth Veda*, written in Sanskrit, that for a century and a half it was regarded as genuine. De Nobili frankly accepted the Hindu caste system and would not associate with those of the lower castes. Separate churches were built for the higher and lower castes. This admission of caste into the church has been the problem of Christian missions to this day.

It is but natural that long years of contact between the Syrian and Roman Catholic Christians and their non-Christian neighbors should have led the first two to adopt many of the customs of the latter. For example, the many splits which occurred in the Syrian church over ecclesiastical matters have become endogamous sects, with no intermarriage permitted between them. Then, again, Hindu influence is seen in the practices connected with marriage customs which prevail in many sections of the Syrian church. A *pandal*, or booth, is erected in front of the bride's house at the time of the wedding. On the night before the wedding the bride is given a ceremonial bath. During the ceremony of marriage the *tali*, or amulet, always used in Hindu marriages in South India, is blessed by the priest, who hands it to the bridegroom to be tied by him around the bride's neck. The bride is veiled as a protection against the evil eye. When the bridal party leaves the church, a lamp is lighted with the object of frightening away evil spirits, or firecrackers are set off for the same purpose. There are also numerous parallels in the birth and death rites of the Syrians and Hindus. Astrology, magic, sorcery, and witchcraft are not unknown.[15] But in most sections of the Syrian church, especially those which have been in contact with the British missions, these practices have disappeared.

While the social customs of the Syrian Christians have been largely affected by the Hindu environment, in matters of worship and religious belief the influence of Hinduism has been surprisingly small. The architecture of church buildings is unlike that of Hindu temples. Instrumental music and flowers, which play a large part in Hindu temple worship, are conspicuously

[15] An admirable treatment of this subject will be found in Ananthakrishna Ayyar, *Anthropology of the Syrian Christians* (Ernakulam: Cochin Government Press, 1926).

absent from Syrian churches. Indian philosophies have left the theology of the Syrians practically untouched. After nineteen centuries of contact with India's rich culture the worship experience of the Syrian church remains largely foreign and aloof. The same may be said of Roman Catholicism also. Both of these branches of the Christian church have been too thoroughly under the domination of ecclesiastical authorities residing outside India to have had any large freedom in adapting their worship to indigenous forms.

IV

The relation of Protestant Christianity to Indian culture has been conditioned to a large degree by commerce, imperialism, and racial antipathies. Although the first Protestant missionaries, Ziegenbalg and Plütschau, were sent by Frederick IV of Denmark, their work was hampered on all sides by the officials of the Dutch East India Company. The story of the early opposition of the British East India Company to William Carey, the first English missionary, is well known.[16] The directors of these trading companies professed the fear of a general uprising on the part of the "natives" if their ancestral religions should be tampered with. Thus, they not only opposed the work of Christian missionaries but actively supported the worship of their Hindu subjects. Yet their motives were suspect, and the mutiny occurred in 1857, bringing to an end the era of the company, for India passed under the control of the British crown, and the proclamation of the queen empress promised religious liberty to all her subjects.

But the suppression of the mutiny and the measures taken to prevent a recurrence caused a breach between Englishmen and Indians which has not yet been healed. A flood of Englishmen came out to India after 1860 filled with a strong racial antipathy

[16] It is impossible to understand the course which Christian history in India has followed without taking into account the economic aspects of the British rule in India. A most comprehensive study of the relation of commerce and politics to the Christian movement is found in Arthur Mayhew, *Christianity and the Government of India* (London: Faber & Gwyer, 1929). See also my "A Bibliography for the Study of the Relation of Politics to Missions in India" (unpublished MS in the Divinity School Library, University of Chicago).

to the inhabitants of the country. Indians and their culture were treated with scorn or contempt.[17] Early Protestant missionaries were more largely influenced by the attitude of British officials than they realized. Many took the stand either that Hindu civilization was satanic and must be rooted out or that it was utterly inferior and must be replaced. The number who made a careful and sympathetic study of India's cultural heritage was relatively small. It is but natural that ardent Indian nationalists should have looked upon Christianity as a part of the British imperialistic policy (even today certain chaplains of the Church of England are supported by the government),[18] and that Christian Indians have often looked upon themselves as foreigners in their own country! They have largely adopted the attitudes of the officials and missionaries with whom they work and live daily and look upon Indian culture as either evil or inferior.

Within the Protestant churches in India there is an almost infinite variety of worship and polity, yet it will serve our present purpose to think of Protestant Christians as divided into two great and fairly distinct categories—rural and urban. Fully 85 per cent of the three million Protestant Christians of India belong to the lower or outcaste groups and live for the most part in villages scattered throughout the country. The great majority of rural Christians have entered the church within the last fifty years through mass movements—or "group movements," as Bishop Pickett would prefer to call them.[19] Whenever a group, larger than a family, accustomed to exercise a measure of control over the social and religious life of the individuals that compose it, accepts the Christian religion, the essential principle of the mass movement is manifest. Such movements have generally been castewise, that is, all the individuals of the particular group who enter the church at the time are

[17] So says G. T. Garratt, "Indo-British Civilization," *op. cit.*, pp. 394-422.

[18] This attitude if forcefully expressed by Jawaharlal Nehru, a recent president of the Indian National Congress, in *An Autobiography* (London: Bodley Head, 1936).

[19] J. W. Pickett, *Christian Mass Movements in India* (New York: Abingdon Press, 1933), p. 22.

members of the same caste. Their conversion produces a far smaller rupture in their social structure than is the case of those who enter the church as individuals. Until the movements among the high-caste groups began recently in the south, the great majority of Christian converts had come from the low-caste or outcaste groups. Thus, in rural areas caste is the central and dominating factor which creates and controls the social environment of Christian Indians.

In northern India the *birādari*, or caste brotherhood of the village, is a formidable social barrier to the progress of the Christian church. Christian converts cannot get out of the *birādari* without leaving the profession in which their caste has traditionally engaged. The rules of the *birādari*, if the majority of its members have not become Christian, often come into conflict with the teachings of the church. Should a Christian who is still a member of the old *birādari* be called to a feast for the dead or a wedding where pagan rites are performed, he must go or come under the discipline of the *panchāyat*, or governing body of the caste *birādari*. His fear of the discipline of the *panchāyat* is greater than his concern for the discipline of the church. Should he determine to break with the *birādari*, he must face almost certain financial ruin.[20] His only hope seems to lie in the conversion of the whole *birādari!*

Until a considerable number of families belonging to one caste have become Christian, their conversion does not free low-caste converts immediately from the social disabilities under which they have suffered for ages at the hands of the higher castes. Bishop Pickett has described the social disabilities under which thousands of village Christians live as unapproachability, untouchability, inability to live in certain sections of the village, limitations upon the use of roads, restriction of trading rights, deprivation of the services of the village washerman, barber, sewing-man, etc., difficulties in securing water from village wells

---

[20] *Report of the Conference of the Depressed Classes Committee* (Lucknow: Lucknow Publishing House, 1928). See also B. L. Rallia Ram, "The Caste System and Its Influence upon the Christian Church in North India," *National Christian Council Review*, November, 1938.

or tanks, denial of the privilege of sending their children to the village school, and an enforced attitude of inferiority.

The economic disabilities of village Christians are no less serious than their social hardships. These they share with their non-Christian neighbors of the lower castes. There is probably no group in all the world more desperately poor than is the Indian farmer. It has been estimated that the total annual per capita income from all sources for the rural Christian is about thirty-three rupees ($11). Here again the caste system plays a distinctive part, for it radically affects the distribution of wealth. Each individual has a fixed economic as well as social status, established by his birth in any given caste.[21] The connection between occupation and religion is thus very close and is a vital factor in any consideration of conversion to Christianity. Other factors which loom large on the economic horizon of the village Christian, in addition to his caste restrictions, are disease, illiteracy, frequent unemployment, antiquated methods of agriculture, poverty, and debt. The indebtedness of the Indian peasant is proverbial. More than 85 per cent of village Christians, it is estimated, are in debt beyond any hope of recovery!

The enormous numbers involved, inaccessibility, illiteracy, poverty, inertia, and lack of adequate missionary forces to cope with the situation have all prevented the Christian church from making the impact upon the life and worship of rural Christians which might have been desired. As a consequence, even as pagan converts in the early centuries "baptized many of their pagan customs and made them Christian," so have Indian converts brought with them into the church many elements which are contrary to traditional Christianity. The customs which they find it hardest to abandon are those which relate to birth, marriage, and death rites, belief in spirits, worship of images, and participation in the numerous festivals which have to do

[21] W. H. Wiser, in *Behind Mud Walls* (London, 1932), has given a fascinating picture of village life, and in *The Hindu Jajmani System* (Lucknow: Lucknow Publishing House, 1936) a scientific study of the social and economic structure of rural Indian society. See also G. J. Lapp, *The Christian Church and Rural India* (Calcutta: Y.M.C.A. Publishing House, 1938).

with fertility and prosperity. Yet in areas where supervision has been thorough and education adequate these non-Christian practices have been dropped, and, while living in a manner in other respects similar to that of their neighbors, rural Christians have attained a high degree of Christian life. An outstanding example is to be seen in the area of Bishop Azariah of Dornakal, where a strong church, indigenous in the best sense of the word, yet thoroughly Christian, has grown up.[22]

Although an overwhelming proportion of Protestant Christians are to be found in rural areas, urban Christianity undoubtedly supplies the intellectual and social leadership of the Protestant Christian movement in India. Yet the social organization of urban Christians is in many respects artificial. Because converts from Hindu and Muslim homes have been ostracized by their own families, the Christian community has grown up very largely around the missionary's bungalow, the church, or the school building. With the growth of the community there has resulted a Christian quarter in many cities. Family life and organization show clearly the influence of contact with missionaries and Western officials. The joint-family system, still common among Hindus and Muslims, has largely given way to the Western single-family system. Western manners and customs in many areas of life have been adopted or adapted. The economic position of the urban church is far from sound. Even those who were born in homes of privilege have usually had to sacrifice wealth, position, and influence upon becoming Christian. Converts have, in general, been drawn from social circles without business or commercial experience, and the missions have felt obliged to provide positions within the Christian movement for them. Thus, as Merle Davis has pointed out,[23] from the very beginning of the church in India the natural leaders of the new community were to a large extent absorbed into the clerical, educational, and spiritual activities of the church, instead of becoming established in independent business enter-

[22] *International Review of Missions*, XVIII, 511 ff.; XXI, 406 ff.

[23] J. Merle Davis, *The Economic and Social Environment of the Younger Churches* (Calcutta: Baptist Mission Press, 1938), p. 67.

prises. Decreases in mission appropriations are now forcing many Christians to seek employment elsewhere in competition with highly qualified non-Christians. The community is now paying in social isolation and economic insecurity the penalty of long years of separation from the heart of Indian life.

The organized worship of urban Christians is also largely Western. Church buildings, music, sermons, orders of worship, and theology as well as church bells, benches, and handshaking stamp the church as a foreign institution. Many years will probably elapse before any general use of indigenous modes of worship will find wide acceptance in the urban church, for Christian Indians are themselves most conservative in abandoning those Western forms to which they have become accustomed.

V

Fortunately, there has always been a small group—increasing in numbers and influence in recent years—within the Protestant community which insists that Christian life and worship be Christian *and* Indian. Drawing on their own rich cultural heritage for inspiration, they have determined to help Christianity become deeply rooted in the soil of India. They are sincerely concerned that the Christian movement become so natural a part of India that it may attract yet larger numbers of Hindus and Muslims to the Christian way of life.

The buildings in which Christians worship have long been a source of dismay to this group. They feel the need for creating a form of church architecture which will embody the best of Indian expression and yet be distinctively Christian. A few of the notable experiments which have been made in this connection are described and illustrated in Fleming's *Heritage of Beauty*.[24] Among the best of these are the chapel at the Women's Christian College, Madras; the church of the Christu-kula Ashram at Tirupatur; and the chapel of the Christa Seva Sangha Ashram at Poona—all of which are adaptations of the Hindu temple architecture to Christian needs—and the All

[24] D. J. Fleming, *Heritage of Beauty* (New York: Friendship Press, 1937).

Saints' Church at Peshawar, which has adapted the scalloped arch, the dome, and the minaret of the Muslim mosque.

It is only natural that Christian Indians should have turned their attention to music also. Probably no nation loves music more than India, and India's heritage in song is rich. In the words of Popley, "The great preachers of Hinduism have left us, not books of sermons, but books of songs." Among the Christian Indians who have made a signal contribution to the treasure of indigenous Christian hymns an outstanding figure is Narayan Vaman Tilak, the Marathi poet-saint. In the style of Tukaram and other Hindu *bhaktas* he sang of his love for Christ. His *Abanganjali* is a "wreath of song" which has greatly enriched the worship in the Marathi church.[25] A similar service was rendered for the Malayalam churches by Moses Walsalam, the poet-preacher of the south, in his *Garland of Prayer* and other collections. The lyrics and *kalekshepam* (dramatic setting of the Gospel stories to folk tunes) of the Tamil singer Vedanayaga Śastriar[26] are also noteworthy. The *katha* in North India and the *kirtan* in Maharasthra follow the Hindu practice of singing the Scripture with frequent pauses for extempore explanations.

As yet, very little progress has been made in developing indigenous Christian art, but A. D. Thomas has made a promising beginning with such scenes from the life of Christ as "Christ the Guru," "The Christ of the Indian Road," and "The Madonna of the Lotus."[27]

Experimentation in adapting Christian worship to Indian modes of devotion are being made in various centers, especially in college chapel services and in Christian ashrams, or hermitages. Notable success has been achieved in congregational worship in the diocese of the Indian bishop of Dornakal. Stephen Neill, in *Builders of the Indian Church*,[28] records this and other interesting experiments in Indianizing worship.

[25] J. C. Winslow, *Narayan Vaman Tilak* (Calcutta: Association Press, 1923).

[26] A. Parker, *Children of the Light in India* (New York: Fleming H. Revell Co., 1919).

[27] Reprints of some of these appeared in *Asia*, December, 1936.

[28] London: Edinburgh House.

From early times Christian missionaries, preachers, and teachers have tried to present the Christian message in terms that would appeal to the Hindu and Muslim mind. Among the first literary efforts along this line were the *Fifth Veda*, written in Sanskrit by De Nobili (or possibly by De Britto), already referred to, and the *Christian Purana* in Marathi, produced by the English Jesuit, Thomas Stephens (1615). A second European Jesuit, Father Beschi, wrote in Tamil the *Tembavani*, which ranks as a classic. The best of Christian Indian thought today is being given to this task of interpreting Christian theology in Indian thought-forms. In the words of J. M. Kumarappa:

> With the rise of cultured nationalism in India, there has come into being what may be called a new Indian "Protestant" Movement, which on the one hand protests against all meaningless forms and antiquated doctrines in the Christian faith and, on the other, makes a plea for separating Christianity from its Western connections and giving it an Indian expression.[29]

The first step in this process has been the substitution of Sanskrit words for their English equivalents in theological works produced in India. This is somewhat the method used by Chakkarai in his *Jesus the Avatar* [Incarnation] and *The Cross and Indian Thought*.[30] There is grave danger in this method, however, for the Hindu or Muslim is inclined to read his own traditional content into the Christian doctrine in this word-for-word substitution. A. J. Appasamy, in his *What Is Moksha* [Salvation]? and *Christianity as Bhakti Marga* [Way of Devotion],[31] has attempted to re-write Christian theology in thought-forms which will be familiar to Hindus and yet to avoid the danger just mentioned. A younger writer who is trying to bridge the gap between the Hindu cultural heritage and Christian thought is Cyril Modak, who believes that certain fundamental Hindu concepts, as, for example, *ahimsa* (the sacramental view of all life) and *bhakti* (the rapturous devotion of the disciple for

[29] "Christianity in India," *Asia*, December, 1936, p. 807.

[30] V. Chakkarai, *Jesus the Avatar* (Madras: Christian Literature Society, 1926), and *The Cross and Indian Thought* (Madras: Christian Literature Society, 1932).

[31] Madras: Christian Literature Society, 1927.

his Lord), are nearer to the heart of the "Christ of the Saffron Robe"[32] than some doctrines which have adhered to Christianity since it left the Galilean shores. We may expect the next few years to witness the emergence of a truly Indian Christianity, for groups of young Indian Christian philosophers in many sections of the church are deeply concerned with the task of helping Christianity take deep root in the soil of India.

Two notable developments, which are quite in line with India's ancient heritage, have taken place in many parts of the country. The first of these is the appearance of Indian Christian *sādhus* and *sannyāsīs*. A splendid example is Sādhu Sundar Singh, who lived a life of world-renunciation and at the same time was thoroughly Christian.[33] The second development is the ashram. The Christian ashram[34] usually combines the Hindu idea of a retreat for the cultivation of the spiritual life and religious study with the European idea of a settlement for service to the community. Among the best-known Christian ashrams are the Christu-kula Ashram at Tirupatur, the Christa Prema Seva Sangha Ashram at Poona, the Lal Bagh Ashram at Lucknow, and the Chakraverti Ashram at Brindaban. Although there are many others, Kraemer is right when he says that the ashram movement has not yet struck deep roots, for few Christian Indians seem attracted to this form of religious expression.[35]

A final problem engages the attention of leaders in the Indian church—the isolation of the church from national life.[36] A

[32] Cyril Modak, "The Christ of the Saffron Robe," *The Fellowship* (Lucknow: Lucknow Publishing House), February, 1935.

[33] H. Kraemer, *The Christian Message in a Non-Christian World* (London: Edinburgh House Press, 1938), p. 374; C. F. Andrews, *Sadhu Sundar Singh* (London, 1934).

[34] S. Jesudason, *Ashrams, Ancient and Modern* (Vellore: Sri Ramchandra Press, 1937); E. Stanley Jones, "The Ashram Ideal," in *Indian Church Problems*, ed. B. T. Badley (Lucknow: Lucknow Publishing House).

[35] *Op. cit.*, p. 375.

[36] See a discussion of this by R. M. Chetsingh in *The Isolation of the Church from the Life of the Nation* (Mysore: Wesley Press, 1938).

charge constantly brought against the work of Christian missions is that it has denationalized those who enter the Christian church. During the nationalist movement of the last twenty years very few Christian Indians have identified themselves with the Indian National Congress or with other parties. In very recent days, however, under the spell of nationalism, young Christians have been spurred to greater efforts to make the Christian movement effective in the national life of India.[37] As never before, they are becoming conscious and proud of their rich cultural heritage.

Some few discerning Christians are becoming aware of the fact, also, that the contact of Christianity with the culture of India is not merely intellectual, though it must be that in part. Nor is it merely religious, though religion must continue to be the chief concern of the church. Christianity is a socioreligious movement which is in vital contact with a culture rich in religious and social values. In its struggle with its rivals—for Hinduism, Islam, and Animism are definitely antagonistic—Christianity must prove herself superior not primarily as an intellectual propaganda but rather as a vital and complex movement in society. Christianity must indeed answer the intellectual questions of India's millions, but the real demands made upon the Christian movement in India, like those made upon the early church in the Roman Empire,[38] are of a different sort. India's masses are seeking satisfactions to deep emotional and religious urges; they desire the more abundant physical life; they yearn for fellowship in an institution which will insure safety and security over the whole range of human experience, present and future. These longings they have found only partially fulfilled in their old environment. Thus, the problems, facing the Christian church in India today are only partially religious. They are as fundamentally social and economic. If

[37] See M. H. Harper, *The Methodist Episcopal Church in India* (Lucknow: Lucknow Publishing House, 1937), chap. vi.

[38] See S. J. Case, *The Social Origins of Christianity* (Chicago: University of Chicago Press, 1923), chap. vi.

the Christian movement, deep rooted in the soil of India's culture, can function vitally in India's religious, social, economic, and national life, in harmony with India's traditions, its future in this country is assured. And further, like the Indian *raja* of old, who, we are told, laid his rich gift at the feet of the Christ-child, so may Indian Christianity contribute a rich tradition to the church universal.

CHRISTIANITY IN THE MODERN JAPANESE ENVIRONMENT

D. C. HOLTOM

Aoyama Gakuin Theological School
Tokyo, Japan

NO CONSIDERATION of the Christian movement in relation to its Japanese environment is possible apart from recognition of the all-embracing demands of a highly sensitive nationalism. This means that the most difficult problem lying before the Christian church in Japan today is to be found in the area of the adjustment of loyalties. Christians in Japan have always been suspected of a divided loyalty; this in spite of a devotion to the highest interests of the state second to that of no other group in the nation. Agencies and individuals lying outside the Christian church, and moving in areas untouched by Christian influences and ignorant of its purposes and activities, have often noted with suspicion an irreconcilable disparity between the obligations of Christian universalism and the exclusiveness of Japanese nationalism. How can the single devotion to the state required of all good citizens be positively related to the ideal world-brotherhood of Jesus? How can the obligations of devotion to a Heavenly Father who loves all mankind be harmonized with the demands of unquestioning subordination of personal will and intelligence demanded by an all-powerful state? Monotheism is under suspicion as arrogating a totalitarian dominion over life that excludes patriotic devotion to the ancestral gods. If this is the crisis of Christianity in the world today, it is acutely so in Japan. In a summary such as this only a few of such facts as give peculiar significance and interest to the Japanese situation can be reviewed.

Present-day Japanese discussion of the basis of all sound national morality invariably seeks to find its fundamental principles in the Imperial Rescript on Education, promulgated by the Meiji Emperor on October 30, 1890. Herein we may discover the chief sacred scripture of modern Japanese nationalism, and no integration of the Christian movement with the foundations of contemporary Japanese life is possible apart from a careful reference to this brief but highly important document. The text of the official English translation follows:

Know Ye, Our Subjects:

Our Imperial Ancestors have founded Our Empire on a basis broad and everlasting, and have deeply and firmly implanted virtue; Our subjects ever united in loyalty and filial piety have from generation to generation illustrated the beauty thereof. This is the glory of the fundamental character of Our Empire, and herein also lies the source of Our education. Ye, Our subjects, be filial to your parents, affectionate to your brothers and sisters; as husbands and wives be harmonious, as friends true; bear yourselves in modesty and moderation; extend your benevolence to all; pursue learning and cultivate arts, and thereby develop intellectual faculties and perfect moral powers; furthermore, advance public good and promote common interests; always respect the Constitution and observe the laws; should emergency arise, offer yourselves courageously to the State; and thus guard and maintain the prosperity of Our Imperial Throne coeval with heaven and earth. So shall ye be not only Our good and faithful subjects but render illustrious the best traditions of your forefathers.

The Way here set forth is indeed the teaching bequeathed by Our Imperial Ancestors, to be observed alike by Their Descendants and the subjects, infallible for all ages and true in all places. It is Our wish to lay it to heart in all reverence, in common with you, Our subjects, that we may attain to the same virtue.

The 30th day of the 10th month of the 23rd year of Meiji.
[October 30, 1890]   [Imperial Sign Manual, Imperial Seal]

The tendency to glorify this document into the realm of sacred perfection of form and spirit, where all criticism is transcended, has increased with the years that have passed since it was issued. This tendency has grown to crescendo volume under the stimulus of the ethnocentric war psychology that has developed with ever rising intensity since the early autumn of 1931. The contemporary ethical field is flooded with avowals of the superlative all-sufficiency of the rescript as an instrument of moral and nationalistic education. It is "perfect in spirit and in form, especially in fostering the spirit of loyalty and patriotism."[1] It is "the clearest and most definite statement of the essential features of the Japanese national life, an authoritative formulation of the virtues of the individual, the home and the nation."[2] In 1916 Dr. Shinkichi Uesugi, professor at the time in Tokyo Imperial University, wrote: "The Imperial Rescript on Education supplies the bones of Japanese morality and the foundation of the spirit of the nation. It transcends criticism."[3] More recent writers have reiterated and amplified these enthusiastic observations. The particular point which we need to note here, however, is not that of laudation of the document but rather the manner in which various writers have placed the rescript in irreconcilable opposition to the teachings of Christianity.

The sharpness of this issue is given unusually significant expression in the book, *Our National Organization and Christianity* [*Waga Kokutai to Kirisutokyo*], written by the late Dr. Hiroyuki Katō, former professor of Tokyo Imperial University, and first published in 1907. Regarding the matter before us he writes:

The doctrines of Christianity are quite irreconcilable with the Imperial Rescript on Education. In the Imperial Rescript on Education there is not a single word about the Heavenly Father who is the object of absolute love and reverence in Christianity. The Rescript speaks only of the Imperial Ancestors. For this reason they [the Christians] cannot have it in their hearts at all to read the Rescript acceptably. [In reading it] they must practice deception [p. 63].

Again, he says:

It is altogether impossible to assimilate Christianity to the national organization of Japan. If Christianity were to be assimilated to the national organization of Japan, the fundamental teachings of Christianity would have to be completely destroyed. As long as Christianity possesses its characteristic nature, it can never be said that it is not injurious to our national organization. Sovereignty in Japan is vested in a single Race-father, a form of government without peer among all the nations of the world. It is, therefore, not to be tolerated that a sovereign should be accepted who receives reverence above and beyond the Emperor and the Imperial Ancestors. Our national organiza-

[1] N. Katō, "The Educational System of Japan," *Transactions of the Japan Society of London*, XVI, 142.

[2] Danjō Ehina, *Shinjin*, December 27, 1910.

[3] *Kokutai Kempō oyobi Kensei* ["The National Organization, the Constitution, and Constitutional Government"] (Tokyo, 1916), p. 82.

tion makes it impossible to permit the acceptance of a "one true God" above the Emperor. For this reason it is entirely clear that the teachings of Christianity and our national organization can never stand together [p. 56].

The foregoing statements might lead to the inference that the Imperial Rescript on Education was actually drafted as a nationalistic corrective of the universalism of Christianity. Such an inference would not be entirely wrong. Evidence can be cited to show that it would cover a part of the original situation that called the rescript into being. For example, a Japanese writer has recently said:

> One reason for the promulgation of the Imperial Rescript on Education was undoubtedly the fear that Christian thought was destructive of the ancient and beautiful Japanese teachings of loyalty and filial piety, righteousness and benevolence.[4]

The same author then adds significantly: "Furthermore, this idea has survived to the present day."[5] This statement must be recognized as partial, however. Reference to a wider range of facts goes to show that the rescript originated in an attempt to rescue Japan from the danger of the impact of occidental culture as a whole and not merely in its religious aspects.

The history of modern Japan sets forth a striking picture of progress through the more or less violent adjustment of the forces of liberalism and reaction, of universalism and conservatism. Periods of cordiality toward occidental culture have given place, sometimes with almost sudden abruptness, to periods of antiforeign nationalism. The opening of the reign of the Meiji Emperor saw the promulgation of an imperial oath (April 6, 1868), declaring that knowledge should be sought throughout the whole earth and thereby the foundations of the state strengthened. True to the implications of this oath, it was not long before foreign influences began to pour into the land in a mighty stream. An army of foreign experts in all departments of human specialization, ranging from military science to cookery, was imported. Another army made up of the most brilliant of the youth of Japan invaded the West and attempted to take its

---

[4] Toraji Tsukamoto, *Gendai Nihon to Kirisuto-Kyō* (Tokyo, 1932), p. 123.
[5] *Ibid.*

learning captive. Under such circumstances a favorable attitude toward Christianity was almost inevitable. Early persecution and suspicion gave way to toleration and this, in turn, to an ever widening appreciation. The eighties of the last century saw the enthusiasm for things Western reach unprecedented intensity. Christianity attained a popularity that has made possible the writing of the history of the decade up to the year 1887 as the period of rapid growth for the Christian movement. Then came an inevitable reaction, centering in the final stages of the struggle for the removal of unequal treaties with foreign powers. This made the story of the next ten years one of retarded growth and difficulty. The *Japan Mail* in its issue of April 27, 1889, describes this situation in words that have a surprisingly recent flavor:

The fall of 1887 found the nation beginning to be pervaded by the apprehension that it had travelled too rapidly; that it was in danger of losing its individuality altogether; and that the way to compete with foreign countries was not to follow in their wake by copying their example, but rather to strengthen and develop the faculties that belong especially to the genius of the country. This conviction has now passed into the cry of the day. Under the name of *Kokusai Hozon* ("Preservation of the National Excellencies") it is recognised as the guiding principle, the first duty of the present generation.

The accuracy of the analysis just given is confirmed by what may be taken as an official exposition of the origin of the Imperial Rescript on Education. For this account we are indebted to a remarkable statement made public by Mr. Akimasa Yoshikawa, the man who was serving as minister of education at the time of issuance. The statement appeared in the press of August 5, 1912, shortly after the death of Meiji Tennō. This was twenty-two years after the rescript itself was first promulgated. Mr. Yoshikawa says:

At the time of the Restoration the late Emperor declared it would be the guiding principle of his government to introduce western civilization into the country and to establish New Japan upon that civilization. Consequently every institution in Japan was westernized and the atmosphere of the "new civilization" was felt in almost every stratum of society. Indeed, the process of westernization was carried to extremes. Thus, those who advocated the virtues of righteousness, loyalty and filial duty brought down on themselves the cynical laughter of the men who professed as their first principle the westernization of Japan every way, and who declared that the champions of the old-fashioned virtues were ignorant of the changed social condition of the Empire.

But if any tendency is carried too far, inevitably there comes a reaction. The excessive westernization of Japan very naturally aroused strong opposition among conservative people, especially scholars of the Japanese and Chinese classics, who thought it dangerous for the moral standard of this Empire to see this process carried even into the moral teachings of the people. Thus a hot controversy followed between scholars, publicists and teachers, who were divided into many schools. The question was so keenly agitated that it was taken up at a meeting of the Governors at the Home Office in 1890. At that time Prince Yamagata was Minister of Home Affairs and I was the Vice-Minister of the same department and personally witnessed the heated debate at the Governor's conference. It was, however, agreed in the end among the Home Office authorities that as the question concerned the peoples' thought, it must be dealt with rather by the educational authorities than by the Home Office officials.

His Majesty at once instructed the Minister of Education, Viscount Enomoto, to frame some principles for education. Viscount Enomoto, however, resigned for some reason before he had completed the task and I succeeded him and had to complete the work. I consulted the late Viscount Ki Inouye, then Director of the Legislation Bureau on the matter and the draft was finally drawn up. While, however, the draft was under compilation we frequently approached the Emperor, and asked his gracious advice upon the moral principles which were to be embodied in the new moral standard for the nation.

As people know, the Imperial Rescript on Education was based on the four virtues: benevolence, righteousness, loyalty and filial piety [*jingi chūkō*]. The making of these four virtues the foundation of the national education was, however, strongly criticized at that time, and some scholars even declared that these virtues were imported from China and ought never to be established as the standard of the nation's morality. Others again said that should such old-fashioned virtues be encouraged among the people it would mean the revival of the old form of virtue typified by private revenge, etc. But I strongly upheld the teaching of these four principal virtues, saying that the essence of man's morality is one and the same irrespective of place or time, although it might take different forms according to different circumstances, and that therefore the aforesaid four virtues could well be made the moral standard of the Japanese people.

The Imperial Rescript was issued in its original form, and, in spite of the criticism and opposition before its promulgation, which caused much fear about its future, the Rescript, once issued, soon came to be the light of the people in their moral teaching and is now firmly established as the standard of the nation's morality.[6]

A reference to the text of the Imperial Rescript on Education confirms Mr. Yoshikawa's recognition of dependence upon Con-

---

[6] *Japan Advertiser*, August 6, 1912. Translated from the *Kokumin Shimbun* of August 5, 1912.

fucianism. It is obvious that the relations of ruler and subject, parent and child, husband and wife, brothers and sisters, and of friends with which the rescript concerns itself merely repeat the *gorin*, or five human relationships, of Confucian ethics. This Confucianism is, however, fully assimilated to Japanese norms in its historical and practical references. It is made to center in state and dynastic loyalty, and its foundations are established in the character and will of the Japanese imperial ancestors. Though it is true that one can perceive here an implied recognition of a habitual inability of Japanese culture to construct a satisfactory ethic apart from a Confucian foundation that is characteristic in the long history of the nation, yet the justification alleged by Mr. Yoshikawa that the essentials of human morality are the same the world over, irrespective of time and place, is undoubtedly cogent, and accordingly the Confucian formulation may well be taken as the moral standard for the Japanese people. This sounds like true universalism, and there are those, especially among Japanese Christians, who would take it thus. On the other hand, the much more numerous group which espouses exclusive nationalism as a doctrine, goes to great pains to point out that an unusually definite and self-sufficient manifestation of these universal virtues is embodied in the unique Japanese social and political organization. The Imperial Rescript on Education is to them a moral and spiritual declaration of independence on the part of the Japanese people, and— inconsistent though the statement may seem in view of what we know of the manner in which the rescript was drafted—the registration of a determination to find the wellsprings of spiritual inspiration completely within the Japanese tradition itself.

We have noted, on good authority, that the Imperial Rescript on Education had its origin in an attempt to establish a nationalistic correction to the decentralizing excesses that appeared in Japan in connection with the overrapid Westernization that took place in the eighties of the last century.

Now, fifty years later, nationalist sentiment in Japan is once again at flood tide. The main reasons for this situation are fairly obvious and have been reviewed often. In spite of the fact that there was a rapid growth in pro-foreign feeling in Japan in the years immediately following the World War, the first step in the recent development of reactionary attitudes may be found in the rejection of Japan's demands for racial equality at Versailles. Events conspired to add to this in quick succession a sense of unfairness over treatment received at the Washington and London naval conferences, apprehensions arising from the scrapping of the Anglo-Japanese alliance in 1922, bitterness over the American immigration law of 1924, resentment toward the attitude of foreign powers in the Manchurian affair, frustrations in international markets arising partly out of the world-depression and partly out of a foreign economic nationalism that discriminated against the products of Japanese industry with disastrous repercussions in domestic business, and, finally, a continuous and dangerously adverse foreign-trade balance that threatened to make national bankruptcy merely an affair of years. On top of all this must be heaped a widespread unrest both on the farms and in the industrial areas and acute population problems. Such was the situation until the development of long-premeditated plans on the continent of Asia demanded the sublimation of internal difficulties in the total mobilization of the national resources, material and spiritual, to meet an external foe.

In summary: the rapid Westernization of the land had produced an extraordinary rise in the standard of living, but to continue life at this standard, extend and refine it, and, above all, pay its bills—here were problems that seemed almost insoluble. Japan has found it to be the curse of the white man's burden that, once shouldered, it could never afterward be laid down.

It would be a great mistake, however, to regard Japan's present disquiet as merely economic. It goes deeper than this to the inner beliefs of the nation. To the Japanese nationalist it is not simply the self-sufficiency of the physical life of the people that must be guaranteed and safeguarded. First and foremost the indigenous national spirit itself—viewed as the real source of all things external—must be protected and fostered. Too

much democracy, too much socialism, too much international-
ism, too much of everything foreign, have corrupted the inner
life. The soul of the nation must be fed and restored to itself.

Writing in the spring of 1933, M. D. Kennedy summarized
this spiritual situation in words that are even more pertinent
now:

The fact is that the rapidity with which Japan has become industrialized
and modernized since she opened her doors to foreign intercourse, little more
than seventy years ago, has wrought such vast changes in the whole social
and economic structure of the country, and has played such havoc with the
old ideals, traditions, and beliefs of the people, that there is now a general
spiritual yearning and groping for something to take the place of the ancient
gods and of the old conceptions of life that have been destroyed in the process.
The doctrines of Marx and Moscow have proved unsatisfying to the hungry
soul. Christianity, too, fails to make any appeal to the masses in the Westernized form in which it is served up to them. The people are therefore questioning whether, after all, they would not be better served by a return to their old
gods, which, in their scramble for wealth and material gain, they have, to a
large extent, forsaken.[7]

Whether or not Christian influence in Japan is rightly evaluated in these words is a matter that lies outside our immediate
purpose here. Certainly, a positive and wholesome relationship
with "the masses" is not altogether lacking. Our interest, however, is in the reality of Japan's present-day quest for spiritual
satisfaction as revealed in an officially sponsored return to the
old and tested. More specifically, we have to note that the inspiration of this fervent endeavor to build secure foundations,
unmixed with foreign straw and stubble, exists in the determination of the directors of the thought of the people to realize the
undeniable material advantages of the West and, at the same
time, to replace the widespread bewilderment and uncertainty
of the nation with loyalties and convictions constructed strictly
according to home-drawn patterns. Evidence that this situation is accompanied by fears that Christian teachings threaten
the weakening of the national structure is not far to seek. It
may make the issue clearer if we examine a little more of this
evidence.

[7] "The Reactionary Movement of 1932," Contemporary Japan, I, No. 4 (March,
1933), 632–33.

Writing in the spring of 1935, a Japanese pastor said:

However its advocates may defend Japanism, at present it is nationalistic, ultra-nationalistic and militaristic, in natural opposition to Christianity as international, progressive, and peace-loving. Besides, on the part of Japanism there is a strong tendency to criticize Christianity as an imported doctrine, out of harmony with Japan's national genius, and thus to try to stamp it out quickly by an attack on the emotional plane. On the part of Christianity, further, there has been an unfavorable attitude which regards Japanism as stubbornly-mistaken ancient ideas, and refuses to observe its strong and weak points calmly and impartially, giving it its due.[8]

If the events of the years that have elapsed since these words were written suggest the need of any qualification, it is only in the direction of noting an intensification of the characteristics of "Japanism" mentioned by this writer, together with an increasing difficulty in speaking thus frankly.

Late in 1937 a professor in Dōshisha University said:

Among the intelligentsia and patriots of Japan today there are not a few who are prone to conclude that the views entertained by Christians are difficult to harmonize with convictions that make up the basis of our empire, that is, with conceptions relating to the fundamental character of our national life (*kokutai kan*). In extreme cases there are even those who have definitely made up their minds that Christianity as a whole and the fundamental character of the Japanese Empire can never be mutually adjusted with each other.[9]

Interrogations have been made in the national Diet regarding the adjustment of the universalism taught in Christian schools to the claims of Japanese nationalism. This situation, together with the accompanying fear lest it be made the grounds for a widespread criticism of Christian education, has been cited by officials of the central government as lying behind the interest of the department of education in securing changes in the statement of educational purpose on the part of Christian schools so as to give first place to the Imperial Rescript on Education. The importance of this development justifies a few further words of explanation.

The distinctive feature of Japanese education lies in the suc-

[8] Rinzō Onomura, "Christianity and Current Japanese Thought," *Japan Christian Quarterly*, X, No. 4 (autumn number, 1935), 334.

[9] Masami Hino, "Kokutai no Hongi to Kirisutokyō no Shinzui" ["The Foundation Principles of Our National Life and the Essence of Christianity"], *Nihon Shingakkai Kiyō* ["Records of the Theological Society of Japan"], 1937, p. 169.

cess that it has attained in imparting necessary knowledge and skill within the limits of the safe amalgamation of the individual into the activities and purposes of the Japanese state. This is only to say that Japanese education is predominantly and avowedly nationalistic, both in regard to its legal foundations and in regard to its spirit and method. The regulations of the central department of education are very specific in this respect. From primary school to university the officially defined purpose of education is always that of imparting a specified grade of education within limits imposed by an attention to the fostering of "national morality" (*kokumin dōtoku*) that is always given priority. Meanwhile Christian schools have emphasized the fundamental character of Christian principles in their statement of educational objectives. This has inevitably laid Christian education in Japan open to the risk of being interpreted as an unabsorbed alien element within an otherwise well-integrated national whole. To correct this situation the national department of education is now securing as rapidly as possible a revision of the statement of educational purpose on the part of Christian schools so as to give first place to the Imperial Rescript on Education and at the same time effect the minimizing or total elimination of any reference to Christian principles.

The most recent developments indicate that from now on it will be impossible to secure official approval of school charters that make any reference whatsoever to the principles of Christianity in their statement of educational purpose. How long older charters containing such references will be permitted to stand is not clear. Officials in the department of education have taken pains to point out that Christian schools are still free to impart Christian teaching inside the curriculum as heretofore. It was undoubtedly the situation just passed in review that led the National Christian Educational Association of Japan to declare in a recent statement:

The promotion of the welfare of the nation is dependent on the development of national morality.

The Imperial Rescript on Education promulgated in Meiji 23 (1890), sets forth the ends of national morality. This, together with the issuing of the Imperial Constitution in Meiji 22 (1899) and the establishment of the National Diet in Meiji 23 are the most important of the unprecedented achievements of the time, and ever since its proclamation the Imperial Rescript on Education has been the source of national morality, with the result that the national progress has manifested a brilliance without parallel in past or present.

We of the Christian schools who believe with regard to all ethics that the beauty thereof is more and more revealed in proportion as morality is spiritualized by religion, hereby register our purpose to introduce religious feeling into our conformity to the Imperial Rescript on Education and our expression thereof in actual life.[10]

There are numerous straws in the wind that show the existence of a considerable amount of anxiety in certain quarters lest this attempt to spiritualize morality by the power of religion find itself diverted from an exclusive support of purely national interests to a dangerous infatuation with delusions that transcend the state and its sacred traditions. We can note here only one of these indications, but that an important one.

On March 4, 1938, the head of the thought-control office of the Osaka gendarmery sent out to some of the Christian pastors and educators of that city, both Japanese and foreign, a questionnaire in which they were asked to discuss certain points of Christian teaching in relation to Japanese nationalism. Although this questionnaire was first distributed merely to a small group of Christian leaders, twenty-four in number, resident in a single city, it quickly found its way throughout the nation, and various individuals and some groups sent in replies. A point of special significance lies in the fact that these questions did not originate in the Osaka gendarmery itself. They are reported to have been compiled from some ten thousand communications asking for clarification of various matters in the relation of Christianity to the national life received by the army office in Osaka from representatives of all walks of life in the nation. They thus afford an unrivaled opportunity to gauge the immediate status of the problem of the adjustment of Christianity to its nationalistic environment in Japan. The statement of replies to the Osaka questionnaire translated below is that made out by a number of Christian leaders having membership in a

[10] Resolutions of the Twenty-fourth Session of the National Christian Educational Association of Japan, Kyoto, Dōshisha, November 7–9, 1935.

group known as the Christian Patriotic Movement. The ideas set forth may be taken as thoroughly representative of the tenets entertained by Japanese Christianity in its attempted accommodation to the primary principles of nationalism in this country.

In the translation made here, the subject of investigation as sent out by the Osaka gendarmery is first printed after its appropriate number. Immediately after this is given the Christian reply.

1. The Christian idea of God
    The God of Christianity is the Creator of the Universe revealed in Jesus Christ. He is a Being with the attributes of uniqueness, absoluteness and personality. Jesus called Him the Lord of Heaven and Earth and the Father of mankind. God is Spirit, existing above all things, through all things and in all things. He is all-holy, all-loving, omniscient and omnipotent.
2. Views regarding the eight hundred myriads of deities of Japan (*yao-yorodzu no kami*)
    As is set forth in the ancient classics, we interpret "the eight hundred myriads of deities" of our country to mean the ancestors of our race who lived in the Age of *Takama-ga-Hara*.[11]
3. The relation of the Emperor of Japan and the God of Christianity
    In the Charter Oath of Five Articles pronounced by the Meiji Emperor on April 6, 1868, are the words: "We, in Our own person and as an example to the people, take oath to the God of the Universe (*Tenchi Shinmei*)[12] to fix the policy of the state and establish principles for the welfare of the people." Again, in the Imperial Message to Soldiers and Sailors promulgated in 1882, the Emperor said: "We believe that in guarding the nation, whether or not response is manifested for the mercies of God (*Jōten*) and gratitude shown for mercies received from ancestors, depends on how you soldiers and sailors do your duty." Again, the Empress Dowager has said in a poem: "The God of the Universe (*Tenchi no Kami*) clearly knows the secret good and bad in our hearts." Again, the reigning Emperor has also written a poem containing the words: "We pray to the God of the Universe (*Tenchi no Kami*) for a world where all is like the sea in a morning calm, where waves arise no more."
    The God who is here called *Tenchi Shinmei*, *Jōten* and *Tenchi no Kami* is, we respectfully conclude, probably the same as the God in whom we believe.
4. The relation of the emperors of foreign countries (for example, England) and God
    The coronation ceremony of the English Sovereign is carried out according to Christian rites. In the course of the rites, the master of cere-

---

[11] The mythological age.   [12] This may be plural.

monies [the Archbishop of Canterbury] presents a newly printed volume of the Scriptures to the King and makes the following statement: "Our gracious King, we present you, with this book, the most valuable thing that this world affords. Here is wisdom; this is the royal Law; these are the living Oracles of God." After listening to these words, the King lays his hands carefully on the Bible, then kisses it and takes an oath to be obedient to God. These facts are self-explanatory of the relation of the English King and God. The cases of foreign rulers in Christian Countries apart from England are in general the same as this.

5. The relation of Imperial Rescripts and the Bible

The Imperial Rescripts are the exalted words bestowed upon the nation by the Emperor as the embodiment of the Will of Heaven and as the Ruler of the Japanese Empire. And as such they are to be reverently obeyed by the nation.

The Bible (Sacred Scripture) is the sacred writing brought into existence by divine revelation, that is, by the Will of Heaven. It sets forth duty of man toward the supreme God, and the way of salvation for man both in the present and in the future.

6. The difference between the educational policy of the Imperial Rescript on Education and education according to the principles of Christianity

All education directed toward the Japanese people must be carried out according to the purposes of the Imperial Rescript on Education. In this respect there is not the slightest difference between educational policy according to the Imperial Rescript on Education and education according to the principles of Christianity. In the case of the latter, however, the attempt is made to foster religious sentiment in addition to general education.

7. Views regarding ancestor worship (that is, ideas relating to participation in the ceremonies of the Shintō shrines of Japan)

The government has declared that the shrines are places of national veneration and reverence and not religious in nature. Accordingly, participation in shrine ceremonies differs in meaning from religious worship, and therefore, it is the duty of subjects, without regard to religion, to participate in shrine ceremonies out of feelings of reverence for the shrines as places of national veneration. There are people who say that Christianity is a religion that treats ancestors with contempt, but this is a serious misunderstanding. A yearning after the virtues of ancestors and a desire to reveal that which has been received from them are natural human emotions and the Bible gives powerful expression to this fact for various periods of the past.

8. Ideas regarding the divine spirits of the Imperial Ancestors

Just as in our attitude towards the Emperor, so also towards the Imperial Ancestors we should manifest a supreme reverence.

9. What is the supreme condition of faith?

In Christianity the supreme condition of faith does not mean what is commonly known as "god possession." It means rather, a state of oneness between God and man that includes healthy ethical aspects. It is what Christ meant when he said, "I and the Father are one." We are not gods,

however, but as babes we follow the direction of the spirit of God and with
prayer and thanksgiving live lives of service according to His will.

10. Ideas regarding freedom of faith

Article XXVIII of the Constitution says: "Japanese subjects shall,
within limits of law, not prejudicial to peace and order, and not antagonistic to their duties as subjects, enjoy freedom of religious belief." We,
therefore, within limits that do not violate our duties as subjects and with
high regard for peace and order, interpret this as a guarantee of the right
to establish free churches for the purpose of free religious worship with
religious faith as an object, and also the right to freedom of propaganda.

11. Reasons why Christianity calls Japanese Shintō and Buddhism idolatrous
superstitions.

The Christians of Japan today do not say indiscriminately that Shintō
and Buddhism are idolatrous superstitions. All religions, however, are
apt to tend to fall easily into superstition, and we should mutually
take warning to strive to avoid falling into these evils.

12. The relation of Christianity and the Japanese Spirit

Both Christianity and the Japanese Spirit have their origins in the
great principles of the universe, and therefore there is no conflict whatsoever between them in essence. The Japanese Spirit manifests itself
by permeating the unique Japanese national organization (*kokutai*) and
is the center of reverence and of veneration for ancestors, as well as of
loyalty to ruler and love of country. As revealed in history, however, the
Japanese Spirit is exceedingly rich in its power of assimilation [lit. *hōyō*,
"to comprehend, to include"], and we believe that by virtue of taking
in Christianity and effecting harmonization therewith the content of
the Japanese Spirit will be more and more enriched and its glory exalted
throughout the world.

13. Other items for information

(1). Having over us an Emperor who rules the Japanese empire in a
single line unbroken for all ages, we cherish the national Constitution
and obey the laws of the land. Our Scriptures also highly enjoin this same
thing. We Christians therefore believe that it is the divine command
that we always be loyal and worthy subjects of the Emperor, and we
resolve to give our lives for our country.[13]

Further replies under this heading can only be summarized
briefly here. Rom. 13:1–2 and Tim. 2:1–3 are cited to show the
nature of authoritative Christian teaching on the proper relation of believers to the state; undying opposition to communism
is affirmed; and, finally, various passages of Scripture are adduced to show how the fundamentals of Christianity are permeated by the teaching of filial piety.

[13] Daikichirō Tagawa, *Kokka to Shūkyō* ["The State and Religion"] (Tokyo, 1938),
pp. 123–36.

In our study of the relations of Christianity to its Japanese environment we have merely glanced at a few examples that have been selected because of their value in throwing light on a much greater whole. Fragmentary though the discussion has been, it may suffice to show that in Japan, as in other totalitarian states, Christians find themselves in a position in which they must make certain politico-religious affirmations in the interests of national unity as conceived by the ruling classes or else take the consequences of an alleged disloyalty. While much greater attention has been attracted by the struggles of Christian groups in totalitarian states other than Japan, partly because of the remoteness of this land and partly because of the greater strength of the church in the West, nevertheless, the difficulties of the Christians in Japan are peculiarly acute because here alone they must strive for adjustment with an official purpose that attempts to reinforce the structure of the national life with a carefully integrated framework which, functionally at least if not legally, is nothing other than a state religion.

RELIGIOUS BEARINGS OF THE MODERN SCIENTIFIC MOVEMENT

EDWIN EWART AUBREY

Divinity School, University of Chicago

P HYSICAL science will not console me for the ignorance of morality in the time of affliction." When Blaise Pascal[1] wrote these words, he stated the problem of modern man. But in our own day we have added an appendix: Morality will not console me for ignorance of religion in the time of affliction. Because of this, we stand at the second remove from physical science and are more concerned with the bearings of social science.

It is a truism fully exploited by A. D. White[2] and J. W. Draper[3] that the theologians have not been conspicuous for hospitality to new scientific ideas. It is not so clearly understood why this should be so. The modern scientific movement came into being as a sort of stepchild of medieval thought. From its mother, Western theology, it had inherited a firm belief in the orderly, rational structure of the world; and from its stepfather, the Levantine mentality, it acquired a strange collection of data and speculations about the natural world: Arabian alchemy and astrology and a number system useful for big calculations and Greek theories of a materialistic sort. That the Schoolmen in their way, and Francis of Assisi in his, should have developed a new interest in the world of nature is not surprising. It should be no more surprising that the dislocating effect of these new composite views upon traditional theology should have been resented.

---

[1] *Pensées* (Everyman ed.; London, 1931), § 67.

[2] *A History of the Warfare of Science with Theology* (2 vols.; New York, 1898).

[3] *A History of the Conflict between Science and Religion* (New York, 1862).

For attacks upon specific doctrines were attacks upon a structure of thought so highly organized and unified that all parts would suffer: in other words, they would undermine the faith as a whole. In this theology the flat earth, with its dome of heaven above, was the center of the universe. To it Christ and the angels descended, and from it Christ ascended and the Virgin was taken up to glory. When Christ came again, his arrival would be visible from all parts of the earth. Under the earth was hell, that hell into which Columbus' mutinous sailors feared to fall. If a few believed in the sphericity of the earth, it was for Aristotle's speculative reason that a perfect solid *must* be a sphere, rather than from experimental evidence. The centrality of the earth was the guaranty of man's centrality in the divine concern, and God was therefore willing to sacrifice his only begotten Son for human redemption. In the ordinary affairs of life disease was still regarded as due to supernatural influence, so that cure might be a religious rite, while insanity was treated as demonic possession. Since man hoped for a physical resurrection, anatomical dissection was a dreadful thing and heavily punished. Exorcism and torture were used, penance often took the place of medicine, and prayers were substitutes for hygiene.

The Greek interest in natural processes had given way to Roman concern with speculative origins: *physis* to *natura*.[4] And the absolute origin, the First Cause, was supernatural. Man had been created perfect, in the goodness of God, but had since the Fall of Adam lost the power to establish union with God or to achieve ultimate knowledge—these were now dependent on divine grace. Born in nature but endowed with a divine soul inbreathed at the creation, man stood always in two worlds which tore him apart in the conflict of flesh with spirit. On this asceticism had been built—the backbone of ecclesiastical discipline. On this rested man's confidence in a happier life beyond for those who obeyed the behests of the church.

Whatever we may today think of these views, we must re-

[4] C. Singer in J. Needham (ed.), *Science, Religion and Reality* (New York, 1925), p. 94.

member that they were firmly lodged in the world into which modern science was born. The slowness with which even scientists themselves became emancipated from such preconceptions should give us pause. Kepler, for all his careful mathematical observations of the planets, believed they were moved by angels, in accord with the underlying mathematical harmony appropriate to the Great Geometer; and Galilei shared this latter view. Descartes, who laid the foundations of analytical geometry, still believed in God as an innate idea implanted in the human mind.

I

More significant, however, than particular doctrinal controversies was the growing tendency to separate science from metaphysics. For side by side with the pious acknowledgments of a Pascal or a Spinoza or a Leibnitz, there was growing up a different tradition in thought. Francis Bacon had expounded, though not actually employed, it. The method of induction was explained in his *Novum organum*, and its social implications for a culture scientifically controlled were written down as *The New Atlantis*. But Bacon had a place for theology at the conclusion, though not the culmination, of his *Advancement of Learning*, for, said he, "In human laws, there be many grounds and maxims which are *placita juris*, positive upon authority, and not upon reason, and therefore not to be disputed. . . . . Such therefore is that secondary reason, which hath place in divinity [i.e., theology], which is grounded upon the *placets* of God."[5] Hobbes, in following Bacon, allowed faith in God and angels but reserved the term "knowledge" for sensation produced by motion and held that philosophy was to deal with "composable and decomposable things." At the same time the Accademia del Cimento in Florence was based on "abjuration of all faith." Yet Newton, despite his celebrated declaration on the last page of the *Principia* that he does not indulge in speculations,[6] in a letter says of the centrifugal motion that cuts athwart the law

[5] *Advancement of Learning* (Everyman ed.; New York, 1934), pp. 211 f.

[6] *Hypotheses non fingo.*

of gravitation: "I do not know any Power in Nature which would cause this transverse Motion without the divine Arm."[7]

The collapse of scientific metaphysics came with Berkeley and Hume. Bishop Berkeley employed a logical *via negativa* to God, seeking to show that, because we cannot prove the independent objectivity of the things we sense, we must posit a supreme cosmic consciousness to give them reality. But alas, the pious conclusion was lost sight of in the excitement over his denial of objectivity to the data of sensory observation. When Hume applied the argument to the fundamental concept of causality, and was led to a rejection of objective causal connections, the demolition seemed complete. It is little wonder that Kant was roused from his dogmatic faith in science to examine the foundations of our knowledge, with the hope of restoring objective truth; but he fathered positivism as much as idealism.

In the nineteenth century came the revolt of the sciences against philosophy. The allies who had made common cause against the theological dogmatism of the church now looked askance at one another. Hegel attempted a reconciliation, but it was a proposal to absorb the *atman* of science into the *brahman* of philosophy. And, besides, he held the painstaking fact-gathering of the scientists in low esteem, preferring to extract a priori the results they so laboriously sought. In the natural sciences he failed completely. His fatal error was to have attacked Newton, the real founder of contemporary physical science. The result was, as Helmholtz wrote,[8] that

the philosophers accused the scientific men of narrowness; the scientific men retorted that the philosophers were crazy. And so it came about that men of science began to lay some stress on the banishment of all philosophic influences from their work; . . . . no regard was paid to the rightful claims of philosophy, that is, the criticism of the sources of cognition, and the definition of the functions of the intellect.

This is not to say that there were no philosophic implications in their science. On the contrary the attacks of the philosophical

[7] Letter to Bentley, quoted by M. Maeterlinck, *The Supreme Law* (New York, 1935), p. 65.

[8] *Popular Lectures on Scientific Subjects*, English trans. (London, 1873), p. 5.

critics[9] made it abundantly clear that the scientists were attached to a mechanistic world-view; and Büchner, in his *Kraft und Stoff*, had in 1855 made this position quite explicit. Furthermore, the underlying assumptions of scientific method were never examined by scientific men, who remained naïve realists in their epistemology. The logical studies of Boole, Jevons, and Clifford were ignored in scientific circles, while the work of Ernst Mach received some attention.[10] Later the critical studies of Karl Pearson[11] and Henri Poincaré[12] stimulated a closer examination of the adequacy of the methods of scientific observation and validation; and the limitations of scientific knowledge have been popularized in theological circles through the Gifford Lectures of the English physicist, A. S. Eddington, on *The Nature of the Physical World*.[13] In his Swarthmore Lecture on *Science and the Unseen World*[14] the same author ventured still farther to assert the reality of the world apprehended in the mystical experience.

While such reassurances have given a consolation to many religious people which was perhaps premature, yet they have served as reminders not only that science and metaphysics are not the same thing but also that science suffers loss by its divorce from metaphysics. Here the theme has been more thoroughly treated by A. N. Whitehead, who has attempted to frame the organic conception of nature as a resolution of the conflict between science and metaphysics.[15]

The successive stages have had their reflections in theology. The earlier influence of Ockhamist nominalism had been for the separation of philosophy from theology; but the philosophy was built upon particulars after the nominalist manner, and that meant the incipience of inductive method. But this had been

[9] See A. Aliotta, *The Idealistic Reaction against Science in the Nineteenth Century* (London, 1914).

[10] W. Dampier, *A History of Science* (New York, 1936), p. 316.

[11] *Grammar of Science* (London, 1892).   [13] Cambridge and New York, 1928.

[12] *La Science et l'hypothèse* (Paris, 1903).   [14] New York, 1929.

[15] *Science and the Modern World* (New York, 1925), p. 226; *Process and Reality* (New York, 1929), *passim*.

snowed under in religious circles by the ecclesiastical problem presented first by the Lutheran revolt and then by the internal strife of the wars of religion. In France the Gallican church was breaking away from papal control even while Louis XIV was establishing his absolute monarchy; and England was engaged in its dual civil struggle between religious tolerance and bigotry, on the one hand, and between king and parliament, on the other. It was this religious strife which helped the modern revolt of philosophy against rival claims to revealed truth; and in the transitional period Deism became a potent name.

II

The Deists were seeking a natural religion in the same way that contemporaneous social philosophers were seeking the natural roots of government, and the psychologists the foundations of human intelligence. Herbert of Cherbury had in 1624 published his *De veritate* in an attempt to promote toleration by setting down five fundamental truths which all men (*sic*) share; that there is a supreme God, that he is to be worshiped, that the principal part of his worship is virtue, that men ought to repent of sin, and that there are rewards and punishments here and hereafter. The effect of this was to minimize the special revelatory value of Christianity; and, in the works of John Toland[16] and Anthony Collins,[17] this position was further developed, and the authority of the Bible was attacked. The attempt made by such Christian apologists as Grotius[18] and Tillotson[19] to rest the superiority of Christian truth on the prophecies and miracles of the Bible invited the attacks of Blount, Whiston, Collins, Woolston, and Hume.[20]

[16] *Christianity Not Mysterious* (London, 1696). (Published anonymously.)

[17] *Discourse on Freethinking* (London, 1713).

[18] *De veritate religionis Christianae* (London, 1788).

[19] *Sermons* (London, 1694–1710).

[20] Charles Blount, *Oracles of Reason* (London, 1693); W. Whiston, *Restoring the True Text of the Old Testament* (London, 1722); A. Collins, *Grounds and Reasons of the Christian Religion* (London, 1724); T. Woolston, *Discourses on the Miracles of Our Saviour* (London, 1727–29); D. Hume, *Enquiry concerning Human Understanding* (London, 1748), Sec. X.

Thereupon the Christian theologians responded in four different ways: Locke in his *Reasonableness of Christianity* and Chubb in *The True Gospel of Jesus Christ Asserted* sought to differentiate true rational Christianity from false Christianity. Others, like Jonathan Edwards in his *Divine Supernatural Light*, Jenyns in his *A View of the Internal Evidences of the Christian Religion*, and Paley in his *Evidences of Christianity*, shifted the ground from the evidential value of the now disputed prophecies and miracles to the intrinsic merits of the New Testament itself which presents, through the medium of ignorant men, a system of morality and religion which is so sublime that it must be attributed to divine interposition.[21] (It is said that Patrick Henry was persuaded by Jenyns' book to accept the Christian faith.[22]) A third reaction was that typified in Paley's *Natural Theology*, where the argument from design was employed; but a fourth group removed the faith from attack by placing it beyond reason. Thus Joseph Butler's *Analogy of Religion* argued that it was absurd to demand that revelation be intelligible to the finite human mind which is restricted to judgments of probability; and William Law in *The Case of Reason* (1731) and Dodwell in his *Christianity Not Founded on Argument* (1743) sounded the same note.

Meanwhile, the efforts to establish knowledge on the basis of mathematical demonstration had been developing from Giordano Bruno, Da Vinci, and Galilei into the pretentious systems of Spinoza, Leibnitz, and Newton. It was a search for "the most exact and most economical mathematical description of sensory experience";[23] and in Newton's *Principia* this mathematical form of demonstration was related to a body of experimental knowledge accumulated by Galilei, Kepler, Huygens, Halley, and Boyle. The effect of the *Principia* on religious thought lay, first of all, in its metaphysical implications. As Burtt has said, "The gloriously romantic universe of Dante and Milton, that

[21] Soame Jenyns, *A View of the Internal Evidences of the Christian Religion* (London, 1776), Introd.

[22] *Evangelical Family Library* (New York, 1833), XIV, 2.

[23] F. Orestano, *Verita dimostrate* (Naples, 1937), p. 140.

set no bounds to the imagination of man as it played over space and time, had now been swept away. . . . . The really important world outside was a world hard, cold, colorless, silent and dead; a world of quantity, a world of mathematically computable motions in mechanical regularity."[24] Furthermore, the discovery of a unitary principle operative on all planets removed man from his unique centrality in the scheme of things and also seemed to many like Laplace to dispense with need for a God.

In Kant these two streams of thought met, and his philosophy sought both to re-establish the creative role of human reason and will (after the skepticism of Hume) and to assert the existence of God by appeal to the inner witness of conscience. At the same time his critical rejection of rationalist metaphysics paved the way for the romantic movement with its "experiential" theology and, on the other hand, gave a charter to modern positivism.

III

The nineteenth century opened, therefore, with several possibilities in the relation of theology to science. One possibility was to abstract religion from the realm of scientific verification; another was to claim for the data of religious experience the same scientific status as the data of the physical sciences and to build thereon an empirical science of theology; and the third was to build a religion out of the materials furnished by the several sciences.

Schleiermacher, Kierkegaard, and Ritschl in their different ways followed the first procedure. In the first, the inner witness, which in Kant's philosophy had been the moral imperative of the sense of duty, took a more aesthetic form; and he defined religion as "the feeling of absolute dependence," to which we are led back by all our reasoning but which is intuitive in character. This emphasis on intuitive feeling is characteristic of the romanticists and may be seen also in Coleridge and Bushnell. In the work of Bushnell on *God in Christ* we find a theory of language employed which differentiates an incomprehensible dogmatic

[24] E. A. Burtt, *The Metaphysical Foundations of Modern Science* (New York: Harcourt, Brace & Co., 1925), p. 236.

formulation from the true spiritual experience which it embodies,[25] the implication of which is that science might criticize a theological dogma without affecting the religious experience expressed therein. Here Bushnell anticipates a familiar attitude of twentieth-century modernism.

Kierkegaard passes in his thought from an earlier aesthetic stage to a later stage in which the paradoxes of Christian faith defy reason and thereby convict reason of inadequacy.[26] Consequently, the attacks of scientific reason do not touch the essentials of faith.

In Ritschl a Kantian distinction is drawn between judgments of fact and judgments of value. The objective facts of science constitute one order of knowledge. But even these are discovered by virtue of assumptions regarding their interest and value to human beings, by "concomitant value judgments." Yet there are also "independent value judgments" which relate to an ideal order of things and not to perceived data: these are the materials of religion.[27]

But in Ritschl we have also the attitude of a second group which proposed to build an empirical theology out of the data of religious experience. Affected as he was by the developments in historical method which Baur and his Tübingen associates had applied to the life of Christ, Ritschl proposed to base theology on history rather than on metaphysics.[28] The religious experience of Christ in the early Christian community is the historical foundation, as the practical spiritual import in contemporary experience is the empirical foundation, of Christian faith. This dual basis is accepted by Herrmann.[29]

Further development of this "theology of experience" is found in the development of the psychology of religion in the United

[25] H. Bushnell, *God in Christ* (Hartford, 1849), p. 301.

[26] See W. Ruttenbeck, *Sören Kierkegaard: der christliche Denker und sein Werk* (Berlin, 1929), pp. 126, 138, 158 n.; and J. Wahl, "Hegel et Kierkegaard," *La Revue philosophique*, CXII (1931), 343–62.

[27] A. Ritschl, *The Christian Doctrine of Justification and Reconciliation*, English trans. (Edinburgh, 1902), pp. 204 f.

[28] A. E. Garvie, art. "Ritschlianism," *ERE*, X, 814 and 816.

[29] *The Communion of the Christian with God* (London, 1906), pp. 102 f.

States. The work of Leuba, Starbuck, James, Coe, Ames, King, and Pratt[30] represents the effort to examine the data of religious experience as a means to the achievement of a scientific discipline in the theological field. Comparable studies by the Frenchmen Murisier, Delacroix, Flournoy, Bois, and Frommel represent the same tendency, though not always with the same theological interest.

The third attitude parallels the movement among nineteenth-century empiricists to construct philosophy out of the established findings of the various sciences. Against the background of Auguste Comte's *Philosophie positive*, which utilized the intervening scientific developments to elaborate the theme of Francis Bacon's *New Atlantis* by making sociology the climax of the sciences, there arose in England the philosophy of J. S. Mill, who sought to demonstrate the utility of religion in the enrichment of the happiness of men and who found in Christ the embodiment of a noble ideal of human life.[31] In similar fashion Frederic Harrison expounded religious devotion to human values. Herbert Spencer's regard for the penumbra of mystery surrounding the lighted area of scientific knowledge modified his religious outlook, so that he and Harrison fell into disagreement. The contemporary movement of religious humanism carries forward the empirical approach into an interpretation of religion as devotion to the socially discovered values of ideal human living.[32]

IV

All attempts to establish a co-operative relation between religion and science, however, are influenced by the relativistic

[30] J. H. Leuba, "Studies in the Psychology of Religion," *American Journal of Psychology*, VII (1896), 309–85; E. D. Starbuck, *The Psychology of Religion* (New York, 1899); G. A. Coe, *The Spiritual Life* (New York, 1900); W. James, *Varieties of Religious Experience* (New York, 1902); J. B. Pratt, *Psychology of Religious Belief* (New York, 1905); E. S. Ames, *Psychology of Religious Experience* (Boston, 1910); I. King, *Development of Religion* (New York, 1910). The general methodological problem is well stated in G. B. Foster, *The Finality of the Christian Religion* (Chicago, 1906), and D. C. Macintosh, *Theology as an Empirical Science* (New York, 1919).

[31] *The Utility of Religion* (London, 1858); *Theism* (London, 1870).

[32] E. S. Ames, *Religion* (New York, 1929); J. Dewey, *The Quest for Certainty* (New York, 1929); *A Common Faith* (New Haven, 1934); A. E. Haydon, *The Quest of the Ages* (New York, 1929); and others.

character of modern scientific thought. Mathematical studies in the theory of probability were inaugurated by Pascal's study of games of chance, continued by Gauss's investigations of the collisions of molecules and by the Maxwell-Boltzmann experiments in the velocity of molecules, applied to human problems by Laplace and Quetelet, and received formal logical application to the whole problem of induction in J. M. Keynes's *Theory of Probability*. They reached the fundamental assumptions of modern physical science in the quantum theory associated with the researches of A. H. Compton, Planck, and Heisenberg, and taken up into the celebrated treatises of Einstein. The mention of Einstein recalls, in addition, the recent geometries of Riemann and Lobatchewsky which are offered as alternatives to the more familiar system of Euclid, and the axioms of which are self-consistent while contradicting those of each other and of Euclid. Certainty here gives way to probability: a result the theological bearings of which were explored by John Dewey in his Gifford Lectures[33] in a manner not fully grasped apparently by his theological critics.

Dewey was, however, influenced more by the relativism which emerged within the area of social sciences. The eighteenth century was a time of taking intellectual inventory: men re-examined their stock-in-trade of assumptions, and there followed essays in the foundations of government, of economics, of ethics, of religion, of reason. The life of peoples did not escape this scrutiny; and historiography in the hands of Voltaire, Montesquieu, and Rousseau, of Gibbon and Bolingbroke, and later, of Herder, and Hegel, turned to theories of the *esprit du peuple* and the laws of human change. The nineteenth-century development of historical research showed two tendencies: the construction of elaborate interpretations of history by such writers as Comte, Spencer, Marx, and Buckle and the confinement to accurate factual representation exemplified by Leopold von Ranke and his followers. Despite differences of attitude toward *Geschichtsphilosophie*, there was general recognition of the relativity of human thought and action to cultural and physical

<hr>

[33] *The Quest for Certainty.*

milieus. The new discipline of sociology, fathered by Saint-Simon, publicized by Comte and systematized speculatively by Spencer, lent further support to social relativism. Men and their doings were explained by so-called sociological "laws," and various forms of determinism appeared within historiography: geographic, racial, economic, etc.

The accepted verities of moral and religious belief were inevitably affected; and in histories of morals or religion the thesis was elaborated that all such beliefs are relative to social conditions. Mores were declared to be changing formulations of what a group, within the limits of its experience, deemed best for its group welfare. Conscience was no longer the categorical imperative of Kantian ethics but the voice of the group echoed in the judgments of the individual whom it had "conditioned." The word God was a relative term, depending for its meaning upon the cultural experience of the adherents of a variety of religions. Indeed, religion itself had lost its exclusively Christian connotation, and even popular thought began to wonder about the validity of introducing occidental religion into oriental cultures.

The influence of Darwin on philosophical thought cannot be too strongly emphasized. There had been theories of dynamic change before, but they were expressions of an Absolute. What Darwin did was to destroy a fundamental postulate of the inherited philosophy: the immutable "forms."[34] The vitalism inherent in the views of Duns Scotus, and combined with alchemy in the curiously profound system of Jakob Boehme, here appears in scientific form with painstaking factual support from biological research. To Herbert Spencer, Darwin furnished unwittingly a key to general philosophy, an amplified basis for the old Heraclitean apotheosis of process. All is in the flux of evolution, in a dynamic equilibrium which defines the apparent stability of any object or idea or situation. Our stage is a temporary adjustment; and our truths are functional ideas which

[34] G. H. Mead, *Movements of Thought in the Nineteenth Century* (Chicago, 1936), chap. viii.

are tested by their efficiency in the continual adaptation which is life.[35]

When truths are viewed in this way, a new tendency appears: to trace an idea back not to its logical foundations but to its psychological foundations. Thus Dewey in his most recent book on logic opens the treatise with chapters on the biological and cultural matrixes of inquiry.[36] Recent studies in "compulsive thinking" have been directed toward the discovery of motives behind thought, and this has led many people to abandon logic entirely for psychology and sociology. We are all familiar with the strictures of Freudians and Marxists upon "rationalization."

This whole relativistic trend has had two important bearings upon religious thought. In the first place, it has suggested a new approach to the history of religious thought and thus to the problem of finality in religious belief; and, in the second place, it has created an attitude in which conviction is, by the very nature of its fixity, suspect. Students of the Bible have long been familiar with the efforts to understand biblical passages by reference to the cultural situation in which they arose, but the idea that they are adequately interpreted in that historical context of the past is relatively new. Its culmination is found in the *Formgeschichte* school, which traces the erstwhile *ipsissima verba* of Jesus to special interests of the early church.[37] In similar fashion, historians of the early church had already sought the key to New Testament theology in adaptation to the gentile or the Jewish environment;[38] and historians of doctrine had portrayed the changes in Christian theology through the centuries as reactions to new cultural factors encountered in successive epochs.[39] The implication was clear: there can be no

---

[35] See J. Dewey, *The Influence of Darwin on Philosophy and Other Essays* (New York, 1910), chap. i; *Logic: The Theory of Inquiry* (New York, 1938), chap. v.

[36] *Logic*, chaps. ii and iii.   [37] F. C. Grant, *Form Criticism* (Chicago), 1934.

[38] See, e.g., S. J. Case, *The Evolution of Early Christianity* (Chicago, 1914), and the literature cited therein.

[39] S. Mathews, *The Atonement and the Social Process* (New York, 1930); *The Growth of the Idea of God* (New York, 1931); S. J. Case, *Highways of Christian Doctrine* (Chicago, 1936).

final Christian belief in a changing world. The search for the essence of Christianity was therefore abandoned,[40] and truth was identified with greatest probability.

A reaction against all this may be seen in the writings of Karl Barth. In fact, his first work, which called attention to his "dialectical theology," was an unconventional commentary on the Epistle to the Romans[41] which insisted on going beyond the historical relativities in Paul's letter to ask what they mean for our day. He has tried to rescue the absolute by individualistic recoil from social conditioning as his spiritual forebear, Kierkegaard, did a century before. The probabilistic character of rational truth was attacked by Kierkegaard as follows:

. . . . The man of understanding uses his understanding to feel before him after the probability, and he finds God where probability indicates. . . . . To believe against the understanding is a sheer impossibility. . . . . Whereas faith *always* gives thanks to God, always is in the midst of mortal peril, in that conflict between the infinite and the finite which is the special peril of him who is constituted of both. Probability, therefore, is so far from being dear to the believer that he fears it most of all, knowing well that his interest in the probabilities is an indication that he is in the process of losing his faith.[42]

We are here face to face with a crucial problem raised by the development of relativistic thinking for the religious attitude. The situation is a dilemma: on the one hand, the feeling of the relativity of all our beliefs reinforces the attitude of tentativeness as it has done in the area of scientific knowledge; but, on the other hand, the commitment of a life in religious devotion at any given point of decision seems to require a fixed center of action. We must act as though the accepted plan of action were absolutely true, even while we know it is only relatively true. An attempt has been made to solve this problem in the fictionalism of Hans Vaihinger[43] and in an article by E. S. Ames on "The Practical Absolute."[44] Their proposal was to act

[40] M. H. Krumbine (ed.), *The Process of Religion* (New York, 1933), pp. 24–31.

[41] *Epistle to the Romans*, English trans. (London, 1933).

[42] Quoted in W. Lowrie, *Kierkegaard* (New York, 1938), pp. 317 f.

[43] *Die Philosophie des Als Ob* (Berlin, 1911; English trans., London and New York, 1924).

[44] *International Journal of Ethics*, XXXII (1922), 347–65.

in the immediate situation as though something were true and thus to open the way through action to future discovery. But the psychological possibility of doing this depends on one's ability to neglect the other possibilities of action confronting one at the moment of decision. This question is dealt with in Tillich's discussion of the idea of one's fatality,[45] and the acute sense of the cosmic implications in a personal decision lends a tragic quality to his presentation. He would have us penetrate beneath the relativities of thinking to "the Unconditioned," which is always ambiguous to reason, but which is the source of all tensions in our human existence—tensions which are the mark of life itself. "The Kairos, the fateful moment of knowledge, is absolute in so far as it places one at this moment before the absolute decision for or against the truth, and it is relative, in so far as it knows that this decision is possible only as a concrete decision, as the fate of the time."[46]

Face to face with this subtle problem alike of logic and of religious commitment, one feels that problems of reconciling scientific theories with particular theological doctrines are peripheral. But such is not actually the case. Fundamentalist attacks on the Darwinian theory of evolution are not mere superstitious recalcitrance; they are based on sound suspicions that to yield an inch is to expose the citadel of their system to destruction. It is not merely the origin of man which is involved but the scientific approach as such; and the evolutionary point of view spells destruction of dogmatic finality. That issue at least is clearly drawn; and its full import requires further examination at the hands of theologians.

But in the meantime science has been creating a host of problems for religion by supplying the basis for important technological changes in modern life. The Industrial Revolution, with the rapid process of urbanization which followed, has presented to the churches an unprecedented task.

45 P. Tillich, *The Interpretation of History* (New York: Charles Scribner's Sons, 1936), pp. 123–75.

46 *Ibid.*, p. 175.

V

The evils which ensued upon the Industrial Revolution and the factory system provoked a humanitarian reaction, which expressed itself within Christianity in the social gospel. In 1826 Thomas Chalmers published his *Christian and Civic Economy of Large Towns*, in the opening chapter of which he pleads for the unity of science and religion in the service of man—a unity which, as a mathematician and economist, he was able to achieve in himself. Meanwhile, in America, the field of moral philosophy in the universities was being used more and more for development of incipient social science in the interests of human welfare. John McVickar and Francis Wayland were paving the way.[47] The preaching of men like J. F. D. Maurice and Charles Kingsley and Washington Gladden was reinforced by the literary work of Carlyle and Ruskin. Gladden and Josiah Strong led the way in the United States to be followed by Francis Peabody, Shailer Mathews, C. R. Henderson, and Graham Taylor. Later came Walter Rauschenbusch, Harry F. Ward, and Reinhold Niebuhr—all prophets of radical social reform. In 1891 Leo XIII issued his encyclical *De rerum novarum*.[48]

But a strange situation appeared in the relations between sociology and the Christian social reformers. In the earlier stage the Christian writers had rested their case either on a priori considerations of moral theology or on the teachings of Jesus. But, with the growing influence of biblical critical methods, it became increasingly difficult to rely upon the alleged social principles of Jesus. Yet at the very time when the Christian thinkers were inclining toward an empirical approach to social ethics, the sociologists were moving away from ethics to scientific detachment despite the warnings of early leaders like C. H. Cooley and E. C. Hayes. An analysis of the contents of the *American Journal of Sociology*, the official organ of the American Socio-

[47] J. McVickar, *Outlines of Political Economy* (New York, 1825); F. Wayland, *Elements of Moral Science* (New York, 1835). See G. Bryson, "The Emergence of the Social Sciences from Moral Philosophy," *International Journal of Ethics*, XLII (1932), 304–23.

[48] E. Troeltsch, *Gesammelte Schriften*, Vol. I: *Die Soziallehren der christlichen Kirchen und Gruppen* (Tübingen, 1912), pp. 965–86.

logical Society, recently showed the presence of this trend.[49]
Whether Christian social ethics will persist in empirical methods
of seeking social reorganization or turn away from social science
to moral theology again remains to be seen. After a period of
active organizational attack on social evils, there is now an inclination to relate the programs of Christian social action to
their theological presuppositions.

This shift is symptomatic of an important trend in society
today: the drift toward a conflict of ideologies embodied in rival
political forces. The situations in Russia and Germany have
forced the issue upon the Christian churches in a direct political
form; but the deeper problems of the relation of Christian theological presuppositions to the philosophical assumptions of
communism and fascism are already being seriously examined.
At the Oxford Conference on Life and Work in 1937 one of the
most remarkable features was the extent to which social problems were treated in theological terms.[50] Scholars are active in
all three of the great branches of Christianity today: among the
Roman Catholics may be mentioned J. Maritain, C. Dawson,
and F. X. Millar;[51] the Eastern Orthodox are led in this field by
S. Bulgakoff and N. Berdyaev;[52] and within Protestantism the
Anglo-Catholic writings of W. G. Peck, V. A. Demant, M. B.
Reckitt, and A. G. Hebert[53] represent one radical approach, and
the "dialectical" approach of P. Tillich, E. Brunner, and Rein-

[49] H. P. Becker, "Distribution of Space in the *American Journal of Sociology*, 1895–1927," *American Journal of Sociology*, XXXVI (1930), 461–66.

[50] See the *Oxford Conference Library* (Chicago, 1938).

[51] J. Maritain *et al.*, *Essays in Order* (New York, 1931); J. S. Zybura, *Present Day Thinkers and the New Scholasticism* (St. Louis, 1926); C. Dawson, *Progress and Religion* (London, 1929); Pope Pius XI, *The Social Order: Its Reconstruction and Perfection* (London, 1931).

[52] S. Bulgakoff, *Social Teaching in Modern Russian Orthodox Theology* (Lancaster, Pa., 1934); N. Berdyaev, *The Bourgeois Mind* (New York, 1934); *The Origins of Russian Communism* (New York, 1937).

[53] W. G. Peck, *The Divine Society* (London, 1925); V. A. Demant, *This Unemployment, Disaster or Opportunity* (London, 1931); M. B. Reckitt, *Faith and Society* (London, 1932); A. G. Hebert, *Liturgy and Society* (London, 1935).

hold Niebuhr another;[54] while the empirical studies of H. P. Douglass, S. C. Kincheloe, and M. H. Leiffer remain closer to social-science methods and issue in more concrete and cautious proposals.[55]

Side by side with these trends in social thinking in Christian circles goes a growth of the application of modern psychology to the cure of souls. The recent development of psychotherapy has revealed the role of deep conflict in the tensions which many associate with religious disturbances. A recent book by C. G. Jung has attracted wide attention by its frank recognition of the role of religious belief in emotional adjustment.[56] The relations of religion and mental hygiene have been hailed, but so far little critical writing in this field has been done. It is possible that further co-operation may be stopped from two directions: the recognition that many psychotherapists work with assumptions regarding man and his needs which contradict fundamental positions of Christian thought and the charge leveled by radical social critics that the psychiatrists are seeking merely to adjust man to the present social order which he should be reconstructing.

The attitudes of contemporary theologians to science are as varied as they have ever been. Some relegate science to the area of immediate physical adjustments reserving for religion the realm of ends. Some hope to find in scientific method the key to religious truth. Some work within the metaphysical framework of naturalism, while to others a naturalistic Christianity is a contradiction in terms. The prospect is that of a re-examination of basic assumptions and methods of thought comparable to the realist-nominalist controversy of the Middle Ages.

There are many who believe that Christianity cannot survive the impact with modern science, and they may prove to be

[54] P. Tillich, *Die sozialistische Entscheidung* (Potsdam, 1933); *The Interpretation of History*; E. Brunner, *Das Gebot und die Ordnungen* (Tübingen, 1933); R. Niebuhr, *Reflections on the End of an Era* (New York, 1934).

[55] H. P. Douglass, *The Church in the Changing City* (New York, 1929); S. C. Kincheloe, *The American City and Its Church* (New York, 1938); M. H. Leiffer, *City and Church in Transition* (Chicago, 1938).

[56] *Modern Man in Search of a Soul* (New York, 1933).

right. But whether they are or not remains to be seen, and the most hopeful fact is that in Protestantism the issues raised are being met with increasing directness and profundity. The solution will be found only as Christian belief is related to the basic assumptions of science which are penetrating contemporary culture. By such a relationship I do not mean acceptance. It may be that experience will require abandonment of some of those assumptions; but only a profoundly critical theology dare attempt that task and furnish the foundations for a reconstruction of faith.

THE FRONTIER IN AMERICAN CHRISTIANITY

WILLIAM WARREN SWEET

Divinity School, University of Chicago

WHAT the Mediterranean was to the Greeks in "breaking the bond of custom, offering new experiences, calling out new institutions and activities,"[1] the frontier was to America. And, as the influence of the Mediterranean basin affected every phase of Greek life—political, economic, and religious—so the frontier influence has been manifest in every department of American life. When men leave the beaten paths and plunge into the unknown, there always must be a frontier of human endeavor, "submitting what is old and accepted to conditions that are new and untried." Frontiers thus become seed plots "where new forms of life, whether of institutions or types of thought, are germinated."[2] The Christian church throughout its long history has pioneered on many frontiers. It is the purpose of this essay to trace in broad outline the ways in which organized Christianity accommodated itself to the peculiar conditions prevailing on the American frontier and to try to understand both what the Christian church meant to the West and what the West meant to the church.

In the Introduction to his monumental work on the *Colonial Period of American History*, Professor Charles M. Andrews states: "The seventeenth century shows us an English world in America with little in it that can strictly be called American."[3]

[1] Frederick Jackson Turner, *The Frontier in American History* (New York: Henry Holt & Co., 1920), p. 38.

[2] Carl L. Becker, *Essays in American History* (New York: Henry Holt & Co., 1910), chap. iv: "Kansas," p. 88.

[3] *The Colonial Period of American History*, Vol. I: *The Settlements* (New Haven: Yale University Press, 1934), p. 13.

Though the author is thinking primarily in terms of the political and economic situations prevailing in seventeenth-century America, yet his generalization applies with almost equal force to the cultural and religious conditions. Some important religious innovations had come about in America by the end of the seventeenth century,[4] but as a whole there was little that could be called distinctly American until well along in the eighteenth. It was not until population began to move away from the Atlantic seaboard and, as a consequence, to turn its back more and more upon European influence that a distinctively American religious scene begins to appear.

Though the Puritans had departed from their motherland in order to be free to go their own way religiously, yet, when they came to draw up their first discipline and to adopt their first doctrinal statement after a generation of experience in America, they drew upon European models, incorporating the doctrinal portion of the Westminster Confession in their Cambridge Platform. "Early Congregationalism in America stood uncriticisingly on the doctrinal basis of the great Puritan party in the home land," and neither the Cambridge Synod nor the churches of New England at the time of the adoption of the Platform "felt in any critical spirit toward the Confession, which Parliament had just made the doctrinal standard of England."[5] Even in church polity the Cambridge Platform presents little that is distinctively American, leaning heavily upon Barrowist ideas as to what constitutes a true church.[6] The outstanding American development in seventeenth-century Congregationalism was its establishment as a state church, though even in this respect, inconsistent as it was with true Congregational prin-

[4] An example of such innovation is that presented by the development of the Colonial vestry in Virginia and Maryland in the Anglican church (see W. W. Manross, *The Episcopal Church in the United States, 1800–1840* [New York: Columbia University Press, 1938], p. 23).

[5] Williston Walker, *A History of the Congregational Churches in the United States* (New York: Christian Literature Co., 1894), pp. 160–61.

[6] Cf. the Cambridge Platform with H. A. Barrow, *A Brief Discovery of the False Church* (Dort, 1590).

ciples,[7] it was to find an Old World justification in its dominance under Cromwell.

Early American Presbyterianism was identical in both discipline and doctrine with the Irish and Scottish churches and indeed looked to the General Assembly of Scotland for its precedents until well toward the end of the Colonial period.[8] All the non-English-speaking Colonial religious bodies were closely tied to their European backgrounds throughout the entire Colonial era, with the exception of some of the small sects such as the Mennonites and Dunkers. But the German and Dutch Reformed bodies, the Moravians, and the Lutherans, both German and Swedish, maintained strong Old World ties throughout the entire eighteenth century. There was, therefore, little opportunity for them to develop distinctively American traits until their Old World connections had been severed. Colonial Quakerism likewise maintained an Old World relationship and looked to the Yearly Meeting of London for guidance.[9] The most distinctively American religious development in seventeenth-century Colonial America was among the Baptists, where in Rhode Island their influence was responsible for the separation of church and state and for the establishment of complete religious liberty. While this development was in the realm of politics as much as in religion, it yet was a principle that was primarily developed among religious minority groups

[7] In John Cotton's *Questions and Answers upon Church Government* (1634?), and his *The Doctrine of the Church to Which Are Committed the Keys of the Kingdom of Heaven*, etc. (London, 1643 [pamphlet]), and Richard Mather's *Church Government and Church Covenant Discussed, etc.* (London, 1643), the polity set forth is identical with the Congregationalism of Barrow and Robinson (cf. W. B. Selbie, *Congregationalism* [London: Methuen & Co., 1927], pp. 62–63).

[8] Cf. Richard Webster, *A History of the Presbyterian Church in America from Its Origin until the Year 1760, etc.* (Philadelphia: Joseph M. Wilson, 1857), IV, 121–31: "The Methods in use in Ireland and Scotland were all introduced on the erection of congregations."

[9] Cf. Rufus M. Jones, *The Quakers in the American Colonies* (London: Macmillan & Co., 1911), p. 438: "While in local matters the American meetings were supreme each within its limits, they all paid great respect to the letters of George Fox and the official epistles of the London Yearly Meeting. These were both doctrinal and practical, stating the theory of the meeting for worship, setting up the church machinery, giving directions as to the treatment of delinquents and of the poor, advice as to business, dress, and language, and a multitude of other details."

and was vigorously advocated by Baptists from the beginning of their appearance in the New World. Since the Baptists had no Old World connections, they went forward more rapidly than perhaps any other American Colonial religious body in developing distinctive American characteristics.

The first three colleges founded in Colonial America—Harvard (1636), William and Mary (1692), and Yale (1701)—were to a large degree transplantations of Cambridge and Oxford colleges. Harvard was an American duplicate of Emmanuel College, Cambridge;[10] Yale was patterned after Harvard; while, in the founding of William and Mary, Oxford influence was dominant. It was not until the great Colonial awakenings had strengthened and revived the religious forces in America that the remaining six Colonial colleges came into existence. Their establishment, largely as a result of revival influence, marked the beginning of what might be called the college movement in America. The forces of frontier democracy were already at work demanding the decentralization of educational facilities.

I

The rise of revivalism[11] at the end of the first third of the eighteenth century was the first clear manifestation of frontier influence in American Christianity. In fact, revivalism grew out of a situation which is peculiar to newly settled lands.[12] And

[10] In spite of Professor Morison's prejudice against his Puritan ancestors, the founders of Harvard College, he has to admit that Harvard was the child of that hotbed of English Puritanism, Emmanuel College, Cambridge (S. E. Morison, *The Founding of Harvard College* [Cambridge: Harvard University Press, 1935], pp. 100, 107, 432; cf. also his *The Puritan Pronaos* [New York: New York University Press, 1936], and *Three Centuries of Harvard, 1636–1936* [Cambridge: Harvard University Press, 1936]).

[11] I am using the term "revivalism" to mean a method of presenting evangelical truth and with only an incidental doctrinal connotation. See W. W. Sweet, "Religious Revivals," *Encyclopaedia Britannica* (14th ed.), for a brief discussion of the distinction between "evangelism" and "revivalism."

[12] At the very time revivalism was beginning to manifest itself in the colonies the evangelical awakening was beginning in England under John Wesley's leadership. This would seem to be a refutation of the statement that revivalism is peculiar to new lands and newly settled regions. As a matter of record the evangelical awakening in England had its greatest success in the new industrial centers arising, such as Manchester, Leeds, Sheffield, and Bristol, where new population was pushing in from the rural sections. Thus the situation in England was in a way comparable to that on the American

perhaps more than through any other channel, at least until some fifty or so years ago, it was the principal means of bringing the impact of the gospel to bear upon the problems of American society.

In the American colonies, for the first time in the history of Christendom since the Reformation, there had come to be a group of civil states in which a majority of the people were without church affiliation. In all the European countries, on the other hand, there were everywhere state churches, and in these countries church membership came about more or less as a matter of course. There, church membership was almost co-extensive with citizenship, and few people were unchurched. In the colonies the situation was radically different. Here, from the very beginning, church membership had been a matter of the few and not of the masses and was difficult to attain.[13] The lower economic classes among the colonists, especially those who had come over as servants or redemptioners, had had in many cases slight attachment to the church before leaving the motherland, and in the new land conditions gave little encouragement for close church relationship. Though the religious motive was strongly present in the establishment of the majority of the English colonies in America, yet, as a matter of fact, the economic motive was far more powerful in bringing individual colonists to the New World. Coming as they did primarily to better their economic status, religion, for the time being, for the vast majority was pushed into the background.

It was out of the urge to find some way of winning this large unchurched element to the Christian life and to church fellowship that revivalism arose. It is significant that revivalism had its largest success in the colonies in the newer sections rather than in the older regions where church life had firmer roots. It

---

frontiers. In both cases people were leaving their old homes and their old social and religious relationships and were taking up their lives under new conditions (cf. Maximin Piette, *John Wesley in the Evolution of Protestantism* [London: Sheed & Ward, 1937], pp. 343–52).

[13] For a discussion of church membership in the colonies see W. W. Sweet, "The American Colonial Environment and Religious Liberty," *Church History*, IV (March, 1935), 52–54.

is also significant that Colonial revivalism found its principal opposition in the older settled sections.[14]

The Colonial revivalism which bore the stamp of the frontier most distinctly was the Baptist phase of the Virginia awakening.[15] Here it was almost exclusively a frontier movement under the leadership of uneducated "farmer-preachers." In its extravagance, in its effective emotional appeals, and in its widespread influence among the lower economic classes, it presaged the great revivals in the trans-Allegheny West of the early years of the nineteenth century. One of the most famous and successful of the Virginia Baptist preachers was James Ireland, whose work covered several frontier counties. He states that "there were not many places upon the waters among the back mountains that were then inhabited but what I visited."[16] John Leland, a co-worker of Ireland's, preached about three thousand sermons and baptized more than seven hundred persons; John Waller baptized more than two thousand persons and assisted in the formation of eighteen churches. Under the preaching of these men and many others like them the revival spread in successive waves through the new communities from 1760 to 1770.[17]

Previous to the Colonial awakenings, religion had made but slight impress upon the great majority of the people; from now on it became increasingly concerned with reaching the common man. In other words, it marks the beginning of an aggressive American Christianity. The appeal of revivalism from the be-

[14] The principal opposition to the New England awakening under the leadership of Jonathan Edwards and George Whitefield came from Boston and from Harvard and Yale colleges (see Charles Chauncy, *The Later Religious Commotion in New England Considered* [Boston, 1743]; see also Joseph Tracy, *A History of the Revival of Religion in the Time of Edwards and Whitefield* [Boston, 1842], chap. xvii: "Opposition to the Revival in Connecticut"). When Whitefield preached in Boston, the physical exercises common in other sections were discouraged and were absent (C. H. Maxson, *The Great Awakening in the Middle Colonies* [Chicago: University of Chicago Press, 1920], pp. 69–70).

[15] Wesley M. Gewehr, *The Great Awakening in Virginia* (Durham, N.C., 1930), chap. v: "The Baptist Revival," contains the best account of this phase of the great Virginia awakening.

[16] James Ireland, *Life* (Winchester, Va., 1819), quoted in Gewehr, *op. cit.*, p. 118.

[17] Brief biographies of many of these early Virginia Baptist farmer-preachers will be found in J. B. Taylor, *Virginia Baptist Preachers* (1st ser.; New York, 1860).

ginning was admittedly primarily to the emotions. Even Jonathan Edwards stated that "our people do not so much need to have their heads stored as to have their hearts touched."

Perhaps the most remarkable of the revival movements which have swept over the nation was that which occurred in the latter years of the eighteenth and early years of the nineteenth centuries, often called the "second awakening." Its most spectacular manifestations and its greatest successes were won in the West, where in great out-of-door meetings people gathered by the thousands and remained, often for several days, encamped upon the ground while preaching went on, more or less continuously, under a corps of ministers representing several different denominations. Thus arose the camp meeting, which became one of the most influential social as well as religious institutions of the frontier.[18] The revival resulted in adding tens of thousands of new members to the revivalistic churches, and frontier communities noted for lawlessness, drunkenness, Sabbathbreaking, and general "cussedness" were, in many instances, completely transformed.[19]

From this time forward revivalism became the recognized method of all the more aggressive American religious bodies— Baptists, Methodists, Presbyterians, Congregationalists, and, later, the Disciples—in attempting to reach the unconverted and to win them to church affiliation.[20] A mistaken notion,

[18] There are numerous accounts of the western phase of the second awakening: C. C. Cleveland, *The Great Revival in the West, 1797–1805* (Chicago: University of Chicago Press, 1916); Robert Davidson, *History of the Presbyterian Church in Kentucky* (New York, 1847), chaps. v, vi, and vii; B. W. McDonnold, *History of the Cumberland Presbyterian Church* (Nashville, 1888), chaps. iii, iv, v, and vi; William Speer, *The Great Revival of 1800* (Philadelphia, 1872). A contemporary account from a Shaker viewpoint is that of Richard McNemar, *The Kentucky Revival: Or a Short History of the Late Extraordinary Out-pouring of the Spirit of God in . . . . America . . . . etc.* (Cincinnati, 1807). This was the first book published under Shaker auspices.

[19] For a summary of the results of the great Kentucky revival see W. W. Sweet, *Religion on the American Frontier*, Vol. I: *The Baptists* (New York: Henry Holt & Co., 1931), pp. 209–612; Vol. II: *The Presbyterians* (New York: Harper & Bros., 1936), chap. iv: "Revivalism and Presbyterian Controversy"; F. M. Davenport, *Primitive Traits in Religious Revivals: A Study in Mental and Social Evolution* (New York: Macmillan Co., 1905).

[20] Revivalism also made inroads among the people of German background and gave rise to two revivalistic German bodies, the United Brethren in Christ and the Evangeli-

widely held, is that revivalism has been confined almost exclusively to the Methodists, Baptists, and Disciples, while Presbyterians and Congregationalists were consistently opposed to the revivalistic methods. Nothing can be farther from the truth. As a matter of fact, these two bodies, Congregationalists and Presbyterians, have furnished the most spectacular and widely known of all American revivalists. Jonathan Edwards, Gilbert Tennent, Samuel Davies, James McGready, Barton W. Stone, Charles G. Finney, Asahel Nettleton, Dwight L. Moody, and, finally, William A. ("Billy") Sunday were all from these two communions. Lyman Beecher, perhaps the most widely known preacher of his day and a "Presbygationalist," was an advocate of continuous revivalism, as were practically all his Presbyterian and Congregational contemporaries.[21]

II

Revivalism in America has been intimately related both to education and to reform. The great college movement which was in full swing from 1800 to the Civil War and which continued for a generation thereafter has a direct relationship to the revivalism of the time since the revivalistic appeal not only increased church membership and multiplied the number of churches but also led numerous young men to think of the ministry as a lifework. This was the period also of the greatest development of the "anti-everything-wrong" movements, such as the temperance, the antitobacco, and the antislavery movements; prison reform; antitea and anticoffee crusades, and a host of others. The period from 1836 to 1860 has been termed the "sentimental years" by a present-day historian, a delightfully descriptive phrase.[22]

---

cal church (cf. Paul H. Eller, "Revivalism and the German Churches of Pennsylvania, 1783–1816" [University of Chicago dissertation, 1933]).

[21] For Henry Ward Beecher's part in the great revival of 1857 see Paxton Hibben, *Henry Ward Beecher: An American Portrait* (New York: Doubleday, Doran Co., 1927), pp. 172–73.

[22] Douglas E. Branch, *The Sentimental Years, 1836–1860* (New York: Appleton-Century Co., 1934), pp. 227–53.

A large majority of the colleges founded before the Civil War were established on some frontier by the several denominations with the primary purpose of training young men for the ministry. In 1855 approximately ten thousand of the forty thousand graduates of American colleges whose records were studied became ministers. Here we have striking verification of the dominant purpose of the college founders. The forces of frontier democracy demanded the decentralization of educational facilities and determined that America should be a land of colleges rather than one confining higher education to a few institutions located at distant centers.²³ There can be no doubt but that the religious forces at work on the frontier were the primary agencies, and, in fact, almost the only agencies, which determined the pattern of American higher education previous to the Civil War.²⁴

During these years the frontier churches were the most active in college-founding. Lyman Beecher in his famous *A Plea for the West*²⁵ declared that civil and religious liberty could be secured for the West only by establishing "permanent, powerful, literary and moral institutions." He insisted that teachers for the West must be educated in the West and that the type of preachers demanded in the West must be talented and eloquent as well as pious, for, said he, nowhere on earth is "talent and learning, and argument and eloquence more highly appreciated, and regarded." While the Presbyterians were the most active in this

---

²³ G. F. Magoun, *The West: Its Culture and Its Colleges* (1855 [pamphlet]), p. 30 (quoted in Donald G. Tewkesbury, *The Founding of American Colleges and Universities before the Civil War with a Particular Reference to the Religious Influences Bearing upon the College Movement* [New York: Columbia University Press, 1932], pp. 84–87). See also W. W. Sweet, *Indiana-Asbury-DePauw University, 1837–1937: A Hundred Years of Higher Education in the Middle West* (New York: Abingdon Press, 1937), chap. i, pp. 11–24.

²⁴ Tewkesbury's study (*op. cit.*) contains conclusive support for this statement. Even the state institutions established before the Civil War were dependent upon the religious bodies, primarily the Presbyterians. In 1851 it was affirmed that "two thirds of the colleges in the land were directly or indirectly under the control of the Presbyterian Church" (M. S. Snow, *Higher Education in Missouri* [U.S. Bureau of Education Circular of Information, No. 2 (Washington, 1888)], p. 93). For Presbyterian influence in the pre-Civil War college movement see Tewkesbury, *op. cit.*, pp. 92–103.

²⁵ Lyman Beecher, *A Plea for the West* (3d ed.; Cincinnati and New York, 1836), pp. 22, 23, 24, 141.

respect, after 1830 the Methodists and Baptists, and a little later the Disciples, entered the educational field and were soon establishing colleges in every section of the land, but particularly in the newer regions. In 1830 the Methodists had not established a single permanent college; by 1860 they had founded thirty-four institutions of college grade, twenty-six of which were located on what might be termed the frontier. Before 1820 the Baptists had established but one institution, Brown University (1765); in 1860 there were twenty-five colleges under Baptist control, twenty-one of which were in frontier communities. Of the forty-nine colleges founded before 1860 with a Presbyterian background, more than three-fourths of them were in relatively new sections of the country. There were, in 1860, five Disciples colleges, all of them, of course, in the West.[26]

The direct relationship between revivalism and the rise of reform movements and benevolent enterprises on a great scale has been clearly set forth in a recent study of the antislavery movement by Professor Gilbert H. Barnes.[27] He shows conclusively that the principal leaders of the antislavery movement after 1835 came out of the revivalism of the time, and especially out of that of Charles G. Finney. "As the number of the new-born in the Kingdom increased by the thousands, the ten thousands and, after the Great Revival year of 1830, by the hundred thousands, their enthusiasm overflowed into 'all the great objects of Christian benevolence.' " Finney's appeal was primarily to the minds of his hearers. But, having won their minds, he addressed himself to their sympathies. His central doctrinal emphasis was upon "disinterested benevolence,"

[26] For lists of colleges established by the several denominations before the Civil War see Tewkesbury, *op. cit.*, pp. 93–95, 104–5, 115–16, 129–32. Of the fourteen Catholic institutions of college grade established before 1860, six were located west of the Alleghenies. Of the twenty-one Congregational colleges, only four, which were entirely independent of the Presbyterians (Oberlin, Marietta, Beloit, and Olivet) were established west of the Alleghenies previous to the Civil War (*ibid.*, pp. 121–22). See also P. G. Mode, *The Frontier Spirit in American Christianity* (New York: Macmillan Co., 1923), chap. iv: "The Small Colleges," pp. 59–78.

[27] *The Anti-slavery Impulse, 1830–1844* (New York: Appleton-Century Co., 1933), chap. i: "The Great Revival, 1830," and chap. ii: "The New York Philanthropists, 1830–1831."

which had been the principal emphasis in the Hopkinsian school of New England thought. It was the influence of this revivalistic theology which had its origin in Jonathan Edwards and the New England revival which furnished a good share of the dynamic back of the great home and foreign missionary movement of the early years of the nineteenth century.[28] Coupled with this influence was the other type of revivalistic preaching which had its chief development among the Methodists in which the emphasis was upon the infinite love and pity of God and the incalculable worth of every immortal soul. Here are to be found the roots of the social gospel emphasis which was to appear a century later.

III

The frontier was to prove the testing-ground where it was to be determined which among the American churches were to become the most numerous and influential as well as the most typically American religious bodies. The greatest task which faced the American churches at the beginning of the national period of our history was that of following the population westward. The greatest accomplishment of the American people has been the conquest of the continent;[29] and sharing in that conquest were the religious and cultural forces of the nation.

It is a significant fact that neither of the churches which were established by law during the Colonial period—the Congregationalists in New England and the Episcopalians in the colonies south of Pennsylvania—succeeded in maintaining their positions of leadership as population pushed westward, and both churches have remained relatively small bodies. Neither of these bodies developed any adequate method of following population westward. On the other hand, those churches which suc-

[28] *Ibid.*, pp. 10–12; see also O. W. Elsbree, *The Rise of the Missionary Spirit in America* (Williamsport, Pa., 1928).

[29] Accounts of the western movement of population and the development of the West may be found in Robert E. Riegel, *America Moves West* (New York: Henry Holt & Co., 1930); Frederick L. Paxson, *History of the American Frontier* (Boston and New York: Houghton Mifflin Co., 1924); John B. McMaster, *A History of the People of the United States* (8 vols.; New York: Appleton, 1885–1913), esp. Vols. III and IV.

ceeded in finding an adequate technique in dealing with restless and moving populations in the early West were those churches which became the most evenly distributed as well as the most numerous religious bodies in America. I am, of course, leaving out of account the Roman Catholic and the newer Lutheran churches which arose as a result of nineteenth-century immigration because neither were important factors during the early years of the last century. Both were to a large degree direct European transplantations, and neither was modified in any marked degree by frontier influence.

The principal frontier churches were the Baptist, the Methodist, the Presbyterian, and, after 1830, the Disciples. Each of these bodies developed frontier methods of its own and achieved success in the West just in proportion to the adequacy with which it met the peculiar problems which the new West presented. The Presbyterians emphasized an educated ministry, a proud tradition which was maintained on the American frontier in the face of almost insuperable difficulties.[30] As a result of this emphasis the Presbyterians introduced into the West the first large group of college-trained men. Naturally many of their ministers became schoolmasters, carrying on the work of the church and the school at the same time. They thus became the great college founders in the early West, and until 1830 a large majority of the higher educational institutions west of the Alleghenies were under their control.[31] The very fact, however, that their ministers divided their time and energies between religion and education proved a handicap in the expansion of Presbyterianism in the West.

Presbyterianism was also handicapped in dealing with the new situations presented by the frontier by the rigidity of both its creed and its polity. Lack of elasticity brought on frontier controversies, created divisions, and produced heresy trials

[30] Sweet, *Religion on the American Frontier*, Vol. II: *The Presbyterians*. For materials on Presbyterianism on the frontier see the Bibliography, pp. 888–917.

[31] See *ibid.*, chap. iii: "Cultural and Educational Influence of the Presbyterians in the Early West"; see also Tewkesbury, *op. cit.*; Sweet, *Indiana-Asbury-DePauw University, 1837–1937: A Hundred Years of Higher Education in the Middle West*.

which sapped its energies and divided its forces.[32] Any attempt to adapt Presbyterianism to the new conditions in the West made by such leaders as Barton W. Stone or James McGready or Finis Ewing was almost sure to result in controversy and finally schism. On the other hand, the Presbyterians organized nationally immediately on independence, and the Presbyterian system of church government, with its national assembly, regional synods, and presbyteries, gave them a nation-wide conception of their task.[33]

Congregationalists, however, failed to secure any national or centralized organization until after 1852, and their close cooperation with the Presbyterians under the Plan of Union of 1801 resulted in their partial absorption into the more highly organized Presbyterian body as Congregational and Presbyterian people came together in frontier communities west of the Hudson.[34] The American Home Missionary Society and other eastern home missionary agencies poured men and money into the West primarily in the interest of establishing Presbyterian churches, but on the whole with disappointing results. The policy of the missionary societies resulted in long-distance control and developed a dependent attitude on the part of frontier communities and a migratory ministry, or, to put it in another way, Presbyterianism and Congregationalism did not as a rule spring out of the soil of the frontier to the same extent as did the Baptists, Methodists, and Disciples.[35]

The very looseness of their organization was an asset in fitting the Baptists to deal with frontier conditions. Their ministry was drawn from among the people to whom they ministered; in the early days they were farmer-preachers, cultivating their fields during the week and ministering to their neighbors "in holy

[32] Sweet, *Religion on the American Frontier*, Vol. II: *The Presbyterians*, pp. 42, 82–83.

[33] *Ibid.*, chaps. i and ii.

[34] For the operation of the Plan of Union and the resultant effect upon frontier Congregationalists see Sweet, *ibid.*, chaps. iv and v; see also James H. Hotchkin, *A History of the Purchase and Settlement of Western New York and the Rise, Progress, and Present State of the Presbyterian Church in That Section* (New York, 1848); R. H. Nichols, "The Plan of Union in New York," *Church History*, Vol. V, No. 1 (1936).

[35] Charles T. Thrift, Jr., "Frontier Missionary Life," *Church History*, June, 1937.

things" on the Sabbath. Theirs was an unsalaried and an uneducated ministry. In fact, in many frontier communities the
Baptists were bitterly opposed to educated and salaried ministers. This humble but sincere lay ministry moved out with the
advancing frontier; and in most new communities springing up
numerously along the creeks and rivers in the West, especially
south of the Ohio, Baptist churches were most often the first to
be formed and their log meeting-houses the first places of worship to be erected.[36] Though the preaching of these humble
farmer-preachers left much to be desired, their churches were
centers of religious and moral influence in the midst of rough
and rowdy communities where life was in the raw and drunkenness, swearing, and loose morals were often the order of the
day.[37]

After its formation in 1830 the Church of the Disciples of
Christ, or the Christian church, performed in much the same
way as did frontier Baptists. Though their great leader, Alexander Campbell, was a man of high educational attainments, their
ministry likewise was drawn from among the people, many of
them farmer-preachers and without formal education. But they
were steeped in Scripture and were literalists to the last degree,
and what they lacked in education they made up in zeal and
devotion.[38]

The Methodists, with their highly centralized organization
with its circuit system, class leaders, and local preachers, seemed
ideally suited to meet the immediate needs of a moving and
restless population. A circuit rider often traveled over a region
several hundred miles in circumference, having as many as
twenty-five or thirty preaching places, where, at each place as
rapidly as converts were made, classes were organized under

[36] Sweet, *Religion on the American Frontier*, Vol. I: *The Baptists*, esp. chap. ii:
"Baptist Expansion and Migration Westward," and chap. iii: "The Frontier Baptist
Preacher and the Frontier Baptist Church"; see also John Taylor, *History of Ten Bap-
tist Churches* (Frankfort, Ky., 1823), and the various documents in Sweet, *The Baptists*.

[37] See the long list of discipline cases in Sweet, *The Baptists*, pp. 248–416.

[38] W. E. Garrison, *Religion Follows the Frontier: A History of the Disciples of Christ*
(New York: Harper & Bros., 1931); G. L. Peters, *Disciples of Christ in Missouri:
1837–1937* (n.p., 1937), esp. chap. iv: "The First Churches."

the supervision of "class leaders." Over all the circuits on a "district" was the presiding elder, always an ordained man and one chosen because of his especial qualifications to supervise the younger men on their circuits. Four times a year he visited each circuit, when he held the quarterly conference at which every class on the circuit was represented, and where he preached and administered the sacraments. At the end of the summer came the camp meetings when the whole countryside, non-church members as well as church members, gathered at an appointed place in the woods, erected their booths or set up their tents, and for several days together experienced the joy of congenial social intercourse interspersed with numerous religious meetings. Though originating among the Presbyterians, the camp meeting had its largest development among the Methodists, who made it one of the most influential social and religious institutions of the frontier. Once a year came the annual conference presided over by the bishop, when all circuit preachers were assigned to their circuits for the coming year. Such was the closely knit Methodist system which soon covered the entire nation with a network of circuits, districts, and annual conferences. No community was too remote, no region too wicked, but that a Methodist circuit rider soon made his appearance to preach the gospel of free grace and individual responsibility, and, in the words of one of the popular camp-meeting songs, "To shout old Satan's kingdom down."[39]

In the 1830's a deputation of Congregational ministers from England and Wales came to America to make a survey of the status of organized religion. They traveled extensively throughout the country and recorded their observations in a series of letters.[40] The Baptists, they state, are a large and flourishing

[39] For an account of the impact of Methodism on the American West see W. W. Sweet, *The Rise of Methodism in the West* (New York and Nashville, 1920); *Circuit-Rider Days in Indiana* (Indianapolis, 1916); *Circuit-Rider Days along the Ohio* (New York: Methodist Book Concern, 1923); W. B. Posey, *The Development of Methodism in the Old Southwest, 1783–1824* (Tuscaloosa, Ala., 1933); W. E. Arnold, *A History of Methodism in Kentucky*, Vol. I: *1783–1820* (Louisville, 1936).

[40] Andrew Reed and James Mateson, *A Narrative of the Visit to the American Churches by the Deputation from the Congregational Union of England and Wales* (2 vols.; New York: Harper & Bros., 1835), II, 60–81.

body, with their principal strength lying in the West and South, but "they want exceedingly an enlightened ministry." In spite, however, of numerous handicaps, of which ignorance is the chief, they have "contributed most honourable" their "share in overtaking the wants of an empire, which has been advancing with a giant's pace and power." Of the Methodists, they report:

They depend here, as everywhere, rather on their method than the talent of their ministry. . . . . They are a hive of bees in which each one has his place, and each one has his work to do. . . . . Whatever may have been their failings, they have done more, both in America and Canada, than any other body of Christians, to carry the means of instruction and worship to the most neglected and scattered portions of these regions.

The deputation considered the Presbyterians the strongest religious body in America, if not in numbers at least in standing and consideration. The co-operation of the Presbyterians and Congregationalists in the Plan of Union, while it led almost to the complete absorption of Congregationalism in the West, yet was regarded by the visitors as good in that it supplied "an edifying and scarce example of two religious bodies dwelling in amity and oneness."

Such were the principal forces of organized Christianity at work on the early frontier. There were differences, of course, in doctrinal emphasis and method. The Presbyterians were at first staunchly Calvinistic, until frontier influences began to Arminianize such groups as the Cumberland Presbyterians and the New Lights. On the whole, Arminianism, with its emphasis upon man's part in the work of salvation, was more at home on the frontier than predestinarian Calvinism. The Presbyterians had an aristocratic theology but a democratic system of church government; the Methodists had a democratic theology and an autocratic system of church government. The main body of frontier Baptists were mildly Calvinistic; the Disciples were decidedly anti-Calvinistic, while both Baptists and Disciples carried democracy to its utmost limits in their church polity. But they were all engaged in the same task—all attempting to bring the softening influences of Christianity to bear upon the life of the raw, rough, and often blasphemous communities of the great new West.[41]

IV

We have been, until more or less recent times, a race of pioneers. And the pioneer is always an individualist.[42] But the individualism of the American frontier was "one of achievement, not of eccentricity." There was in the frontier type of individualism a certain uniformity, an absence of deep-seated differences. It was an individualism marked by self-reliance, a buoyant faith in one's own ability to achieve. And, while frontier individualism was one of the important factors which has produced religious diversity, it was a diversity underlaid with a certain uniformity which has made possible a much larger unity of action than on the surface would seem possible.

In the early West there was little interest in theology. There, the emphasis was upon the practical application of Christianity. All the frontier churches became agencies for promoting morality; all were engaged in fighting the evils which were everywhere in evidence. They were all united in a common struggle to save the vast new West from sinking into semibarbarism.[43] It was the simple gospel—a gospel that even uneducated preachers might proclaim and the humblest frontiersman might understand—which found widest acceptance. While the multiplication of denominations, which is one of the characteristics of American Christianity, is a thing to be deplored, yet it was after all a natural development where there has been complete free-

---

[41] "The first generation [in the West] can hardly be said to live. They let go life, throw it away, for the benefit of the generation to come after them. And these will be found, in most cases, to have grown up in such rudeness and barbarity, that it will require one or two generations more to civilize their habits. . . . . Whatever man or family removes to any new country should understand that he makes a large remove also toward barbarism . . . . he has gone beyond the pale of society" (Horace Bushnell, *Work and Play: Or Literary Varieties* [New York, 1864], pp. 246–50).

[42] For a discussion of frontier individualism see Becker, *op. cit.*, pp. 90–95.

[43] W. W. Sweet, "The Churches as Moral Courts of the Frontier," *Church History*, March, 1933, pp. 3–21; see also J. T. McNeill, *Religious and Moral Conditions among the Canadian Pioneers* ("Papers of the American Society of Church History: Second Series," Vol. VIII [New York, 1928]). See also Sweet, *Religion on the American Frontier*, Vol. I: *The Baptists;* Vol. II: *The Presbyterians,* for long lists of disciplinary cases.

dom of thought, of speech, and of religion. From the standpoint of human happiness it is far better to have two hundred and thirteen free churches[44] than to have one church to which all are compelled to conform. What seems to be an absurd diversity is better than any enforced uniformity. The freedom of the human spirit is far more to be desired than a uniformity of religious expression.

A recent writer has pointed out that in America there has been little interest or concern over a doctrine of the church.[45] Here, we have been accustomed to speak of "the churches" and not of "the church." The lack of religious unity from the beginning and the rapid increase of new religious bodies as a result of revivalism and frontier individualism were largely responsible for this failure to develop a "sense of the Church as the one transcendent body of Christ." And there would be no difficulty in pointing out other lacks in American Christianity, if lacks they be, due to frontier influence, both theological and otherwise, if judged by Old World standards. But American Christianity cannot be judged by Old World criteria, for the New World demanded a new spirit as well as a new method.

It has often been remarked that American Christianity has been weak in theology; that it has substituted action for meditation; that it has been principally activistic; that quietism has had small chance. Our European friends are contemptuous of the American churches for this reason. In their opinion they have nothing to offer. Those Americans attending the recent European conferences at Oxford and Edinburgh (1937) have remarked this attitude of indifference, if not of contempt. They report that the European delegates knew little as to what organized Christianity had accomplished in America, and, what is more, they cared less. Perhaps the dependence of our contemporary American theologians upon European leadership, even more in recent years than formerly, and the failure of their

44 The *Federal Census of Religious Bodies* (Washington: United States Department of Commerce, Bureau of the Census, 1930) lists 213 denominations in the United States.

45 Cyril C. Richardson, *The Church through the Centuries* (New York: Charles Scribners' Sons, 1938), pp. 222–23.

theology to reflect American developments and American needs, has been one of the reasons for this unfavorable opinion toward everything pertaining to American Christianity. But some day, I fully believe, in the not too distant future, our European brethren will be awakened, and perhaps rudely so, to the fact that the future of Protestant Christianity, just as the future of democracy, does not lie with them but with the vigorous new churches across the western ocean, born of the American frontier.

BIBLIOGRAPHY OF THE WRITINGS OF SHIRLEY JACKSON CASE

ALLEN CABANISS

A. BOOKS

1. *The Historicity of Jesus: A Criticism of the Contention That Jesus Never Lived; a Statement of the Evidence for His Existence; an Estimate of His Relation to Christianity.* Chicago: University of Chicago Press, 1912. Pp. vii+352. 2d ed., 1928. Pp. vii+352.
2. *The Evolution of Early Christianity: A Genetic Survey of First-Century Christianity in Relation to Its Religious Environment.* Chicago: University of Chicago Press, 1914. Pp. x+386.
3. *The Millennial Hope: A Phase of War-Time Thinking.* Chicago: University of Chicago Press, 1918. Pp. x+254.
4. *The Revelation of John: A Historical Interpretation.* Chicago: University of Chicago Press, 1919. Pp. xii+419.
5. *The Social Origins of Christianity.* Chicago: University of Chicago Press, 1923. Pp. vii+263.
6. *Jesus: A New Biography.* Chicago: University of Chicago Press, 1927. Pp. ix+453. Translated into Japanese by NAOSHIGE SATAKE. Tokyo: Shinshado Publishing Co., 1931.
7. *Experience with the Supernatural in Early Christian Times.* New York: Century Co., 1929. Pp. vii+341.
8. *Jesus through the Centuries.* Chicago: University of Chicago Press, 1932. Pp. vii+382.
9. *Report of the Church History Deputation to the Orient, September, 1931, to March, 1932.* New York: International Missionary Council, 1932. Pp. 82.
10. *The Social Triumph of the Ancient Church.* New York: Harper & Bros., 1933. Pp. 250. English ed. London: Allen & Unwin, 1934.
11. *Makers of Christianity: From Jesus to Charlemagne.* New York: Henry Holt & Co., 1934. Pp. xii+256.
12. *Highways of Christian Doctrine.* Chicago: Willett, Clark & Co., 1936. Pp. vii+201.

B. ARTICLES

1. "Some Wit and Wisdom of the Arab," *Acadia Athenaeum*, April, 1903.
2. "Coins of Jesus' Time and Country," *Pilgrim Teacher*, XXII (1906), 571–73.
3. "Paul's Historical Relation to the First Disciples," *American Journal of Theology*, XI (1907), 269–86.
4. "Authority for the Sacraments," *Biblical World*, XXIX (1907), 357–60.

399

5. "Κύριος as a Title for Christ," *Journal of Biblical Literature*, XXVI, Part II (1907), 151–61.
6. "The Historical Method in the Study of Religion," *Yale Divinity Quarterly*, IV (1908), 121–33.
7. "The Circumstances of Jesus' Baptism," *Biblical World*, XXXI (1908), 300–302.
8. "Was Christianity a New Religion?" *ibid.*, XXXII (1908), 417–27.
9. "The First Christian Community," *ibid.*, XXXIII (1909), 54–64.
10. "The Essential Unity of the Christian Religion" (an editorial), *ibid.*, pp. 75–78.
11. "The Resurrection Faith of the First Disciples," *American Journal of Theology*, XIII (1909), 169–92.
12. "Jesus and Historical Inquiry" (an editorial), *Biblical World*, XXXIV (1909), 75–78.
13. "The Origin and Purpose of the Gospel of Matthew," *ibid.*, pp. 391–402.
14. "The Legalistic Elements in Paul's Religion," *ibid.*, XXXV (1910), 151–58.
15. "The Personal Religion of Jesus," *American Journal of Theology*, XIV (1910), 234–52.
16. "The Missionary Idea in Early Christianity," *Biblical World*, XXXVI (1910), 113–25.
17. "Modern Belief about Jesus," *ibid.*, XXXVII (1911), 7–18.
18. "The Historicity of Jesus," *American Journal of Theology*, XV (1911), 20–42.
19. "Is Jesus a Historical Character?" *ibid.*, pp. 205–27.
20. "Jesus' Historicity: A Statement of the Problem," *ibid.*, pp. 265–68.
21. "The Scribes' Interpretation of the Old Testament," *Biblical World*, XXXVIII (1911), 28–40.
22. "The New Testament Writers' Interpretation of the Old Testament," *ibid.*, pp. 92–102.
23. "To Whom Was 'Ephesians' Written?" *ibid.*, pp. 315–20.
24. "Jesus in the Light of Modern Scholarship," *ibid.*, pp. 262–71, 331–40, 409–15, XXXIX (1912), 55–62.
25. "The Religious Value of the Apostolic Age" (an editorial), *ibid.*, XXXIX (1912), 291–94.
26. "The Nature of Primitive Christianity," *American Journal of Theology* XVII (1913), 63–79.
27. "The Rehabilitation of Pharisaism," *Biblical World*, XLI (1913), 92–98.
28. "The Problem of Christianity's Essence," *American Journal of Theology*, XVII (1913), 541–62.
29. "Christianity and the Mystery Religions," *Biblical World*, XLIII (1914), 3–16.
30. "Divorce and Remarriage in the Teaching of Jesus," *ibid.*, XLV (1915), 18–22.
31. "The Religion of Lucretius," *American Journal of Theology*, XIX (1915), 92–107.
32. "Religion and War in the Graeco-Roman World," *ibid.*, pp. 179–99.
33. "John Mark," *The Expository Times*, XXVI (1915), 373–76.

34. "The Authority of the Spirit in the Religion of Paul," in *University of Chicago Sermons* (Chicago: University of Chicago Press, 1915), pp. 143–62.

35. "Allegory" and "Interpretation," in *Dictionary of the Apostolic Church*, ed. JAMES HASTINGS (Edinburgh: T. & T. Clark, 1918), I, 191–209, 575, 619.

36. "The Study of Early Christianity," chap. v of *A Guide to the Study of the Christian Religion*, ed. G. B. SMITH (Chicago: University of Chicago Press, 1916), pp. 239–326.

37. "Gentile Forms of Millennial Hope," *Biblical World*, L (1917), 67–68.

38. "The Book of Revelation," *ibid.*, pp. 192–200, 257–64, 321–28, 382–90.

39. "The Premillennial Menace," *ibid.*, LII (1918), 1–8.

40. "The Historical Study of Religion," *Journal of Religion*, I (1921), 1–17.

41. "Second Adventism," in *Hastings' Encyclopedia of Religion and Ethics* (Edinburgh: T. & T. Clark; New York: Scribner's, 1921), Vol. XI.

42. "Angels," "Demons," "Devil," "Emperor Worship," "Gentile Christianity," "Gnosticism," "Healing and Healing Gods," "Heroes and Hero-Worship," "Jewish Christianity," "Marcion and Marcionism," "Mother Goddesses," "Mystery Religions," "Spirits," "Synoptic Gospels," "Timothy," "Titus," "Virgin Birth," in *A Dictionary of Religion and Ethics*, ed. S. MATHEWS and G. B. SMITH (New York: Macmillan Co., 1921), pp. 17, 128 f., 130, 146, 181, 183, 198, 202, 237, 272, 296 f., 300–302, 425, 434, 467.

43. "The Use of ἄμφοδον in the Septuagint and the New Testament," *Classical Philology*, XVII (1922), 117.

44. "Contributions of the Yale Divinity School to Theological Literature," in *The Centennial Anniversary of Yale Divinity School* (New Haven: Yale University Press, 1923), pp. 19–24.

45. "Gentile Religions of the Ancient Mediterranean World," *Journal of Religion*, III (1923), 64–68.

46. "The Art of Healing in Early Christian Times," *ibid.*, pp. 238–55.

47. "The Rehabilitation of Church History in Ministerial Education," *ibid.*, IV (1924), 225–42.

48. "The Next 'Life of Jesus,'" *Canadian Journal of Religious Thought*, I (1924), 371–79.

49. "The Religious Meaning of the Past," *Journal of Religion*, IV (1924), 576–91.

50. "Josephus' Anticipation of a Domitianic Persecution," *Journal of Biblical Literature*, XLIV (1925), 10–20.

51. "The Life of Jesus during the Last Quarter Century," *Journal of Religion*, V (1925), 561–75.

52. "Jesus and Sepphoris," *Journal of Biblical Literature*, XLV (1926), 14–22.

53. "The Problem of Teaching Bible to Undergraduates," *Journal of Religion*, VI (1926), 154–62.

54. "The Roman Christians and the Way," *Institute*, X (1926), 85–95.

55. "The Christian Way in the Second Generation," *ibid.*, pp. 101–11.

56. "The Alleged Messianic Consciousness of Jesus" (president's address), *Journal of Biblical Literature*, XLVI (1927), 1–19.

57. "The Acceptance of Christianity by the Roman Emperors" (president's address), in *Papers of the American Society of Church History* (New York: Putnam, 1928), pp. 43–64.
58. "The Jewish Bias of Paul," *Journal of Biblical Literature*, XLVII (1928), 20–31.
59. "Character Education in the Early Church," *Religious Education*, XXIV (1929), 28–33.
60. "Jude" and "Second Peter," in *The Abingdon Bible Commentary* (New York: Abingdon Press, 1929), pp. 1345–49, 1361–63.
61. "Popular Competitors of Early Christianity," *Journal of Religion*, X (1930), 55–73.
62. "Exploiting Religious Gullibility," *Christian Century*, March 26, 1930, p. 402.
63. "Education in Liberalism," in *Contemporary American Theology*, ed. Vergilius Ferm (New York: Round Table Press, 1932), pp. 107–25.
64. "Religion and Patriotism," *University of Chicago Magazine*, XXV (1932), 72–75.
65. "Whither Historicism in Theology?" in *The Process of Religion: Essays in Honor of Dean Shailer Mathews*, ed. by M. H. KRUMBINE (New York: Macmillan Co., 1933), pp. 55–71.
66. "Stabilizing Our Civilization," *Bulletin of Crozer Theological Seminary*, XXVI (1934), 159–68.
67. "The Ethics of Jesus from Strauss to Barth," *Journal of Religion*, XV (1935), 389–99.
68. "The Task of the Preacher," in *The Church at Work in the Modern World*, ed. W. C. BOWER (Chicago: University of Chicago Press, 1935), pp. 210–35.
69. "Finding Our Way," *Divinity School News*, V, No. 1 (1938), 1–4.
70. "Law and Gospel" (convocation address), *ibid.*, No. 2, pp. 1–6.

C. TRANSLATIONS

FROM GERMAN

1. "Hellenistic Ideas of Salvation in the Light of Ancient Anthropology," by PAUL WENDLAND, *American Journal of Theology*, XVII (1913), 345–51.
2. "Buddhistic Influence in the New Testament," *ibid.*, XX (1916), 536–48.
3. "The Sect of the Nicolaitans and Nicolaus the Deacon in Jerusalem," by A. VON HARNACK, *Journal of Religion*, III (1923), 413–22.
4. "Jesus in Contemporary German Theology," *ibid.*, XI (1931), 179–211.
5. "What Is Wrong with the Dialectic Theology?" by PAUL TILLICH, *ibid.*, XV (1935), 127–45.

FROM ITALIAN

1. "Orphism and Paulinism," by V. MACCHIORO, *Journal of Religion*, VIII (1928), 337–70.

D. BOOKS AND JOURNALS EDITED

American Journal of Theology (with G. B. SMITH), 1912–20.
Journal of Religion, 1927–1939.

Divinity School News, 1934–38.
Studies in Early Christianity. New York: Century Co., 1928. Pp. ix+467.
(Author of article: "The Rise of Christian Messianism," pp. 311–32.)
A Bibliographical Guide to the History of Christianity. Chicago: University of
Chicago Press, 1931. Pp. xi+265. (Author of chaps. i, ii, iii, and ix.)

E. BOOK REVIEWS

1908

Knopf, *Die Zukunftshoffnungen des Urchristentums* (*American Journal of Theology*, XII, 486, 487).

1909

Jülicher, *Paulus und Jesus* (*American Journal of Theology*, XIII, 114–16);
Wustmann, *Jesus und Paulus* (*ibid.*); Meyer, *Wer hat das Christentum
begründet?* (*ibid.*); Warschauer, *Jesus: Seven Questions* (*ibid.*, pp. 459–63);
Denney, *Jesus and the Gospel* (*ibid.*); Gregory, *Einleitung in das Neue Testament* (*ibid.*, pp. 611–13); Huck, *Synopse der drei ersten Evangelien* (*ibid.*,
pp. 119, 120); Miller, *Zur Synopse* (*ibid.*); Garvie, *Studies in the Inner Life
of Jesus* (*Biblical World*, XXXIII, 137–39); Scott, *Apologetic of the New
Testament* (*ibid.*, pp. 212–14); Goodspeed, *Epistle to the Hebrews*; Gilbert,
Acts; Smith, *The Gospel of St. Matthew*; Clark, *The Gospel of St. John*;
Andrews, *The Acts of the Apostles*; McFadyen, *The Epistles to Corinthians
and Galatians* (*ibid.*, pp. 64–67); Harnack, *The Sayings of Jesus* (*ibid.*, pp.
68, 69); Scott, *The Pauline Epistles* (*ibid.*, pp. 355–57); Robertson, *Grammar of the Greek New Testament* (*Classical Journal*, IV, 282–83).

1910

Preuschen, *Vollständiges Griechisch-Deutsches Handwörterbuch zu den Schriften
des Neuen Testaments und der übrigen urchristlichen Literatur* (*American
Journal of Theology*, XIV, 296–99); Feine, *Theologie des Neuen Testaments* (*ibid.*, pp. 448–50); Spitta, *Jesus und die Heidenmission* (*ibid.*, pp.
450–51); Goguel, *L'Evangile de Marc et ses rapports avec ceux de Mathieu et
de Luc* (*ibid.*, pp. 458–59); Zahn, *Introduction to the New Testament* (*ibid.*,
pp. 459–62).

1911

Montefiore, *The Synoptic Gospels* (*American Journal of Theology*, XV, 116–
17); Mangenot, *La Résurrection de Jésus, suivie de deux appendices sur la
crucifixion et l'ascension*; Durand, *The Childhood of Jesus Christ according
to the Canonical Gospels*; *Le Dogme et l'évangile* (*par un groupe de prêtres
catholiques*); Goguel, *Les Sources du récit johannique de la passion*; Goguel,
L'Eucharistie, des origines à Justin Martyr (*ibid.*, pp. 118–21); J. Weiss,
Die Aufgaben der neutestamentlichen Wissenschaft in der Gegenwart; Bultmann, *Der Stil der Paulinischen Predigt und die kynisch-stoische Diatribe*;
Huck, *Synopse der drei ersten Evangelien*; Souter, *Novum Testamentum
Graece*; Milligan, *Selections from the Greek Papyri* (*ibid.*, pp. 286–89);
Alexander, *The Ethics of Paul* (*ibid.*, pp. 291–92); Drews, *The Christ Myth*;

Smith, *Ecce Deus;* Clemen, *Der geschichtliche Jesus;* Troeltsch, *Die Bedeutung der Geschichtlichkeit Jesu für den Glauben (ibid.,* pp. 626-28); Valensin,
Jésus-Christ et l'étude comparée des religions (Biblical World, XXXVIII,
428).

1912

Moffatt, *Introduction to the Literature of the New Testament (American Journal
of Theology,* XVI, 119-22); Feine, *Theologie des Neuen Testaments;* Holtz-
mann, *Lehrbuch der neutestamentlichen Theologie;* Weinel, *Biblische Theologie des Neuen Testaments;* Hertlein, *Die Menschensohnfrage;* Abbott, *The
Son of Man;* Scott, *The Kingdom and the Messiah;* Emmet, *The Eschatological Question in the Gospels;* Von Dobschutz, *The Eschatalogy of the Gospels;*
Lake, *The Earlier Epistles of St. Paul;* Robertson and Plummer, *A Critical
and Exegetical Commentary on the First Epistle of St. Paul to the Corinthians
(ibid.,* pp. 290-302); Wendt, *Die Schichten im vierten Evangelium;* Overbeck,
Das Johannesevangelium; Buchsel, *Der Begriff der Wahrheit (ibid.,* pp.
462-64); Koch, *Die Abfassungszeit des lukanischen Geschichtswerkes;* Harnack, *Neue Untersuchungen zur Apostelgeschichte;* Westberg, *Zur neutestamentlichen Chronologie (ibid.,* pp. 465-67); Kent, *Makers and Teachers of
Judaism (Biblical World,* XXIX, 356).

1913

Goblet d'Alviella, *L'Evolution du dogme catholique;* Achelis, *Das Christentum
in den ersten drei Jahrhunderten;* Müller, *Die Entstehung des persönlichen
Christentums der Paulinischen Gemeinden;* Friedlander, *Hellenism and
Christianity;* Hall, *The Historical Setting of the Early Gospels;* Heitmüller,
Taufe und Abendmahl im Urchristentum (American Journal of Theology,
XVII, 122-28); Drews, *Witness to the Historicity of Jesus;* W. Smith, *Ecce
Deus;* D. Smith, *The Historic Jesus;* Thoburn, *Jesus the Christ;* Van den
Bergh van Eysinga, *Die holländische radikale Kritik des Neuen Testaments;*
Dujardin, *Sources of Christian Tradition;* Hamilton, *The People of God;*
Clemen, *Primitive Christianity and Its Non-Jewish Sources;* Perdelwitz,
Die Mysterienreligion und das Problem des I. Petrusbriefes (ibid., pp. 279-
85); Böhlig, *Die Geisteskultur von Tarsos;* Gardner, *The Religious Experience
of St. Paul;* Rostron, *The Christology of St. Paul;* Deissner, *Aufersteh-
ungshoffnung und Pneumagedanke bei Paulus (ibid.,* pp. 285-88); Clemen,
Die Entstehung des Johannesevangeliums; Weiss, *Das Johannesevangelium
(ibid.,* pp. 288-91); Spitta, *Die synoptische Grundschrift (ibid.,* pp. 431-32);
Loofs, *What Is the Truth about Jesus Christ?;* Linck, *De antiquissimis
veterum quae ad Jesum Nazarenum spectant testimoniis (ibid.,* pp. 627-30).

1914

Clemen, *Der Einfluss der Mysterienreligionen auf das älteste Christentum;*
Kennedy, *St. Paul and the Mystery Religions (American Journal of The-
ology,* XVIII, 147-48); Focke, *Die Entstehung der Weisheit Salomos (ibid.,*
pp. 300-301); Abelson, *The Immanence of God in Rabbinical Literature;*
Abelson, *Jewish Mysticism;* Montefiore, *Judaism and St. Paul;* Justen,
Les Juifs dans l'empire romain (ibid., pp. 433-35); Norden, *Agnostos Theos;*
Bousset, *Kyrios Christos;* J. Weiss, *Das Ur-Christentum (ibid.,* pp. 440-45);

Wernle, *Die Quellen des Lebens Jesu;* Heitmüller, *Jesus;* Schweitzer, *Geschichte der Leben-Jesu-Forschungen;* Weinel and Widgery, *Jesus in the Nineteenth Century and After;* Schweitzer, *Die psychiatrische Beurteilung Jesu;* Martin, *The Life of Jesus in the Light of Higher Criticism;* Conybeare, *The Historical Christ;* Klostermann, *Die neuesten Angriffe auf die Geschichtlichkeit Jesu;* Hammer, *Traktat vom Samaritanermessias;* Jackson, *The Eschatology of Jesus;* Davies, *The Miracles of Jesus;* Browne, *The Parables of the Gospels in the Light of Higher Criticism;* Murray, *Jesus and His Parables;* Groton, *The Christian Eucharist and the Pagan Cults;* Cobb, *Mysticism and the Creed (ibid.,* pp. 609–16); Bornhöffer, *Epiktet und das Neue Testament (Classical Philology,* IX, 223–24); Thoburn, *Jesus the Christ: Historical or Mythical? (Harvard Theological Review,* VII, 625).

1918

Moore, *Religious Thought of the Greeks (American Journal of Theology,* XXII, 593–94); Cobern, *The New Archaeological Discoveries and Their Bearing upon the New Testament and upon the Life and Times of the Primitive Church (Biblical World,* LI, 305–6).

1919

Swete, *Essays on the Early History of the Church and the Ministry (Biblical World,* LIII, 323–24).

1920

Alfaric, *Les Ecritures manichéennes,* Vol. I: *Vue général;* Vol. II: *Etude analytique (American Journal of Theology,* XXIV, 302–4); Whittaker, *The Neoplatonists (ibid.,* pp. 304–5); Inge, *The Philosophy of Plotinus (ibid.,* pp. 305–6); Alfaric, *L'Evolution intellectuelle de Saint Augustin (ibid.,* pp. 468–70); Robertson, *The Jesus Problem (Harvard Theological Review,* XIII, 295–96).

1921

Weiss, *Das Urchristentum;* Lake, *Landmarks in the History of Early Christianity;* Jackson and Lake, *Beginnings of Christianity (Journal of Religion,* I, 97–100); Charles, *A Critical and Exegetical Commentary on the Revelation of St. John (ibid.,* pp. 433–37).

1922

Farnell, *Greek Hero Cults and Ideas of Immortality (Journal of Religion,* II, 441–43).

1924

Dougall and Emmet, *The Lord of Thought;* Headlam, *The Life and Teaching of Jesus the Christ;* Dickey, *The Constructive Revolution of Jesus;* Berguer, *Some Aspects of the Life of Jesus from the Psychological and Psychoanalytic Point of View (Journal of Religion,* IV, 97–102); McGiffert, *The God of the Early Christians (ibid.,* pp. 322–24); Deissmann, *Licht von Osten;* Stählin, *Die altchristliche-griechische Literatur;* Von Dobschütz, *Eberhard Nestle's Einführung in das griechische Neue Testament;* Knopf, *Einführung in das Neue Testament;* Preuschen and Krüger, *Handbuch der Kirchengeschichte für Studierende;* Hennecke, *Neutestamentliche Apokryphen;* Dibelius, *Der Hirt des Hermas;* Grill, *Untersuchungen über die Entstehung des vierten Evangeliums;* ΕΥΧΑΡΙΣΤΗΡΙΟΝ; Bousset, *Apophthegmata (ibid.,* pp. 424–31).

1925

Streeter, *The Four Gospels;* Fascher, *Die formgeschichtliche Methode (Journal of Religion,* V, 428–31); Scott, *Hermetica;* Horner, *Pïstis Sophia;* Schmidt, *Pïstis Sophia;* De Faye, *Gnostique et Gnosticisme;* Harnack, *Marcion (ibid.,* pp. 640–45).

1926

Goguel, *Jesus the Nazarene (Nation,* CXXIII, 179); Farnell, *The Attributes of God (ibid.,* pp. 380–81); Foakes-Jackson, *The Life of St. Paul (New Republic,* XLVIII, 279).

1927

Workman, *John Wyclif (Nation,* CXXIV, 454–55); Moore, *Judaism in the First Centuries of the Christian Era (ibid.,* CXXV, 183–84); Foakes-Jackson, *The Rise of Gentile Christianity (Christian Century,* XLIV, 434); Guignebert, *Christianity Past and Present (ibid.,* pp. 1521–22); McNeile, *An Introduction to the Study of the New Testament (New York Herald Tribune Books,* III, No. 4, 33); Cadbury, *The Making of Luke-Acts (ibid.,* No. 14, p. 16).

1928

Gilbert, *Greek Thought in the New Testament (Christian Century,* XLV, 733–34); Dalton, *The History of the Franks (Journal of Religion,* VIII, 139); More, *Christ the Word (Nation,* CXXVI, 127–28); Shotwell and Loomis, *The See of Peter (ibid.,* p. 647).

1929

Odelberg (ed.), *The Hebrew Book of Enoch (Journal of Religion,* IX, 130–32); Rand, *Founders of the Middle Ages (ibid.,* pp. 135–36); Leclercq, *La Vie chrétienne primitive;* Siouville, *Hippolyte de Rome;* De Faye, *Origène: la doctrine (ibid.,* pp. 306–9).

1930

Reitzenstein, *Die Vorgeschichte der christlichen Taufe (Journal of Religion,* X, 129–30); Rosen, *Juden und Phönizier;* Goodenough, *The Jurisprudence of the Jewish Courts in Egypt;* Stein, *Die allegorische Exegese des Philo aus Alexandria;* Lewy, *Sobria ebrietas (ibid.,* pp. 412–16); *The History of Christianity in the Light of Modern Knowledge (ibid.,* pp. 444–47).

1931

Kirsch, *Kirchengeschichte: Die Kirche in der antiken griechisch-römischen Kulturwelt (Journal of Religion,* XI, 450–51).

1933

McConnell, *The Christian Ideal and Social Control* (*Journal of Religion*, XIII, 101–2); *Christian Education in Japan;* Anderson and Whitehead, *Christian Education in India* (*ibid.*, pp. 103–4); Lietzmann, *Geschichte der alten Kirche: Die Anfänge* (*ibid.*, pp. 334–35); Niebuhr, *The Contribution of Religion to Social Work;* Niebuhr, *Moral Man and Immoral Society* (*ibid.*, pp. 359–61); *Rethinking Missions, Laymen's Foreign Missions Inquiry: Fact-Finders Reports: India-Burma* (*ibid.*, pp. 361–63).

1934

Conway, *Ancient Italy and Modern Religion;* Jacks, *The Revolt against Mechanism* (*Journal of Religion*, XIV, 464–65).

1935

Day, *Jesus and Human Personality;* Bultmann, *Jesus and the Word* (*Journal of Religion*, XV, 82–86); Lake, *Paul, His Heritage and Legacy* (*ibid.*, pp. 91–93); *The Education of American Ministers* (4 vols., various authors) (*ibid.*, pp. 101–2); Jonas, *Gnosis und spätantiker Geist: Die mythologische Gnosis* (*ibid.*, pp. 325–26); Bailey, *Religion in Vergil* (*ibid.*, pp. 483–84); Goodenough, *By Light, Light: The Mystic Gospel of Hellenistic Judaism* (*ibid.*, pp. 484–85).

1936

Grant, *Frontiers of Christian Thinking* (*Journal of Religion*, XVI, 205–6); Lietzmann, *Geschichte der alten Kirche: Ecclesia catholica* (*ibid.*, pp. 210–11); Robson, *Civilization and the Growth of Law* (*ibid.*, pp. 357–58); Adolph, *Entbürgerlichung des Protestantismus?* Maritain, *Freedom in the Modern World* (*ibid.*, pp. 476–78).

1937

Orosius, *Seven Books of History against the Pagans,* trans. Raymond; Berdyaev, *The Meaning of History;* Tillich, *The Interpretation of History;* Matthews, *The Purpose of God* (*Journal of Religion*, XVII, 213–21); Heard, *The Source of Civilization* (*ibid.*, pp. 324–26); Fabricius, *Positive Christianity in the Third Reich;* Hauer, Heim, and Adam, *Germany's New Religion: The German Faith Movement;* Lichtenberger, *The Third Reich;* Niemoeller, *First Commandment* (*ibid.*, pp. 478–80); Hocking, *The Lasting Elements of Individualism* (*ibid.*, pp. 483–84); *Church and State in the Modern World* (several authors) (*ibid.*, pp. 492–93); Pickman, *The Mind of Latin Christendom* (*Christendom*, II, 617–20).

1938

Atkinson, *Prelude to Peace* (*Journal of Religion*, XVIII, 82–84); Curtis, *Civitas Dei* (*ibid.*, pp. 311–13); Gavin, *Seven Centuries of the Problem of Church and State* (*ibid.*, pp. 314–15); Oldham, *The Oxford Conference* (official report); Leiper, *World Chaos or World Christianity: Reports of the Commission on the Church's Unity in Life and Work* (*ibid.*, pp. 340–42).

INDEX